Fodor's 96
Arizona

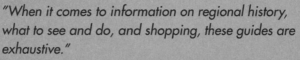

"When it comes to information on regional history, what to see and do, and shopping, these guides are exhaustive."

—*USAir Magazine*

"Usable, sophisticated restaurant coverage, with an emphasis on good value."
—Andy Birsh, *Gourmet Magazine* columnist

"Valuable because of their comprehensiveness."
—*Minneapolis Star-Tribune*

"Fodor's always delivers high quality...thoughtfully presented...thorough."

—*Houston Post*

"An excellent choice for those who want everything under one cover."

—*Washington Post*

D0354620

Fodor's Travel Publications, Inc.
New York • Toronto • London • Sydney • Auckland

Fodor's Arizona

Editor: Stephen Wolf

Editorial Contributors: Steven K. Amsterdan, Rob Andrews, Suzanne Carmichael, William Hafford, Mark Hein, Edie Jarolim, Bevin McLaughlin, Tracy Patruno, Trudy Thompson Rice, M. T. Schwartzman, and Dinah Spritzer

Creative Director: Fabrizio LaRocca

Cartographers: David Lindroth, Mapping Specialists

Cover Photograph: Rob Boudreau/TSW

Text Design: Between the Covers

Copyright

Special Sales

Fodor's Travel Publications are available at special discounts for bulk purchases for sales promotions or premiums. Special editions, including personalized covers, excerpts of existing guides, and corporate imprints, can be created in large quantities for special needs. For more information, contact your local bookseller or write to Special Markets, Fodor's Travel Publications, 201 E. 50th Street, New York, NY 10022. Inquiries from Canada should be directed to your local Canadian bookseller or sent to Random House of Canada, Ltd., Marketing Dept., 1265 Aerowood Drive, Mississauga, Ontario L4W 1B9. Inquiries from the United Kingdom should be sent to Fodor's Travel Publications, 20 Vauxhall Bridge Road, London, England SW1V 2SA.

MANUFACTURED IN THE UNITED STATES OF AMERICA

10 9 8 7 6 5 4 3 2 1

CONTENTS

ON THE ROAD WITH FODOR'S

A GOOD TRAVEL GUIDE is like a wonderful traveling companion. It's charming, it's brimming with sound recommendations and solid ideas, it pulls no punches in describing lodging and dining establishments, and it's consistently full of fascinating facts that make you view what you've traveled to see in a rich new light. In the creation of *Arizona '96*, we at Fodor's have gone to great lengths to provide you with the very best of all possible traveling companions— and to make your trip the best of all possible vacations.

About Our Writers

The information in these pages is a collaboration of two extraordinary writers.

In 1992, **Edie Jarolim** abandoned her senior editor's desk at Fodor's in New York to settle among the saguaros in Tucson. Born to the vertical vistas of Manhattan, she is still adjusting to horizontal space while she roams her adopted state searching for the best burritos and the most garish cowboy boots.

Susana C. Sedgwick is a writer and explorer. She has traveled all over the world, particularly in South America, where among other adventures she paddled 2,000 miles down the Amazon River in a dugout canoe. She is a member of the Explorer's Club in New York and a Fellow of the Royal Geographical Society in London, England. When she is not traveling, Susana makes her home between New York and Arizona.

We'd also like to thank the people who have assisted in preparing this guide: Marjorie Magnusson of the Arizona Office of Tourism, whose helpfulness is matched only by her cheerfulness, Jean E. McKnight of the Tucson Convention & Visitors Bureau, Frank Miller of the Sedona Chamber of Commerce, L. Greer Price, Information Specialist at Grand Canyon National Park, and City of Phoenix Park Ranger Dave Stamper for his expertise on rattlesnakes, Gila monsters, and scorpions.

What's New

This edition we've added a couple of kitsch items on Old Route 66 to our chapter on the northeast, included a great spot for birding at Ramsey Canyon Preserve in the southeast part of the state, recommended more hiking, and tried to make this as entertaining a guide as it is informative.

You'll also find a new portrait in this year's guide—a historical sketch on Arizona's founding mothers and fathers that we hope will foster a better understanding of human history in the region and pique your curiosity about the fascinating cultures of the Hopi, the Navajo, the Tohono O'odham, the Pima, and the Yaqui. It should help to dispel some of the mysteries that have surrounded, in particular, the groups that archaeologists have called the Anasazi.

A New Design

If this is not the first Fodor's guide you've purchased, you'll immediately notice our new look. More readable and easier to use than ever? We think so—and we hope you do, too.

Let Us Do Your Booking

Our writers have scoured Arizona to come up with an extensive and well-balanced list of the best B&Bs, inns, resorts, and hotels, both small and large, new and old. But you don't have to beat the bushes to come up with a reservation. Now we've teamed up with an established hotel-booking service to make it easy for you to secure a room at the property of your choice. It's fast, it's free, and confirmation is guaranteed. If your first choice is booked, the operators can line up your second right away. Just call 800/FODORS–1 or 800/363–6771 (0800/89–1030 when in Great Britain; 0014/800–12–8271 when in Australia; 1800/55–9109 when in Ireland).

Travel Updates

In addition, just before your trip, you may want to order a Fodor's Worldview Travel Update. From local publications all over Arizona, the lively, cosmopolitan editors at Worldview gather information on concerts, plays, opera, dance performances, gallery and museum shows, sports competitions, and other special events that coincide with your visit. See the order blank at the back of this book, call 800/799–9609, or fax 800/799–9619.

And in Arizona

Sports are a draw for visitors and residents alike, and football festivities loom large in Arizona's future. January 1, 1996, will mark the 25th anniversary of college football's Fiesta Bowl at Tempe's Sun Devil Stadium, and November and December 1995 will see celebrations throughout the state—everything from televised parades and battles of the bands to black-tie balls. Also at Sun Devil Stadium, the National Football League's **Super Bowl XXX** will inspire lots of hoopla before the January 28, 1996, game.

How to Use This Book

Organization

Up front is the **Gold Guide,** comprising two sections on gold paper that are chock-full of information about traveling within your destination and traveling in general. Both are in alphabetical order by topic. **Important Contacts A to Z** gives addresses and telephone numbers of organizations and companies that offer destination-related services and detailed information or publications. Here's where you'll find information about how to get to Arizona from wherever you are. **Smart Travel Tips A to Z,** the Gold Guide's second section, gives specific tips on how to get the most out of your travels, as well as information on how to accomplish what you need to in Arizona.

Chapters in *Arizona '96* are arranged from the top of the state down, starting with the Grand Canyon, moving to the Navajo and Hopi reservations in the northeast, then looking at the center of the state before moving to Phoenix, Tucson, and the south. Each chapter covers exploring, shopping, sports, dining, lodging, and arts and nightlife and ends with a section called Essentials, which tells you how to get there and get around and gives you important local addresses and telephone numbers.

At the end of the book you'll find Portraits, wonderful essays about Native American history, desert life, and shopping, followed by suggestions for pretrip reading, both fiction and nonfiction.

Stars

Stars in the margin are used to denote highly recommended sights, attractions, hotels, and restaurants.

Restaurant and Hotel Criteria and Price Categories

Restaurants and lodging places are chosen with a view to giving you the cream of the crop in each location and in each price range.

Hotel Facilities

Note that in general you incur charges when you use many hotel facilities. We wanted to let you know what facilities a hotel has to offer, but we don't always specify whether or not there's a charge, so when planning a vacation that entails a stay of several days, it's wise to ask what's included in the rate.

Dress Code in Restaurants

Look for an overview in the Dining section of Smart Travel Tips A to Z in the Gold Guide pages at the front of this book. Individual chapters' dining sections tell you what's most common in that area. In general, we note a dress code only when men are required to wear a jacket or a jacket and tie.

Credit Cards

The following abbreviations are used: **AE,** American Express; **D,** Discover; **DC,** Diners Club; **MC,** MasterCard; and **V,** Visa.

Please Write to Us

Everyone who has contributed to *Arizona '96* has worked hard to make the text accurate. All prices and opening times are based on information supplied to us at press time, and the publisher cannot accept responsibility for any errors that may have occurred. The passage of time will bring changes, so it's always a good idea to call ahead and confirm information when it matters—particularly if you're making a detour to visit specific sights or attractions. When making reservations at a hotel or inn, be sure to mention if you have a disability or are traveling with children, if you prefer a private bath or a certain type of bed, or if you have specific dietary needs or any other concerns.

Were the restaurants we recommended as described? Did our hotel picks exceed your expectations? Did you find a museum we recommended a waste of time? We would love your feedback, positive and negative. If you have complaints, we'll look into them and revise our entries when the facts warrant it. If you've happened upon a special place that we haven't included, we'll pass the information along to the writers so they can check it out. So please send us a letter or postcard (we're at 201 East 50th Street, New York, New York 10022). We'll look forward to hearing from you. And in the meantime, have a wonderful trip!

Karen Cure
Editorial Director

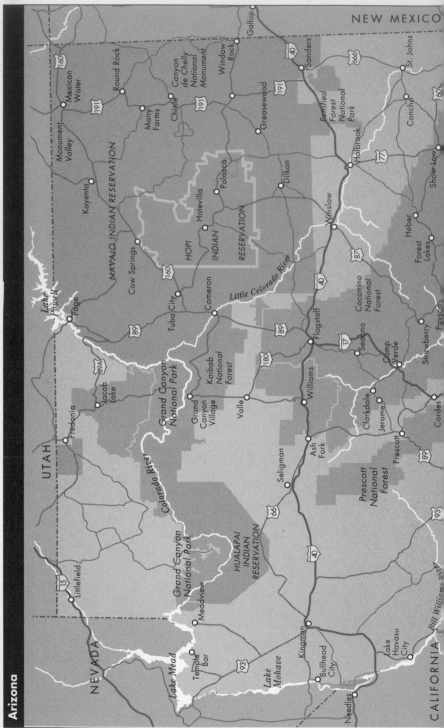

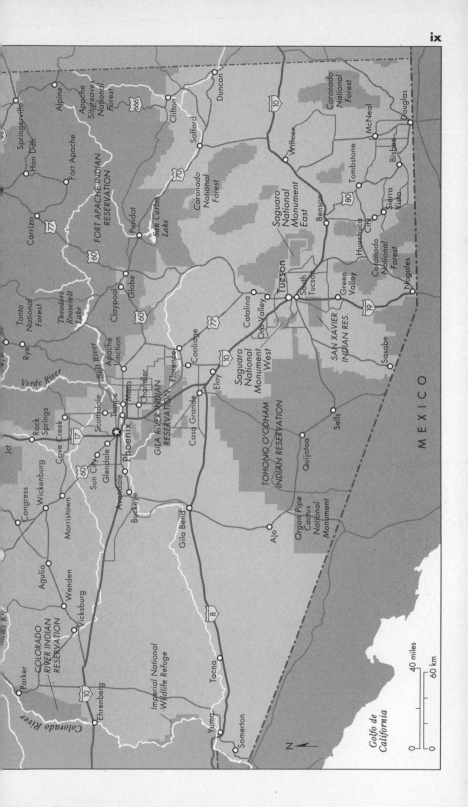

The United States

World Time Zones

Numbers below vertical bands relate each zone to Greenwich Mean Time (0 hrs.).
Local times frequently differ from these general indications,
as indicated by light-face numbers on map.

Algiers, **29**
Anchorage, **3**
Athens, **41**
Auckland, **1**
Baghdad, **46**
Bangkok, **50**
Beijing, **54**

Berlin, **34**
Bogotá, **19**
Budapest, **37**
Buenos Aires, **24**
Caracas, **22**
Chicago, **9**
Copenhagen, **33**
Dallas, **10**

Delhi, **48**
Denver, **8**
Djakarta, **53**
Dublin, **26**
Edmonton, **7**
Hong Kong, **56**
Honolulu, **2**

Istanbul, **40**
Jerusalem, **42**
Johannesburg, **44**
Lima, **20**
Lisbon, **28**
London
(Greenwich), **27**
Los Angeles, **6**
Madrid, **38**
Manila, **57**

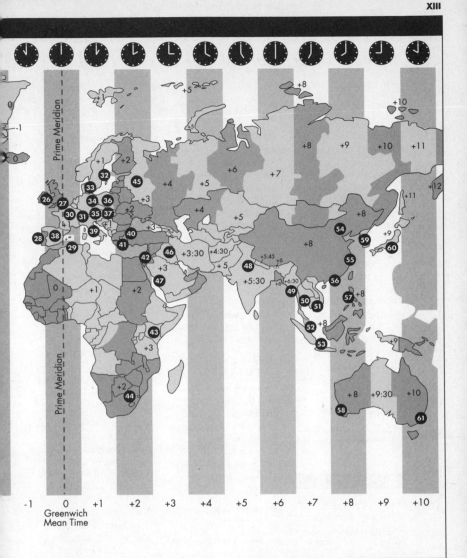

Mecca, **47**	Ottawa, **14**	San Francisco, **5**	Toronto, **13**
Mexico City, **12**	Paris, **30**	Santiago, **21**	Vancouver, **4**
Miami, **18**	Perth, **58**	Seoul, **59**	Vienna, **35**
Montréal, **15**	Reykjavík, **25**	Shanghai, **55**	Warsaw, **36**
Moscow, **45**	Rio de Janeiro, **23**	Singapore, **52**	Washington, D.C., **17**
Nairobi, **43**	Rome, **39**	Stockholm, **32**	Yangon, **49**
New Orleans, **11**	Saigon (Ho Chi Minh City), **51**	Sydney, **61**	Zürich, **31**
New York City, **16**		Tokyo, **60**	

IMPORTANT CONTACTS A TO Z

An Alphabetical Listing of Publications, Organizations, and Companies That Will Help You Before, During, and After Your Trip

No single travel resource can give you every detail about every topic that might interest or concern you at the various stages of your journey—when you're planning your trip, while you're on the road, and after you get back home. The following organizations, books, and brochures will supplement the information in *Arizona '96*. For related information, including both basic tips on visiting Arizona and background information on many of the topics below, study Smart Travel Tips A to Z, the section that follows Important Contacts A to Z.

A

AIR TRAVEL

The major gateways to Arizona include Phoenix Sky Harbor International, about 3 miles east of Phoenix city center, and Tucson International Air Terminal, about 8½ miles south of the central business area. Flying time is 5½ hours from New York (most airlines have stopovers), 3½ hours from Chicago, and 1¼ hours from Los Angeles.

CARRIERS

Carriers serving Arizona include **Alaska** (☎ 800/426–0333), **American** (☎ 800/433–

7300), **America Trans Air** (☎ 800/225–2995), **America West** (☎ 800/235–9292), **Arizona Airways** (☎ 800/274–0662), **Continental** (☎ 800/525–0280), **Delta** (☎ 800/221–1212), **Northwest** (☎ 800/225–2525), **Reno Air** (☎ 800/736–6247), **Southwest** (☎ 800/435–9792), **TWA** (☎ 800/221–2000), **United** (☎ 800/241–6522), and **USAir** (☎ 800/428–4322).

LOW-COST CARRIERS

For inexpensive, no-frills flights, contact **MarkAir** (☎ 800/627–5247), **Midwest Express** (☎ 800/452–2022), **Reno Air** (☎ 800/736–6247), and **Southwest Airlines** (☎ 800/444–5660).

WITHIN ARIZONA

Within the state, **America West Express/Mesa** (☎ 800/235–9292) operates regularly scheduled flights from Phoenix to Flagstaff and Yuma; **Skywest** (☎ 800/453–9417) flies from Phoenix to Yuma and to Page/Lake Powell. **Scenic Airlines** (☎ 800/535–4448) offers flights from Phoenix to the Grand Canyon Airport.

COMPLAINTS

To register complaints about charter and scheduled airlines, contact the U.S. Department of Transportation's **Office of Consumer Affairs** (400 7th St. NW, Washington, DC 20590, ☎ 202/366–2220 or 800/322–7873).

PUBLICATIONS

For general information about charter carriers, ask for the Office of Consumer Affairs' brochure **"Plane Talk: Public Charter Flights."** The Department of Transportation also publishes a 58-page booklet, **"Fly Rights"** ($1.75; Consumer Information Center, Dept. 133-B, Pueblo, CO 81009).

For other tips and hints, consult the Consumers Union's monthly **"Consumer Reports Travel Letter"** ($39 a year; Box 53629, Boulder, CO 80322, ☎ 800/234–1970) and the newsletter **"Travel Smart"** ($37 a year; 40 Beechdale Rd., Dobbs Ferry, NY 10522, ☎ 800/327–3633); *The Official Frequent Flyer Guidebook,* by Randy Petersen ($14.99 plus $3 shipping; 4715-C Town Center Dr., Colorado Springs, CO 80916, ☎ 719/597–8899 or 800/487–8893); *Airfare Secrets Exposed,* by Sharon Tyler and Matthew Wonder (Universal Information Publishing; $16.95 plus $3.75 shipping from Sandcastle Publishing, Box 3070-A, South Pasadena, CA 91031,

☎ 213/255–3616 or 800/655–0053); and *202 Tips Even the Best Business Travelers May Not Know,* by Christopher McGinnis ($10 plus $3 shipping; Irwin Professional Publishing, 1333 Burr Ridge Pkwy., Burr Ridge, IL 60521, ☎ 708/789–4000 or 800/634–3966).

BETTER BUSINESS BUREAU

Contact the **Better Business Bureau** in Phoenix (4428 N. 12th St., Phoenix, AZ 99503, ☎ 602/264–1271) and Tucson (3620 N. 1st Ave., Suite 136, Tucson, AZ 85719, ☎ 602/888–5353). For other local contacts, consult the **Council of Better Business Bureaus** (4200 Wilson Blvd., Arlington, VA 22203, ☎ 703/276–0100).

BUS TRAVEL

Greyhound (☎ 800/231–2222) provides service to many Arizona destinations from most parts of the United States.

C

CAR RENTAL

Major car-rental companies represented in Arizona include **Alamo** (☎ 800/327–9633, 0800/272–2000 in the U.K.), **Avis** (☎ 800/331–1212, 800/879–2847 in Canada), **Budget** (☎ 800/527–0700, 0800/181–181 in the U.K.), **Hertz** (☎ 800/654–3131, 800/263–0600 in Canada, 0181/679–1799 in the U.K.), and **National** (☎ 800/227–7368, 0181/950–5050 in the U.K., where it is known as Europ-

car). In Phoenix, rates begin at $29 a day and $115 a week for an economy car with unlimited mileage. Prices do no include sales tax, which in Arizona is 8.8%.

CHILDREN AND TRAVEL

FLYING

Look into **"Flying With Baby"** ($5.95 plus $1 shipping; Third Street Press, Box 261250, Littleton, CO 80126, ☎ 303/595–5959), cowritten by a flight attendant. **"Kids and Teens in Flight,"** free from the U.S. Department of Transportation's Office of Consumer Affairs, offers tips for children flying alone. Every two years the February issue of *Family Travel Times* (*see* Know-How, *below*) details children's services on three dozen airlines.

KNOW-HOW

Family Travel Times, published 10 times a year by Travel with Your Children (TWYCH, 45 W. 18th St., New York, NY 10011, ☎ 212/206–0688; annual subscription $55), covers destinations, types of vacations, and modes of travel.

The *Family Travel Guides* catalog ($1 postage; ☎ 510/527–5849) lists about 200 books and articles on family travel. Also check *Take Your Baby and Go! A Guide for Traveling with Babies, Toddlers and Young Children,* by Sheri Andrews, Judy Bor-

deaux, and Vivian Vasquez ($5.95 plus $1.50 shipping; Bear Creek Publications, 2507 Minor Ave., Seattle, WA 98102, ☎ 206/322–7604 or 800/326–6566). *The 100 Best Family Resorts in North America,* by Jane Wilford with Janet Tice ($12.95), and the two-volume *50 Great Family Vacations in North America* ($18.95 per volume), both from Globe Pequot Press (plus $3 for shipping; Box 833, 6 Business Park Rd., Old Saybrook, CT 06475, ☎ 203/395–0440 or 800/243–0495, 800/962–0973 in CT) help plan your trip with children, from toddlers to teens.

LOCAL INFO

A Family Guide to Arizona, by Catherine Dunes (Kids Touring Arizona, 4201 W. Villa Maria Dr., Glendale, AZ 85308, ☎ 602/439–2324; $6.95), contains Arizona-related fun facts, games, puzzles, and palatable educational information.

LODGING

All **Holiday Inns** (☎ 800/465–4329) allow children under age 19 to stay free when sharing a room with an adult, and some offer family plans, whereby children under 12 can eat free from special children's menus. **Westin La Paloma Hotel** in Tucson (☎ 800/228–3000) has supervised activities year round for children ages 6 months–12, as well as junior tennis camps for kids 5–14 years old in summer. From Thanksgiving through April, the **Tanque Verde Guest Ranch** (☎ 800/234–3833), also in Tucson, offers activities for children 4–11, including horseback-riding lessons, tennis, and nature walks in the daytime, and arts and crafts and games in the evening. In the Phoenix area, the **Pointe Hilton Resort at Squaw Peak** (☎ 800/934–1000) runs its Coyote Camp for children ages 4–12 year-round, including such activities as hiking, swimming, arts and crafts, and cooking. The **Phoenician Resort** (☎ 800/888–8234) in Scottsdale has supervised indoor and outdoor activities for children 5–12 as well as junior golf and tennis clinics for kids 5–14 throughout the year; Scottsdale's **Hyatt Regency** (☎ 800/233–1234), also offers a full range of supervised daytime activities, geared for kids 3–12; in addition, there are evening sessions each Friday and Saturday. All of the above resorts also have baby-sitting services.

TOUR OPERATORS

Contact **Grandtravel** (6900 Wisconsin Ave., Suite 706, Chevy Chase, MD 20815, ☎ 301/986–0790 or 800/247–7651), which has tours for people traveling with grandchildren ages 7 to 17; or **Rascals in Paradise** (650 5th St., Suite 505, San Francisco, CA 94107, ☎ 415/978–9800 or 800/872–7225).

CUSTOMS

CANADIANS

Contact **Revenue Canada** (2265 St. Laurent Blvd. S, Ottawa, Ontario, K1G 4K3, ☎ 613/993–0534) for a copy of the free brochure **"I Declare/Je Déclare"** and for details on duties that exceed the standard duty-free limit.

U.K. CITIZENS

HM Customs and Excise (Dorset House, Stamford St., London SE1 9NG, ☎ 0171/202–4227) can answer questions about U.K. customs regulations and publishes **"A Guide for Travellers,"** detailing standard procedures and import rules.

D
FOR TRAVELERS
WITH DISABILITIES

COMPLAINTS

To register complaints under the provisions of the Americans with Disabilities Act, contact the U.S. Department of Justice's **Public Access Section** (Box 66738, Washington, DC 20035, ☎ 202/514–0301, TDD 202/514–0383, FAX 202/307–1198).

DISCOUNT PASSES

The **National Park Service** (Box 37127, Washington, DC 20013–7127) provides a Golden Access Passport free to those who are legally blind or have a permanent disability; the passport covers the entry fee for the holder and anyone accompanying the holder in the same private vehicle and a 50% discount

on camping and some other user fees. Apply for the passport in person at a national recreational facility that charges an entrance fee; proof of disability is required.

LOCAL INFO

For information on accessible facilities at specific parks and sites in northern Arizona (Wupatki, Sunset Crater, Walnut Canyon, Canyon de Chelley, and Navajo national monuments), contact the **National Park Service, Southwest Regional Office** (☎ 505/988–6012); for sites in the rest of Arizona, contact the **Southern Arizona Group Office** (☎ 602/640-5250).

GETTING AROUND

BY BUS➤ **Greyhound** (☎ 800/752–4841; TTY 800/345–3109), which provides service to many destinations in Arizona, will carry a person with disabilities and a companion for the price of a single fare.

BY TRAIN➤ **Amtrak** (National Railroad Passenger Corp., 60 Massachusetts Ave., NE, Washington, DC 20002, ☎ 800/872–7245) advises that you request Redcap service, special seats, or wheelchair assistance when you make reservations. Also note that not all stations are equipped to provide these services. All passengers with disabilities are entitled to a 15% discount on the lowest fare, and there are special fares for children with disabilities as well. Contact Amtrak for a free brochure that outlines services for older travelers and people with disabilities.

BY CAR➤ **Avis** (☎ 800/331–1212), **Hertz** (☎ 800/654–3131), and **National** (☎ 800/328–4567) can provide hand controls on some rental cars with advance notice.

ORGANIZATIONS

FOR TRAVELERS WITH HEARING IMPAIRMENTS➤ Contact the **American Academy of Otolaryngology** (1 Prince St., Alexandria, VA 22314, ☎ 703/836–4444, FAX 703/683–5100, TTY 703/519–1585).

FOR TRAVELERS WITH MOBILITY IMPAIRMENTS➤ Contact the **Information Center for Individuals with Disabilities** (Fort Point Pl., 27–43 Wormwood St., Boston, MA 02210, ☎ 617/727–5540, 800/462–5015 in MA, TTY 617/345–9743); **Mobility International USA** (Box 10767, Eugene, OR 97440, ☎ and TTY 503/343–1284; FAX 503/343–6812), the U.S. branch of an international organization based in Belgium (*see below*) that has affiliates in 30 countries; **MossRehab Hospital Travel Information Service** (1200 W. Tabor Rd., Philadelphia, PA 19141, ☎ 215/456–9603, TTY 215/456–9602); the **Society for the Advancement of Travel for the Handicapped** (SATH, 347 5th Ave., Suite 610, New York, NY 10016, ☎ 212/447–7284, FAX 212/725–8253); the **Travel Industry and**

Disabled Exchange (TIDE, 5435 Donna Ave., Tarzana, CA 91356, ☎ 818/344–3640, FAX 818/344–0078); and **Travelin' Talk** (Box 3534, Clarksville, TN 37043, ☎ 615/552–6670, FAX 615/552–1182).

FOR TRAVELERS WITH VISION IMPAIRMENTS➤ Contact the **American Council of the Blind** (1155 15th St. NW, Suite 720, Washington, DC 20005, ☎ 202/467–5081, FAX 202/467–5085) or the **American Foundation for the Blind** (15 W. 16th St., New York, NY 10011, ☎ 212/620–2000, TTY 212/620–2158).

IN THE U.K.

Contact the **Royal Association for Disability and Rehabilitation** (RADAR, 12 City Forum, 250 City Rd., London EC1V 8AF, ☎ 0171/250–3222) or **Mobility International** (Rue de Manchester 25, B1070 Brussels, Belgium, ☎ 00–322–410–6297), an international clearinghouse of travel information for people with disabilities.

PUBLICATIONS

Several free publications are available from the U.S. Information Center (Box 100, Pueblo, CO 81009, ☎ 719/948–3334): **"New Horizons for the Air Traveler with a Disability"** (address to Dept. 355A), describing legally mandated changes; the pocket-size **"Fly Smart"** (Dept. 575B), good on flight safety; and the Airport Operators Council's worldwide **"Access**

Travel: Airports" (Dept. 575A).

Fodor's *Great American Vacations for Travelers with Disabilities* ($18; available in bookstores, or call 800/533–6478) details accessible attractions, restaurants, and hotels in U.S. destinations. The 500-page *Travelin' Talk Directory* ($35; Box 3534, Clarksville, TN 37043, ☎ 615/552–6670) lists people and organizations who help travelers with disabilities. For specialist travel agents worldwide, consult the *Directory of Travel Agencies for the Disabled* ($19.95 plus $2 shipping; Twin Peaks Press, Box 129, Vancouver, WA 98666, ☎ 206/694–2462 or 800/637–2256). The Sierra Club publishes *Easy Access to National Parks* ($16 plus $3 shipping; 730 Polk St., San Francisco, CA 94109, ☎ 415/776–2211 or 800/935–1056).

TRAVEL AGENCIES, TOUR OPERATORS

The Americans with Disabilities Act requires that travel firms serve the needs of all travelers. However, some agencies and operators specialize in making group and individual arrangements for travelers with disabilities, among them **Access Adventures** (206 Chestnut Ridge Rd., Rochester, NY 14624, ☎ 716/889–9096), run by a former physical-rehab counselor. In addition, many general-interest operators and agencies (*see* Tour Operators, *below*) can arrange vacations for travelers with disabilities.

FOR TRAVELERS WITH HEARING IMPAIRMENTS➤ One agency is **International Express** (7319-B Baltimore Ave., College Park, MD 20740, ☎ TDD 301/699–8836, FAX 301/699–8836), which arranges group and independent trips.

FOR TRAVELERS WITH MOBILITY IMPAIRMENTS➤ A number of operators specialize in working with travelers with mobility impairments: **Access Tours** (Box 2985, Jackson, WY 83001, ☎ 307/733–6664 in summer; 2440 S. Forest, Tucson, AZ 85713, ☎ 602/791–7977 winter–mid-May), which organizes national park tours; **Hinsdale Travel Service** (201 E. Ogden Ave., Suite 100, Hinsdale, IL 60521, ☎ 708/325–1335 or 800/303–5521), a travel agency that will give you access to the services of wheelchair traveler Janice Perkins; and **Wheelchair Journeys** (16979 Redmond Way, Redmond, WA 98052, ☎ 206/885–2210), which can handle arrangements worldwide.

FOR TRAVELERS WITH DEVELOPMENTAL DISABILITIES➤ Contact the nonprofit **New Directions** (5276 Hollister Ave., Suite 207, Santa Barbara, CA 93111, ☎ 805/967–2841).

DISCOUNTS

Options include **Entertainment Travel Editions** (fee $28–$53, depending on destination; Box 1068, Trumbull, CT 06611, ☎ 800/445–

4137), **Great American Traveler** ($49.95 annually; Box 27965, Salt Lake City, UT 84127, ☎ 800/548–2812), **Moment's Notice Discount Travel Club** ($25 annually, single or family; 163 Amsterdam Ave., Suite 137, New York, NY 10023, ☎ 212/486–0500 or 212/486–0503), **Privilege Card** ($74.95 annually; 3391 Peachtree Rd. NE, Suite 110, Atlanta, GA 30326, ☎ 404/262–0222 or 800/236-9732), **Travelers Advantage** ($49 annually, single or family; CUC Travel Service, 49 Music Sq. W, Nashville, TN 37203, ☎ 800/548–1116 or 800/648–4037), and **Worldwide Discount Travel Club** ($50 annually for family, $40 single; 1674 Meridian Ave., Miami Beach, FL 33139, ☎ 305/534–2082).

DRIVING

For up-to-date information on highway conditions and road closings throughout the state, call 520/573-7623.

G

GAY AND
LESBIAN TRAVEL

ORGANIZATION

The **International Gay Travel Association** (Box 4974, Key West, FL 33041, ☎ 800/448–8550), a consortium of 800 businesses, can supply names of travel agents and tour operators.

PUBLICATIONS

The premier international travel magazine for gays and lesbians is

Our World ($35 for 10 issues; 1104 N. Nova Rd., Suite 251, Daytona Beach, FL 32117, ☎ 904/441–5367). The 16-page monthly **"Out & About"** ($49 for 10 issues; ☎ 212/645–6922 or 800/929–2268), covers gay-friendly resorts, hotels, cruise lines, and airlines.

TOUR OPERATORS

Toto Tours (1326 W. Albion, Suite 3W, Chicago, IL 60626, ☎ 312/274–8686 or 800/565–1241) has group tours worldwide.

TRAVEL AGENCIES

The largest agencies serving gay travelers are **Advance Travel** (10700 Northwest Freeway, Suite 160, Houston, TX 77092, ☎ 713/682–2002 or 800/695–0880), **Islanders/Kennedy Travel** (183 W. 10th St., New York, NY 10014, ☎ 212/242–3222 or 800/988–1181), **Now Voyager** (4406 18th St., San Francisco, CA 94114, ☎ 415/626–1169 or 800/255–6951), and **Yellowbrick Road** (1500 W. Balmoral Ave., Chicago, IL 60640, ☎ 312/561–1800 or 800/642–2488). **Skylink Women's Travel** (746 Ashland Ave., Santa Monica, CA 90405, ☎ 310/452–0506 or 800/225-5759) works with lesbians.

I

INSURANCE

Travel insurance covering baggage, health, and trip cancellation or interruptions available from **Access America** (Box 90315, Richmond,

VA 23286, ☎ 804/
285–3300 or 800/284–
8300), **Carefree Travel
Insurance** (Box 9366,
100 Garden City Plaza,
Garden City, NY
11530, ☎ 516/294–
0220 or 800/323–
3149), **Near** (Box 1339,
Calumet City, IL 60409,
☎ 708/868–6700 or
800/654–6700), **Tele-
Trip** (Mutual of Omaha
Plaza, Box 31716,
Omaha, NE 68131,
☎ 800/228–9792),
**Travel Insured Interna-
tional** (Box 280568,
East Hartford, CT
06128-0568, ☎ 203/
528–7663 or 800/243–
3174), **Travel Guard
International** (1145
Clark St., Stevens Point,
WI 54481, ☎ 715/345–
0505 or 800/826–
1300), and **Wallach &
Company** (107 W.
Federal St., Box 480,
Middleburg, VA 22117,
☎ 703/687–3166 or
800/237–6615).

IN THE U.K.

The **Association of
British Insurers** (51
Gresham St., London
EC2V 7HQ, ☎ 0171/
600–3333; 30 Gordon
St., Glasgow G1 3PU,
☎ 0141/226–3905;
Scottish Provident Bldg.,
Donegall Sq. W, Belfast
BT1 6JE, ☎ 01232/
249176; and other
locations) gives advice
by phone and publishes
the free **"Holiday Insurance,"** which sets out
typical policy provisions
and costs.

L

LODGING

APARTMENT AND
VILLA RENTALS

Among the companies
to contact are **Rent-a-
Home International**

(7200 34th Ave. NW,
Seattle, WA 98117,
☎ 206/789–9377 or
800/488–7368) and
**Vacation Home Rentals
Worldwide** (235 Kens-
ington Ave., Norwood,
NJ 07648, ☎ 201/
767–9393 or 800/
633–3284). Members
of the travel club **Hideaways International**
($99 annually; 767
Islington St., Ports-
mouth, NH 03801,
☎ 603/430–4433 or
800/843–4433) receive
two annual guides plus
quarterly newsletters,
and arrange rentals
among themselves.

B&BS

Arizona B&B organiza-
tions include **Mi Casa Su
Casa** (Box 950, Tempe
85280, ☎ 602/990–
0682 or 800/456–0682,
FAX 602/990–3390), **Bed
& Breakfast Inn Arizona**
(8900 East Via Linda,
Suite 101, Scottsdale
85258, ☎ and fax 602/
860–9338, reservations
only 800/266–7829),
and the **Arizona Asso-
ciation of Bed and
Breakfast Inns** (Box
7186, Phoenix 85012,
☎ 602/277–0775).
The Arizona Office of
Tourism (*see* Visitor
Information, *below*) has
a statewide list of bed
and breakfasts.

CAMPING

Individual campgrounds
should be contacted
before travel for sugges-
tions as to specific
equipment to bring, as
well as necessary reser-
vations, advance de-
posits, and permits.
Most state parks have a
15-day maximum-stay
limit. For further de-
tails, contact the **Na-
tional Park Service** (202
E. Earll Dr., Suite 115,

Phoenix 85012, ☎ 602/
640–5250), **Bureau of
Land Management** (Box
16563, Phoenix 85011,
☎ 602/650–0528),
**Arizona State Parks
Department** (*see* State
Parks, *above*), **Apache
Sitgreaves National
Forest** (309 S. Mountain
Ave., Springerville
85938, ☎ 520/333–
4301), **Coconino Na-
tional Forest** (2323 E.
Greenlaw La., Flagstaff
86004, ☎ 520/527–
3600), **Coronado Na-
tional Forest** (Federal
Bldg., 300 W. Congress
St., Tucson 85701,
☎ 520/670–4552),
**Williams-Forest Service
Visitor Center** (200 W.
Railroad Ave., Williams
86046, ☎ 520/635–
4061), **Prescott National
Forest** (344 S. Cortez,
Prescott 86303, ☎ 520/
771–4700, 520/771–
4792 TTY), or **Tonto
National Forest** (2324
E. McDowell Rd.,
Phoenix 85006, ☎ 602/
225–5200). The **Na-
tional Forest Service hot
line** (☎ 602/225–5296)
gives recorded informa-
tion and campground
updates.

DUDE RANCHES

Contact the Arizona
Office of Tourism (*see*
Visitor Information,
below) for the names
and addresses of dude
ranches throughout the
state.

HOME EXCHANGE

Principal clearinghouses
include **Intervac International** ($65 annually;
Box 590504, San
Francisco, CA 94159,
☎ 415/435–3497),
which has three annual
directories; and **Loan-a-
Home** ($35–$45 annu-
ally; 2 Park La., Apt.
6E, Mount Vernon, NY

10552-3443, ☎ 914/664–7640), which specializes in long-term exchanges.

M
MONEY MATTERS

ATMS

For specific **Cirrus** locations in the United States and Canada, call 800/424–7787. For U.S. **Plus** locations, call 800/843–7587 and enter the area code and first three digits of the number from which you're calling (or of the calling area where you want an ATM).

WIRING FUNDS

Funds can be wired via **American Express MoneyGram** (☎ 800/926–9400 from the U.S. and Canada for locations and information) or **Western Union** (☎ 800/325–6000 for agent locations or to send using MasterCard or Visa, 800/321–2923 in Canada).

N
NATIONAL AND STATE PARKS

The **Golden Eagle Pass,** available to anyone, provides admission to all national parks within a one-year period for $25 and is available at any park charging admission or by mail from the **National Park Service** (Dept. of the Interior, Washington, DC 20240). The Park Service's Southwest regional office (☎ 505/988–6012) can answer regional questions. For seniors, the **Golden Age Passport** provides free admission and other benefits (*see* Senior Citizens, *below*).

For a complete listing of all state parks and their facilities, contact the **Arizona State Parks Department** (1300 W. Washington St., Phoenix 85007, ☎ 602/542–4174).

P
PASSPORTS AND VISAS

U.K. CITIZENS

For fees, documentation requirements, and to get an emergency passport, call the **London passport office** (☎ 0171/271–3000). For visa information, call the **U.S. Embassy Visa Information Line** (☎ 0891/200–290; calls cost 49p per minute or 39p per minute cheap rate) or write the **U.S. Embassy Visa Branch** (5 Upper Grosvenor St., London W1A 2JB). If you live in Northern Ireland, write the **U.S. Consulate General** (Queen's House, Queen St., Belfast BTI 6EO).

PHOTO HELP

The **Kodak Information Center** (☎ 800/242–2424) answers consumer questions about film and photography.

R
RAIL TRAVEL

The *Southwest Chief* operates daily between Los Angeles and Chicago, stopping in Kingman, Flagstaff, and Winslow. The *Sunset Limited* travels three times each week between Los Angeles and Miami, with stops at Yuma, Phoenix, Tempe, Coolidge, Tucson, and Benson. For details, contact **Amtrak** (☎ 800/872–7245).

ROCKHOUNDING

The **Department of Mines and Mineral Resources** (1502 W. Washington St., Phoenix 85007, ☎ 602/255–3795) is an excellent source of information about specimens that can be found in each part of the state.

S
SENIOR CITIZENS

DISCOUNT PASSES

For $10, U.S. residents age 62 or older can pick up a Golden Age Passport. In addition to lifetime free admission to national parks, the pass allows a 50% discount on park facilities and services (excluding those run by private concessionaires).

EDUCATIONAL TRAVEL

The nonprofit **Elderhostel** (75 Federal St., 3rd Floor, Boston, MA 02110, ☎ 617/426–7788), for people 60 and older, has offered inexpensive study programs since 1975. The nearly 2,000 courses cover everything from marine science to Greek myths and cowboy poetry. Fees for programs in the United States and Canada, which usually last one week, run about $300, not including transportation.

ORGANIZATIONS

Contact the **American Association of Retired Persons** (AARP, 601 E St. NW, Washington,

DC 20049, ☎ 202/434–2277; $8 per person or couple annually). Its Purchase Privilege Program gets members discounts on lodging, car rentals, and sightseeing, and the AARP Motoring Plan furnishes domestic trip-routing information and emergency road-service aid for an annual fee of $39.95 per person or couple ($59.95 for a premium version).

For other discounts on lodgings, car rentals, and other travel products, along with magazines and newsletters, contact the **National Council of Senior Citizens** (membership $12 annually; 1331 F St. NW, Washington, DC 20004, ☎ 202/347–8800) and **Mature Outlook** (subscription $9.95 annually; 6001 N. Clark St., Chicago, IL 60660, ☎ 312/465–6466 or 800/336–6330).

PUBLICATIONS

The 50+ Traveler's Guidebook: Where to Go, Where to Stay, What to Do, by Anita Williams and Merrimac Dillon ($12.95; St. Martin's Press, 175 5th Ave., New York, NY 10010, ☎ 212/674–5151 or 800/288–2131), offers many useful tips. **"The Mature Traveler"** ($29.95; Box 50400, Reno, NV 89513, ☎ 702/786–7419), a monthly newsletter, covers travel deals.

SPORTS

BASEBALL

During spring training, the **Chicago Cubs** play at Hohokam Park in Mesa (☎ 602/964–4467), the **Oakland**

Athletics at Phoenix Municipal Stadium (☎ 602/392–0074), the **San Francisco Giants** at Scottsdale Stadium (☎ 602/990–7972), the **California Angels** at Diablo Stadium in Tempe (☎ 602/438–9300), and the **Milwaukee Brewers** at the Compadre Stadium in Chandler (☎ 602/895–1200). Both the **San Diego Padres and the Seattle Mariners** train at Peoria Stadium (☎ 602/878–4337) in another Phoenix suburb. The **Colorado Rockies** play at Tucson's Hi-Corbett Field (☎ 520/327–9467). For current information on all aspects of Cactus League baseball, contact the **Mesa Convention and Visitor's Bureau** (120 North Center St., Mesa 85201, ☎ 602/827–4700 or 800/283–6372).

BICYCLING

Call the county **Parks and Recreation Department** in the area you're visiting for information on nearby bike paths. **The Arizona Bicycle Club, Inc.** (Box 7191, Phoenix, AZ 85011, ☎ 602/264–5478 or 602/279–6674) publishes a schedule of the many bicycle races that take place throughout the state.

FISHING

Fishing licenses are required and can be obtained from the **Arizona Game and Fish Department** (2221 W. Greenway Rd., Phoenix 85023, ☎ 602/942–3000). For permission to fish San Carlos Lake on the San Carlos Indian reservation call 520/475–2343.

GOLF

For a list of Arizona's golfing facilities, contact the **Arizona Golf Association** (7226 N. 16th St., Suite 200, Phoenix 85020, ☎ 602/944–3035 or 800/458–8484).

HIKING

The **Backcountry Office** (☎ 602/638–7888) provides hikers with trail details, weather conditions, and packing suggestions. For hikers who prefer to travel with a group, the **Sierra Club** (602/253–8633) leads a variety of wilderness treks. Contact the local chapters in Phoenix, Tucson, Kingman, Prescott, Sedona, Flagstaff, and Yuma for information on guided hikes in these area.

RIVER RAFTING

Contact the **Arizona Office of Tourism** (*see* Visitor Information, *below*) for an extensive list of rafting outfits, or *see* Tour Operators, *below*.

SKIING

For cross-country skiing, **Flagstaff Nordic Center** (☎ 520/779–1951), **Mormon Lake Ski Touring Center** (☎ 520/354–2240) southeast of Flagstaff, **North Rim Nordic Center** (☎ 602/526–0924 or 800/525–0924 outside AZ), and miles of crisscrossing trails around **Alpine** (☎ 602/339–4384) are recommended. Equipment and instruction are readily available. We advise making reservations in the busy season.

Important Contacts A to Z

THE GOLD GUIDE / IMPORTANT CONTACTS

Sunrise Park Resort in McNary (☎ 800/772–7669), owned and operated by the White Mountain Apache Indians, encompasses three mountain peaks and is the state's largest ski area. Other popular resorts are **Arizona Snowbowl,** near Flagstaff (☎ 520/779–1951), and **Mt. Lemmon Ski Valley,** near Tucson (☎ 520/576–1321). Though they aren't as impressive as the Rockies, ski resorts cater to all levels and provide instruction and equipment rental.

TENNIS

Arizona offers a multitude of tennis opportunities, from hard courts at city parks and university campuses to full-scale programs at ultraposh tennis-oriented resorts such as **John Gardiner's Tennis Ranch** (5700 E. McDonald Dr., Scottsdale 85253, ☎ 602/948–2100 or 800/245–2051), one of the country's best. Most hotels either have their own courts or are affiliated with a private or municipal facility.

STUDENTS

GROUPS

Major tour operators include **Contiki Holidays** (300 Plaza Alicante, Suite 900, Garden Grove, CA 92640, ☎ 714/740–0808 or 800/466–0610).

HOSTELING

Contact **Hostelling International–American Youth Hostels** (733 15th St. NW, Suite 840, Washington, DC 20005, ☎ 202/783–6161) in

the United States, **Hostelling International–Canada** (205 Catherine St., Suite 400, Ottawa, Ontario K2P 1C3, ☎ 613/237–7884) in Canada, and the **Youth Hostel Association of England and Wales** (Trevelyan House, 8 St. Stephen's Hill, St. Albans, Hertfordshire AL1 2DY, ☎ 01727/855215 and 01727/845047) in the United Kingdom. Membership ($25 in the U.S., C$26.75 in Canada, and £9 in the U.K.) gets you access to 5,000 hostels worldwide that charge US$7–$20 nightly per person.

I.D. CARDS

To get discounts on transportation and admissions, get the **International Student Identity Card** (ISIC) if you're a registered student or the **International Youth Card** (IYC) if you're under 26. In the United States, the ISIC and IYC cards cost $16 each and include basic travel accident and illness coverage, plus a toll-free travel hot line. Apply through the Council on International Educational Exchange (*see* Organizations, *below*). Cards are available for $15 each in Canada from Travel Cuts (187 College St., Toronto, Ontario M5T 1P7, ☎ 416/979–2406 or 800/667–2887) and in the United Kingdom for £5 each at student unions and student travel companies.

ORGANIZATIONS

A major contact is the **Council on International**

Educational Exchange (CIEE, 205 E. 42nd St., 16th Floor, New York, NY 10017, ☎ 212/661–1450) with locations in Boston (729 Boylston St., Boston, MA 02116, ☎ 617/266–1926), Miami (9100 S. Dadeland Blvd., Miami, FL 33156, ☎ 305/670–9261), Los Angeles (1093 Broxton Ave., Los Angeles, CA 90024, ☎ 310/208–3551), 43 college towns nationwide, and the United Kingdom (28A Poland St., London W1V 3DB, ☎ 0171/437–7767). Twice a year, it publishes *Student Travels* magazine. The CIEE's Council Travel Service offers domestic air passes for bargain travel within the United States and is the exclusive U.S. agent for several student-discount cards.

Campus Connections (325 Chestnut St., Suite 1101, Philadelphia, PA 19106, ☎ 215/625–8585 or 800/428–3235) specializes in discounted accommodations and airfares for students. The **Educational Travel Centre** (438 N. Frances St., Madison, WI 53703, ☎ 608/256–5551) offers rail passes and low-cost airline tickets, mostly for flights departing from Chicago.

In Canada, also contact **Travel Cuts** (*see above*).

T

TOUR OPERATORS

Among the companies selling tours and packages to Arizona, the following have a proven reputation, are nationally known, and offer plenty of options.

GROUP TOURS

For escorted deluxe tours to Arizona, contact **Maupintour** (Box 807, Lawrence, KS 66044, ☎ 913/843–1211 or 800/255–4266) and **Tauck Tours** (11 Wilton Rd., Westport, CT 06880, ☎ 203/226–6911 or 800/468–2825). Another operator falling between deluxe and first-class is **Globus** (5301 South Federal Circle, Littleton, CO 80123-2980, ☎ 303/797–2800 or 800/221–0090). In the first-class and tourist range, try **Collette Tours** (162 Middle Street, Pawtucket, RI 02860, ☎ 401/728–3805 or 800/832–4656), **Domenico Tours** (750 Broadway, Bayonne, NJ 07002, ☎ 201/823–8687 or 800/554–8687), and **Mayflower Tours** (1225 Warren Ave., Downers Grove, IL 60515, ☎ 708/960–3430 or 800/323–7604). For budget and tourist class programs, try **Cosmos** (*see* Globus, *above*).

PACKAGES

Independent vacation packages are available from major tour operators and airlines. Carriers to contact include: **American Airlines Fly AAway Vacations** (☎ 800/321–2121), **SuperCities** (139 Main St., Cambridge, MA 02142, ☎ 617/621–0099 or 800/333–1234), **Continental Airlines' Grand Destinations** (☎ 800/634–5555), **Delta Dream Vacations** (☎ 800/872–7786), **Certified Vaca-**

tions (Box 1525, Ft. Lauderdale, FL 33302, ☎ 305/522–1414 or 800/233-7260), **TWA Getaway Vacations** (☎ 800/438–2929), **United Vacations** (☎ 800/328–6877), **Kingdom Tours** (300 Market St., Kingston, PA 18704, ☎ 717/283–4241 or 800/872–8857), and **USAir Vacations** (☎ 800/455–0123). **Funjet Vacations,** based in Milwaukee, Wisconsin, and Gogo Tours in Ramsey, New Jersy, sell packages to Arizona only through travel agents.

FROM THE U.K.➤ Companies offering packages to Arizona include **British Airways Holidays** (Astral Towers, Betts Way, London Rd., Crawley, West Sussex RH10 2XA, ☎ 01293/518–022); **Jetsave Travel Ltd.** (Sussex House, London Rd., East Grinstead, West Sussex RH19 1LD, ☎ 01342/312033); **Key to America** (1–3 Station Rd., Ashford, Middlesex TW15 2UW, ☎ 01784/248–777); **Kuoni Travel** (Kuoni House, Dorking, Surrey RH5 4AZ, ☎ 01306/742222); and **Premier Holidays** (Premier Travel Centre, Westbrook, Milton Rd., Cambridge CB4 1YG, ☎ 01223/516–688).

Travel agencies that offer cheap fares to Arizona include **Trailfinders** (42–50 Earl's Court Rd., London W8 6FT, ☎ 0171/937–5400), **Travel Cuts** (295a Regent St., London W1R 7YA, ☎ 0171/637–3161; *see* Students, *above*), and

Flightfile (49 Tottenham Court Rd., London W1P 9RE, ☎ 0171/700–2722).

THEME TRIPS

ADVENTURE➤ **All Adventure Travel** (5589 Arapahoe #208, Boulder, CO 80303, ☎ 800/537–4025) can book hiking, walking, kayaking, and rafting programs in the Southwest. Packages from **American Southwest Tours** (Box 4300, Durango, CO 81302, ☎ 303/247–2955 or 800/644–5755) combine rafting, mountain biking, and horseback riding. **World Wide River Expeditions** (153 E. 7200 South, Midvale, UT 84047, ☎ 800/231–2769) combines rafting with mountain biking and hiking. **Trek America** (Box 470, Blairstown, NJ 07825, ☎ 908/362–9198 or 800/221–0596) includes hiking and camping in several of its Westerner treks.

ARCHAEOLOGY➤ **Southwest Ed-Ventures** (Four Corners School of Outdoor Education, Box 1029, Dept. ST, Monticello, UT 84535, ☎ 801/587–2156, FAX 801/587–2193) visits rarely viewed Native American ruins and rock art in the Southwest. **American Southwest Tours** (*see* Adventure, *above*) will arrange for you to join a professional dig. **The Archaeological Conservancy** (5301 Central NE, Suite 1218, Albuquerque, NM 87108-1517, ☎ 505/266–1540) is a nonprofit organization that conducts tours of Southwestern ruins with an emphasis on Native American culture. **Crow Canyon Archaeological Center** (23390 Country Rd. K, Cortez, CO 81321, ☎ 800/422–8975, FAX 303/565–4859) visits ancestral Pueblo sites and investigates the symbolism behind Southwestern rock art. **Earthwatch** (680 Mount Auburn St., Watertown, MA 02272, ☎ 617/926–8200 or 800/776–0188) recruits volunteers to serve in its EarthCorps as short-term assistants to scientists or research expeditions.

BICYCLING➤ Bike tours of Arizona are available from **Backroads** (1516 5th St., Suite A550, Berkeley, CA 94710-1470, ☎ 510/527–1555 or 800/462–2848).

CULTURAL➤ **Southwest Ed-Ventures** (*see* Archaeology, *above*) employs local artists and authors as tour guides. Art and culture are the focus of several itineraries planned by **American Southwest Tours** (*see* Adventure, *above*).

DRIVING➤ Custom-tailored itineraries for independent travelers can be arranged by **Off The Beaten Path** (109 E. Main, Bozeman, MT 59715, ☎ 800/445–2995). Itineraries include stays at distinctive inns and ranches, visits to unique cultural attractions such as ruins and historical sites, and meals in the region's best restaurants.

DUDE RANCHES➤ **American Wilderness Experience** (Box 1486, Boulder, CO 80306,

☎ 303/444–2622 or 800/444-DUDE) books ranches from luxurious to rustic. Also contact **Off The Beaten Path** (*see* Driving, *above*).

GOLF➤ Packages including accommodations, confirmed tee-times, and golfing fees are sold by **Golfpac** (Box 162366, Altamonte Springs, FL 32716-2366, ☎ 407/260–2288 or 800/327–0878) and **Golftrips** (Box 2314, Winter Haven, FL 33883-2314, ☎ 813/314–1300 or 800/428–1940).

KAYAKING➤ Inflatable kayaking trips in the Grand Canyon are sold by **Orange Torpedo Trips** (Box 1111, Dept. STI, Grants Pass, OR 97526, ☎ 503/479–5061 or 800/635–2925).

MOTORCYCLING➤ **Western States Motorcycle Tours** (1823 W. Seldon La., Phoenix, AZ 85021, ☎ and fax 602/943–9030) leads rides through the Southwest, including the Grand Canyon.

NATIVE AMERICAN HISTORY➤ **Southwest Ed-Ventures** (*see above*) explores Navajo, Hopi and Ute culture. **American Southwest Tours** (*see above*) emphasizes Native American history in its various itineraries. **Crow Canyon Archaeological Center** (*see above*) visits the homes and studios of Native American jewelers, potters, weavers, sand painters, and kachina carvers.

RIVER RAFTING➤ For trips on the Colorado River, try **Grand Canyon Dories** (Box 216, Al-

taville, CA 95221, ☎ 209/736–0805 or 800/877–DORY) and **Canyoneers** (Box 2997, Flagstaff, AZ 86003, ☎ 602/526–0924 or 800/525–0924), OARS (Box 67, Angels Camp, CA 95222, ☎ 800/346–6277). Rafting on the Salt River Canyons is the specialty of Far Flung Adventures (Box 377, Terlingua, TX 79852, ☎ 915/371–2489 or 800/359–4138).

WALKING➤ **Country Walkers** (Box 180S, Waterbury, VT 05676, ☎ 802/244–1387) takes a leisurely look at the Sonoran Desert.

ORGANIZATIONS

The **National Tour Association** (546 E. Main St., Lexington, KY 40508, ☎ 606/226–4444 or 800/682–8886) and **United States Tour Operators Association** (USTOA, 211 E. 51st St., Suite 12B, New York, NY 10022, ☎ 212/750–7371) can provide lists of member operators and information on booking tours.

PUBLICATIONS

Consult the brochure **"Worldwide Tour & Vacation Package Finder"** from the National Tour Association (*see above*) and the Better Business Bureau's **"Tips on Travel Packages"** (publication No. 24-195, $2; 4200 Wilson Blvd., Arlington, VA 22203.

TRAVEL AGENCIES

For names of reputable agencies in your area, contact the **American Society of Travel Agents** (1101 King St., Suite

200, Alexandria, VA 22314, ☎ 703/739–2782).

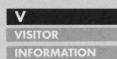

VISITOR INFORMATION

The **Arizona Office of Tourism** (1100 W. Washington St., Phoenix 85007, ☎ 602/542–8687 or 800/842–8257, FAX 602/542–4068) can send a comprehensive tourist kit as well as information on the 14 tribal councils, a map of reservations, and a list of addresses and phone numbers. The **Hopi Tribe Office of the Chairman** (Box 123, Kykotsmovi 86039, ☎ 520/734–2441, FAX 520/734–2435) and the **Navajoland Tourism Department** (Box 663, Window Rock 86515, ☎ 520/871–6659 or 871–7371, FAX 520/871–7381) can inform you of upcoming tribal activities.

In the U.K., also contact the **United States Travel and Tourism Administration** (Box 1EN, London W1A 1EN, ☎ 0171/495–4466). For a free USA pack, write the USTTA at Box 170, Ashford, Kent TN24 0ZX). Enclose stamps worth £1.50.

WEATHER

For current conditions and forecasts, plus the local time and helpful travel tips, call the **Weather Channel Connection** (☎ 900/932–8437; 95¢ per minute) from a touch-tone phone.

SMART TRAVEL TIPS A TO Z

Basic Information on Traveling in Arizona and Savvy Tips for Making Your Trip a Breeze

The more you travel, the more you learn about how to make trips run like clockwork. To help make your travels hassle-free, Fodor's editors have rounded up dozens of tips from our contributors and travel experts all over the world, as well as basic information on visiting Arizona. For names, addresses, and phone numbers of organizations to contact and publications that can give you more information, *see* Important Contacts A to Z, *above.*

A
AIR TRAVEL

If time is an issue, **always look for nonstop flights,** which require no change of plane and make no stops. If possible, **avoid connecting flights,** which stop at least once and can involve a change of plane, although the flight number remains the same; if the first leg is late, the second waits.

CUTTING COSTS

The Sunday travel section of most newspapers is a good source of deals.

MAJOR AIRLINES➤ The least-expensive airfares from the major airlines are priced for round-trip travel and are subject to restrictions. You must usually re-serve in advance and **buy the ticket within 24 hours** to get cheaper fares, and you may have to **stay over a Saturday night.** The lowest fare is subject to availability, and only a small percentage of the plane's total seats are sold at that price. It's good to **call a number of airlines, and when you are quoted a good price, reserve it on the spot**—the same fare on the same flight may not be available the next day. Airlines generally allow you to change your return date for a $25 to $50 fee, but most low-fare tickets are nonrefundable. However, if you don't use it, you can apply the cost toward the purchase price of a new ticket, again for a small charge.

CONSOLIDATORS➤ Consolidators, who buy tickets at reduced rates from scheduled airlines, sell them at prices below the lowest available from the airlines directly—usually without advance restrictions. Sometimes you can even get your money back if you need to return the ticket. Carefully read the fine print detailing penalties for changes and cancellations. If you doubt the reliability of a consolidator, **confirm your reservation with the airline.**

ALOFT

AIRLINE FOOD➤ If you hate airline food, **ask for special meals** when booking. These can be vegetarian, low choles-terol, or kosher, for example; commonly prepared to order in smaller numbers than standard catered fare, they can be tastier.

SMOKING➤ Smoking is banned on all flights within the U.S. of less than six hours' duration and on all Canadian flights; the ban also applies to domestic segments of international flights aboard U.S. and foreign carriers. Delta has banned smoking system-wide.

C
CAMERAS, CAMCORDERS, AND COMPUTERS

LAPTOPS

Before you depart, **check your portable computer's battery,** because you may be asked at security to turn on the computer to prove that it is what it appears to be. At the airport, you may prefer to **request a manual inspection,** although security X-rays do not harm hard-drive or floppy-disk storage.

PHOTOGRAPHY

If your camera is new or if you haven't used it for a while, **shoot and develop a few rolls of film** before you leave. Always **store film in a cool, dry place**—never in a car's glove compartment or on the shelf under the rear window.

Every pass through an X-ray machine increases film's chance of clouding. To protect it, carry it in a clear plastic bag and **ask for hand inspection** at security. Such requests are almost always honored at U.S. airports, and usually are accommodated abroad. Don't depend on a lead-lined bag to protect film in checked luggage—the airline may increase the radiation to see what's inside.

VIDEO

Before your trip, **test your camcorder, invest in a skylight filter to protect the lens, and charge the batteries.** (Airport security personnel may ask you to turn on the camcorder to prove that it's what it appears to be).

Videotape is not damaged by X-rays, but it may be harmed by the magnetic field of a walk-through metal detector, so **ask that videotapes be hand-checked.**

CHILDREN
AND TRAVEL

Many large resorts and dude ranches offer special activities for children, and many offer baby-sitting services. Children of all ages are enthralled by the Wild West flavor around Tucson and the southeastern part of the state, with Tombstone ranking as a particular favorite. If you're driving on long desert stretches, take along plenty of games and snacks.

BABY-SITTING

For recommended local sitters, **check with your hotel desk.**

DRIVING

If you are renting a car, **arrange for a car seat when you reserve.** Sometimes they're free.

FLYING

On domestic flights, children under 2 not occupying a seat travel free. Older children currently travel on the lowest applicable adult fare.

BAGGAGE➤ In general, the adult baggage allowance applies for children paying half or more of the adult fare.

SAFETY SEATS➤ According to the FAA, it's a good idea to **use safety seats aloft.** Airline policy varies. U.S. carriers allow FAA-approved models, but airlines usually require that you buy a ticket, even if your child would otherwise ride free, because the seats must be strapped into regular passenger seats.

FACILITIES➤ When making your reservation, **ask for children's meals and a freestanding bassinet** if you need them; the latter are available only to those with seats at the bulkhead, where there's enough legroom. If you don't need a bassinet, **think twice before requesting bulkhead seats**—the only storage for in-flight necessities is in the inconveniently distant overhead bins.

LODGING

Most hotels allow children under a certain age to stay in their parents' room at no extra charge, while others charge them as extra adults; be sure to **ask about the cut-off age.**

CUSTOMS
AND DUTIES

IN ARIZONA

U.K. CITIZENS➤ British visitors age 21 or over may import the following into the United States: 200 cigarettes or 50 cigars or 2 kilograms of tobacco; 1 U.S. liter of alcohol; gifts to the value of $100. Restricted items include meat products, seeds, plants, and fruits. Never carry illegal drugs.

BACK HOME

IN CANADA➤ Once per calendar year, when you've been out of Canada for at least seven days, you may bring in C$300 worth of goods duty-free. If you've been away less than seven days but more than 48 hours, the duty-free exemption drops to C$100 but can be claimed any number of times (as can a C$20 duty-free exemption for absences of 24 hours or more). You cannot combine the yearly and 48-hour exemptions, use the C$300 exemption only partially (to save the balance for a later trip), or pool exemptions with family members. Goods claimed under the C$300 exemption may follow you by mail; those claimed under the lesser exemptions must accompany you.

Alcohol and tobacco products may be included in the yearly and 48-hour exemptions but not in the 24-hour exemption. If you meet the age requirements of the province through which you reenter Canada, you may bring in, duty-free, 1.14 liters (40 imperial ounces) of wine or liquor *or* 24 12-ounce cans or bottles of beer or ale. If you are 16 or older, you may bring in, duty-free, 200 cigarettes, 50 cigars or cigarillos, and 400 tobacco sticks or 400 grams of manufactured tobacco. Alcohol and tobacco must accompany you on your return.

An unlimited number of gifts valued up to C$60 each may be mailed to Canada duty-free. These do not count as part of your exemption. Label the package "Unsolicited Gift— Value under $60." Alcohol and tobacco are excluded.

IN THE U.K.➢ From countries outside the EU, including the United States, you may import duty-free 200 cigarettes, 100 cigarillos, 50 cigars or 250 grams of tobacco; 1 liter of spirits or 2 liters of fortified or sparkling wine; 2 liters of still table wine; 60 milliliters of perfume; 250 milliliters of toilet water; plus £136 worth of other goods, including gifts and souvenirs.

D

DINING

Make advance reservations at better restaurants, and don't be misled by the casual lifestyle—**ask about** **dress codes** first to avoid being turned away at the door. Some establishments, including some at more elegant resorts, require men to wear a jacket and tie.

FOR TRAVELERS
WITH DISABILITIES

Most of the region's national parks and recreation areas have wheelchair-accessible visitor centers, rest rooms, campsites, and trails, and more are being added every year. Even so, when discussing accessibility with an operator or reservationist, **ask hard questions.** Are there *any* stairs, inside *or* out? Are there grab bars next to the toilet *and* in the shower/tub? How wide is the doorway to the room? To the bathroom? For the most extensive facilities, meeting the latest legal specifications, **opt for newer facilities,** which more often have been designed with access in mind. Older properties or ships must usually be retrofitted and may offer more limited facilities as a result. Be sure to **discuss your needs before booking.**

DISCOUNT CLUBS

Travel clubs offer members unsold space on airplanes, cruise ships, and package tours at as much as 50% below regular prices. Membership may include a regular bulletin or access to a toll-free hot line giving details of available trips departing from three or four days to several months in the future. Most also offer 50% discounts off hotel rack rates. Before booking with a club, **make sure the hotel or other supplier isn't offering a better deal.**

DRIVING

Major approaches from the east and west are I–40, I–10, I–8, and U.S. 60. Main north–south routes are I–17, I–10 (from Phoenix to Tucson), and U.S. 89. Other artery roads are U.S. 70 and U.S. 64 (U.S. 160 in Arizona) from the east.

Most highways into the state are good to excellent, with easy access, roadside facilities, rest stops, and scenic views. The speed limit is 65 miles per hour, but **don't drive much faster than the limit**—police use sophisticated detection systems to catch violators.

At some point you will probably pass through one or more of the state's 23 Indian reservations. Roads and other areas within reservation boundaries are under the jurisdiction of reservation police and governed by separate rules and regulations. **Observe all signs and respect Indians' privacy.**

PRECAUTIONS

DUST STORMS➢ These usually occur mid-July to mid-September (the monsoon months), just before thunderstorms hit, causing extremely low visibility. If you're on the highway, **pull as far off the road as possible, turn off your headlights, and wait for the storm to subside.**

FLASH FLOODS➤ They may sound apocalyptic or overly cautious, but warnings about flash floods should not be taken lightly. Sudden downpours send torrents of water racing into low-lying areas so dry that they are unable to absorb such a huge quantity of water so quickly. The result is powerful walls of water suddenly descending upon these low-lying areas, devastating anything in their paths. If you see rainclouds or thunderstorms in the area, stay away from dry riverbeds (also called arroyos or washes). If you find yourself in one, get out quickly. If you're with a car in a long gulley, leave your car and climb out of the gulley. You simply won't be able to outdrive a speeding wave. The idea is to **get to higher ground immediately when it rains.** Major highways are mostly floodproof, but some smaller roads dip through washes. If showers are nearby, look before you cross. Washes filled with water should not be crossed until you can see the bottom. By all means, don't camp in these areas at any time, interesting as they may seem.

DESERT HEAT➤ Vehicles and passengers should be well equipped for searing summer heat in the low desert. If you're planning to drive through the desert, **carry plenty of water, a good spare tire, a jack, and emergency supplies.** If you get stranded, stay with your vehicle and wait for help to arrive.

FRAGILE DESERT LIFE➤ The dry and easily desecrated desert floor takes centuries to overcome human damage. Consequently, it is illegal for four-wheel-drive and all-terrain vehicles and motorcycles to travel off established roadways.

H
HIKING

Be sure to take the following precautions when you go for a hike of any length.

SUN PROTECTION

Wear a hat and sunglasses and put on sun block to protect against the burning Arizona sun. And **watch out for heatstroke.** Symptoms include headache, dizziness, and fatigue, which can turn into convulsions, unconsciousness, and can lead to death. If someone in your party develops any of these conditions, have one person seek emergency help while others move the victim into the shade, wrap him or her in wet clothing (is a stream nearby?) to cool him or her down.

DEHYDRATION

This underestimated danger can be very serious, especially considering that one of the first major symptoms is the inability to swallow. It may be the easiest hazard to avoid, however; simply **drink every 10–15 minutes,** up to a gallon of water per day in summer.

ANIMAL BITES

Wherever you're hiking, particularly between April and October, **keep a lookout for rattlesnakes.** You're likely not to have any problems if you maintain distance from snakes that you see—they can strike only half of their length, so a 6-foot clearance should allow you to stay unharmed, especially if you **don't provoke them.** If you are bitten by a rattler, don't panic. Just get to a hospital within 2–3 hours of the bite. Keep in mind that 30–40% of bites are dry bites, where the snake uses no venom (still, get thee to a hospital). **Avoid night hikes without rangers,** when snakes are on the prowl and less visible. You may want to pick up a kit called The Extractor for use if bitten.

Scorpions and Gila monsters are really less of a concern, since they strike only when provoked. To avoid scorpion encounters, **don't put your hands where you can't see with your eyes:** under rocks and in holes. Likewise, if you move a rock to sit down, make sure that scorpions haven't been exposed. Campers should shake out shoes in the morning, since scorpions like warm, moist places. If you are bitten, see a ranger about symptoms that may develop. Chances are good that you won't need to go to a hospital. Children are a different case, however, for whom scorpion stings can be fatal. Always try to keep an eye on what they may be getting their hands into to avoid the scorpion's sting. Gila monsters are relatively rare, but they are most active between April and June when they do most of their hunting.

HYPOTHERMIA

Temperatures in Arizona can vary widely from day to night—as much as 40°F. Be sure to **bring enough warm clothing for hiking and camping, along with wet weather gear.** Exposure to the degree that body temperature dips below 95° F produces the following symptoms: chills, tiredness, then uncontrollable shivering and irrational behavior, with the victim not always recognizing that he or she is cold. If someone in your party is suffering from any of this, wrap him or her in blankets and/or a warm sleeping bag immediately and try to keep him or her awake. The fastest way to raise body temperature is through skin-to-skin contact in a sleeping bag. Drinking warm liquids also helps.

POTABLE WATER

Never drink from any stream, no matter how clear it may be. Giardia organisms can turn your stomach inside out. The easiest way to purify water is to **dissolve a water purification tablet** in it. Camping equipment stores also carry purification pumps. **Boil water for 15 minutes,** a reliable method, if time- and fuel-consuming.

I
INSURANCE

Travel insurance can protect your monetary investment, replace your luggage and its contents, or provide for medical coverage should you fall ill during your trip. Most tour operators, travel agents, and insurance agents sell specialized health-and-accident, flight, trip-cancellation, and luggage insurance as well as comprehensive policies with some or all of these features. Before you make any purchase, **review your existing health and homeowner policies** to find out whether they cover expenses incurred while traveling.

BAGGAGE

Airline liability for your baggage is limited to $1,250 per person on domestic flights. On international flights, the airlines' liability is $9.07 per pound or $20 per kilogram for checked baggage (roughly $640 per 70-pound bag) and $400 per passenger for unchecked baggage. However, this excludes valuable items such as jewelry and cameras that are listed in your ticket's fine print. You can buy additional insurance from the airline at check-in, but first **see if your homeowner's policy covers lost luggage.**

FLIGHT

You should **think twice before buying flight insurance.** Often purchased as a last-minute impulse at the airport, it pays a lump sum when a plane crashes, either to a beneficiary if the insured dies or sometimes to a surviving passenger who loses eyesight or a limb. Supplementing the airlines' coverage described in the limits-of-liability paragraphs on your ticket, it's expensive and basically unnecessary. Charging an airline ticket to a major credit card often automatically entitles you to coverage and may also include bus, train, and ship travel.

HEALTH

FOR U.K. TRAVELERS➤ According to the Association of British Insurers, a trade association representing 450 insurance companies, it's wise to **buy extra medical coverage when you visit the United States.** You can buy an annual travel-insurance policy valid for most vacations during the year in which it's purchased. If you go this route, make sure it covers you if you have a preexisting medical condition or are pregnant.

TRIP

Without insurance, you will lose all or most of your money if you must cancel your trip due to illness or any other reason. Especially if your airline ticket, cruise, or package tour is nonrefundable and cannot be changed, it's essential that you **buy trip-cancellation-and-interruption insurance.** When considering how much coverage you need, look for a policy that will cover the cost of your trip plus the nondiscounted price of a one-way airline ticket should you need to return home early. Read the fine print carefully, especially sections defining "family member" and "preexisting medical conditions." Also **consider default or bankruptcy insurance,** which protects you against a supplier's failure to deliver. However, such policies often do not cover default by a travel agency, tour operator, airline, or cruise line if you bought your tour and the coverage directly from the firm in question.

L
LODGING

Arizona's hotels and motels run the gamut—from world-class resorts to budget chains, and from historic inns, bed-and-breakfasts, and mountain lodges, to dude ranches, campgrounds, and RV parks providing even more options. And there is plenty of camping. Most nationwide and international companies are represented within the state. Large resorts offer extensive recreational and dining facilities, while modest motels may provide nothing more than a small swimming pool and complimentary coffee. **Make reservations well in advance for the high season—** winter in the desert south and summer in the high country. Tremendous bargains

can be found off-season, when even the most exclusive establishments cut their rates by half.

APARTMENT AND VILLA RENTALS

If you want a home base that's roomy enough for a family and comes with cooking facilities, **consider a furnished rental.** It's generally cost-wise, too, although not always—some rentals are luxury properties (economical only when your party is large). Home-exchange directories do list rentals—often second homes owned by prospective house swappers—and some services search for a house or apartment for you and handle the paperwork. Some send an illustrated catalogue and others send photographs of specific properties, sometimes at a charge; up-front registration fees may apply.

CAMPING

You can choose from a feast of federal, state, Native American, or private campgrounds in virtually all parts of the state. Facilities range from deluxe parks with swimming pools and recreation rooms to primitive backcountry wilderness sites. Most campgrounds provide toilets, drinking water, showers, and hookups. Camping is also permitted in Arizona's seven national forests, but be forewarned that they have no facilities whatsoever.

GEAR➤ **Pack according to season, region, and length of trip.** Basics

include a sleeping bag, a tent (optional, and forbidden in some RV parks), a camp stove, cooking utensils, food and water supplies, a first-aid kit, insect repellent, sunscreen, a lantern, trash bags, a rope, and a tarp. In case you forget something, almost every camping item is available for sale or rent at one of Arizona's many sporting-goods shops.

PRECAUTIONS➤ Don't forget to **shake out your shoes** in the morning after climbing out of your sleeping bag, since scorpions like warm, moist places. Also, keep in mind that flash floods after sudden rain showers are extremely dangerous, sending water hurtling through low-lying areas. For your safety, **avoid camping in or next to dry riverbeds, washes, arroyos, etc.**

DUDE RANCHES

Down-home Western lifestyle, cooking, and activities are the focus of guest ranches, situated primarily in Tucson and Wickenburg. Some are resortlike properties where guests are pampered, while smaller family-run ranches expect *everyone* to join in the chores. Horseback riding and other outdoor recreational activities are emphasized. Most dude ranches are closed in summer.

HOME EXCHANGE

If you would like to find a house, an apartment, or other vacation property to exchange for your own while on vacation, **become a member of a home-exchange organization,** which will send you its annual directories listing available exchanges and will include your own listing in at least one of them. Arrangements for the actual exchange are made by the two parties to it, not by the organization. (*See* Lodging *in* Important Contacts A to Z, *above,* for specific organizations.)

M
MONEY AND EXPENSES

ATMS

Chances are that you can **use your bank card at ATMs** to withdraw money from an account and get cash advances on a credit-card account if your card has been programmed with a personal identification number (PIN). Before leaving home, **check in on frequency limits** for withdrawals and cash advances.

On cash advances you are charged interest from the day you receive the money from ATMs as well as from tellers. Transaction fees for ATM withdrawals outside your home turf may be higher than for withdrawals at home.

Plan accordingly for remote parts of Arizona where you won't be able to find banks or ATMs—most notably the Navajo and Hopi Indian reservations and the North Rim of the Grand Canyon and surrounding Arizona Strip country.

TRAVELER'S CHECKS

Whether or not to buy traveler's checks depends on where you are headed; **take cash to rural areas and small towns, traveler's checks to cities.** The most widely recognized are American Express, Citicorp, Thomas Cook, and Visa, which are sold by major commercial banks for 1% to 3% of the checks' face value—it pays to **shop around.** Both American Express and Thomas Cook issue checks that can be counter-signed and used by you or your traveling companion. Record the numbers of the checks, cross them off as you spend them, and keep this information separate from your checks.

WIRING MONEY

You don't have to be a cardholder to send or receive funds through MoneyGram^{SM} from American Express. Just go to a MoneyGram agent, located in retail and convenience stores and in American Express Travel Offices. Pay up to $1,000 with cash or a credit card, anything over that in cash. The money can be picked up within 10 minutes in cash or check at the nearest MoneyGram agent. There's no limit, and the recipient need only present photo identification. The cost, which includes a free long-distance phone call, runs from 3% to 10%, depending on the amount sent, the destination, and how you pay.

You can also send money using Western Union. Money sent from the United States or Canada will be available for pickup at agent locations in 100 countries within 15 minutes. Once the money is in the system, it can be picked up at any one of 25,000 locations. Fees range from 4% to 10%, depending on the amount you send.

P
PACKAGES AND TOURS

A package or a tour to Arizona can make your vacation less expensive and more convenient. Firms that sell tours and packages purchase airline seats, hotel rooms, and rental cars in bulk and pass some of the savings on to you. In addition, the best operators have local representatives to help you out at your destination. (*See* Important Contacts A to Z, *above,* for specific tour operators.)

A GOOD DEAL?

The more your package or tour includes, the better you can predict the ultimate cost of your vacation. Make sure you know exactly what is included, and **beware of hidden costs.** Are taxes, tips, and service charges included? Transfers and baggage handling? Entertainment and excursions? These can add up.

Most packages and tours are rated deluxe, first-class superior, first class, tourist, and budget. The key difference is usually accommodations. If the package or tour you are considering is priced lower than in your wildest dreams, **be skeptical.** Also, **make sure your travel agent knows the hotels** and other services. Ask about location, room size, beds, and whether it has a pool, room service, or programs for children, if you care about these. Has your agent been there or sent others you can contact?

BUYER BEWARE

Each year consumers are stranded or lose their money when operators go out of business—even very large ones with excellent reputations. If you can't afford a loss, take the time to **check out the operator**—find out how long the company has been in business, and ask several agents about its reputation. Next, **don't book unless the firm has a consumer-protection program.** Members of the United States Tour Operators Association and the National Tour Association are required to set aside funds exclusively to cover your payments and travel arrangements in case of default. Nonmember operators may instead carry insurance; look for the details in the operator's brochure—and the name of an underwriter with a solid reputation. Note: When it comes to tour operators, **don't trust escrow accounts.** Although there are laws governing those of charter-flight operators, no

governmental body prevents tour operators from raiding the till.

Next, **contact your local Better Business Bureau and the attorney general's office** in both your own state and the operator's; have any complaints been filed? Last, **pay with a major credit card.** Then you can cancel payment, provided that you can document your complaint. Always **consider trip-cancellation insurance** (*see* Insurance, *above*).

BIG VS. SMALL➤ An operator that handles several hundred thousand travelers annually can use its purchasing power to give you a good price. Its high volume may also indicate financial stability. But some small companies provide more personalized service; because they tend to specialize, they may also be experts on an area.

USING AN AGENT

Travel agents are an excellent resource. In fact, large operators accept bookings only through travel agents. But it's good to **collect brochures from several agencies,** because some agents' suggestions may be skewed by promotional relationships with tour and package firms that reward them for volume sales. If you have a special interest, **find an agent with expertise in that area;** the American Society of Travel Agents can give you leads in the United States. (Don't rely solely on your agent, though; agents may be unaware of small niche opera-

tors, and some special-interest travel companies only sell direct).

SINGLE TRAVELERS

Prices are usually quoted per person, based on two sharing a room. If traveling solo, you may be required to pay the full double occupancy rate. Some operators eliminate this surcharge if you agree to be matched up with a roommate of the same sex, even if one is not found by departure time.

PACKING FOR ARIZONA

Wear casual clothing and resort wear in Arizona. When in more elegant restaurants in larger cities, as well as in dining rooms of some resorts, most men wear jackets and appropriate pants (few places require ties). Dressy casual wear is appropriate for women even in the nicest places—take along a silky blouse and chunky silver jewelry and you'll fit in almost anywhere.

Stay cool in cotton fabrics and light colors. T-shirts, polo shirts, sundresses, and lightweight shorts, trousers, skirts, and blouses are right for summer. **Bring sun hats, swimsuits, sandals, and sunscreen**—mandatory warm-weather items. **Bring a sweater and a warm jacket in winter,** particularly for high-country travel—anywhere around Flagstaff and north of it. And **don't forget jeans and sneakers or sturdy walking shoes;** they're important year-round.

Take along appropriate sports gear, although tennis, golf, ski, and horseback-riding equipment are readily available for rental.

Bring an extra pair of eyeglasses or contact lenses in your carry-on luggage, and if you have a health problem, pack enough medication to last the trip. In case your bags go astray, don't put prescription drugs or valuables in luggage to be checked.

BAGGAGE

Free airline baggage allowances depend on the airline, the route, and the class of your ticket; ask in advance. In general, on domestic flights you are entitled to check two bags—neither exceeding 62 inches, or 158 centimeters (length + width + height), or weighing more than 70 pounds (32 kilograms). A third piece may be brought aboard; its total dimensions are generally limited to less than 45 inches (114 centimeters), so it will fit easily under the seat in front of you or in the overhead compartment. In the U.S., the Federal Aviation Administration (FAA) gives airlines broad latitude to limit carry-on allowances and tailor them to different aircraft and operational conditions. Charges for excess, oversize, or overweight pieces vary.

SAFEGUARDING YOUR LUGGAGE➤ Before leaving home, itemize your bags' contents and their worth, and label them with your name, address, and phone number. (If you use your home address, cover it so that potential thieves can't see it.) Inside your bag, pack a copy of your itinerary. At check-in, make sure that your bag is correctly tagged with the airport's three-letter destination code. If your bags arrive damaged or not at all, file a written report with the airline before leaving the airport.

PASSPORTS AND VISAS

CANADIANS

No passport is necessary to enter the United States.

U.K. CITIZENS

British citizens need a valid passport. If you are staying fewer than 90 days and traveling on a vacation, with a return or onward ticket, you will probably not need a visa. However, you will need to fill out the Visa Waiver Form, 1-94W, supplied by the airline. While traveling, keep one photocopy of the data page separate from your wallet and leave another copy with someone at home. If you lose your passport, promptly call the nearest embassy or consulate, and the local police; having the data page can speed replacement.

R RENTING A CAR

CUTTING COSTS

To get the best deal, book through a travel agent and shop around. When pricing cars, ask where the rental lot is located. Some off-airport locations offer lower rates—even though their lots are only minutes away from the terminal via complimentary shuttle. You may want to price local car-rental companies, whose rates may be lower still, although service and maintenance standards may not be up to those of a national firm. Also ask your travel agent about a company's customer-service record. How has it responded to late plane arrivals and vehicle mishaps? Are there often lines at the rental counter, and, if you're traveling during a holiday period, does a confirmed reservation guarantee you a car?

INSURANCE

When you drive a rented car, you are generally responsible for any damage or personal injury that you cause as well as damage to the vehicle. Before you rent, see what coverage you already have by means of your personal auto-insurance policy and credit cards. For about $14 a day, rental companies sell insurance, known as a collision damage waiver (CDW), that eliminates your liability for damage to the car; it's always optional and should never be automatically added to your bill.

SURCHARGES

Before picking up the car in one city and leaving it in another, ask about drop-off charges or one-way service fees, which can be substantial. Note, too, that some rental agencies charge extra if you return the car before the time specified on your contract. To avoid a hefty refueling fee, **fill the tank just before you turn in the car.**

FOR U.K. CITIZENS

In the United States you must be 21 to rent a car; rates may be higher for those under 25. Extra costs cover child seats, compulsory for children under 5 (about $3 per day), and additional drivers (about $1.50 per day). To pick up your reserved car you will need the reservation voucher, a passport, a U.K. driver's license, and a travel policy covering each driver.

S

SENIOR CITIZENS

The state's healthful environment and many retirement communities make it a popular destination for older travelers. As such, Arizona has a multitude of recreational, sports, and entertainment facilities geared especially to senior citizens' needs and interests.

DISCOUNTS

Discounts are offered on public transportation, museum entrance fees, fishing and hunting licenses, cinemas, musical and theatrical performances, and a wide variety of other services. The minimum age limit varies between 55 and 65 years. To qualify for age-related discounts, **mention your senior-citizen status up front** when booking hotel reservations, not when checking out, and before you're seated in restaurants, not when

paying your bill. Note that discounts may be limited to certain menus, days, or hours. When renting a car, **ask about promotional car-rental discounts**—they can net lower costs than your senior-citizen discount.

SHOPPING

Keep in mind that the high quality of Native American arts and crafts is reflected in the prices they fetch. Bargaining is the exception, not the rule. In general, the best buys are to be had in the fall, after most of the tourists have gone home.

STUDENTS

ON THE ROAD

To save money, **look into deals available through student-oriented travel agencies.** To qualify, you'll need to have a bona fide student I.D. card. Members of international student groups also are eligible. *See* Students *in* Important Contacts A to Z, *above.*

T

TELEPHONES

LONG-DISTANCE

The long-distance services of AT&T, MCI, and Sprint make calling home relatively convenient and let you avoid hotel surcharges; typically, you dial an 800 number.

TIME

Arizona sets its clocks to mountain standard time—two hours earlier than eastern standard, one hour later than Pacific standard. However, from April to

October, when other states switch to daylight saving time, Arizona does *not* change its clocks; during this portion of the year, the mountain standard hour in Arizona is the same as the Pacific daylight hour in California. To complicate matters, the vast Navajo reservation in the northeastern section of the state *does* observe daylight saving time, so that from April to October it's an hour later on the reservation than it is in the rest of the state. Finally, to add to the confusion, the Hopi reservation, whose borders fall within those of the Navajo reservation, stays on the same non-Navajo, non-daylight saving clock as the remainder of the state.

W

WHEN TO GO

When you travel to Arizona depends on whether you prefer scorching desert or snowy slopes, elbow-to-elbow resorts or wide-open territory. Our advice: **visit during spring and autumn,** when the temperatures are milder and the crowds have thinned out.

Winter is prime time in the central and southern parts of the state. The weather is sunny and mild, and the cities bustle with travelers escaping the cold. Conversely, northern Arizona—including the Grand Canyon—can be wintry, with snow, freezing rain, and subzero temperatures;

the road to the Grand Canyon's North Rim is closed during this time.

Arizona's desert regions sizzle in summer, and travelers and their vehicles should be adequately prepared. Practically every restaurant and accommodation is air-conditioned, though, and you can get great deals on tony southern Arizona resorts you might not be able to afford in high season. Summer is also a delightful time to visit northern Arizona's high country, when temperatures are 18°F–20°F lower than they are down south.

CLIMATE

Phoenix averages 300 sunny days and 7 inches of precipitation annually. Tucson gets all of 11 inches of rain each year, and the high mountains see about 25 inches. The Grand Canyon is usually cool on the rim, and about 20°F warmer on the floor. During winter months, approximately 6–12 inches of snow fall on the North Rim, while the South Rim receives half that amount.

The following average daily maximum and minimum temperatures for two major cities in Arizona offer a representative range of temperatures in the state.

Climate in Arizona

TUCSON

Jan.	64F	18C	May	89F	32C	Sept.	96F	36C
	37	3		57	14		68	20
Feb.	68F	20C	June	98F	37C	Oct.	84F	29C
	39	4		66	19		57	14
Mar.	73F	23C	July	101F	38C	Nov.	73F	23C
	44	7		73	23		44	7
Apr.	82F	28C	Aug.	96F	36C	Dec.	66F	19C
	51	11		71	22		39	4

FLAGSTAFF

Jan.	41F	5C	May	66F	19C	Sept.	71F	22C
	14	−10		33	1		41	5
Feb.	44F	7C	June	77F	25C	Oct.	62F	17C
	17	− 8		41	5		30	− 1
Mar.	48F	9C	July	80F	27C	Nov.	51F	11C
	23	− 5		50	10		21	− 6
Apr.	57F	14C	Aug.	78F	26C	Dec.	42F	6C
	28	− 2		48	9		15	− 9

1 Destination: Arizona

THE GRAND CANYON STATE

ARIZONA IS an ancient land, visibly etched by the passage of the Earth and the human race through time. Aeons of our planet's story are written in the deep, multicolored walls of the Grand Canyon and the cathedral-like stone spires of Monument Valley. Ages of human history echo in the hidden grandeur of Canyon de Chelly, the "sky villages" perched atop Hopi reservation mesas, and the prehistoric ruins of Montezuma Castle and Casa Grande.

At the same time, Arizona is a lively hub of modern life, a quickening center in the emerging web of communications and trade, travel, and recreation that links western North America with the Pacific Rim. Phoenix, the state capital and the metropolitan center of the Southwest, is America's ninth-largest and fastest-growing city.

Visitors usually wonder about the desert: How hot is it? What should we wear? Is it safe? These are intelligent questions about a place where summer daytime temperatures often exceed 100°F (38°C), major rivers run underground, and the native flora are spiny cactus and thorny scrub.

What few people realize is that Arizona has two deserts. The low desert (roughly the southwestern third of the state) is indeed arid and dotted with tall saguaro cacti, but the high desert—the northeastern tier, with the Grand Canyon and Navajo and Hopi lands—is a savanna-like plain, thousands of feet above sea level and mantled in snow all winter. The middle third of Arizona is not desert at all but rather mountainous terrain, with alpine lakes and the world's largest ponderosa pine forest.

Even with—and partly because of—its low-desert climate, Arizona has an irresistible draw. Long one of the nation's prime tourist destinations, visited annually by millions from around the world, in the past two decades Arizona has been one of America's fastest-growing states, with tens of thousands of immigrants arriving each year.

That growth transformed Phoenix from a farming town of 60,000 in 1940 to an urban center of 1 million by 1990. It also doubled and redoubled the population of Tucson, the "Old Pueblo" in the southern part of the state. Yet Arizona remains a place of boundless vistas, with more than 80% of its land in U.S. and state parks and preserves or Native American reservations. Whether they are in the deserts or the mountains, Arizona's small towns still have vast spaces between them.

The state has also retained much of its rich Native American and Spanish colonial heritage. More Native Americans live here than in any other state, and the Hopi village of Oraibi is the oldest continually inhabited community in North America. Mexican and Central American families continue to immigrate, many following routes opened by Spanish explorers a century before the Pilgrims landed. Numerous Tucson families trace their lineage to Mexican pioneers who arrived in the days of the American Revolution.

Visitors can readily see some of the gifts modern Arizona has received from these ancient cultures: the Native American and Spanish names of most of its mountains and rivers, plants, and animals, even its streets and the pervasive influence of Hopi and Mexican architecture in homes and public buildings. Other aspects of this heritage appear only after some study: in the canals that carry Arizona's mountain streams into the low desert and the legal system that gives husband and wife equal shares in their "community property."

One part of Arizona's cultural heritage that almost everyone gets to share is the relaxed pace and style of living: In almost everything, from clothing to art, from home decor to meals, the desert dwellers of each era have learned to prize the unhurried and the informal, to accept the calming lessons of the heat and the majestic landscape. Leave your tie and tails at home and, even if you're on business, plan to take time out: Lean back for a leisurely late lunch during the hottest part of the day; stretch out under a patio awning beside a pool or fountain during the long, cool evenings.

And wherever you take your siesta, cast your eye toward the horizon: You'll see deep skies and luminous, gold-edged sunsets; the towering silhouettes of buttes and mountain ranges, their rugged surfaces subtly alive with shifting shadows and pastel colors; a forest of widely spaced saguaro cacti, standing firm like many-armed sentinels amid sketchy creosote and ocotillo bushes while birds and lizards dart from one spiny haven to the next; or the long, green bowl of a mountain meadow, dusted with poppy clusters and blue lupine beds, edged with shimmering aspens. Arizonans and visitors alike never tire of watching the play of sun and shadows on some corner of this magnificent land.

— *Mark Hein*

Mark Hein is an editor and a writer in the features department of the Arizona Republic.

WHAT'S WHERE

The Grand Canyon and Northwest Arizona

In the face of this vast marvel, words can be hard to come by—except on the subject of recommendations: Go to the North Rim. It may take longer to get there, and it is closed in winter to all but cross-country skiers, but you will be rewarded by having a wonder of the world more to yourself. In and around the state's northwest corner, Lake Mead, the Hoover Dam, and the gambling halls of Laughlin, Nevada, have their appeals, too.

The Northeast

This sprawling corner of the state is the home of the Navajo Nation and Hopi Reservation. Native American crafts draw some visitors, as does interest in getting an understanding of the lives, past and present, of some of our land's true founding mothers and fathers. Along with the living Navajo and Hopi reservations, ancient Pueblo ruins at Betatakin, Keet Seel, and Canyon de Chelly are haunting, unforgettable sights. (*See* The First Arizonans *in* Chapter 7, Portraits, for cultural background

to ancestral and contemporary inhabitants.) And don't forget about Monument Valley, the bizarre and fascinating Petrified Forest National Park and Painted Desert, and activities at another manmade lake, Lake Powell, when planning your trip.

North Central Arizona and Flagstaff

Jerome and Prescott are two of the state's most popular towns, for their wild west history, some of it bawdy and outrageous, all of it interesting, and for their place in yet another wondrous, beautiful locale. Sedona's red rocks, recognizable for the roles that they played in numerous Hollywood westerns, are as captivating as they are easy to hike. Flagstaff has become more of a destination in its own right, with historical buildings, an increasing number of good restaurants, and nightlife. Outside of the city, ancient Native American dwellings at Wupatki and Walnut Canyon National Monuments and Sunset Crater are windows onto the world of a thousand years past.

Phoenix and Central Arizona

The ever-widening Phoenix metropolitan area provides a tremendous variety of activities for almost all interests—from hiking in superb parks on some of the country's most-traveled trails to golfing on championship courses, and from dining at the restaurants where Southwestern cuisine was born to the last word in pampering at world-class resorts. The White Mountains are a nearby escape, with Old West towns, the stunning Salt River Canyon, and more great hiking.

Tucson and Southern Arizona

Tucson may have buried most of its Mexican roots, but some remnants of the adobe days in its El Presidio neighborhood provide a pleasant architectural diversion. And there is great Mexican food. Outside of town, the Mission San Xavier del Bac is an architectural and art historical masterpiece, set in the midst of the Tohonó O'odham Reservation, where Native American crafts are also available. Farther from the city, visit the legendary Tombstone and other mining towns, pop over the border to Agua Prieta, Mexico, and for nature and bird lovers, Ramsey Canyon, Organ Pipe National Monument, and

Chiracahua National Monument have fascinating flora and fauna and great hiking. Chiracahua is a particularly unique zone where species from the Southwest, the Chiracahua Mountains, and Mexico all live amid forests and volcanic rock formations.

PLEASURES & PASTIMES

Ballooning

If you're so inclined, floating in a balloon can be a delight. In both Phoenix and Tucson pilots will take you up over metropolitan areas as well as the Sonoran Desert. Some go up year-round, though most fly only in cooler months. Tours last about an hour and are customarily followed by a champagne celebration.

Baseball

Baseball fans visiting Arizona in March have a chance to watch major-league teams during spring training. Exhibition games begin in early March, but the eight Cactus League teams start practice at training camps as much as three weeks earlier. Their free drills—held in the morning before an exhibition game—are fun to watch, and there's a good chance you might be able to chat with the players before or after these sessions. In some cases, reserved seats sell out the fall before an upcoming season, but you can almost always get general admission seats on the day of the games.

Bicycling

Desert trails, the open road, and mountain passes provide a tremendous variety of great cycling. We recommend riding in cooler months, of course—a desert road in summer is like a frying pan.

Boating and Lake Activities

You may be surprised to find so many lakes in what most consider a desert state. In fact, Arizonans own more boats per capita than residents of any other state. The two national recreational areas, Glen Canyon (Lake Powell) in north-central Arizona and Lake Mead (including Lake Mohave) in the northwest have marinas, launching ramps, and boat and ski rentals. At both lakes you can take a paddle-wheeler tour or take the wheel yourself in a fully equipped houseboat. Lake Havasu, fed by the Colorado River in the western part of the state, is another favored site for boating, waterskiing, windsurfing, and jet-skiing. London Bridge, which was moved block by block from England and reassembled here, is a surreal vision at this lakeside resort. Be sure to call ahead on the availability of rental equipment.

Saguaro and Canyon lakes, just east of Scottsdale, offer good boating and waterskiing for those based in the Phoenix area who are looking for a convenient day trip.

Canoeing. Swift currents without rapids make the day-long Topock Gorge trip on the Colorado River a favorite outing. Beginning at Topock, canoeists travel through a wildlife refuge to Castle Rock at the top end of Lake Havasu. Another route, made dramatic by the Black Canyon cliffs, is along the Colorado River below Hoover Dam to Willow Beach.

River Rafting. Rafting and kayaking trips down the Colorado River and through the Grand Canyon keep some visitors returning year after year. Trips run from one day to two weeks and operate during the summer season. Other rafting expeditions run on the Salt and Verde rivers, through the Sonoran Desert, near Scottsdale.

Other Water Sports. Swimmers can plunge into a cool mountain lake or splash in the acres and acres of water at one of the recreational mega-resorts. Virtually every hotel and motel has a swimming pool of some size, and nearly all Arizona cities have at least one public pool. Or, cavort in man-made waves at a number of water parks around Phoenix, including Water World and Golfland/Sunsplash (in Mesa), and even surf the 3- to 5-foot-high waves at Big Surf in Tempe. Tubing is popular along the Salt River, east of Mesa.

Dining

Outside of major cities, Arizona cuisine leans mainly toward Western-style steaks, barbecued ribs and beans, biscuits with gravy, and chuck wagon–type fare. The Navajo taco (beans, tomatoes, lettuce, and cheese on Indian fry bread) and a few Hopi recipes served on the reservation combine Native American and Mexican food traditions. Mexican food is plentiful everywhere in the state. Phoenix and Tucson offer Continental dining, an eclectic mix of ethnic eateries, and, most important, the acclaimed Southwestern cuisine, using local ingredients with a style at once classic and innovative.

Fishing

Fish virtually jump out of Arizona's cool mountain streams, major rivers, and man-made lakes and are especially plentiful at Colorado River resorts. Rainbow, brown, brook, and cutthroat trout, as well as catfish, crappie, bass, pike, and bluegill, are the primary game. San Carlos Lake is tops for bass, and trout are plentiful at Lees Ferry. Fishing licenses *are* required.

Golf

Your clubs certainly won't gather dust in Arizona. Aside from the big-draw Phoenix and Tucson opens (*see* Festivals and Seasonal Events, *below*), golfers flock to this state to tee off at the myriad top-rank private and municipal courses. Year-round desert courses offer cheaper greens fees during the summer, and those in the northern part of the state usually shut down for winter. Just about every resort has its own course or is affiliated with a private club.

Hiking

Throughout the state, hikers can choose from trails that wind through the desert, climb mountains, meander past supernal rock formations, delve deep into forests, or circumnavigate cities. Whatever your choice of direction, you'll find thousands of miles of marked paths through unforgettable landscapes, many of which you'll find in parks and around national monuments.

Be prepared when you do hike—please *see* Smart Travel Tips A to Z *in* the Gold Guide for important precautions to take before setting out.

Horseback Riding

Traveling by horseback through the somewhat wild West or the scenic high country is perhaps the most appropriate way to explore Arizona. Stables offer a selection of mountain or desert trail rides lasting a half day, two days, or as long as two weeks. In northern regions the season is from May through October. If riding is the focus of your Arizona holiday, you might consider staying at a dude ranch where you can saddle up every day.

National and State Parks and Monuments

National Parks. Arizona's three national parks are the granddaddy Grand Canyon National Park (1,218,375 acres), Petrified Forest National Park (93,533 acres), and the U.S.'s newest, Saguaro National Park (91,327 acres). The Grand Canyon, northwest of Flagstaff, has achieved status as one of the Seven Natural Wonders of the World. Travelers come from all parts of the globe to hike, camp, raft, helicopter, or simply "ooh and aah" at the spectacular views and ever-changing colors, shadows, and light. Petrified Forest National Park, east of Flagstaff, features rainbow-colored petrified logs, tree fragments, and chunks of rock—preserved-in-stone remnants of a forest dating from the dinosaur age. Saguaro National Park, which flanks Tucson's east and west sides, supports the most specimens in the United States of the towering saguaro (suh-*wah*-ro) cactus, which can live over 200 years.

National Monuments. Southwest of Tucson on the Mexican border, Organ Pipe National Monument abounds in examples of the saguaro's many-armed cactus cousin. For Native American ruins in scenic settings, visit Canyon de Chelly near the New Mexico border, Walnut Canyon National Monument and Wupatki National Monument in the Flagstaff area, Tuzigoot National Monument south of Sedona, and Navajo National Monument's Keet Seel and Betatakin (beh-*tah*-tah-kin) near Monument Valley. Little-visited spots of unusual beauty include Sunset Crater Volcano National Monument, west of Flagstaff, its black lava flows contrasted against a lush green forest. And Chiricahua National Monument in the southeast, where odd rock formations preside over woods that simultaneously celebrate spring and autumn.

State Parks. Arizona's state parks range from relatively small Slide Rock (54 acres), near Sedona, to 13,000-acre Lake Havasu; both feature water-based activities. Boating and water-sports enthusiasts also like to congregate at Alamo Lake State Park, north of Wenden, Roper Lake State Park, at the foot of Mt. Graham in the southeast, and Lyman Lake State Park, in the

White Mountains area. Catalina and Pi-
cacho Peak state parks, near Tucson, and
Lost Dutchman State Park, east of Phoenix,
are the best bets for desert activities.
Painted Rocks State Park, west of Gila Bend,
is distinctive for its Indian rock carvings.
Those interested in the lively frontier his-
tory of this state should enjoy Riordon His-
torical State Park in Flagstaff, Jerome
State Historic Park and Fort Verde State
Historic Park in north-central Arizona, and
Tombstone Courthouse State Historic
Park and Yuma Territorial Prison State His-
toric Park, both in the south.

Fragile Life. Don't be tempted to pull any
of Arizona's century-old saguaro cacti
out by the roots. The state flower is protected by law, as are most slow-growing
desert plants and flowers. Theft or van-
dalism carries stiff penalties. Similarly,
the dry and easily desecrated desert floor
takes centuries to overcome human damage. Consequently, it is illegal for four-wheel-
drive and all-terrain vehicles and motorcycles
to travel off established roadways.

Native American Culture

Watching Indian festivals and exploring
the remains of earlier settlements can be
a rewarding part of a trip to Arizona—
we recommend any effort to enhance your
understanding of aspects of Native American culture on your trip. (For more information on Native Americans past and
present, *see* The First Arizonans *in* Chapter 7, Portraits.)

Rockhounding

Arizona is rock-hound heaven, its deserts
and mountains laden with a dazzling variety of rocks and minerals: agate, jasper,
tourmaline, petrified wood, quartz,
turquoise, amethyst, precious opal, and fire
agate, and more. The department has a
fine Mining and Mineral Museum as well
as a rockhounding reference library. Remember, however, to inquire about restrictions before you fill your pockets.
Taking rocks is illegal on the Navajo and
Hopi reservations, for example.

You can purchase rocks and minerals at
specialty shops or at one of the state's year-
round rock and gem shows. The largest
shows are held in Quartzsite, about 19 miles
from the California border, and in Tucson, generally from late January to mid-
February.

Shopping

Many tourists come to Arizona for no
other reason than to purchase fine Native
American jewelry and crafts. Collectibles
include Navajo rugs and sand paintings,
Hopi kachina dolls (intricately carved
and colorful representations of Hopi spiritual beings) and pottery, Tohonó O'odham (Papago) basketry, and Apache
beadwork, as well as the highly prized silver and turquoise jewelry produced by several different tribes. Many of these items
are sold in big-city shops and malls, but
going directly to the reservation often
gives shoppers additional rewards.

Museums and trading posts on the Navajo
and Hopi reservations in the state's northeastern region offer introductions to crafts
and their history and have gift shops
where you can make purchases; especially
worth visiting are the Hubbell and Cameron
trading posts, the Navajo Arts and Crafts
Enterprises, and the Hopi Cultural Center. Demonstrations of silversmithing, rug-
weaving, and pottery-making techniques
are often held on the premises. Roadside
stands also offer wares for sale.

You can find exquisite baskets and other
crafts of the Tohonó O'odham at the
plaza outside the San Xavier Mission on
the outskirts of Tucson, as well as at shops
in Sells, the tribe's headquarters, about 60
miles southwest of Tucson. Apache beadwork, baskets, wood carvings, and jewelry are sold at reservation trading posts
in the eastern part of the state.

Skiing

Cross-country and downhill skiing are
both worthy winter pastimes in Arizona,
even if they don't quite match the scale
of the Rockies. Flagstaff Nordic Center,
Mormon Lake Ski Touring Center southeast of Flagstaff, the North Rim Nordic
Center, and miles of crisscrossing trails around
Alpine are good places for cross-country
skiing. The three peaks of Sunrise Park Resort in McNary are owned and operated
by the White Mountain Apache Indians
and constitute the state's largest ski area.
Other popular areas are Arizona Snowbowl near Flagstaff and Mt. Lemmon Ski
Valley near Tucson.

Tennis

Tennis lovers abound in Arizona, and
you can find numerous opportunities to

play the game. The dryness of the air makes for some of the best climate for tennis anywhere.

FODOR'S CHOICE

Activities and Wonders

★ **Grand Canyon, North Rim.** The only way to get to know the canyon, to feel the force of it open you right up, is to hike or ride a mule down through all of those geological years to the bottom of the great chasm.

★ **Canyon de Chelly National Monument, Navajo Nation, The Northeast.** The silence and harmony with which these ancient cliff dwellings exist in their surroundings are truly profound—as they must have been for the Canyon's inhabitants 700 and more years past.

★ **Sedona's red rocks.** Picnic or hike among Sedona's natural monuments and just feel the wonder of the place—it's the real reason to visit here.

★ **Desert Botanical Gardens, Phoenix.** An early morning walk through the desert gives perhaps the best, and most pleasant, view of the lives of its flora and fauna.

★ **Signal Hill, Saguaro National Monument, Tucson.** The fascinating petroglyphs (rock art) made by Hohokam tribespeople are among the state's numerous living testaments of the mythological figures and symbols of the first Americans.

Scenic Drives

★ **Point Sublime, North Rim, Grand Canyon.** The dirt road out to the point provides one of the most awe-inspiring panoramic views you'll have from a car, anywhere.

★ **U.S. 163 from Kayenta, Arizona, to the Goosenecks of the San Juan River in southern Utah.** This drive through the archetypal wild west landscape of Monument Valley ends in a winding, water-carved canyon of the San Juan River, a unique counterpart to the Grand Canyon.

★ **Flagstaff to Sedona via Oak Creek Canyon, North-Central Arizona.** Another stunning canyon, this one quiet and tree lined on its low end, towering and majes-

tic as it looks toward Sedona, marks the transition from northern Arizona's Colorado Plateau to the southern desert landscape.

★ **Jerome to Prescott, North-Central Arizona.** The winding road through Prescott National Forest is one of Arizona's most breathtaking mountain drives—precipitous at times, but beautiful.

★ **Texas Canyon, Southern Arizona.** Does one ever tire of canyons? We don't think so, especially when they are hung with giant boulders apparently defying their great mass in astonishing formations, as in this one, east of Tucson.

★ **Tucson to Kitt Peak, Tucson and Southern Arizona.** About 20 miles southwest of Tucson, upon entering the Tohonó O'odham reservation, you enter the heart of the desert. In the distance looms the sacred Baboquivari Peak, a symbol of the deepfeeling Native American worldview that remains in view as you climb the sides of Kitt Mountain.

Shopping

★ **Cameron Trading Post, Grand Canyon.** One of the state's historic trading posts, this one has a wide variety of Hopi, Navajo, and Pueblo jewelry, rugs, baskets, and pottery, along with Navajo tacos at its restaurant next door.

★ **Hubbell Trading Post, Ganado, The Northeast.** Established in 1878 by a bighearted New Mexican, this National Historic Site specializes in Navajo rugs, existing, as it does, on the Navajo Reservation.

★ **Tlaquepaque Mall, Sedona, North-Central Arizona.** Worth a visit as much for its architecture and Mexican village design as for its shopping, Tlaquepaque houses Sedona's most exclusive boutiques and their variety of splendid wares.

★ **Main Street, Scottsdale.** From the touristy to the genuine, including Mexican imports and Thursday evening Art Walks (October–May), this is Scottsdale's own Western version of one of America's favorite pastimes.

★ **Tubac, Southern Arizona.** Arizona's first Euramerican town, Tubac is a great town, with an artist's community, lots of history, numerous shops, and good values.

Restaurants

★ **Vincent's on Camelback, Phoenix.** One of the very first practitioners of "Southwestern" cooking, Vincent Guerithault masterfully grafts Mexican traditions onto his classic French training to the great delight of followers and newcomers alike. *$$$$*

★ **La Hacienda, Scottsdale, Central Arizona.** Perhaps the most elegant Mexican restaurant in the state, the much-loved Hacienda serves the finest Sonoran cuisine in a richly decorated setting at the Scottsdale Princess Resort. *$$$–$$$$*

★ **Heartline Café, Sedona, North-Central Arizona.** What some might call hippie haute cuisine—because they love it, of course—serves tasty grilled food, inventive pizza, and Southwestern dishes in a pleasant, friendly atmosphere. *$$–$$$*

★ **Brix Grill & Wine Bar, Flagstaff.** With home-made bread and dessert, a good selection of wine by the glass, and innovative Southwestern cooking, Brix may be Flagstaff's most interesting, if modestly set, restaurant. *$$*

★ **Such Is Life.** Come to Moises Treves' corner of Phoenix to taste cactus, chicken Maya, garlic shrimp—yes, delicious regional Mexican food. *$$*

★ **Café Poca Cosa, Tucson.** Ooh, those tropical colors, and ooh, what fantastic Sonoran Mexican cooking—especially if you like chicken mole. You won't find any excesses of cheese here. *$–$$*

★ **Adrian's, Phoenix.** When local Hispanic families keep coming back for dishes like broiled pike with fresh lime or a seafood cocktail whose name translates as "Return to Life," why waste time trying to decide where to go for dinner? *$*

Hotels and B&Bs

★ **Briar Patch Inn, Sedona, North-Central Arizona.** It may not be in the heart of Sedona's red rocks, but its lovely Oak Creek Canyon location alongside the laughing water, and so many touches, set the Briar Patch apart. *$$$$*

★ **Arizona Inn, Tucson.** With almost all that you would want from a landmark inn—period furnishings, fireplaces, quiet, friendly service, even a downtown location on property of its own—you won't be disappointed with a stay here. *$$$–$$$$*

★ **The Buttes, Phoenix and Central Arizona.** Desert views and interesting architecture and design are part of the Buttes' appeal, as are the comfortable rooms, two elegant restaurants, and jogging and hiking trails. *$$$–$$$$*

★ **Wahweap Lodge at Lake Powell, The Northeast.** A central and well-equipped location for Lake Powell recreation, Wahweap's cruises, river excursions, boat, ski, and tackle rentals, and restaurant make for a nearly all-in-one resort. *$$$*

★ **Cameron Trading Post at Cameron, Grand Canyon.** This may well be the best base, or even jumping-off point, for both the Grand Canyon, North and South Rims, and Navajo-Hopi country, all with its own trading-post-style charm. *$$*

★ **Grand Canyon Lodge, North Rim, Grand Canyon.** We've said it once, and we'll say it again—come to the North Rim to avoid the crowds and *enjoy* the mighty abyss. While you're here, why not stay in the historic, rustic, Grand Canyon Lodge, with spectacular views of you-know-what. *$$*

★ **Casa Tierra Bed & Breakfast, Tucson.** In an adobe brick building, this friendly bed and breakfast outside of town is a great desert getaway, highly recommended. *$–$$*

FESTIVALS AND SEASONAL EVENTS

WINTER

JAN. 1➤ Tempe's nationally televised **Fiesta Bowl Footbowl Classic** kicks off the year with a match between the nation's top two college teams.

JAN.➤ At the **Phoenix Open Golf Tournament** in Scottsdale, top players compete at the Tournament Players Club. The **Northern Telecom Tucson Open,** the other top PGA event, is co-hosted by Tucson National Golf & Conference Resort and Starr Pass Golf Club.

JAN.➤ The **Dixieland Jazz Festival** at Lake Havasu City uses London Bridge as the backdrop to traditional Dixieland sounds and more, including a parade, dancing on a riverboat, and Sunday morning gospel.

JAN.–FEB.➤ **Parada del Sol Rodeo and Parade,** a popular state attraction on Scottsdale Road, features lots of dressed-up cowboys and cowgirls, plus horses and floats.

EARLY FEB.➤ The **Quartzsite Pow Wow Gem and Mineral Show** is a gigantic flea market, held the first Wednesday through Sunday of the month, attracting more than 100,000 buyers and sellers of rocks, minerals, gems, and related crafts and supplies.

FEB.➤ At **O'odham Tash** in Casa Grande Native American tribes from around the country host parades, native dances, a rodeo, costume displays, and food stands.

FEB.➤ History comes to life during **Wickenburg Gold Rush Days,** when the Old West town puts on a rodeo, dances, gold-panning demonstrations, a mineral show, and other activities.

FEB.➤ **La Fiesta de los Vaqueros** features the world's longest "non-mechanized" parade—horses pull floats and carry dignitaries—launching a four-day rodeo at the Tucson Rodeo Grounds.

FEB.➤ The huge **Tucson Gem and Mineral Show** attracts rock hounds—amateur and professional—from all over the world who come to buy, sell, and display their geological treasures and to attend lectures and competitive exhibits.

SPRING

MAR.➤ The highlight of the **Ostrich Festival** in Chandler is a race of the big birds; it also features a parade, crafts and food booths, and a petting zoo.

MAR.➤ For the **Lost Dutchman Gold Mine Superstition Mountain Trek** in Apache Junction, the Dons of Arizona search for the legendary lost mine, pan for gold, and eat lots of barbecue to keep up their strength. There are crafts demonstrations and fireworks, too.

MAR.➤ In Phoenix, the **Heard Museum Guild Indian Fair and Market** is a prestigious juried show of Native American arts and crafts that brings together participants from all over the Southwest. Visitors can also enjoy Native American foods, music, and dance.

APR.➤ Tucson hosts the **International Mariachi Conference,** four days of mariachi music, along with cultural and educational exhibits.

APR.➤ During the **Route 66 Fun Run Weekend,** in Seligman/Topock, the historic road between Chicago and Los Angeles is feted with classic car rallies, hot rod and antique-car shows, and various other events—including a 1950s hop.

APR.➤ **Yaqui Easter** is celebrated in old Pasqua village (Tucson) on the Saturday nights preceding Palm Sunday and Easter Sunday. Visitors are welcome to watch traditional Yaqui dances and ceremonies.

APR.➤ Bisbee's **La Vuelta de Bisbee** is Arizona's largest bicycle race and attracts top racers from around the country to the hills of the historic mining town. The 1995 race was used to select riders for the 1996 U.S. Olympic cycling team.

MAY➤ On **Rendezvous Days,** the townspeople of Williams reenact the annual trek to town by 1800s mountain traders. Events include a steak fry and a Buckskinners black powder shoot.

MAY➤ A two-day tournament, the **Lake Havasu Western Outdoor News Striper Derby** is the largest in Arizona, drawing fishing teams from as far away as Michigan and Idaho.

MAY–JUNE➤ At Flagstaff's **Trappings of the American West Festival,** the featured attraction is cowboy art—everything from painting and sculpture to cowboy poetry readings.

SUMMER

JUNE➤ Festivities of **Old West Day/Bucket of Blood Races,** in Holbrook, include arts and crafts, western dress, and Native American song and dance, in addition to the 10-kilometer fun run and 20-mile bike ride from Petrified Forest National Park to Holbrook.

LATE JUNE OR EARLY JULY➤ **All Indian Powwow** and **Native American Arts Fair** are held in Flagstaff the weekend before July 4. Tribes from around the world present dance performances and competitions, and an international array of crafts is displayed and sold.

JULY➤ **Prescott Frontier Days and Rodeo,** billed as the world's oldest rodeo, finds big crowds and an equally big party on downtown Whiskey Row.

JULY➤ At the **Loggers/ Sawdust Festival** in Payson, loggers from the United States and Canada test their skills and strength. Family fun includes a greased pole

climb and a fire extinguisher water fight.

JULY➤ The **Native American Arts & Crafts Festival,** in Pinetop/Lakeside brings storytellers, dancers, musicians, and artists together for two days in a beautiful mountain setting.

AUG.➤ The **Payson Rodeo** draws top cowboys from around the country to compete for top prizes in calf- and steer-roping contests at what they call the world's oldest continuous rodeo.

AUG.➤ Flagstaff's **Festival in the Pines** is a gathering of painters, potters, musicians, and other artists from around the United States. They vie with carnival rides, and food vendors for the crowd's attention.

AUTUMN

SEPT.➤ At the **Jazz on the Rocks Festival** in Sedona, six or seven ensembles perform in a spectacular red rock setting.

SEPT.➤ The **Navajo Nation Annual Tribal Fair** is the world's largest Native American fair. Held in Window Rock, it includes a rodeo, traditional Navajo music and dances, food booths, and an intertribal powwow.

OCT.➤ Phoenix's massive **Arizona State Fair** features games, rides, exhibits, livestock, art shows, and other entertainment.

OCT.➤ Spicy food lovers revel at **La Fiesta de Los Chiles,** Tucson's two-day salute to the chile, which

is cooked, hung, made into art, and otherwise celebrated.

OCT.➤ At **Tombstone's Helldorado Days,** the town relives the spirited Wyatt Earp era and the shoot-out at the OK Corral.

OCT.➤ A week-long event, **London Bridge Days,** includes a triathlon, a parade, and a variety of contests in Lake Havasu City.

NOV.➤ Exhibits at the **Heard Museum Native American Art Show** in Phoenix feature fine tribal arts and crafts from across the state.

NOV.➤ In Lake Havasu City's **Havasu Classic Outboard World Championships,** various classes of racing boats tear up the water competing for prize money and trophies.

NOV.➤ During the **Thunderbird Balloon Classic & Air Show,** one hundred or more balloons participate in Glendale's colorful race.

DEC.➤ The **Arizona Temple Christmas Lighting** in Mesa finds over 300,000 lights illuminating the walkways, reflection pool, trees, and plants at the Arizona Temple Gardens and Visitors Center.

DEC.➤ The waters of Lake Powell alight with the **Festival of Lights Boat Parade** as dozens of illuminated boats glide from Wahweap Lodge to Glen Canyon Dam and back.

DEC.➤ For the three days of **Old Town Tempe Fall Festival of the Arts,** the downtown area closes to traffic for art exhibits, food booths, music, and other entertainment.

2 The Grand Canyon and Northwest Arizona

In the face of this vast marvel, words can be hard to come by—except on the subject of recommendations: Go to the North Rim. It may take longer to get there, and it is closed in winter to all but cross-country skiers, but you will be rewarded by having a wonder of the world more to yourself. In and around the state's northwest corner, Lake Mead, the Hoover Dam, and the gambling halls of Laughlin, Nevada, have their appeals, too.

By William E.
Hafford and
Edie Jarolim

ALTHOUGH MILLIONS of words have been devoted to describing the Grand Canyon, writers have generally conceded that the Earth's greatest gorge is beyond the scope of language. Southwestern author Frank Waters has come closer than most to capturing its power. "It is the sum total," he writes, "of all the aspects of nature combined in one integrated whole. It is at once the smile and frown upon the face of nature. In its heart is the savage, uncontrollable fury of all the inanimate Universe, and at the same time the immeasurable serenity that succeeds it. It is Creation."

To appreciate the Grand Canyon, you must see it. Not even the finest photographs pack a fraction of the impact of a personal glimpse of this vast, beautiful scar on the surface of our planet—277 miles long, 18 miles across at its widest spot, and more than a mile below the rim at its deepest point. The Grand Canyon is the quintessence of the high drama of the American western landscape.

More than 65 million years ago, a great wrenching of the earth pushed the land in the region of the canyon up into a domed tableland, today called the Colorado Plateau. Then the Colorado River, racing south through present-day Utah, began chewing at the uplifted region. The river is responsible for much of the erosion, but many side gullies and canyons were formed by melting snow and fierce rainstorms that sent water rushing into the gorge through smaller tributaries. Softer rock formations were washed away by the Colorado and carried to the distant sea; the harder formations remained as great cliffs and buttes. Above the twisting line of river are otherworldly stone monuments with colors that range from muted pastels to deep purples, vibrant yellows, fiery reds, and soft blues. This palette shifts with the hours: What you see at mid-morning is repainted by the setting sun.

This is also a land of ancient peoples. In some of the deepest, most inaccessible reaches of the Grand Canyon, evidence of early human habitation exists. Stone ruins high in the cliffs reveal the archaeological secrets of cultures some 8,000 to 10,000 years old. In higher country above both north and south rims are the remains of prehistoric Pueblo settlements active until about AD 1300. It is believed that a period of harsh and sustained drought, coupled with the effects of climatic change, soil erosion, and heavy use of local resources, caused the people to seek more favorable lands. Today's Hopi Indians, who live on mesas about 150 miles east of the canyon, along with New Mexican Pueblo people, view themselves as descendants of the earlier inhabitants. The former dwellings are, as a result, sacred homes of ancestral spirits.

In the year 1540, a band of Spanish soldiers under the command of Captain García López de Cárdenas became the first white men to look into the canyon. The members of the expedition, dispatched by Francisco Coronado to find an Indian village, were disinclined to stay very long—or to return. Spanish Franciscan missionary and explorer Francisco Tomás Garcés visited a Havasupai Indian village in the canyon in 1776, and Lieutenant Joseph Ives went on an official mission for the U.S. government to explore the area in 1857. But no one thought it worth much attention until 1869, when John Wesley Powell, a one-armed adventurer and scholar, put rough-hewn boats into the Colorado and let the swirling white water of the mighty river take him along its length.

During the last years of the 19th century, almost all development at or near the canyon was related to mining. In fact, the earliest trails down into the canyon were built by miners searching for precious minerals. Shortly after the beginning of the 20th century, the Santa Fe Railroad completed a line to the South Rim of the canyon, ushering in the era of tourism. In 1903 Theodore Roosevelt visited and drew public interest to the site. It was declared a national park in 1919. Today close to 5 million visitors come each year from around the world to peer into this gorge in amazement.

The Fred Harvey Company opened the world-famous El Tovar Hotel on the rim of the canyon in 1905, heralding the beginning of Grand Canyon Village. Now there are more than 900 motel and hotel rooms in the Village, but the ever-increasing visitor population makes even that number of accommodations insufficient in summer. If you can arrange it, try to visit the Grand Canyon in the fall or spring. You might encounter cold weather during those periods, but chances are good that most of the days will be clear and will range from pleasantly cool to warm. In autumn and spring, when the crowds have thinned, reservations are much easier to arrange, and, in some cases, prices drop. Or consider a winter visit. Snow on the ground only enhances the site's sublime beauty.

The North Rim, in the isolated Arizona Strip, draws only about 10% of the Grand Canyon's visitors but is every bit as gorgeous as the South Rim. From southern Arizona, there's only one highway into this area, 210 miles of lonely road to the north and west of Flagstaff. Set in deep forest near the 9,000-foot crest of the Kaibab Plateau, the North Rim is, for many visitors, worth the extra miles. But truth to tell, there's virtually no place along either rim or in the depths of the Grand Canyon that will fail to startle and impress you.

THE GRAND CANYON

From the rim of this awesome creation, your first view of the canyon will last a lifetime. After a half dozen lookouts, however, your sense of wonder will begin to diminish—it's difficult to establish a personal relationship with so much grandeur. Traveling along the rim, you will soon tire of putting your nose up against all of this beauty, safely, almost antiseptically, peering in. By all means stop along the rim, but we can't encourage you strongly enough to take a walk, however brief, into the canyon itself. A 20-minute descent into the maw of this abyss will open up a totally new perspective and permit you to get close to the canyon in a way that is impossible at the rim.

Both the South Rim and the North Rim areas of the Grand Canyon were established as recreational and sightseeing enclaves under the direction of the National Park Service. Unfortunately, most of Grand Canyon Village at the South Rim was laid out before the Park Service existed, so the area is not well equipped to accommodate the large crowds that converge on the area every summer (and increasingly throughout the spring and fall).

In truth, the South Rim is a bit of a circus in summer. It's hard to commune with one of nature's great spectacles when you've just spent two hours looking for a parking spot (there are only 1,400 spaces for the approximately 6,000 cars that enter each day) and are now being asked to step out of the range of someone's video camera. Not even a descent into the canyon itself guarantees a getaway at this time of year. For your sake as well as that of the canyon, it's best to avoid the South Rim in its busiest season. The North Rim is the better alternative.

Grand Canyon National Park

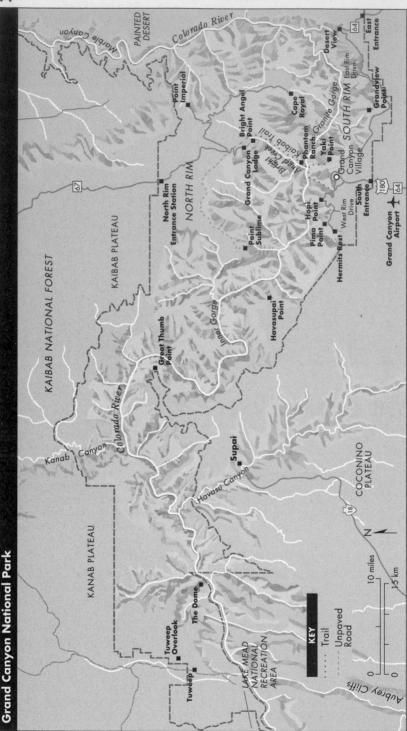

PAINTED DESERT

Marble Canyon

Colorado River

East Entrance

64

Desert View

East Rim Drive

Point Imperial

Cape Royal

Grandview Point

Grand Granite Gorge

SOUTH RIM

Bright Angel Point

Phantom Ranch

Bright Angel Creek / Kaibob Trail

Yaki Point

Grand Canyon Village

67

North Rim Entrance Station

NORTH RIM

Grand Canyon Lodge

Hopi Point

South Entrance

180

64

KAIBAB PLATEAU

Point Sublime

Pima Point

West Rim Drive

Grand Canyon Airport

KAIBAB NATIONAL FOREST

Hermits Rest

Inner Gorge

Havasupai Point

Great Thumb Point

Colorado River

Kanab Canyon

Colorado River

Supai

Havasu Canyon

COCONINO PLATEAU

KANAB PLATEAU

18

N

The Dome

Tuweep Overlook

KEY

Trail

Unpaved Road

10 miles

15 km

Tuweep

LAKE MEAD NATIONAL RECREATION AREA

0

0

Aubrey Cliffs

Exploring

There are two ways to discover the canyon: walk or drive along the rim (Tours 1–6), and/or hike into its depths (*see* Hiking *in* Sports and the Outdoors, *below*). For a short hike, Bright Angel Trail is easiest; South Kaibab Trail is steeper but more spectacular. Tours 1–4 cover the South Rim, Tours 5 and 6 the North Rim.

Tour 1: Approaching the South Rim

Numbers in the margin correspond to points of interest on the South Rim: Tours 1 and 2 map.

Because the approach to the South Rim of the Grand Canyon is across the relatively level surface of the 7,000-foot Coconino Plateau, you won't see the great gorge until you're practically at its edge. If you're coming in from the south (AZ 64/180), Mather Point gives you the first glimpse of the canyon from one of the most impressive and accessible vista points on the rim. If you're arriving from the east (AZ 64 from Cameron), you might be tempted to stop at Desert View, just inside the park, but we suggest that you save this and other vista points on the eastern approach for a later East Rim tour (*see* Tour 2, *below*).

Whether you enter the park from the east or south, you'll arrive at the junction of AZ 64 and AZ 180. Proceed in the direction of Grand Canyon Village for less than a mile, and you'll see a large parking area with a

❶ sign for **Mather Point,** approximately 4 miles from the south entrance and 24 miles from the east entrance. This overlook of the canyon, named for the National Park Service's first director, Stephen Mather, affords an extraordinary view of the Inner Gorge of the canyon and of numerous buttes that rise out of the eroded chasm: Wotan's Throne, Brahma Temple, Zoroaster Temple, and many others. The Grand Canyon Lodge, on the North Rim, is almost directly north from Mather Point and only 10 miles away—yet you have to drive nearly 210 miles to get from one spot to the other.

After your first view of the canyon, proceed to Grand Canyon Village,

★ ❷ and stop in at the **National Park Service's Visitor Center,** which has something for even the most independent traveler. The center orients you to many facets of the site, and it's an excellent place for gathering information, whether you're interested in escapist treks or group tours. Park rangers are on hand to answer questions and aid in planning Grand Canyon excursions, short movies and slide shows on the canyon are presented regularly, and a bookstore carries a wide variety of printed matter and videotapes. A daily schedule for ranger-led hikes and evening lectures is also posted here.

A separate exhibit area offers an intriguing profile of the area's natural and human history. The first inhabitants were probably nomadic Paleo-Indians, arriving more than 10,000 years ago. Artifacts that were found in caves deep in the canyon were left by a later Archaic culture. They are perfectly preserved figurines of animals, made from willow twigs more than 4,000 years ago—thus predating Homeric Greece by 1,000 years. Around 2,200 years ago, ancestral Pueblo culture began to develop around the canyon. The museum also traces the arrival of early Spanish explorers, including Captain García López de Cárdenas, leader in 1540 of the first expedition of white men to see the Grand Canyon, and of John Wesley Powell, the first person to travel through the canyon by boat. Various crafts that have navigated the white-water rapids of the Colorado River are on display. *East side of Grand Canyon Village,*

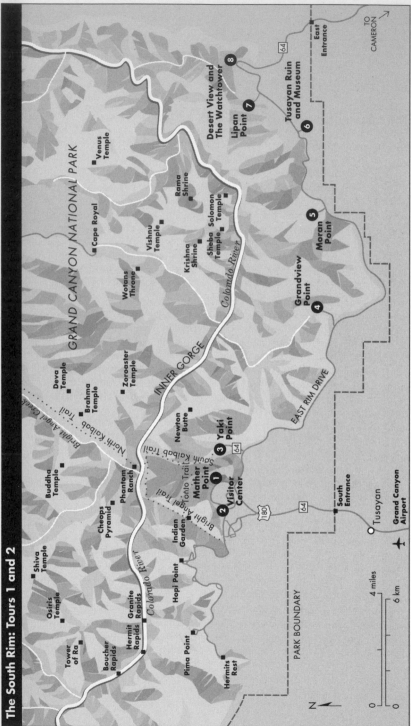

The South Rim: Tours 1 and 2

GRAND CANYON NATIONAL PARK

Venus Temple

Cape Royal

Rama Shrine

Vishnu Temple

Sheba Solomon Temple Temple

Krishna Shrine

Wotans Throne

INNER GORGE

Colorado River

Devassa Temple

Zoroaster Temple

Brahma Temple

Bright Angel Creek Trail

North Kaibab Trail

Buddha Temple

Newton Butte

Cheops Pyramid

Phantom Ranch

South Kaibab Trail

Tonto Trail

Shiva Temple

Osiris Temple

Granite Rapids

Hermit Rapids

Colorado River

Indian Garden

Bright Angel Trail

Hopi Point

Tower of Ra

Boucher Rapids

Pima Point

Hermits Rest

Desert View and The Watchtower

Tusayan Ruin and Museum

Lipan Point

Moran Point

Grandview Point

Yaki Point

Mather Point

Visitor Center

EAST RIM DRIVE

East Entrance

TO CAMERON

South Entrance

Tusayan

Grand Canyon Airport

PARK BOUNDARY

⑧ ⑦ ⑥ ⑤ ④ ③ ① ②

64 64 64 180

N

4 miles
6 km
0
0

about 1 mi east of El Tovar Hotel, ☎ *520/638–7888.* ☛ *Free.* ☉ *Memorial Day–Labor Day, daily 8–6; rest of yr., daily 8–5.*

If you'd like a little exercise and great overlooks of the canyon, it's an easy hike from the back of the Visitor Center to the El Tovar Hotel (*see* Tour 3, *below*). Walk through a pretty wooded area for about a half mile, then the path will parallel to the rim for another half mile or so. The wide dirt trail is more or less level all the way, though at this altitude, even slight inclines require more effort.

Tour 2: East Rim

This breathtaking drive on the East Rim proceeds east for about 25 miles along the South Rim from Grand Canyon Village to Desert View. Before beginning the drive, consider stopping to see the exhibits and attend the free minilectures offered by park naturalists at Yavapai Observation Station, ¾ mile east of the visitor center. There are four posted picnic areas along the route and rest rooms at Tusayan Museum and Desert View.

❸ To get to **Yaki Point** from the village, head east to the junction of AZ 180 and AZ 64. Turn onto AZ 64 and continue east. From this vantage point, look to the northeast for an exceptional view of Wotan's Throne, a majestic flat-top butte named by François Matthes, a U.S. Geological Survey scientist who developed the first topographical map of the Grand Canyon. Due north is Buddha Temple, capped by limestone; Newton Butte, with its flat top of red sandstone, lies to the east. At Yaki Point the popular Kaibab Trail starts the canyon descent to the Inner Gorge, crosses the Colorado over a steel suspension bridge, and wends its way to rustic Phantom Ranch, the only lodging facility at the bottom of the Grand Canyon. You might take this opportunity to hike a short distance down the Kaibab Trail, just to get a feel for a descent into the canyon. If you plan to go more than a mile, carry water with you (*see* Hiking *in* Sports and the Outdoors, *below*). If you encounter a mule train, be aware that the animals have the right-of-way. Move to the inside of the trail and wait as they pass.

❹ About 7 miles east of Yaki Point, **Grandview Point,** at an altitude of 7,496 feet, supports large stands of ponderosa pine, piñon pine, oak, and juniper. The view from here is one of the finest in the canyon. To the northeast is a group of dominant buttes, including Krishna Shrine, Vishnu Temple, Rama Shrine, and Shiva Temple. A short stretch of the Colorado River is also visible. Directly below the point and accessed by the Grandview Trail is Horseshoe Mesa, where you can see ruins of the Last Chance Copper Mine. Grandview Point was also the site of the Grandview Hotel, constructed in the 1890s but closed in 1908; logs salvaged from the hotel were used for the Kiva Room of the Desert View Watchtower (later in this tour).

❺ The next overlook is **Moran Point,** about 5 miles east, named for American landscape artist Thomas Moran, who painted Grand Canyon scenes from many points on the rim but was especially fond of the play of light and shadows from this location. He first visited the canyon with John Wesley Powell in 1873, and his vivid canvases helped convince Congress to create a national park at the Grand Canyon. This is also a favorite spot for photographers.

Three miles east of Moran Point, on the south side of the highway, is ❻ the entrance to **Tusayan Ruin and Museum,** which offers evidence of early habitation in the Grand Canyon and information about the lifestyles of ancestral Pueblo people. The partially intact rock dwellings here were occupied for roughly 20 years by a group of about 30 Indian hunters, farmers, and gatherers. They moved elsewhere, like so many others, pressured by drought and depletion of natural resources to find better settlements. A museum and a bookstore display artifacts, models of the dwellings, and exhibits on modern tribes of the region. Free 30-minute guided tours—as many as five during the summer, fewer in winter—are given daily. ☎ 520/638–2305. ☛ *Free.* ☉ *Daily 9–5; closed Thanksgiving and Dec. 25.*

⑦ Lipan Point, 1 mile east of Tusayan Ruin, is the canyon's widest point. From here you can get an astonishing visual profile of the gorge's geologic history, with a view of every eroded layer of the canyon.

★ At 7,500 feet, the highest point along the tour, **Desert View** and **The Watchtower** offer a climactic final stop. From the top of the 70-foot stone-and-mortar watchtower, built in 1932 by the Fred Harvey Company and the Santa Fe Railroad in the style of Native American structures, even the muted pastel hues of the distant Painted Desert to the east and the 3,000-foot-high Vermilion Cliffs rising from a high plateau near the Utah border are visible. In the chasm below, angling away to the north toward Marble Canyon, a powerful stretch of the Colorado River reveals itself. The Watchtower houses a glass-enclosed observatory with powerful telescopes, as well as galleries decorated with reproductions of ancient Indian pictographs, and a curio shop where paintings, jewelry, and other handicrafts by contemporary Native American artists are sold. *The Watchtower,* ☎ 520/638–2736, *trading post* ☎ 520/638–2360. ☛ *Free, but 25¢ to climb Watchtower.* ☉ *Daily 8–7 or 8–8 in summer, daily 9–6 in winter.*

Tour 3: The Village Rim

Numbers in the margin correspond to points of interest on the South Rim: Tours 3 and 4 map.

① This is a fairly short walking tour (about 1 mile round-trip) over level ground via a paved pathway that runs along the rim. The **Hopi House** is a good place to begin (if you're driving, leave your car at the nearby El Tovar parking lot). This multistoried structure of rock and mortar was modeled after buildings found in the Hopi village of Oraibi, Arizona, the oldest continually inhabited community in the United States (*see* Tour 3 *in* Chapter 3, The Northeast). Part of an attempt by the Fred Harvey Company to encourage Southwest Indian crafts at the turn of the century, Hopi House was established as one of the first curio stores in the Grand Canyon. It has the air of a museum, with some artifacts too priceless to sell today, but it remains one of the best-stocked gift shops in the vicinity.

★ **②** A few yards to the west of Hopi House is the most renowned hotel in the nation's National Park System, the historic **El Tovar Hotel.** Built in 1905 to resemble the great hunting lodges of Europe, this massive log structure underwent a major renovation in 1991, and it retains the ambience of its early days. If the weather is cool, stop in front of the massive stone fireplace to warm your hands. The rustic lobby, with its numerous stuffed and mounted animal heads, is a great place for people-watching, while the back porch affords a front row seat for the spectacle of the canyon.

★ From El Tovar, return to the rim and pick up the trail heading west toward **Lookout Studio.** Built in 1914 to compete with the Kolbs' photographic studio (*see below*), the building was designed by architect

The South Rim: Tours 3 and 4

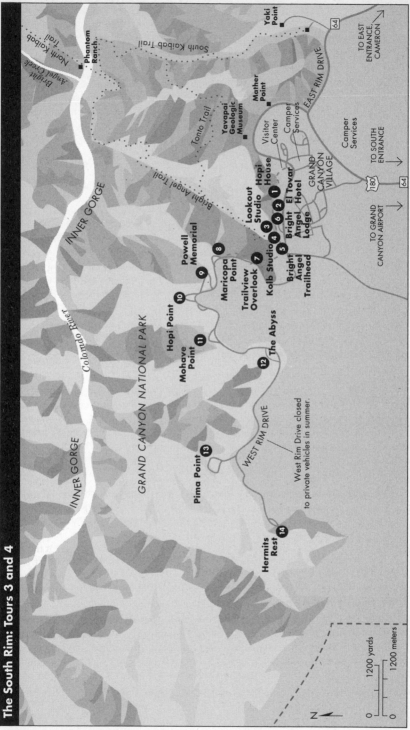

Mary Jane Colter to resemble a Hopi pueblo. Today it's a combination lookout point, museum, and gift shop, and it has an extensive collection of geologic samples from around the world as well as many fossil specimens. An upstairs loft provides another excellent overlook into the mighty gorge below.

4 Walk a half dozen yards west and descend a few steps to the **Kolb Studio,** built in 1904 by the Kolb brothers as a photographic workshop; it's now a bookstore and art gallery. If you look out the window, you can see Indian Gardens, where, in the days before a pipeline was installed, Emery Kolb descended some 3,300 feet each day to get the water he needed to develop his prints. Perhaps the exercise was beneficial; he operated the studio until he died in 1976 at age 95.

★ **5** A few feet from Kolb Studio you'll see **Bright Angel Trailhead,** the starting point for perhaps the best-known of all the trails that descend to the bottom of the canyon. It was originally a bighorn sheep path and was later used by the Havasupai Indians; in 1890–91 it was widened for prospectors trying to reach mining claims in the canyon. Today Bright Angel Trail is a well-maintained avenue for mule and foot traffic. If you intend to go very far—the trail descends 4,460 feet to the Colorado River— you should be prepared with proper shoes, clothing, equipment, and water (*see* Hiking *in* Sports and the Outdoors, *below*); discuss your intentions with the Park Service representatives at the visitor center before you go.

Bright Angel Trailhead is the turnaround point on this short walking tour. (If you'd like to go farther west, *see* Tour 4, *below.*) From Bright Angel Trailhead, walk directly east rather than returning to the rim trail. Across the railroad tracks over which the Santa Fe trains once passed, you'll see the barn that houses some of the tour mules; it's worth a brief

6 stop, especially if children are along. Continue east to **Bright Angel Lodge,** which was built in 1935 of Oregon pine logs and native stone; there are rustic cabins set off from the main building. It's another good place to people-watch, especially in the area of the "geologic" fireplace, made of regional rocks arranged in the order in which they are layered in the Grand Canyon. A history room displays memorabilia from early years at the South Rim.

TIME OUT For light snacks—cold sandwiches, sweets, and soft drinks—try the **Soda Fountain** (☎ 520/638–2631) in the Bright Angel Lodge. It has the distinction of being the spot where the most Breyer's ice cream in the United States is sold.

From Bright Angel Lodge, take the village road back to your parking spot near El Tovar.

Tour 4: West Rim Drive

This tour cannot be made by car in the summer months; at that time the West Rim Road is closed to auto traffic because of congestion. From Memorial Day weekend to October 1, a free shuttle bus makes most of the stops on the described itinerary (*see* Getting Around by Shuttle Bus *in* Grand Canyon Essentials, *below*).

Originally called Hermit Rim Road, **West Rim Drive** was constructed by the Santa Fe Company in 1912 as a scenic tour route. Cars were banned on the road because they frightened horses pulling the open-top touring stages. Ten scenic overlooks spread out over an 8-mile leg. Since you have to return on the same road, consider stopping at half of the overlooks on the way out and the others on the way back; access to the lookout points is easy from both sides of the road.

Start at **Bright Angel Lodge** and head west for about a mile until you **❼** come to **Trailview Overlook.** If you turn and look away from the canyon toward the south you'll have a wonderful, unobstructed view of the distant San Francisco Peaks, Arizona's highest mountains (the tallest is 12,633 feet), as well as of Bill Williams Mountain (on the horizon) and Red Butte (about 15 miles south of the canyon rim). As its name suggests, this overlook also affords a dramatic view of the Bright Angel and Plateau Point trails as they zigzag down the canyon. In the deep gorge to the north flows Bright Angel Creek, one of the few permanent tributary streams of the Colorado River in the region.

❽ **Maricopa Point,** about 7⁄10 mile from Trailview, merits a stop not only for the arresting scenery, which features a clear view of the Colorado River below, but also for its towering headframe of an early Grand Canyon mining operation. On the rim to your left, as you face the canyon, are the Orphan Mine and, in the canyon below, a mine shaft and cable lines leading up to the rim. The copper ore in the mine, which started operations in 1893, was of excellent quality, but the cost of removing it from the canyon finally brought the venture to a halt.

★ **❾** About a half mile beyond Maricopa Point, the large granite **Powell Memorial** stands as a tribute to the first man to ride the wild rapids of the Colorado River through the canyon in 1869. John Wesley Powell, a one-armed Civil War hero and explorer, measured, charted, and named many of the canyons and creeks of the river. It was here that the dedication ceremony for Grand Canyon National Park took place on April 3, 1920.

❿ From **Hopi Point** (elevation 7,071 feet), a half mile down the road, you can see a large section of the Colorado River; although it appears as a thin line from here, the river is nearly 350 feet wide below this overlook. Across the canyon to the north is Shiva Temple, which, until 1937, remained an isolated section of the Kaibab Plateau. In that year, Harold Anthony of the American Museum of Natural History led an expedition to the rock formation in the belief that it supported life that had been cut off from the rest of the canyon. Imagine the expedition members' surprise when they found an empty Kodak film box on top of the temple.

⓫ Four-fifths of a mile to the west, **Mohave Point** also affords spectacular views of the Colorado River. In addition, Granite and Salt Creek rapids can be seen from this point.

⓬ **The Abyss,** 1 mile farther, is one of the most awesome stops on this tour, revealing a sheer canyon drop of 3,000 feet to the Tonto Platform in the gorge below. From this spot, you'll also see several impressive isolated sandstone columns, the largest of which is called The Monument.

⓭ **Pima Point,** 3 miles away, provides a bird's-eye view of the Tonto Platform and the Tonto Trail, which wends its way through the canyon for more than 70 miles. If you look down on the plateau toward the west, you may be able to see the foundations of an old tourist camp built in the first decade of the century and used until 1930. Also to the west, two dark, cone-shape mountains—Mt. Trumbull and Mt. Logan—are visible on clear days. They rise in stark contrast to the surrounding flat-top mesas and buttes.

★ **⓮** **Hermits Rest,** the westernmost viewpoint, and the Boucher Trail that descends from it (*see* Hiking *in* Sports and the Outdoors, *below*) were named for the "hermit" Louis Boucher, a 19th-century prospector who had a number of mining claims and a roughly built home down in the canyon. Canyon views from here include Hermit Rapids and the towering cliffs of the Supai and Redwall formations. The stone building at Hermits Rest sells curios and refreshments and provides the only rest rooms on the West Rim tour.

Tour 5: The Drive to North Rim

Numbers in the margin correspond to points of interest on the North Rim: Tours 5 and 6 map.

This tour is not an option during the winter, when heavy snows close highway access to, and facilities in, the North Rim.

This long excursion—about 210 miles, whether you start out from Grand Canyon Village on the South Rim of the canyon or from Flagstaff—is the best way to get to the North Rim and offers plenty to see along the way. It begins at the **Cameron Trading Post,** on U.S. 89, 1 mile north of the junction with AZ 64 (which you will be on if you're coming from Grand Canyon Village) and 53 miles north of Flagstaff. Founded in 1916, this historic trading post, one of the few remaining in the Southwest, has an extensive stock of Native American jewelry, rugs, baskets, and pottery. Most of the items sold here are made by nearby Navajo and Hopi artisans, but some are created by New Mexico's Zuni and Pueblo Indians. In addition to the main building, which sells wares in all price categories, there's also a separate gallery that offers more expensive, museum-quality goods.

TIME OUT The **Cameron Trading Post** restaurant (☎ 520/679–2231) serves American food that ranges from light snacks to complete dinners; try the huge Navajo tacos on fry bread, heaped with cheese, chopped meat, guacamole, and salad. The high-ceiling room, decorated with Native American art and furniture, is an appealing eatery, but service can be a bit slow; if you're in a rush, try the newer cafeteria next door (open high-season only), where you can get hot and cold sandwiches and other buffet-style fare.

The route north on U.S. 89 affords a wide and unobstructed view of the **Painted Desert** off to the right. The desert, which covers thousands of square miles and extends far to the south and east, is a vision of harsh beauty, with windswept plains and mesas, isolated buttes, and barren valleys in delicate patterns of soft pastels. In the few places in which there is vegetation, it is mostly desert scrub, which provides sustenance for only the hardiest wildlife. Most of the undulating hills belong to the Chinle formation, deposited more than 200 million years ago and containing countless fossil records of ancient plants and animals.

About 30 miles north of the Cameron Trading Post, the Painted Desert country gives way to soaring sandstone cliffs that run for many miles off to the right. Brilliantly hued, and ranging in color from light pink to deep orange, the **Echo Cliffs** rise to well over 1,000 feet in many places. They are also essentially devoid of vegetation, but in a few isolated places high up, you'll spot thick patches of tall cottonwood and poplar trees, nurtured by springs and water seepage from the rock escarpments.

At Bitter Springs, 60 miles north of Cameron, leave U.S. 89 and take U.S. 89A north. Fourteen miles out of Bitter Springs, **Marble Canyon,** actually the beginning of the Grand Canyon, comes into view. Like the rest of the Grand Canyon, Marble Canyon has been carved by the force of the Colorado River. Traversing a gorge nearly 500 feet deep is **Navajo Bridge,** a narrow steel span built in 1929; until the bridge at

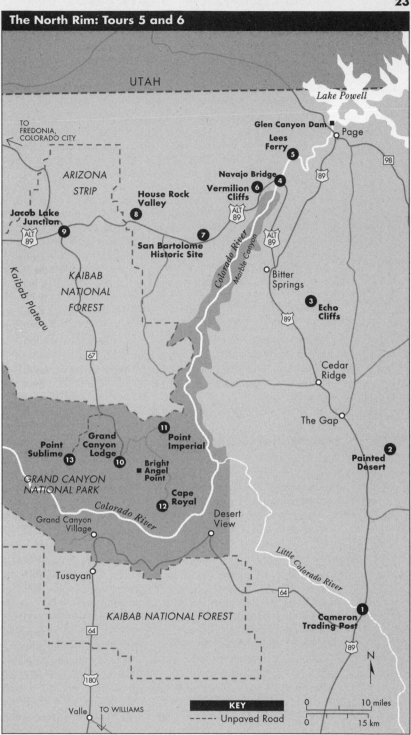

Glen Canyon Dam was constructed in 1959, this was the only bridge crossing the Colorado for the 600 miles from Moab, Utah, to the Hoover Dam. Formerly used for car traffic, it now functions only as a pedestrian overpass; a new, wider bridge, built 120 feet downriver, was dedicated in the summer of 1995. An interpretive area and rest rooms are being designed for a former parking lot near the old bridge, which is listed in the National Register of Historic Places.

★ ❺ When you come to Marble Canyon Lodge, about a mile past Navajo Bridge, you'll see a turnoff for historic **Lees Ferry,** 3 miles away. Situated on a sharp bend in the Colorado River at a break in the surrounding Echo Cliffs, Lees Ferry is considered mile zero of the river, the point from which all distances on the river system are measured. It's also at the eastern edge of Arizona Strip country (*see* Off the Beaten Track, *below*), and it was one of the last areas in the mainland United States to be completely charted. This spot was first visited by non-Indians in 1776, when Spanish priests Fray Francisco Atanasio Domínguez and Fray Silvestre Velez de Escalante tried but failed to cross the Colorado. Explorer John Wesley Powell also visited in 1870 on an expedition with Mormon leaders. After the ferry was established, it became part of the Honeymoon Trail, a gateway to Utah for young couples who wanted their civil marriages in Arizona sanctified at the Latter-Day Saints temple in St. George. It also became a crossing and a supply point for miners and other pioneers who shaped much of the American West.

Lees Ferry retains a number of vestiges of the mining era, but it's now primarily known as the spot where most of the Grand Canyon river rafts put into the water. In addition, huge trout lurk in the river near here, so there are several places to pick up angling gear and/or a guide. If you go out on your own, be sure you have an Arizona fishing license before casting a line (*see* Fishing *in* Sports and the Outdoors, *below*).

★ ❻ Heading west from Navajo Bridge, you'll be treated to views of some of the world's most spectacular geologic formations. Rising to the right of the highway are the sheer **Vermilion Cliffs,** in many places more than 3,000 feet high.

❼ As you continue the journey to the North Rim, the immense blue-green bulk of the Kaibab Plateau stretches out before you. About 18 miles past Navajo Bridge, a sign directs you to the **San Bartolome Historic Site,** an overlook with a series of plaques that tell the story of the Domínguez–Escalante expedition of 1776.

❽ Proceeding about 2 miles west, you'll enter **House Rock Valley,** where a large sign on the road announces the House Rock Buffalo Ranch, operated by the Arizona Division of Wildlife. A 23-mile dirt road leads to the home of one of the largest herds of American bison in the Southwest. You may drive out to the ranch, but be aware that you may not see any buffalo: The expanse of their range is so great that they frequently cannot be spotted from a car.

❾ About 25 miles west of Marble Canyon on U.S. 89A, you'll start climbing to the top of the Kaibab Plateau, heavily forested, rife with animals and birds, and more than 9,000 feet at its highest point. The rapid change from barren desert to lush forest is dramatic. At an elevation of 7,900 feet, the **Jacob Lake junction** is a good place to stop for groceries and gas. Turn left (south) from the junction to access AZ 67. From here to the North Rim, a distance of 44 miles, you drive through one of the thickest stands of ponderosa pine in the United States. Watch for wildlife along the way. Visitors frequently see mule deer and, once in a while, catch a glimpse of rare Kaibab squirrels; you can recognize them by their all-white tails and ears with long tufts of white hair.

Tour 6: The North Rim's Bright Angel Point, Point Imperial, Cape Royal, and Point Sublime

★ ⑩ When you arrive at the historic **Grand Canyon Lodge** you are, literally, at the end of the road; there are no meandering streets as there are at South Rim. A massive stone structure built in 1928 by the Union Pacific Railroad, the lodge is listed in the National Register of Historic Places. Inside, the huge lounge area with hardwood floors and high, beamed ceilings affords a marvelous view of the canyon through massive plate-glass windows. On warm days, visitors sit in the sun and drink in the surrounding beauty at an equally spacious outdoor viewing deck.

★ The trail to **Bright Angel Point,** one of the most awe-inspiring overlooks on either rim, starts on the grounds of the Grand Canyon Lodge and proceeds along the crest of a point of rocks that juts into the canyon for several hundred yards. The walk is only 1 mile round-trip, but the trek is exciting because there are sheer drops just a few feet away on each side of the trail. In a few spots, where the route is extremely narrow, metal railings along the path ensure visitors' safety. The trail is quite safe, but visitors have been known to clamber out to precarious perches to have their pictures taken. Be very careful: There have been tragic falls at the Grand Canyon.

If you'd like to take another walk, this time through the deep forest, head for the beginning of the Transept Trail near the corner of the lodge's east patio. This 3-mile (round-trip) trail stays near the rim for part of the distance, then it plunges into the forest, ending at the North Rim Campground and General Store, 1½ miles from the lodge.

TIME OUT Lunch, dinner, or a snack in the huge, high-ceiling, rock-and-log dining room of the **Grand Canyon Lodge** (☎ 520/638–2611) is an integral part of the North Rim experience; the food is good and reasonably priced. Or, if you don't want to go in for a meal, just buy a drink at the lodge's Pizza Place, sit out on the viewing deck, and watch the sun set over the canyon.

To get to the North Rim's most popular lookouts—Point Imperial and Cape Royal—drive north from Grand Canyon Lodge and veer right ⑪ at the signed fork in the road. **Point Imperial,** 11 miles from the lodge, is the highest vista point (elevation 8,803 feet) on either rim, offering magnificent views of both the canyon and the distant country for many miles around: the Vermilion Cliffs to the north, the 10,000-foot Navajo Mountain to the northeast in Utah, the Painted Desert to the east, and the Little Colorado River canyon to the southeast.

★ ⑫ Return west to the signed junction and turn left (south) to reach **Cape Royal,** about 23 miles from your starting point at the lodge. From the parking lot at the road's end, it's a short, scenic walk on a paved road to this southernmost viewpoint on the North Rim. In addition to another large slice of the Grand Canyon, Angel's Window, a giant, erosion-formed hole can be seen through the projecting ridge of Cape Royal. If you would like to experience a very pleasant walk in this area of the rim, drive north about ⅓ mile to Angel's Window Overlook. At this point, Cliff Springs Trail starts its 1-mile route (round-trip) through a forested ravine. The trail, narrow and precarious in spots, passes ancient dwellings, winds beneath a limestone overhang, and terminates at Cliff Springs, where the forest opens on another impressive view of the canyon walls.

 An excellent option for those who want to get off the beaten path, the trip to **Point Sublime** is intended only for visitors driving vehicles with high-road clearance (pickups and four-wheel-drive vehicles). It is also necessary to be properly equipped for wilderness road travel: Check with a park ranger or at the information desk at Grand Canyon Lodge before taking this journey. The road winds for 17 miles through gorgeous high country to Point Sublime, an overlook that lives up to its name. You may camp here, but only after obtaining a permit from the Backcountry Office at the park ranger station (*see* Hiking *in* Sports and the Outdoors, *below*).

What to See and Do with Children

The Grand Canyon is family vacation country, and most activities can be enjoyed by all ages. However, many of the daily activities at both the North and South rims, detailed in the free Grand Canyon newspaper, *The Guide,* will appeal especially to children. In addition, the Junior Ranger program, geared toward those ages 4 through 12, introduces kids to the concept of caring for the national parks via an activities checklist found in *Young Adventurer,* a publication available at the South Rim Visitor Center and the Tusayan and Yavapai museums.

Animal Rides

You can rent extremely gentle horses at the **Apache Stables** at Moqui Lodge (☎ 520/638–2891 or 520/638–2424) in the village of Tusayan, South Rim. The cost is $22 an hour, $36 for two hours. A four-hour East Rim ride goes for $57.50, a campfire horse and haywagon ride for $27 ($7.50 if you ride in the wagon rather than on your own horse). Children 6 and up are permitted on the hour-long ride, 10 and up on the two-hour ride, 14 and up on the half-day trip. The rides are offered, weather permitting, when Moqui Lodge is open (mid-Feb.–Nov. 30), and sometimes year-round.

Canyon Trail Rides (☎ 801/679–8665 preseason, ☎ 520/638–2292 after May 15 at Grand Canyon Lodge) operates short mule rides suitable for children on the easier trails along the North Rim. A one-hour ride, available to those 6 and older, runs about $12. Half-day trips on the rim or into the canyon (minimum age 8) cost $35; full-day trips (minimum age 12), which include lunch, go for $85. These excursions are very popular, so try to make reservations in advance. Rides are available daily from May 15 to the end of October.

Films of the Canyon

A visually exciting 34-minute historical film, *Grand Canyon—The Hidden Secrets,* is shown on the 70-foot-high screen at the IMAX Theater. The script is informative, and some of the shots—especially those of boats running the rapids—are positively dizzying. *Tusayan,* ☎ *520/638–2203.* ☛ *$7 adults, $4 children ages 3–11.* ☉ *Mar. 1–Oct. 31, daily 8:30–8:30; Nov. 1–Feb. 28, daily 10:30–6:30; shows every hr on the ½ hr.*

The computer-controlled *Over the Edge* multimedia show tells the Grand Canyon story in words and song—with the help of 12 projectors and strobe effects. The photography is often stunning. *Community Building, Grand Canyon Village,* ☎ *520/638–2229.* ☛ *$4 adults, $3.50 senior citizens 55 and older, $2 children 8–15.* ☉ *Mar.–Oct., daily 9–9; Nov.–Feb., daily 10–6; shows every 30 min, on the hr and ½ hr.*

Off the Beaten Track

Arizona Strip

The **Arizona Strip** is the 12,000-square-mile northwestern portion of the state, cut off from the rest of Arizona by the giant scar created by the Colorado River as it comes out of Utah and winds its way through the Grand Canyon to the western border of the state. Sometimes called the American Tibet because it's so isolated, the area boasts only two small towns: the farming and lumbering community of Fredonia and, near the Utah border, the polygamous Mormon town of Colorado City. Their combined population is less than 7,000, and fewer than 700 permanent residents—including 150 members of the Kaibab–Paiute tribe—live in the rest of the strip. The Forest Service's Kaibab Plateau Visitor's Center, a good one- or two-day side trip from the Grand Canyon's North Rim, is open at Jacob Lake (☎ 520/643–7298) from May 1 through mid-October.

The first of the two main destinations in the area is **Pipe Spring National Monument,** 90 miles from the North Rim. Head north from the rim on AZ 67, and at Jacob Lake take AZ 89A to Fredonia; continue 14 miles beyond Fredonia on the same highway (now called AZ 389). Located at Pipe Spring, one of the few reliable sources of water in the Arizona Strip, the park features a restored rock fort and ranch, with exhibits of Southwestern frontier life; in summer there are living-history demonstrations that focus on such things as ranching operations or weaving. The fort was completed in 1871 to fend off Indian attacks (which never came because a peace treaty was signed before it was finished), and it was originally built as a ranch for the managers sent to oversee the Mormon church's tithed herds. It ended up functioning mainly as headquarters for a dairy operation, and in 1871 became the first telegraph station in the Arizona territory. Also on the site are a well-stocked bookstore and gift shop, a coffee shop, and a visitor center with exhibits. About a half mile north of the monument is a campground, picnic area, and—opened in 1994—a casino run by the Kaibab–Paiute tribe. The new slots draw busloads of people to this remote spot. *HC 65, Box 5, Fredonia 86022,* ☎ *520/643–7105.* ☛ *$2 adults, children under 16 free.* ☉ *Historic structures: daily 8–4; Visitor center/museum: daily 8–4:30; closed Thanksgiving, Dec. 25, and Jan. 1.*

After touring the old fort, backtrack on AZ 389 for 6 miles, then take a right turn on the dirt road to **Toroweap Overlook,** a distance of approximately 60 miles. You'll be riding through starkly beautiful, uninhabited country. Toroweap, a lonely and awesome overlook, is one of the narrowest stretches of the canyon (less than 1 mile across) and also the point with the deepest sheer cliff (more than 3,000 feet straight down). From this vantage point, you can see upstream to sedimentary ledges, cliffs, and talus slopes. Looking downstream, you can see miles of the lava flow that forms steep deltas, some of which look like black waterfalls frozen on the cliff.

Be sure you have plenty of gas, drinking water, good tires, and a reliable car; a high-clearance vehicle (one that sits high up off the ground, like a pickup truck) is best for this trip. Don't try to go in wet weather, when the dirt road is likely to be washed out. There's a ranger station near the rim as well as a primitive campground. If you plan to return the same day, you should make motel reservations in advance at one of the Arizona Strip motels (*see* Lodging, *below*).

Havasu Canyon, South Rim

For those who want to get away from the crowds, Havasu Canyon, south of the middle part of the national park, possesses a Shangri-la–like beauty. It is the home of some 500 Havasupai, a tribe that has populated this beautiful, isolated country for centuries. Spectacular waterfalls as high as 200 feet cascade over red cliffs, spilling blue-green water into immense travertine pools surrounded by thick foliage and sheltering trees. Eight-mile-long Hualapai Trail twists into the canyon along the edges of sheer rock walls.

From Grand Canyon Village, head south on U.S. 180 (AZ 64) for 57 miles to Williams, then take I–40 west 44 miles to Seligman. From there, go 34 miles west on AZ 66 until you come to Indian Route 18. This junction will be the last chance to fill up with gas on the final 63 miles north to the head of the Hualapai Trail. Be sure to call ahead if you plan to hike the 8-mile-trail into the canyon—or ride a horse or mule down for about $70. You'll definitely want to spend the night if you're hiking or riding (*see* Dining and Lodging, *below*). All visitors are charged a $12 fee to enter the Havasupai tribal lands. For additional information, contact Havasupai Tourist Enterprise (Supai 86435, ☎ 520/448–2121 for general information or 520/448–2111 for lodging reservations). The hurried—or faint of heart—can take a helicopter; as out of place as that seems. **Papillon Helicopters** (☎ 800/528–2418) offers round-trips for $385 per person, whether you go for a day excursion, or stay overnight.

Sports and the Outdoors

Hiking

Hiking trails are numerous, and scenery is always spectacular around the Grand Canyon. Opportunities range from leisurely walks on well-defined paths through level or easy-rolling country to arduous, multiday treks to the bottom of the canyon—and across to the other rim if you'd like. Easy hikes can be found in Tours 3 and 6 *in* Exploring, *above*. At the very least, a short hike down any of the trails will give you an incredible spatial feeling of the canyon. In addition to some of the most popular trails outlined below, national park rangers or visitor center personnel will gladly provide you with hiking information and local maps of trails of varying difficulty.

Note: Overnight hikes require a permit that can be obtained only by written request to the **Backcountry Office** (Box 129, Grand Canyon, AZ 86023). Permits are limited, so it's wise to make reservations in advance. If you arrive without one, go to the Backcountry Office at either rim: South Rim near the entrance to Mather Campground, North Rim at the ranger station.

BRIGHT ANGEL TRAIL, SOUTH RIM

One of the most popular and scenic hiking paths from the South Rim to the bottom of the canyon (9 miles), the well-maintained Bright Angel Trail was used in the late 1800s as a route to mining claims. There are rest houses for hikers at the 1½-and 3-mile points and at Indian Garden. Plateau Point, about 175 feet below Indian Garden, is a good turnaround point for a day hike. Because the climb out from the bottom of the canyon is an ascent of 4,460 feet, the trip should be attempted only by those in good physical condition. Because of extreme temperatures, it is not recommended during the summer. The top of the trail can be icy in winter.

HERMIT TRAIL, SOUTH RIM

This 9-mile trail beginning at Hermits Rest (8 miles west of Grand Canyon Village) is steep, unmaintained, and suitable only for experienced long-distance hikers; a particularly tricky area is a ⅓-mile section of rock slides. No water is available along the way. The route leads to the Colorado River and has inspiring views of Hermit Gorge and the Redwall and Supai formations. Six miles from the trailhead you'll come across the now-abandoned Hermit Camp, which the Santa Fe Railroad ran as a tourist camp starting around 1912.

SOUTH AND NORTH KAIBAB TRAILS, SOUTH AND NORTH RIMS

South Kaibab Trail, starting near Yaki Point on East Rim Drive near Grand Canyon Village, connects at the bottom of the canyon (after the Kaibab Bridge across the Colorado) with the North Kaibab Trail, the only maintained trail into the canyon on the North Rim. Plan on three days if you want to hike the gorge from rim to rim. South Kaibab Trail is steep, descending 4,800 feet in just 7 miles with no water or campgrounds and very little shade. If you're going back up to the South Rim, ascend Bright Angel Trail. Accommodations for hikers along the way include the campgrounds at Indian Garden and Bright Angel, or Phantom Ranch (*see* Dining and Lodging, *below*).

SAFETY TIPS

You simply must carry water on hikes into the Inner Gorge—at least 1–1½ gallons per day. To avoid dehydration, it is important to drink frequently, about every 10 minutes, especially during summer months. Dehydration can affect you sooner than you think; and it is a serious danger that can be easily avoided. Likewise, take food—preferably energy snacks such as trail mix, bananas, and fig bars. Wear hiking boots or running shoes that have been broken in and proven on previous hikes. In case of a medical emergency, stay with the distressed person and ask the next hiker to go for help. Do not attempt to make the round-trip to the Colorado River in one day. The trek down is deceptively easy; the route back up is much longer than most mountain day-hikes and very fatiguing.

Mule and Horse Trips

Almost everyone who knows anything about the Grand Canyon has heard of the mule rides to the bottom of the canyon. For South Rim rides, *see* Guided Tours *in* Grand Canyon Essentials, *below;* for the North Rim, *see* What to See and Do with Children, *above.* Riding horses in the woods around the South Rim, but not descending into the canyon, might appeal to others. *See* What to See and Do with Children, *above,* for details.

Rafting

Many people who have made the white-water trip down the Colorado River through the Grand Canyon say it is the adventure of a lifetime. White-water trips embark from Lees Ferry, below Glen Canyon Dam near Page, Arizona. Trips that run the length of the canyon (a distance of more than 200 miles) can last from three days to three weeks. Shorter trips, also starting at Lees Ferry, let passengers off at Phantom Ranch at the bottom of Grand Canyon (about 100 miles). These pass through a great amount of white water, including Lava Falls rapids (on longer trips), considered the wildest navigable rapids in North America. For those who would like a more tranquil turn on the Colorado, there are also one-day, quiet-water rafts just below Glen Canyon Dam near Page.

Although more than 25 companies currently offer these excursions, reservations for raft trips (excluding smooth-water, one-day cruises) often need to be made more than six months in advance. For a complete list of river-raft companies, call 520/638–7888 from a Touch-Tone telephone and press 1-3-71, or write Grand Canyon National Park, Box 129, Grand Canyon, AZ 86023 to request a *Trip Planner*. National Park Service white-water concessionaires include **Canyoneers, Inc.** (☎ 520/526–0924 or 800/525–0924 outside AZ), **Diamond River Adventures, Inc.** (☎ 520/645–8866 or 800/343–3121), **Expeditions, Inc.** (☎ 520/779–3769 or 520/774–8176), and **Outdoors Unlimited** (☎ 520/526–4546 or 800/637–7238). Smooth-water, one-day-trip companies include **Fred Harvey Transportation Company** (☎ 520/638–2822 or 502/638–2631) and **Wilderness River Adventures** (☎ 520/645–3279 or 800/528–6154). Prices for river-raft trips vary greatly, depending on type and length. Half-day trips on smooth water run as low as $40 per person; trips that negotiate the entire length of the canyon and take as long as 12 days can cost close to $2,000.

Fishing

In the vicinity of Lees Ferry, just across Marble Canyon Bridge on U.S. 89 (the route to the North Rim), the Colorado River is known for huge trout. Fishing for trout, crappie, catfish, and small-mouth bass is also popular at a number of lakes surrounding Williams, near the South Rim. Many sporting goods stores around the state carry Arizona fishing licenses—Babbitts General Store at the South Rim, and Marble Canyon Lodge near Lees Ferry—but you won't be able to obtain one at the North Rim. If you'd like to apply for a license in advance, contact the **Arizona Game and Fish Department** (2221 W. Greenway Rd., Phoenix, AZ 85023, ☎ 602/942–3000). For details on fishing regulations, check with the Backcountry Office (*see* Hiking, *above*). **Lees Ferry Anglers** (HC-67 Box 2, Marble Canyon, AZ 86036, ☎ 520/355–2261 or 800/962–9755 outside AZ) offers guided fishing trips, including lunch, starting from $225 per day; they're the only guide service in the area that practices year-round catch and release.

Bicycling

Bicycles are not permitted on any of the Grand Canyon trails, but there are miles of scenic paved thoroughfares in the national park. Be aware, however, that the park roads have narrow shoulders and are heavily trafficked; use extreme caution. There are no rentals or tours available at either North or South Rims.

Camping

Camping inside Grand Canyon National Park is permitted only in designated areas. (For information about campgrounds in and around the park, *see* Dining and Lodging, *below*.)

Skiing

Though you can't schuss down into the Grand Canyon, you can cross-country ski in the woods near the rim when there's enough snow. **Babbits General Store** in the South Rim's Grand Canyon Village (☎ 520/638–2234 or 520/638–2262) rents equipment and can guide you to the best trails. In season, when the road to the national park is closed, the **North Rim Nordic Center** (c/o Canyoneers, Inc., Box 2997, Flagstaff 86003, ☎ 520/526–0924 or 800/525–0924 outside AZ) transports visitors via SnowVan from Jacob Lake to the Kaibab Lodge, where they can traverse 25 miles of regularly groomed trails in a spectacular wooded setting. Call or write for information on packages, including one that involves an overnight at a remote yurt (a heated dome-shape cabin).

Unrepentant downhillers can hit the slopes at the nearby **Williams Ski Area** (Box 953, Williams 86046, ☎ 520/635–9330), open when there's snow in the region (usually mid-December through March); take South 4th Street for 2 miles, then turn right at the sign and go another 1½ miles. There are four groomed runs (including one for beginners) and other downhill trails as well as areas suitable for cross-country enthusiasts. For downhill skiing, you may prefer going to the larger (though still small by Rocky Mountain standards) **Arizona Snowbowl** northwest of Flagstaff (*see* the Flagstaff section *in* Chapter 4).

Shopping

At the South Rim, nearly every lodging facility and retail store offers Native American artifacts and Grand Canyon souvenirs. In truth, you'll find that after visiting a few of the curio and jewelry shops, all the merchandise begins to look alike. However, the items at most of the lodges and at major gift shops are authentic. The most interesting places for browsing or buying in the immediate area are **Desert View Trading Post** (East Rim Dr. near The Watchtower at Desert View, ☎ 520/638–2360), which sells a mix of traditional Southwestern souvenirs and authentic Native American pottery; the **El Tovar Hotel Gift Shop** (near the rim in Grand Canyon Village, ☎ 520/638–2631), which carries Native American jewelry, rather expensive casual wear, and souvenir gifts; **Verkamp's** (across from El Tovar Hotel, ☎ 520/638–2242), in a historic (1906) building where a huge buffalo head surveys those browsing the fine artwork and crafts; and **Hopi House** (east of El Tovar Hotel, ☎ 520/638–2631), which opened in 1905 and still offers one of the widest selections of Native American artifacts—some of museum quality and not for sale—in the vicinity of the Grand Canyon. The far less commercial North Rim has only one gift shop, at the Grand Canyon Lodge, where you'll find some better-quality items mixed in with a largely schlocky selection of souvenirs.

The huge **Cameron Trading Post** (*see* Tour 5 *in* Exploring, *above*) stocks crafts of the Navajo, Hopi, Zuni, and New Mexico Pueblo peoples. The vast array of goods and prices will satisfy everyone's taste and purse; but it helps to come armed with knowledge of Native American artisanship if you're looking at high-ticket items. *On U.S. 89 1 mi north of junction with AZ 64,* ☎ *520/679–2231 or 800/338–7385.* ☉ *Apr.–Oct., daily 6 AM–10 PM; Nov.–May, daily 7 AM–9 PM.*

Dining and Lodging

Dining

Throughout Grand Canyon country and the vast areas of northwestern Arizona, restaurants cater to tourists who generally move from one place to another at a good clip. Therefore, most establishments offer standard American fare, prepared quickly and offered at reasonable prices. However, there are a few dining opportunities, noted below, that merit mention. In addition, for a quick meal at reasonable prices, there are cafeterias on the South Rim in Grand Canyon Village at **Yavapai Lodge** and **Maswik Lodge** (☎ 520/638–2401 for both). On the North Rim, the cafeteria is in **Grand Canyon Lodge** (☎ 520/638–2611). Restaurants are open daily unless otherwise noted and dress throughout this recreational area is casual (though you may want to don your hole-free jeans for the tony El Tovar dining room).

CATEGORY	COST*
$$$$	over $25
$$$	$17–$25
$$	$10–$17
$	under $10

per person, excluding drinks, service, and 5% sales tax

Lodging

When it comes to lodging in Grand Canyon country, there is one thing to be aware of above all else. The popular South Rim is very crowded during the summer. The North Rim is less crowded, but that area has limited lodging facilities. You would be well advised to make reservations as soon as your itinerary has been decided, even as early as six months in advance. The South Rim's National Park Service Visitor Center, just outside Grand Canyon Village, posts the availability of hotel rooms inside the park and in the nearby town of Tusayan. (Note: The former tend to be high on rustic atmosphere but low on amenities; if you're looking for modern conveniences, you're better off in Tusayan). If you can't find accommodations in the immediate area of the South Rim, you'll probably find something in the nearby communities of Williams (*see* Northwest Arizona, Lake Mead, and Laughlin, *below*) or Flagstaff (*see* Flagstaff and Environs *in* Chapter 4, North-Central Arizona and Flagstaff). For those going to the North Rim, we list the three lodgings in the sparsely populated Arizona Strip country on the approach to the North Rim on U.S. 89A. Prices at many of the hotels and motels in Grand Canyon country are lower in spring, fall, and winter.

CATEGORY	COST*
$$$$	over $110
$$$	$85–$110
$$	$60–$85
$	under $60

All prices are for a standard double room, excluding 5.5%–6.7% tax.

South Rim

Dining and Lodging

$$$$ **El Tovar Hotel.** Built in 1905 of native stone and heavy pine logs, El
★   Tovar is reminiscent of a grand European hunting lodge. As when it first opened, the hotel is operated by the Fred Harvey Company. It still maintains its excellent reputation for service, though at a time when indoor plumbing is no longer a luxury, rooms don't seem as posh as they might have in the past. Some are rather small, but all are nicely appointed, and a number offer canyon views. For decades the hotel's world-class restaurant ($$$$) has enjoyed a reputation for fine food served in a classic 19th-century room of hand-hewn logs and beamed ceilings. The Southwest-inspired menu changes seasonally but includes a daily vegetarian special along with innovatively prepared fish, poultry, and meat dishes: Free-range chicken breast with smoked tomato pine-nut sauce or grilled salmon with tomatillo salsa might be among your dinner options. ✉ *Box 699, Grand Canyon 86023,* ☎ *520/638–2401 (reservations) or 520/638–2631 (switchboard),* 🖷 *520/638–9247. 70 rooms with bath, 10 suites. Dining room, bar, room service. AE, D, DC, MC, V.*

$–$$$$ **Bright Angel Lodge.** Designed by Mary Jane Colter for the Fred Har-
★   vey Company in 1935, this log-and-native-stone structure sits within a few yards of the canyon rim and offers rooms in the main lodge (most with shared baths) or in the quaint cabins (some with fireplaces and/or canyon views) that are scattered among the pines. Don't come for lux-

ury but for a historic structure that blends superbly with the spectacular natural environment and for bargain prices. The Bright Angel coffee shop is open for breakfast, lunch, and dinner; the more upscale but still casual—especially compared to the El Tovar dining room—Arizona Steak House serves dinner only. ☒ *Box 699, Grand Canyon 86023,* ☏ *520/638–2401 (reservations) or 520/638–2631 (switchboard),* FAX *520/638–9247. 11 rooms with bath, 13 rooms with ½ bath (sink and toilet only), 6 rooms without bath, 42 cabins with bath. Restaurant, bar, coffee shop, beauty salon. AE, D, DC, MC, V.*

Dining

$$ The Steak House. This is a warmly appointed, typical Southwestern steak house—right down to the black-and-white-cowhide–pattern tablecloths, massive brick fireplace, displays of Native American and Western art, and John Wayne bar lined with memorabilia of the actor. The food is Western too, with lots of mesquite-grilled steaks, ribs, and barbecued chicken entrées; the more adventurous might try the rattlesnake appetizer, a recent addition to the menu. Portions are large and service is friendly. ✕ *Tusayan, 2 mi south of Grand Canyon entrance, across from IMAX Theater,* ☏ *520/638–2780. Reservations accepted for 8 or more. No credit cards. Sometimes closed in Jan. No lunch.*

Lodging

$$$$ Best Western Grand Canyon Squire Inn. Located in Tusayan, about 2 miles south of the national park entrance, this motel lacks some of the historic charm of the older lodges at the canyon rim, but it offers a much longer list of amenities—including a bowling alley, a small cowboy museum in the stylish lobby, and an upscale gift shop. The spacious, cheerful rooms are nicely appointed with Southwestern-style furnishings. Ask for one with a view of the woods; others face the highway. ☒ *Box 130, Grand Canyon 86023,* ☏ *520/638–2681 or 800/6–CANYON,* FAX *520/638–2782. 250 rooms with bath. Dining room, coffee shop, lounge, pool, beauty salon, sauna, tennis courts, exercise room, bowling, billiards, video games, travel services. AE, D, DC, MC, V.*

$$$ Quality Inn. The design of this facility in Tusayan is unexpected for a chain motel: First-floor rooms can be entered either from a standard drive-up door or from an attractive atrium featuring a spa and lounge. Accommodations, done in soothing shades of light blue, peach, or tan, are also well designed, offering small seating areas, coffeemakers, two sinks, and (unusual for this area) minibars. An all-you-can eat buffet breakfast at the full-service restaurant is a good way to fortify yourself for a day at the canyon. ☒ *Box 520, AZ 64 and U.S. 180, Grand Canyon 86023,* ☏ *520/638–2673 or 800/221–2222,* FAX *520/638–9537. 176 rooms with bath. Restaurant, lounge, pool. AE, D, DC, MC, V.*

$$–$$$ Grand Canyon National Park Lodges. The Fred Harvey Company has seven lodges on the South Rim. Of them, El Tovar and Bright Angel (*see above*) are outstanding, but Maswik Lodge, Yavapai Lodge, Moqui Lodge, Kachina Lodge, and Thunderbird Lodge are all comfortable, if not luxurious. The setting, rather than the amenities, is the draw here. (Note: it's a good idea to bring a flashlight; the dimly lit, wooded grounds can be rather difficult to negotiate in the evening.) In addition to lodge rooms, Maswik offers rustic cabins ($). Moqui, which is only open from March through November, is on U.S. 180, just outside the national park; the others are in Grand Canyon Village. ☒ *Box 699, Grand Canyon 86023,* ☏ *520/638–2401 (reservations) or 520/638–2631 (switchboard),* FAX *520/638–9247. 855 rooms with bath. Restaurant. AE, D, DC, MC, V.*

Camping

Camping inside Grand Canyon National Park is permitted only in designated areas. Campgrounds at the South Rim are listed below.

Desert View Campground, 23 miles east of Grand Canyon Village off AZ 64, offers RV and tent sites, flush toilets, and water but no hookups. The cost is $10 per site, with no reservations. *Box 129, Grand Canyon 86023,* ☎ *520/638–7888.* ☉ *May–Oct.*

Mather Campground in Grand Canyon Village has 97 RV and 190 tent sites (no hookups), flush toilets, water, showers, and a laundromat; the cost is $10 per site. *Reservations through Mistix, Box 85705, San Diego, CA 92138,* ☎ *800/365–2267 or 619/452–0150 outside the U.S.* ☉ *Year-round; no reservations from Dec. 1–Mar. 1.*

Trailer Village, in Grand Canyon Village, has 78 RV sites with full hookups for $17 per site. *Box 699, Grand Canyon 86023,* ☎ *520/638–2401 (reservations) or 520/638–2631 (switchboard),* ℻ *520/638–9247.* ☉ *Year-round.*

Commercial and Forest Service campgrounds outside the park include:

Flintstone Bedrock City, 30 miles south of the park, offers 28 tent and 32 partial RV hookups in a cartoon kitsch setting off a major thoroughfare. Basic rates are $12 per site for two people; add $2 for electricity hookup, $2 for water hookup, and $1.50 for each additional person. Facilities include a gift shop full of Flintstone-obilia and a diner, as well as pay showers. *Grand Canyon Hwy., HCR 34, Box A, Williams 86046,* ☎ *520/635–2600.* ☉ *Apr.–Oct. (may open earlier or close later, depending on weather).*

Grand Canyon Camper Village in Tusayan, 6 miles south of the rim, has 250 RV hookups, some partial, some full ($22 for two people, plus $2 for each additional person over the age of 12) and 100 tent sites ($15 for two people). *Box 490, Grand Canyon 86023,* ☎ *520/638–2887.*

Ten X Campground is run by the Forest Service about 9 miles south of the park. It offers 70 family sites plus a group site (available for groups of up to 100 people), water, and pit toilets for $10 per day but no hookups. No reservations are accepted (except for the group site). *Kaibab National Forest, Tusayan Ranger District, Box 3088, Grand Canyon 86023,* ☎ *520/638–2443.* ☉ *May 1–Sept. 30.*

Bottom of the Canyon

Dining and Lodging

$ **Phantom Ranch.** Built on the site of an earlier hunting camp in 1932, this group of wood-and-stone buildings is set among a grove of cottonwood trees at the bottom of the canyon. For hikers (who need a backcountry permit to come down here), dormitory accommodations—20 beds for men and 20 for women—are available, as are two cabins (one sleeps 4 people, the other 10). There are also seven cabins reserved exclusively for mule riders; lodging, meals, and mule rides are offered as a package (*see* Guided Tours *in* Grand Canyon Essentials, *below*). The restaurant at Phantom Ranch, probably the most remote eating establishment in the United States, has a limited menu. All meals are served family style, with breakfast, dinner (including a selection for vegetarians), and box lunches available. Arrangements—and payment—for both food and lodging should be made 9 to 11 months in advance. ▣ *Box 699, Grand Canyon 86023,* ☎ *520/638–2401 (reservations) or 520/638–2631 (switchboard). 4 dormitories with shared bath for hikers, 11 cabins with shower outside for mule riders. Dining room. AE, D, DC, MC, V.*

Camping

There are two free campgrounds en route to Phantom Ranch: **Indian Garden,** about halfway down the canyon, and **Bright Angel,** closer to the bottom. Both offer toilet facilities and running water (no showers). A backcountry permit, which serves as a reservation, is required. For information, contact the Backcountry Office (Box 129, Grand Canyon 86023, ☎ 520/638–7888).

En Route to the North Rim/Arizona Strip

Dining and Lodging

$$ Cliff Dwellers Lodge. Originated in 1949 in the Marble Canyon area of the Arizona Strip, this dining and lodging complex sits right at the foot of the Vermilion Cliffs. Rooms in the modern motel building are attractive and clean. In summer, the lodge offers hiking tours of the area, and a river expedition company is headquartered right next door. ⊞ *AZ 89A, 9 mi west of Navajo Bridge, HC 67–30, Marble Canyon 86036, ☎ 520/355–2228 or 800/433–2543, ℻ 520/355–2229. 21 rooms with bath. Restaurant, bar, grocery, gas station. D, MC, V.*

$$ Jacob Lake Inn. This modest but clean complex, on 5 acres in Kaibab National Forest (at the junction of U.S. 89A and AZ 67, 45 mi north of the North Rim), is a good option for lodging in the area. Both basic cabins and standard drive-up units are available. All rooms have modern, motel-style appointments, with some rustic touches; most overlook the highways. The bustling lodge center, a popular stop for those heading to the North Rim, has a grocery, a coffee shop, a restaurant, and a large gift shop. ⊞ *Jacob Lake 86022, ☎ 520/643–7232. 11 motel units, 3 family units, 22 cabins, all with bath. Restaurant, café, grocery. AE, D, DC, MC, V.*

$–$$ Cameron Trading Post. In 1993 the 1930s-era inn abutting the historic
★ trading post was razed and replaced by a two-building motel complex. Rooms still have a Southwestern-style decor, attractive hand-carved oak furniture, tile baths, and balconies overlooking the Colorado, but now have such contemporary amenities as remote-control TVs. The original native-stone landscaping—including fossilized dinosaur tracks—was retained, as was the small, well-kept garden with lilacs, roses, and crab apple trees. A recently built cafeteria, designed to serve the tour-bus trade, is unusually well-fitted, with an antique back bar and light fixtures; the older dining room, with its original tinwork ceilings, kiva fireplace, and beautiful oak sideboards, offers hearty meals at good prices. The trading post is on the Navajo reservation, so no alcohol is served here. ⊞ *Box 339, Cameron 86020, ☎ 520/679–2231 or 800/338–7385, ext. 414, ℻ 520/679–2350. 66 rooms with bath, 3 suites. Restaurant, cafeteria, grocery. AE, DC, MC, V.*

$–$$ Marble Canyon Lodge. This Arizona Strip lodge opened in 1929, on
★ the same day the Navajo Bridge was dedicated. It is currently owned by Jane Foster, who first came here in 1950 with her father. Three types of accommodations are available: rooms with lace curtains, brass beds, and hardwood floors in the original building; standard motel rooms in the newer building across the street; and apartments (which can sleep up to eight) in a 1991 complex. Guests can sit on the porch swing of the native-rock lodge building and look out on the Vermilion Cliffs and the desert, or they can play the piano that was brought over on Lees Ferry in the 1920s. Zane Grey and Gary Cooper are among the well-known guests who have stayed here. ⊞ *½ mi west of Navajo Bridge on AZ 89A, Marble Canyon 86036, ☎ 520/355–2225 or 800/726–1789, ℻ 520/355–2227. 63 units with bath. Restaurant, coin laundry, private airstrip, gas station. D, MC, V.*

$ **Lees Ferry Lodge.** Geared toward the Lees Ferry trout-fishing trade, this lodge will outfit you, guide you, and freeze your catch (if it's legal size). At the end of the day you can sit out on one of the garden patios of this rustic building, constructed of native stone and rough-hewn beams in 1929. Rooms are charming, if a bit quirky in their plumbing. The hotel's Vermilion Cliffs Bar and Grill is a popular gathering spot for the men and women who pilot and guide the river rafts through the Grand Canyon, and it serves good American fare—especially the steaks and seafood—in an authentic Western setting. ⌖ *4 mi west of Navajo Bridge on AZ 89A, HC67, Box 1, Marble Canyon 86036,* ☎ *520/355–2231. 8 rooms with shower, 5-person trailer with bath. Restaurant. MC, V.*

Camping

Jacob Lake Campground, at the junction of U.S. 89A and AZ 67, 45 miles north of the North Rim, has family and group RV and tent sites (no hookups) for $10 per vehicle per day. In summer, rangers present interpretive programs in the evening. No reservations accepted (except for groups of 10 or more). *Southwest Natural and Cultural Heritage Association, Box 620, Fredonia 86022,* ☎ *520/643–7395 (off-season), 520/643–7633 (in season).* ☉ *Year-round, but no running water or other facilities in winter; supervised, with fees charged, mid-April–Oct.*

Kaibab Lodge Camper Village (formerly Jacob Lake RV Park), on AZ 67 ¼ mile south of Jacob Lake junction, has 50 tent sites ($10 for two people) and 80 RV and trailer sites ($20 for a pull-through with full hookups, $10 without hookups). Firepits and more than 70 picnic tables are available in this wooded spot, located near a gas station, store, and restaurant. Reservations are accepted. *Box 3331, Flagstaff 86003 (reservations)* ☎ *520/643–7804 in season, 520/526–0924 or 800/525–0924 (outside AZ) in winter,* FAX *520/527–9398.* ☉ *Mid-May 15–Nov. 1, weather permitting.*

North Rim

Dining and Lodging

$–$$$ **Grand Canyon Lodge.** This historic property offers a range of accom-
★ modations in a setting of extraordinary beauty; constructed mainly in the 1920s and '30s, it's the premier lodging facility in the remote, sparsely populated North Rim area. The main building has massive limestone walls and timbered ceilings. Additional lodging options include small, very rustic cabins; larger cabins (some with a canyon view and some with two bedrooms); and traditional motel rooms in newer units. The hotel's huge, high-ceiling dining room offers spectacular views and very good food; you might find marinated pork kebabs, grilled swordfish, or linguine with cilantro on the surprisingly sophisticated dinner menu. ⌖ *TW Recreational Services, Box 400, Cedar City, UT 84721,* ☎ *801/ 586–7686 (reservations) or 520/638–2611 (switchboard),* FAX *801/586– 3157. 40 rooms, 54 Western cabins (for up to 5 people), 82 Frontier cabins (up to 3 people), 21 Pioneer cabins (4 or 5 people), 4 cabins accessible to travelers with disabilities, all with bath. Dining room, cafeteria, bar. AE, D, MC, V.*

$$ **Kaibab Lodge.** In a lovely wooded setting just 5 miles from the entrance to Grand Canyon National Park's North Rim, this 1920s property offers rustic cabins with plain, motel-style furnishings. When they're not out looking into the abyss, guests can sit around the lodge's huge stone fireplace (it can be chilly up here in spring and early fall). In winter, when the canyon is closed, many folks come up for Nordic skiing (*see* Sports and the Outdoors, *above*). ⌖ *AZ 67, HC 64, Box 30, Fredonia 86022,* ☎ *520/638–2389 or 800/525–0924 (for reservations in winter). 24 cab-*

ins with shower. Restaurant. D, MC, V. ☉ Mid-May–Nov. 1 for summer season, early Dec.–early Apr. for skiing season.

Camping

On the North Rim there is only one designated campground inside Grand Canyon National Park. **North Rim Campground,** located 3 miles north of the rim, has 83 RV and tent sites (no hookups) for $10 per day. *Reservations through Mistix, Box 85705, San Diego, CA 92138, ☎ 800/365–2267 or 619/452–0150 outside the U.S. ☉ May 15–Oct. 26.*

Forest Service campgrounds outside the park include **Demotte Campground,** 16 miles north of the rim, with 22 single-unit RV and tent sites, but no hookups, for $10 per day. There are interpretive campfire programs in summer. No reservations accepted. *Southwest Natural and Cultural Heritage Association, Box 620, Fredonia 86022, ☎ 520/643–7395 (off-season), 520/643–7633 (in season). ☉ Mid-May/early June–Oct.*

Havasu Canyon

Dining and Lodging

$$$ Havasupai Lodge. The lodge and restaurant at the bottom of Havasu Canyon, operated by the Havasupai tribe, offers clean, comfortable rooms at about $80 for a double (this rate is in addition to the $12 per person fee to enter the Havasupai tribal lands). The restaurant serves three meals a day, generally sandwiches and fast-food-type fare, and a special daily meal; dinner prices are about $8–$10. For information about camping in the canyon, call the Havasupai Tourist Enterprise (☎ 520/448–2121). ⌧ *Supai 86435, ☎ 520/448–2111 (lodge), or 520/448–2981 (restaurant). 24 rooms. No credit cards; call for payment guidelines and/or restrictions.*

The Arts and Nightlife

Unless you head for nearby Williams or Flagstaff after dark, nightlife in this part of the Southwest consists of watching a full moon above the soaring buttes of the Grand Canyon, roasting marshmallows over a crackling fire, crawling into your bedroll beside some lonely canyon trail, or attending a free evening program on the history of the Grand Canyon. Dinner at **El Tovar Restaurant** (there is an excellent wine list) would be a memorable evening. In addition, the following Grand Canyon properties have cocktail lounges: **El Tovar Hotel** (piano bar), **Bright Angel Lodge** (live entertainment), **Maswik Lodge** (sports bar). and **Moqui Lodge** (live entertainment). Call 520/638–2401 for reservations and further information.

Similarly, there's little in the way of cultural events in the area, but every September the **Grand Canyon Chamber Music Festival** is held in the Shrine of the Ages auditorium at the South Rim visitor center. For schedule information and advance tickets, call or write Box 1332, Grand Canyon 86023, ☎ 520/638–9215. A **lecture series** on scientific topics, cosponsored by the National Park Service and the Grand Canyon Association is scheduled to coincide with the chamber music festival; ask for details at any of the area lodges or at the visitor center. It's also worth checking out the new **art gallery** at the Kolb Studio, just west of Bright Angel Lodge; a variety of painting, photograph, and craft exhibits are featured here from around April 15 through November 30.

Grand Canyon Essentials

Arriving and Departing

By Plane

Where most of Arizona's scenic highlights are many miles apart and an automobile is the most practical mode of transportation for touring the state, you won't really need a car if you're planning to visit only the Grand Canyon's most popular area, the South Rim. Many people choose to fly to the Grand Canyon and then hike, catch a shuttle or taxi, or sign on for bus tours or mule rides in Grand Canyon Village.

AIRPORTS

McCarran International Airport in Las Vegas (☎ 702/261–5743) is the primary air hub for flights to **Grand Canyon National Park Airport** (☎ 520/638–2446). You can also make connections into the Grand Canyon from **Sky Harbor International Airport** in Phoenix (☎ 520/273–3300).

AIRLINES

The many carriers that fly to the Grand Canyon from Las Vegas include **Air Nevada** (☎ 800/634–6377), **Air Vegas** (☎ 800/255–7474), **Las Vegas Airlines** (☎ 800/634–6851), and **Scenic Airlines** (☎ 800/634–6801).

From Phoenix, **Scenic Airlines** (☎ 800/535–4448) offers two daily flights to Grand Canyon Airport. Phoenix Sky Harbor Airport is served by virtually all the major U.S. commercial airlines (*see* Phoenix Essentials *in* Chapter 5, Phoenix and Central Arizona).

TWA Express (☎ 800/221–2000) has daily service from Los Angeles' LAX to Grand Canyon Village.

FROM THE AIRPORT

The **Tusayan/Canyon Airport Shuttle** (☎ 520/638–0821) operates between Grand Canyon Airport and the nearby towns of Tusayan and Grand Canyon Village; it makes hourly runs daily between 8:15 AM and 5:15 PM, with additional trips in the summer months. Rates are $5 each way. A $25 family pass, which covers two adults and two children, allows unlimited travel back and forth for three days.

Fred Harvey Transportation Company (☎ 520/638–2822 or 520/638–2631) offers 24-hour taxi service at Grand Canyon Airport, Grand Canyon Village, and the nearby village of Tusayan; taxis also make trips to other destinations in and around Grand Canyon National Park.

In summer, transportation services desks are maintained at **Bright Angel Lodge, Maswik Lodge,** and **Yavapai Lodge** in Grand Canyon Village; in winter, the one at Yavapai is closed. The desks provide information and handle bookings, sightseeing tours, taxi and bus services, mule and horseback rides, and accommodations at Phantom Ranch (at the bottom of the Grand Canyon). The concierge at **El Tovar** can also arrange most tours, with the exception of mule rides and lodging at Phantom Ranch.

By Train

Amtrak (☎ 800/872–7245) provides daily service to Arizona from both the east and west, with its most convenient stop (for Grand Canyon access) at Flagstaff. From Flagstaff, bus connections can be made for the final leg of the trip to the South Rim through **Nava-Hopi Tours** (*see* By Bus, *below*).

You can also finish your journey on a scenic rail trip. Travel from Flagstaff to Williams by bus—the cost is included in the price of the Amtrak ticket—then continue to the Grand Canyon on a beautifully restored steam train of the Grand Canyon Railway (*see* Guided Tours, *below*).

By Bus

Greyhound Lines (☎ 800/231–2222) provides bus service from all points in the United States to Flagstaff or Williams, both considered gateway communities to the Grand Canyon.

From either Flagstaff or Williams, bus service to the South Rim of the Grand Canyon is offered by **Nava-Hopi Tours** (☎ 520/774–5003 or 800/892–8687).

Getting Around

By Car

If you are traveling to Arizona by car from the east, or coming up from the southern part of the state, your best access to the Grand Canyon is from Flagstaff. You can take U.S. 180 northwest (81 miles) to Grand Canyon Village on the South Rim. Or, for a scenic route with stopping points along the canyon rim, drive north on U.S. 89 from Flagstaff, then turn left at the junction of AZ 64 (52 miles north of Flagstaff) and proceed west for an additional 57 miles.

To visit the North Rim of the canyon, proceed north from Flagstaff on U.S. 89 to Bitter Springs, then take U.S. 89A to the junction of AZ 67, which leads to the North Rim, a distance of approximately 210 miles from Flagstaff.

If you are crossing Arizona on I–40 from the west, your most direct route to the South Rim is on AZ 64 (U.S. 180), which runs north from Williams for 58 miles to Grand Canyon Village.

Keep in mind that summer car traffic leading to the South Rim is heavy—badly congested in the vicinity of Grand Canyon Village and the various parking areas along the rim. If you visit from October through April, you should experience only light to moderate traffic in the vicinity of the canyon. The more remote North Rim has no services available from late October through mid-May. Reaching elevations of more than 8,000 feet, the road is open for day use only until the first heavy snowfall of the year (generally in November or December), at which point roads close until spring. The South Rim stays open to auto traffic all year, though access to the West Rim is restricted in summer because of overcrowded roads.

RENTAL CARS

It's imperative to make reservations in advance for the busy summer months; for the rest of the year, you'll avoid disappointment if you book a car well ahead of time. Be sure to ask about weekly rates and unlimited mileage opportunities.

Major companies serving Phoenix and Flagstaff include **Avis** (☎ 800/331–1212), **Budget** (☎ 800/527–0700), **Hertz** (☎ 800/654–3131), and **National Interrent** (☎ 800/227–7368). Budget is also represented at the Grand Canyon Airport.

CAUTION: When driving off major highways in low-lying areas, watch for rain clouds. Flash floods from sudden summer rains can be deadly (*see* Driving Precautions *in* The Gold Guide's Smart Travel Tips for more information).

By Shuttle Bus

In summer, free shuttle service on the South Rim is offered by the **National Park Service** (☏ 520/638–7888). Generally this service runs shuttles around Grand Canyon Village and the West Rim approximately every 15 minutes from 6:30 AM to 6:45 PM, late May through September. In addition, during these months free shuttles go to Yaki Point on a more limited basis. **Mayflower,** under the aegis of the National Park Service, runs a year-round shuttle taking hikers from the Backcountry Office (across from the visitor center), Maswik Lodge, and Bright Angel Lodge to South Kaibab Trailhead at Yaki Point; the price is $3, and there are two departures every morning. Check for times upon arrival. From May 15 through the end of October, **Trans Canyon Van Service** (☏ 520/638–2820), a South Rim to North Rim shuttle, leaves from Bright Angel Lodge at 1:30 PM and arrives at the North Rim at about 6 PM; the return from Grand Canyon Lodge is at 7 AM, with arrival at the South Rim at about 11:30 AM. The fare is $60 each way ($100 round-trip), and a 50% deposit is required two weeks in advance.

Guided Tours

By Train

The Grand Canyon Railway began running from Williams to the South Rim in 1989, offering a modern version of a route that was first established in 1901. The railroad had been out of operation since 1968, but an $85 million restoration put the old steam engines and Pullman cars back in business. The ride from the renovated station in Williams, about 2½ hours each way, has refreshments, commentary, and corny but fun on-board entertainment. Upgraded Club Class and Chief Class service is available for an additional $12 and $40, respectively. The company also offers a number of good tour and lodging packages. Even if you don't take the train, the impressive 1908 depot, railroad museum, and gift shop are worth visiting. *518 E. Bill Williams Ave., Williams 86046,* ☏ *800/THE–TRAIN.* ☛ *Round-trip fare: $49 adults, $19 ages 2–16.* ⏲ *Departures from Williams Mar. 15–Oct. 30, daily 9:30 AM, return arrives in Williams at 5:30 PM; more limited schedule rest of yr, so call for details.*

By Plane

Flights over the Grand Canyon by airplane or helicopter are offered by a number of companies operating either from Grand Canyon Airport or from heliports in Tusayan. **Air Grand Canyon** (☏ 520/638–2618 or 800/247–4726) and **Grand Canyon Airlines** (☏ 520/638–2407 or 800/528–2413) fly small planes, while **AirStar Helicopters** (☏ 520/638–2622 or 800/962–3869), **Papillon Helicopters** (☏ 520/638–2419 or 800/528–2418), and **Kenai Helicopters** (☏ 520/638–2412 or 800/541–4537) operate whirlybirds. Prices and length of flights vary greatly with tours, but they start at about $55 per person for short airplane flights and $90 per person for short helicopter runs. Inquiries and reservations can also be made at any Grand Canyon lodge transportation desk (*see* Visitor Information, *below*).

By Bus

From late May to late September, a free **shuttle bus service** is offered by the National Park Service (*see* Getting Around by Shuttle Bus, *above*) in the South Rim area. This does not provide a guided tour, but you can get a good feel for the region by taking advantage of trips through Grand Canyon Village, to Yavapai Museum, and to Hermits Rest on the West Rim. In addition, the **Fred Harvey Transportation Company** (☏ 520/638–2822 or 520/638–2631) in Grand Canyon Village provides a veritable menu of daily motor-coach sightseeing trips along the South Rim and to destinations as far away as Monument Valley on the Navajo reservation. Prices range from $12 for short trips to $80 for all-day tours. Children's half-price fares apply to those under 16 for in-park tours, under 12 on the longer out-of-park tours. For schedules, call the South Rim reservations number (☎ 520/638–2401) or inquire at any transportation desk (*see* From the Airport, *above*). **TW Recreational Services, Inc.** (☎ 801/586–7686) offers an interpretive van tour of the North Rim ($20 adults, $10 children ages 4–12); schedules and other details are available in the lobby of the Grand Canyon Lodge.

By Mule

Mule trips down the precipitous trails to the Inner Gorge of the Grand Canyon are nearly as well known as the canyon itself. But, especially for the summer season, it's very hard to get reservations unless you make them months in advance; write Reservations Department (Box 699, Grand Canyon 86023, ☎ 520/638–2401). These trips have been conducted since the early 1900s, and no one has ever been killed by a mule falling off a cliff. Nevertheless, the treks are not for the faint of heart or people in questionable health. Riders must be at least 4 feet 7 inches tall, weigh less than 200 pounds, understand English, and they cannot be pregnant. Children under 15 must be accompanied by an adult. The all-day ride to Plateau Point costs $102 (lunch included). An overnight with a stay at Phantom Ranch at the bottom of the canyon (*see* Lodging, *above*) is $250.25 ($447.50 for two) for one night, $347.50 ($589 for two) for two nights; meals are included in these prices. (*See* What to See and Do with Children, *above,* for information on the shorter mule rides from the North Rim.)

On Foot

The newly established **Grand Canyon Field Institute** (Box 399, Grand Canyon 86023, ☎ 520/638–2485) leads educational guided hikes around the canyon from April through October. Tour topics include everything from archaeology and backcountry medicine to photography and landscape painting. All levels of hiking expertise are accommodated: Some classes involve easy day hikes, others long backpacking trips over rough terrain. Call or write to GFCI for a current class schedule and price list.

Weather

Weather information and road conditions for both the North and South rims, updated at 7 AM daily, can be obtained by calling 520/638–7888.

In general, the South Rim, with an elevation of 7,000 feet, has summer temperatures that range from lows in the 50s to highs in the upper 80s. There are frequent afternoon thunderstorms. The area cools off quickly when the sun goes down, so be sure to bring a sweater or light jacket for the evening. Winter temperatures have average lows around 20°F and highs near 50°F, with the mercury occasionally dropping below zero. In spring and fall, temperatures generally stay above 32°F and often climb into the 70s. The North Rim, accessed through country that ranges in altitude from 8,000 to 9,000 feet, gets heavy winter snow and is thus open to the public only from mid-May through October. Temperatures during this open season range from lows in the 30s to highs in the 70s. Like the South Rim, afternoon rain is common; in May and October, it occasionally snows as well. As you proceed down either rim toward the canyon's Inner Gorge, temperatures rise. In summer along the Colorado River—at an elevation of about 2,400 feet—temperatures range from lows in the 70s to highs above 100°F. Winter sees lows in the 30s, highs around 50. It rarely snows at the bottom of the Grand Canyon, even in winter; snow on the rims usually turns to rain as it falls into the Inner Gorge.

Telephones

You're likely to have a hard time getting through to the Grand Canyon: Trunk lines into the area are limited and often overloaded with people calling this most popular of Arizona's attractions. You'll get a fast busy signal if this is the case. In addition, when you do get through to the National Park Service or South Rim Reservations numbers—which handle many of the services listed in this chapter—you'll have to punch a lot of numbers on a computer-voice system before you reach the service you want. Be patient; it's possible to get through to a human being eventually. Writing ahead for the information-packed *Trip Planner* (*see* Visitor Information, *below*) is likely to save you a phone call. Remember, too, that the park does not accept reservations for backcountry permits by phone; they must be made in writing.

Safety Tips

Be careful when you or your children are near the edge of the canyon or walking any of the trails that descend into it. Guardrails exist only on portions of the rims. Tragically, a few visitors are killed each year in falls from viewing points. Before engaging in any strenuous exercise, be aware that the canyon rims are more than 7,000 feet in altitude. Being at this height can cause some people—even those in good shape—to become dizzy, faint, or to feel nauseous. Before hiking into the canyon, assess the distance of the proposed hike against your physical condition. Where the descent may not be especially difficult, coming back up can be very strenuous. Be sure to take sufficient water and food on hikes into the canyon (*see* Hiking *in* Sports and the Outdoors, *above*). During summer months, temperatures in the Inner Gorge can climb above 105°F.

Entrance Fees

Fees levied by the National Park Service vary depending on your method of entering Grand Canyon National Park. If you arrive by automobile, the fee is $10, regardless of the number of passengers. Individuals arriving by bicycle or on foot pay $4. The entrance gates are open 24 hours but are generally supervised from about 7 AM until 6:30 or 7 PM. If you arrive when there's no one at the gate, you may enter legally without paying.

Important Addresses and Numbers

Emergencies
Police, fire, or **ambulance** (☎ 911).

Medical
SOUTH RIM
Grand Canyon Health Center (Grand Canyon Village, ☎ 520/638–2551 or 520/638–2469) offers physician services and receives patients weekdays 8–5:30, Saturday 9–noon. After-hours care and 24-hour emergency services are also available. Dental care (☎ 520/638–2395) is offered by appointment only.

The **North Rim Clinic** (Grand Canyon Lodge, Cabin 1, ☎ 520/ 638–2611, ext. 222) is staffed by a nurse practitioner. The clinic is open for walk-ins and appointments Friday through Monday 9–noon and 3–6, and Tuesday 9–noon; it's closed Wednesday. For emergency service dial 911.

Pharmacies

At the South Rim, the well-stocked **Grand Canyon Clinic Pharmacy** (☎ 520/638–2460) in Grand Canyon Village is open weekdays 8:30–5:30 year-round, and also Saturday morning in the summer; it's generally closed for an hour at lunchtime during the week. There is no pharmacy at the North Rim.

Road Service

SOUTH RIM
At Grand Canyon Village, the **Fred Harvey Public Garage** (☎ 520/638–2631) is a fully equipped AAA garage that provides auto and RV repair from 8 to 5 daily (closed 12–1 for lunch) as well as 24-hour emergency service. About ¾ mile down the road, across from the visitor center, **Fred Harvey Chevron** (☎ 520/638–2631) does minor repairs, oil and tire changes, and carries propane and diesel fuel.

NORTH RIM
The **Chevron** service station (☎ 520/638–2611), offering auto repairs, is located inside the park on the access road leading to the North Rim Campground. No diesel fuel is available at the North Rim.

Food and Camping Supplies

SOUTH RIM
Babbitts General Store has three locations in the South Rim area: at Grand Canyon Village (☎ 520/638–2262), in the nearby village of Tusayan (☎ 520/638–2854), and at Desert View (☎ 520/638–2393) near the east park entrance. The main store, in Grand Canyon Village, is a department store that has a deli and sells a full line of camping, hiking, and backpacking supplies in addition to groceries.

NORTH RIM
The **North Rim General Store** (☎ 520/638–2611), inside the park across from the North Rim Campground, carries groceries, some clothing, and travelers' supplies.

Banks

An office of **Bank One** (☎ 520/638–2437) is located at the South Rim across from the visitor center in Grand Canyon Village. Services include a 24-hour teller machine operating with Bank One, Plus (Visa), Star, Arizona Interchange Network, and Cirrus (MasterCard) access cards. The bank cashes traveler's checks and exchanges foreign currency, but it does not usually cash personal checks. Banking hours are weekdays 10–3. No banking facilities are located within Grand Canyon National Park at the North Rim.

Visitor Information

Grand Canyon Lodge (TW Recreational Services, Inc., Box 400, Cedar City, UT 84720, ☎ 801/586–7686, FAX 801/586–3157) has lodging and general information about the North Rim year-round. For information on local services during the season in which the North Rim is open (generally mid-May through late October, depending on the weather), you can phone the lodge directly (☎ 520/638–2611).

Grand Canyon National Park Lodges (Box 699, Grand Canyon 86023, ☎ 520/638–2401, FAX 520/638–9247) can provide information on lodging, tours, and all other recreation inside the park at the South Rim.

Grand Canyon National Park (Box 129, Grand Canyon 86023, ☎ 520/638–7888) is the contact for general information. Write ahead for a complimentary *Trip Planner,* updated regularly by the National Park Service.

Williams and Forest Service Visitor Center (200 W. Railroad Ave., at Grand Canyon Blvd., Williams 86046, ☎ 520/635–4061), run jointly by the National Forest Service, the city of Williams, and the Williams Chamber of Commerce, has information on Williams, Kaibab Forest, and the entire Grand Canyon area.

North and South Rim camping (Mistix, Box 85705, San Diego, CA 92138, ☎ 800/365–2267, or 619/452–0150 outside the U.S.). When you call this computer-operated system, have the exact dates you'd like to camp on hand.

Every arriving visitor at the South or North Rim is given a detailed map of the area. Both rims also publish a free newspaper, *The Guide,* which contains a detailed area map; it is available at the visitor center and many of the lodging facilities and stores.

The park also distributes "Accessibility Guide," a free newsletter that details the facilities available for those with special needs.

NORTHWEST ARIZONA, LAKE MEAD, AND LAUGHLIN

If the Grand Canyon is the most dramatic natural attraction in northwest Arizona, it is by no means all there is to see. Towns like Williams and Kingman hearken back to the glory days of old Route 66, while the ghost towns of Chloride and Oatman bear testament to the mining madness that once reigned in the region. Or you may want to descend into the paradise of quieter Havasu Canyon, north of Seligman (*see* Off the Beaten Track *in* Exploring, *above*). Water-sports fans, or those who just want to laze on a houseboat, will enjoy Lake Mead, just across the Nevada border, or Lake Havasu, over which London Bridge surrealistically presides. Another bridge across the Colorado leads to Nevada and the casinos of Laughlin, more low-key and casual than those of Las Vegas. And if you need an antidote to the Grand Canyon, visit Hoover Dam, the towering monument to that age-old human endeavor: the control of nature.

Exploring

Numbers in the margin correspond to points of interest on the Northwest Arizona and Lake Mead map.

Often considered just a jumping-off point for the Grand Canyon, ❶ **Williams** retains its own funky frontier charm, despite a proliferation of motels and fast-food restaurants on its main street (named, like the town itself, after mountain man Bill Williams). Due to its elevation of 6,700 feet, the area is wooded and pleasantly temperate in summer, and in winter a small ski area operates (*see* Sports and the Outdoors, *above*). Many of the neon signs on Bill Williams Avenue hearken back to the days when it was better known as Route 66. Indeed, Williams was not bypassed by I-40 until 1984, making it the last town in America to be served by the legendary "Mother Road." Reasonably priced antiques shops and retailers selling Native American crafts and jewelry line this main drag, where a number of historic buildings have been restored and period lampposts installed.

Make your first stop the **Williams and Forest Service Visitor Center** (200 W. Railroad Ave., at Grand Canyon Blvd., Williams 86046, ☎ 520/635–4061). Opened in spring 1994, it's a good resource for information about the area—be sure to pick up the Historic Williams Walking Tour and Historic Route 66/Williams to Flagstaff Auto Tour brochures—and an interesting structure in its own right. It was built in 1901 as the original passenger train depot, and its brick walls still show graffiti scrawled by early railroad workers and hoboes.

Although the town is no longer on an east–west rail link, the route north to the Grand Canyon was restored in 1989 (*see* Guided Tours *in* Grand Canyon Essentials, *above*). Even if you don't take the train, it's worth visiting the **Williams Depot** (518 E. Bill Williams Ave., ☎ 520/635–4000), built in 1908 to replace the terminal where the visitor center now resides. Attractions here include a passenger car and the locomotive of a turn-of-the-century steam train, a small but interesting railroad museum, and a gift shop where you can find kitsch souvenirs like a tie that plays "I've Been Working on the Railroad."

The first phase of a new hotel, designed to resemble the depot's original Fray Marcos lodge, is scheduled to open across from the train station in the summer of 1995 (☎ 520/635–4010). At the east entrance to town, the **Ramada Inn,** formerly the Mountain Side Inn & Resort (642 E. Bill Williams Ave., Williams 86046, ☎ 520/635–4431 or 800/462–9381), has comfortable rooms, a good restaurant, and live country-and-western bands in summer. On the west side, the no-frills **Norris Motel** (1001 W. Bill Williams Ave., Williams 86046, ☎ 520/635–2202 or 800/341–8000) offers clean accommodations at good rates (look for the British flag out front).

❷ From Williams, take I–40 west to **Kingman,** surrounded by mountains on three sides and host to the longest remaining stretch of old Route 66. In this town, the neon-lined roadway is named for native son Andy Devine, the gravelly voiced actor who played sidekick to leading men in innumerable Westerns. Because I–40, U.S. 93, AZ 68, and Route 66 all converge in Kingman, which is also served by Amtrak, Greyhound, and America West airlines (offering three flights a day from Phoenix), it is a hub for local attractions like Hoover Dam, Laughlin, and Lake Havasu.

Once in town, the **Kingman Area Chamber of Commerce** (333 W. Andy Devine Ave., Box 1150, Kingman 86402, ☎ 520/753–6106) carries T-shirts, postcards, and the usual brochures to acquaint you with local attractions. The **Mohave Museum of History and Arts** (400 W. Beale St., ☎ 520/753–3195) includes an Andy Devine Room; an exhibit of carved Kingman turquoise; and a diorama depicting the expedition of Lt. Edward Beale, who led his ill-fated camel-cavalry unit to the area in search of a wagon road along the 35th parallel. The **Bonelli House** (430 E. Spring St., call the Mohave Museum for information), an excellent example of the Anglo-Territorial architecture popular in 1915, is one of 62 buildings in the business district listed on the National Register of Historic Places. A 15-mile drive from town up Hualapai Mountain Road will take you to **Hualapai Mountain Park,** where more than 2,200 wooded acres at elevations ranging from 6,000 to 8,400 feet host 6 miles of hiking trails as well as picnic areas, rustic cabins,

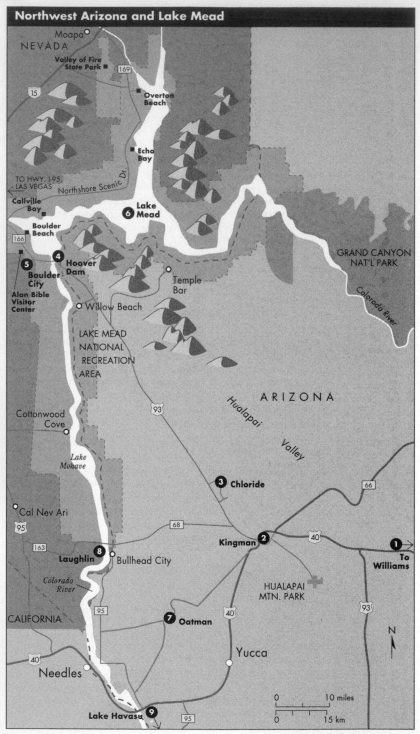

NEVADA

Moapa

Valley of Fire
State Park

169

15

Overton
Beach

Echo
Bay

TO HWY. I-95,
LAS VEGAS

Northshore Scenic Dr.

Callville
Bay

6 Lake
Mead

Boulder
Beach

166

4 Hoover
Dam

5

Boulder
City

Alan Bible
Visitor
Center

Willow Beach

Temple
Bar

GRAND CANYON
NAT'L PARK

Colorado River

LAKE MEAD

NATIONAL

RECREATION

AREA

ARIZONA

Hualapai

Valley

93

Cottonwood
Cove

Lake
Mohave

3 Chloride

66

Cal Nev Ari

95

68

163

8

Laughlin

Bullhead City

Kingman **2**

40

1

To
Williams

Colorado
River

95

HUALAPAI
MTN. PARK

93

CALIFORNIA

7 Oatman

40

N

40

Needles

Yucca

0   10 miles

0   15 km

Lake Havasu **9**

95

and RV and tenting areas; contact the Mohave County Parks Department (☏ 520/753–0739) for details.

There are some 35 motels in this modest (pop. about 13,000) town, most of them along Andy Devine Avenue. The **Quality Inn** (1400 W. Andy Devine Ave., Kingman 86401, ☏ 520/753–4747 or 800/221–2222) has comfortable rooms and a spiffy coffee shop stocked with Route 66 memorabilia.

❸ If you're heading on to Hoover Dam and Lake Mead, take U.S. 93 north; you'll come to a marked turnoff for the ghost town of **Chloride,** which takes its name from a type of silver ore mined in the area. Many buildings were lost to fires that ravaged the town in its heyday, but some historic treasures still stand, including the old bank vault, now a museum; the 1890 Jim Fritz house; and the Tennessee Saloon, now a general store and dance hall. Don't miss the huge murals painted on the rocks at the outskirts of town by Western artist Roy Purcell, who worked the mines here in his youth.

❹ Continue along U.S. 93 to reach **Hoover Dam.** The visual impact of its incredible mass and height often compels visitors to make this the first stop on a visit to the Lake Mead area. Created for flood control and to generate electricity, the dam is 727 feet high (the equivalent of a 70-story building) and 660 feet thick (more than the length of two football fields). Its construction required 4.4 million cubic yards of concrete, enough to build a two-lane highway from San Francisco to New York. Every year more than 700,000 people take the Bureau of Reclamation's guided tour, which takes visitors deep inside the structure for a look at its inner workings; tours leave every few minutes from the exhibit building at the top of the dam. A huge new visitor center, which was scheduled to open on the Nevada side by fall 1995, contains three theaters, an exhibition gallery, an observation tower, and a much-needed five-story parking garage. ☏ 702/293–8367. ☛ *Free. Guided tours: $4 adults, $2 senior citizens over 62 with Golden Age Pass, children under 12 free.* ☉ *Memorial Day–Labor Day, daily 8–7:30 (last tour at 6:15); Labor Day–Memorial Day, daily 9–5 (last tour at 4:15). Closed Dec. 25. Hrs may change; call ahead.*

❺ About 8 miles west of Hoover Dam on U.S. 93, **Boulder City,** Nevada, is a small, pleasant town with a movie theater, numerous gift shops and eateries, and a small hotel. Developed in the early 1930s to house the 4,000 Hoover Dam workers and to deter them from spending their hard-earned dollars on wine, women, and Las Vegas, Boulder City is the only community in Nevada where gambling is illegal. When the dam was completed, the city served as a center for the management and maintenance of the site. The **Boulder City Chamber of Commerce** (1497 Nevada Hwy., Boulder City, NV 89005, ☏ 702/293–2034) has information about the town and nearby attractions.

Just northeast of Boulder City, at the intersection of U.S. 93 (also called Nevada Highway here) and Lakeshore Scenic Drive (NV 166), you'll come to the **Alan Bible Visitor Center** (601 Nevada Hwy., Boulder City, NV 89005, ☏ 702/293–8906), the best place to become acquainted with the Lake Mead area.

Turn left out of the visitor center and go down the hill to pick up Lakeshore Scenic Drive (NV 166). This route wends its way along the
❻ shore of **Lake Mead,** the largest man-made body of water in the United States, with a surface covering 229 square miles and an irregular shoreline extending for 550 miles. It was formed when Hoover Dam was built in 1935 to hold back the Colorado River. Recreation

areas with marinas include Boulder Beach, Callville Bay, Echo Bay, and Overton Beach.

If you didn't bring your own boat, your rental options include house-boats, patio boats, fishing boats, and ski boats—pick up a list of marinas at the Alan Bible Visitor Center (*see above*). Houseboat rentals are available at **Callville Bay Resort and Marina** (☎ 702/565-7340) or at **Echo Bay Resort** (☎ 702/394-4000 or 800/752-9669). Smaller boats are available at these locations and at **Lake Mead Resort** (Boulder Beach, ☎ 702/293-3484), in addition to other marinas.

For those who want to leave the navigating to someone else, a 1½-hour cruise of the Hoover Dam area on a 250-passenger stern-wheeler is available through **Lake Mead Cruises** (Lake Mead Marina, near Boulder Beach, ☎ 702/293-6180) and a 15-mile motorized raft trip on the Colorado from the base of Hoover Dam down Black Canyon to Willow Beach is offered by **Gray Line Tours** (☎ 702/384-1234 or 800/634-6579).

❼ Those of you heading to Laughlin (just over the Nevada border) from Kingman who aren't overanxious to hit the slots might want to look into the ghost town of **Oatman.** A worthwhile detour via old Route 66 (now 68), it's a straight shot across the Mohave Desert valley for a while, but then the road narrows and winds precipitously for about 15 miles through the Black Mountains. The main street of this former gold-mining town is right out of the Old West; in fact, a number of films, including *How the West Was Won,* were shot here. You can wander into one of the three saloons or visit the Oatman Hotel, where Clark Gable and Carole Lombard honeymooned in 1939 after they were secretly married in Kingman, but the burros that often come in from nearby hills and meander down the street are the town's real draw; a couple of stores sell hay to visitors who want to feed these "wild" beasts.

❽ North Oatman Road will take you to Bullhead City, where you can cross the Colorado River to reach **Laughlin,** Nevada. Don Laughlin opened the first casino here in 1966, but the town didn't really take off until the early 1980s. Though often considered just a smaller version of Las Vegas, Laughlin has a character of its own. It generally attracts older, retired travelers who spend at least part of the winter in Arizona, and other folks who prefer the low-pressure, low-minimum tables, the cheap food, the low-cost rooms, and the slots galore. The dealers are generally friendlier, the bettors more relaxed, and, especially compared to the shuttered rooms in Las Vegas, Laughlin casinos have a bright, airy, open feeling, lent by large picture windows that overlook the Colorado. When you've finished at the tables, Laughlin's outdoor activities include water sports, golf, tennis, and strolls along the tree-lined River Walk. The **Laughlin Chamber of Commerce** (1725 Casino Dr., Box 77777, Laughlin, NV 89028, ☎ 702/298-2214 or 800/227-5245) can provide further information on the area, which is served currently served by America West, Arizona Airways, Reno Air, and United Express airlines.

The gambling halls lining Casino Drive include **Riverside Resort** (1650 S. Casino Dr., ☎ 702/298-2535 or 800/227-3849), **Flamingo Hilton** (1900 S. Casino Dr., ☎ 702/298-5111 or 800/FLAMINGO), **Regency Casino** (1950 S. Casino Dr., ☎ 702/298-2439), **Edgewater** (2020 S. Casino Dr., ☎ 702/298-2453 or 800/67-RIVER), **Colorado Belle** (2100 S. Casino Dr., ☎ 702/298-4000 or 800/458-9500), **Pioneer Hotel** (2200 S. Casino Dr., ☎ 702/298-2442 or 800/634-3469), **Ramada Express** (2121 S. Casino Dr., ☎ 702/298-4200 or 800/272-6232), **Golden Nugget** (2300 S. Casino Dr., ☎ 702/298-7111 or 800/237-

1739), **Gold River** (2700 S. Casino Dr., ☎ 702/298–2242 or 800/835–7903), and **Harrah's** (2900 S. Casino Dr., ☎ 702/298–4600 or 800/447–8700). Note: The zip code for the town is 89028, but for the hotel strip it's 89029.

❾ From Bullhead City, drive 19 miles south on AZ 95 to reach **Lake Havasu,** renowned for hosting London Bridge. A brilliant stroke of entrepreneurship turned what might have been just another desert town on the Colorado into a crowd-drawing curiosity: When the City of London put the sinking bridge up for sale in 1967, developer Robert McCulloch decided it would make the perfect centerpiece for the community he had planned on the shores of the lake. He bought the historic bridge for nearly $2.5 million, had it dismantled stone by stone, shipped, and precisely reassembled (all 10,000 tons of it) to span a narrow arm of Lake Havasu.

An Olde English theme is played to the hilt here: A Tudor-style village replete with pub, red London telephone booths, and other Britobilia abuts the base of the bridge. But Havasu City is on a lake, and in Arizona after all, so the sunshine, water sports, and fishing can amuse visitors after they've seen the surprising span. The weather is wonderful in spring, fall, and winter, but summers often see temperatures that exceed 100°F. Among the recreational opportunities on and around 45-mile-long Lake Havasu are houseboat, ski-boat, Jet Ski, and sailboat rentals; marinas, RV parks, and campgrounds; golf, tennis, and guided fishing expeditions. Those who are interested in exploring the desert—including old mines and a wildlife refuge—might consider booking a four-wheel-drive tour with Outback Off-Road Adventures (1350 McCulloch Blvd., ☎ 520/680–6151).

The area has more than 20 lodging establishments—from inexpensive roadside motels to posh resorts—and more than 40 restaurants, from fast-food emporiums to fine dining establishments. For more information on Lake Havasu City, contact the **Lake Havasu Visitor and Convention Bureau** (1930 Mesquite Ave., Suite 3, Lake Havasu City 86403, ☎ 520/453–3444 or 800/242–8278).

CAUTION: When driving off major highways in low-lying, watch for rain clouds. Flash floods from sudden summer rains can be deadly (*see* Driving Precautions *in* The Gold Guide's Smart Travel Tips for more information).

3 The Northeast

This sprawling corner of the state is the home of the Navajo Nation and Hopi Reservation. Native American crafts draw some visitors, as does interest in getting an understanding of the lives, past and present, of some of our land's true founding mothers and fathers. Along with the living Navajo and Hopi reservations, ancient Pueblo ruins at Betatakin, Keet Seel, and Canyon de Chelly are haunting, unforgettable sights. And don't forget about Monument Valley, the bizarre and fascinating Petrified Forest National Park and Painted Desert, and activities at another man-made lake, Lake Powell, when planning your trip.

By William E.
Hafford

*Updated by
Susana C.
Sedgwick*

IF YOU'VE EVER wondered what it felt like to be alive on the first day of Creation, you'll know when you visit northeastern Arizona, a vast and lonely land of shifting red dunes, soaring buttes, and turquoise skies so clear that horizons are almost always 100 miles or more away. Covering more than 30,000 square miles, most of the northeast belongs to the Navajo and Hopi peoples, who have held on to ancient cultural traditions that are based on strong spiritual values and an affinity for nature. Excellent Native American arts and crafts can be found in shops, galleries, and trading posts throughout the region. Visiting here is like crossing into a foreign country—one that is, sadly, less prosperous than much of the rest of the United States. In some respects, life on the Hopi mesas seems to resemble what it must have been in the last century, and it's not uncommon to hear Navajo spoken in towns such as Tuba City and Window Rock.

The Navajo reservation, known to its people as the Navajo Nation, spreads across some 25,000 square miles of the northeastern corner of Arizona. In its approximate center lie 4,000 square miles of Hopi reservation, a series of stone and adobe villages built on high mesas overlooking cultivated land. And on Arizona's northern and eastern borders, where the Navaho Nation continues into Utah, Colorado, and New Mexico, the stunning topographies of Navajo National Monument and Canyon de Chelly contain some of the haunting cliff dwellings of ancient Pueblo people who lived in the four corners area.

Outside of Navajo country, you'll find two of the most popular attractions in the area. Just below the southeastern boundary of the reservation, straddling I–40, Petrified Forest National Park is an intriguing geological open book of the Earth's distant past. The park includes a large portion of the famed Painted Desert, whose name describes the stratified bands of multicolored hills in which ancient life-forms and huge fallen tree trunks have petrified over hundreds of millions of years. Glen Canyon Dam abuts the far northwestern corner of the reservation on U.S. 89. Behind that, more than 120 miles of the emerald waters of Lake Powell are held in precipitous canyons of erosion-carved stone. Many find Lake Powell one of the most serene and beautiful places in the world.

Most of the northeast is arid land, with soil and rock formations ranging in astonishing colors from delicate salmon-pink to rusty orange and even red—this, too, is painted desert. Driving long distances, you'll pass immense mesas, rock spires, canyons, cliffs, and some impressive mountain ranges. Inviting stands of ponderosa pine cover the Chuska Mountains to the north and east of Canyon de Chelly. Navajo Mountain to the north and west in Utah soars above 10,000 feet.

Courtesy in Navajo–Hopi Country

Both the Hopi and Navajo peoples are friendly to tourists. However, their privacy, customs, and laws should be respected.

- Do not wander across residential areas or disturb property.

- Always ask permission before taking photographs of the locals; you may have to pay to take the picture.

- Do not litter.

- No open fires are allowed; fires are permitted only in grills and fireplaces. Bring your own wood or charcoal.

- Observe quiet hours from 11 PM until 6 AM at all camping areas.

- Do not disturb or remove animals, plants, rocks, or artifacts. They are protected by Tribal Antiquity and federal laws, which are strictly enforced.

- The possession and consumption of alcoholic beverages or drugs is illegal.

- No off-trail hiking or rock climbing is allowed.

- A permit is required for fishing in lakes or streams or for hunting game; the use of firearms is otherwise prohibited.

- Off-road travel by four-wheel-drive vehicles, dune buggies, Jeeps, and motorcycles is not allowed.

- Do not wear bikinis or similar scanty clothing in public.

- Pets should be kept on a leash or in a confined area.

- On the Hopi reservation, taking photographs or making videos, tape recordings, and sketches of villages and ceremonies is strictly prohibited. At all sacred events, neat attire and a respectful demeanor are requested. Camping is permitted for a maximum of two nights, but only in designated areas. All Hopi villages have separate rules about visitors; check with the individual village Community Development Offices (*see* Tour 2 *in* Exploring the Northeast, *below*), or call the **Hopi Tribe Office of Public Relations** (☎ 520/734–2441) in advance for information.

Hopi Ceremonies

The Hopi are well known for colorful ceremonial dances, many of which are supplications for rain, fertile crops, and harmony with nature. Most of these ceremonies take place in village plazas and kivas (underground ceremonial chambers) and last two days or longer; outsiders are permitted to watch only certain segments and are never allowed into kivas. Dancers may wear masks and beaded costumes, beat drums, and chant. The snake dance is the best-known, in which participants carry live snakes, including poisonous rattlers. However, this ceremony has not been open to the public in recent years. Seasonal kachina dances have also been restricted: Now only those in Moenkopi, Old Oraibi, Hotevilla, and Kykotsmovi may be observed by those who are not Native American.

Dances that visitors are allowed to watch usually take place on weekends, extending through the day until dusk. Each tribal clan has its own sacred rituals, starting times and dates which are determined by tribal elders. Visitors should be respectful and adhere to the proper etiquette while observing dances. For more information, contact the **Hopi Tribe Office of Public Relations** (*see above*).

EXPLORING THE NORTHEAST

The tours below flow into each other. Choose one or two at a time or string them together with overnight stays to last a week or longer. The first tour starts from Flagstaff. You can use that as a base, but lodging throughout the area will save driving time. If you are coming from Utah or Colorado (*see* Getting Around *in* The Northeast Essentials, *below*), you will need to adjust to a different entry into the tours. Tours 1 and 2 can begin just as easily from Gallup, New Mexico as from Flagstaff.

Tour 1: Petrified Forest National Park and the Painted Desert

Numbers in the margin correspond to points of interest on the North-eastern Arizona map.

❶ From **Flagstaff,** you'll need to get an early start for this tour. Drive east on I–40. Don't miss the 15-foot-tall, red-and-yellow arrows at—yes—Twin Arrows, about 20 miles out of Flagstaff, where there used to be a café and gift shop. You'll also pass Winslow, Arizona, of Eagles' "Take it Easy" fame. This and other towns along the old Route 66 were left on the wayside when I–40 was constructed, depriving them of a fair amount of tourist traffic.

❷ On your way to Petrified Forest, **Homolovi Ruins State Park** (HC 63 Box 5, Winslow 86047, ☎ 520/289–4106), three miles west of Winslow off AZ 87, is the site of five major ancestral Hopi pueblos. There are 40 ceremonial kivas thought to date from AD 900, and one pueblo contains over 700 rooms. The Hopi believe their immediate ancestors inhabited this place, and they still hold the site to be sacred. The Homolovi Visitor's Center is located within the park, about 1½ miles from AZ 87.

TIME OUT Before making your way to Petrified Forest National Park, you may want to·stop in at one of Winslow's Old Route 66 diners for a blast-from-the-past lunch.

★ ❸ Back on I–40, continue east for 54 miles to the north entrance of **Petrified Forest National Park,** a trip back in geological time. In 1984 the fossil remains of one of the oldest dinosaurs ever unearthed—dating from the Triassic period of the Mesozoic era 225 million years ago—were discovered here; other plant and animal fossils in the park date from the same period. Remnants of ancient human beings and their artifacts, dating from some 8,000 years ago, have been recovered at more than 500 sites in this national park.

The park derives its name from the fact that the grounds are also covered with petrified tree trunks whose wood cells were fossilized over centuries by brightly hued mineral deposits—silica, iron oxide, manganese, aluminum, copper, lithium, and carbon. In many places, petrified logs scattered about the landscape resemble a fairy-tale forest turned to stone. Most of the park's 94,000 acres include portions of the vast, pink-hued lunarlike landscape known as the Painted Desert. In the northern area of the park, this colorful but essentially barren and waterless series of windswept plains, hills, and mesas is considered by geologists to be part of the Chinle formation, deposited at an early stage of the Triassic period. Colors are most dramatic at dawn and sunset, when oblique light enhances the earth tones, making smaller chasms glow deep red.

Because so many looters hauled away large quantities of petrified wood in the early years of this century, President Theodore Roosevelt made the area into a national monument in 1906. Since then, it has been illegal (not to mention bad karma) to remove even a small sliver of petrified wood from the park (there are plenty of pieces on sale at the visitor center gift shop if you want a souvenir).

You can easily spend most of a day on the park's 28 miles of paved roads and walking trails. A number of lookouts on the north end of the park provide beautiful Painted Desert vistas. Fascinating Native American petroglyphs survive on boulders at Newspaper Rock. The

Northeastern Arizona

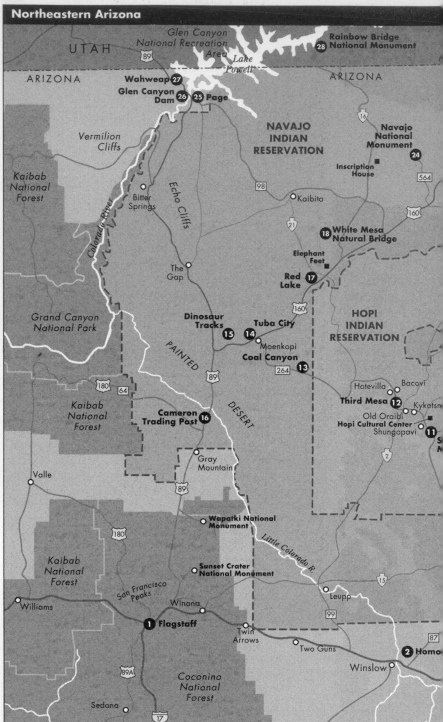

UTAH

ARIZONA

Glen Canyon National Recreation Area
89
Lake Powell

ARIZONA

28 Rainbow Bridge National Monument

Wahweap 27
Glen Canyon Dam 26 25 Page

16

Navajo National Monument

NAVAJO INDIAN RESERVATION

24

Vermilion Cliffs

Inscription House

564

Kaibab National Forest

Bitter Springs

98

Kaibito

160

Colorado River

Echo Cliffs

21

18 White Mesa Natural Bridge

Elephant Feet

The Gap

Red Lake 17

160

HOPI INDIAN RESERVATION

Grand Canyon National Park

PAINTED

Dinosaur Tracks 15   14 Tuba City

Moenkopi
Coal Canyon 264 13

89

Hotevilla   Bacovi

180
64

DESERT

Third Mesa 12   Kykotsn

Old Oraibi
Hopi Cultural Center 11
Shungopavi

Kaibab National Forest

Cameron Trading Post 16

2

Valle

Gray Mountain

89

Williams

Wapatki National Monument

Little Colorado R.

15

180

Kaibab National Forest

Sunset Crater National Monument

Leupp

San Francisco Peaks

Winona

99

1 Flagstaff

Twin Arrows

87

Two Guns

2 Homo

89A

Coconino National Forest

Winslow

Sedona

17

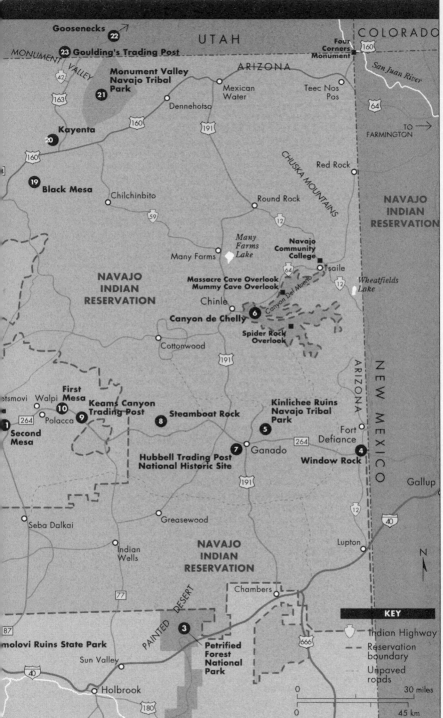

area around **Jasper Forest** contains stunning hunks of petrified trees scattered on the desert floor. Near the southern end of the park, **Agate House** is a structure assembled from pieces of petrified wood. And the self-guided **Giant Logs Trail** starts at the Rainbow Forest Museum and Visitor Center and loops through a half mile of huge fallen trees. One of the ancient, fallen trunks measures over six feet in diameter.

★   At the north entrance of the park, the **Painted Desert Visitor Center** shows a movie entitled *The Stone Forest,* tracing the natural history of the area. The **Rainbow Forest Museum and Visitor Center,** located at the south entrance (off U.S. 180), displays three skeletons from the Triassic period, including that of the ferocious phytosaur, a crocodilelike carnivore. The museum has numerous exhibits relating to the world of cycads (tropical plants), ferns, fish, and other early life, as well as artifacts and tools of ancient humans. Within the park's boundaries, visitors also have access to gift shops, a restaurant, a soda fountain, and a service station. Picnicking is allowed inside the park.

If you don't want to return to Flagstaff (115 miles), go to Holbrook or Winslow for motel accommodations; continue 82 miles to Window Rock where you can stay overnight and begin Tour 2 in the morning; or drive 86 miles to Second Mesa where you can stay overnight and begin Tour 3 in the morning. You may hike into the nearby wilderness areas to camp, but you must obtain a park permit for an overnight stay. Free permits are issued at both visitor centers (*see above*).

North entrance: off I–40, 25 mi east of Holbrook. South entrance: off U.S. 180, 19 mi southeast of Holbrook. Box 2217, Petrified Forest, AZ 86028, ☎ 520/524–6228. ☛ $5 per vehicle, free with Golden Eagle, Golden Age, or Golden Access pass. ☉ Daily 8–5 (budget permitting, 1996 summer hrs may be extended; call ahead to inquire). Park closed Dec. 25 and Jan. 1.

TIME OUT   If you want to shake off some dust after the Petrified Forest, get some kicks on historic Route 66 which runs through the heart of Holbrook. Best seen at night, lit up with neon, Holbrook is a funky, once-booming cowboy town—the kind where you might expect to encounter Thelma and Louise. In fact, Hollywood discovered it in 1990 when several scenes for the movie *Dark Wind,* based on Tony Hillerman's novel, were shot at the kitsch **Wigwam Motel**—just the sort of 50's icon you would expect to find on Route 66. For a typical Route 66 meal, Butterfield Stage Coach Restaurant (609 Hopi Drive [Old Route 66]), with the coach right up there on the roof, serves standard western fare. *See* Dining, *below,* for more information.

Tour 2: Navajo Nation East

To complete this tour, allow at least three days and two nights. It begins in Window Rock, 82 miles from Petrified Forest National Park (*see* Tour 1, *above*), 192 miles from Flagstaff, and 26 miles from Gallup, New Mexico (via NM 666 and 264). If you arrive in the area late in the day, dining and lodging are available at the Navajo Nation Inn (*see* Dining and Lodging, *below*). Be sure to call ahead for reservations.

 From the Petrified Forest, continue east on I–40 to Lupton; turn north on Indian Highway 12, which will take you to **Window Rock.** Named for an immense hole in a massive sandstone ridge nearby, Window Rock is the capital of the Navajo Nation. With a population of less than 5,000, this community serves as the business and social center for countless

Navajo families from the surrounding areas. It is also the home of the **Navajo Nation Council Chambers** (turn east off Indian Hwy. 12, about ½ mi from AZ 264), a handsome structure that resembles a large hogan—the traditional eight-sided, domed Navajo house. Visitors can observe sessions of the council, where 88 delegates representing 100 reservation communities meet on the third Monday of January, April, July, and October. Sessions are conducted mostly in the Navajo language. When the council is not being held, you can walk around the chamber, where colorful murals decorate the walls. Window Rock Navajo Tribal Park is near the Council Chambers. It is a pleasant picnic area with juniper trees and allows for a close view of the huge rock formation.

A short drive south of Tribal Park is the **Navajo Tribal Museum,** a small space devoted to the art and culture of the region and the history of the Navajo people; there's an excellent selection of books on the Navajo Nation here. *On AZ 264, next to Navajo Nation Inn,* ☎ *520/871–6673.* ☛ *Free.* ☉ *Weekdays 8–4:45.*

In the same building, the **Navajo Arts and Crafts Enterprise** displays local art work, including pottery, jewelry, and blankets. ☎ *520/871–4095.* ☛ *Free.* ☉ *Apr.–Oct., Mon.–Sat. 8–6; Nov.–Mar., weekdays 8–5 (often later during busy season from Thanksgiving to Jan. 1).*

If you're curious about wildlife in northeastern Arizona, stop at the **Navajo Nation Zoological Park,** just east of the Navajo Tribal Museum. Set amid sandstone monoliths you'll find indigenous birds and animals that figure in Navajo legends—golden eagles, hawks, elk, wolves, cougars, and coyotes, among others. *East of Navajo Nation Inn and north of AZ 264.* ☛ *Free.* ☉ *Daily 8–5.*

Window Rock is a good place to stop for lunch, supplies, and gas. Restaurants here serve standard American fare and Navajo dishes. There is fast food as well. Near the center of downtown, the **Navajo Tribal Fairgrounds** is the site of many all-Indian rodeos (in the Navajo Nation, many Indians are cowboys). The community hosts the annual July 4 Powwow, with a major rodeo, ceremonial dances, and a parade; and the Navajo Nation Tribal Fair, much like a traditional state fair, in early September. For more information about both events, call the Navajo Nation Fair Office (☎ 520/871–4941).

⑤ Kinlichee Ruins Navajo Tribal Park lies 22 miles west of Window Rock off AZ 264. A marked road leads to this 640-acre park. Ancestral Pueblo people also built these former dwellings. The park, which is always open, has a self-guided trail that takes you past the ruins and trailside exhibits (you are not permitted to descend into the kiva pit). There are also picnic areas and a primitive campground. A camping fee of $1 per person may be collected.

Next, drive 6 miles west on AZ 264, passing through the community of **Ganado,** and continue for another miles until you reach the intersection of U.S. 191 north; turn right and drive 30 miles to **Chinle,** the closest town to Canyon de Chelly. There are three good lodgings with restaurants here (*see* Dining and Lodging, *below*), as well as a large supermarket and a campground. Call ahead for hotel reservations, especially in summer.

★ **⑥** The nearly 84,000-acre **Canyon de Chelly** (pronounced duh-*shay*) near Chinle is one of the most spectacular national monuments in the Southwest. Its main gorges—the 26-mile-long **Canyon de Chelly** and the adjoining 35-mile **Canyon del Muerto**—have sheer, heavily eroded sandstone walls that reach up to 1,000 feet. Ancient pictographs decorate some of the cliffs. Gigantic stone formations rise hundreds of feet above small streams, hogans, tilled fields, peach orchards, and grazing lands. Although the monument is administered by the National Park Service, the land itself belongs to the Navajo.

The first inhabitants of the canyons, ancestral Pueblo people, arrived more than 2,000 years ago and constructed stone cliff dwellings. Their departure around AD 1300 is widely believed to have resulted from changing climatic conditions, soil erosion, and dwindling local resources. Present day Hopis see these people as their ancestors, who quite simply moved to find a better place to live. Beginning around AD 780, Hopi farmers settled here, followed by the Navajo around 1000. Centuries-old traditions have been passed down to the Navajo families who now live, farm, and raise sheep in the area.

Canyon de Chelly and Canyon del Muerto each have a paved rim drive with marvelous views of the great canyon. Prehistoric ruins sometimes can be found near the base of cliffs or perched on high, sheltering ledges. Occasionally you will see the dwellings and cultivated fields of the present-day Navajo in the flatlands between the cliffs. The Navajo who inhabit the Canyon today farm much the way their ancestors did. Each canyon drive takes about two hours.

The **South Rim Drive** (36 miles round-trip) of Canyon de Chelly starts at the visitor center and ends at **Spider Rock Overlook,** where cliffs plunge 1,000 feet. Here you'll have a view of two pinnacles, Speaking Rock and Spider Rock; the latter rises about 800 feet from the canyon floor. Other highlights on the South Rim Drive are **Junction Overlook,** where Canyon del Muerto joins Canyon de Chelly; **White House Overlook,** which allows access to the canyon floor (*see below*); and **Sliding House Overlook,** where you can see ruins on a narrow, sloped ledge across the canyon.

The **North Rim Drive** (34 miles round-trip) of Canyon del Muerto also begins at the visitor center and continues northeast on Indian Highway 64 toward Tsaile, the site of Navajo Community College. Major stops on this drive include **Antelope House Overlook,** the site of a large ruin named for the animals painted on an adjacent cliff; the **Mummy Cave Overlook,** where two mummies were found inside a remarkably unspoiled pueblo dwelling, the monument's largest; and **Massacre Cave Overlook,** the last stop on the drive, which marks the spot where 115 Navajo were killed by the Spanish in 1805.

Within the monument, only one hike—the **White House Ruin Trail,** on the South Rim Drive—can be done without an authorized guide. The easy-to-negotiate trail starts near White House Overlook and runs along sheer walls that drop about 550 feet. The trail leads to the White House Ruin, with dwelling remains of nearly 60 rooms and several kivas. Bring your own water for this 2½-mile hike (round-trip).

Visitors can explore the area of Canyon de Chelly National Monument by hiking with rangers and paid guides (*see* Hiking *in* Sports and the Outdoors, *below*) or by taking truck and Jeep tours (*see* Guided Tours *in* The Northeast Essentials, *below*). The **visitor center** features exhibits on the history of the cliff dwellers and provides information on scheduled hikes, tours, and other programs within the national monument. It also has a good selection of books on the area and on Navajo culture. *Box 588, Chinle 86503,* ☎ *520/674–5500.* ☛ *Free.* ☺ *Memorial Day–Labor Day, daily 8–6; Labor Day–Memorial Day, daily 8–5.*

Retrace your steps after you depart Canyon de Chelly: Head back south for about 30 miles on U.S. 191, turn east onto AZ 264, and continue

❼ for several miles to **Hubbell Trading Post National Historic Site.** This trading post was established in 1878 by John Lorenzo Hubbell, a native of the Southwest who was born in Pajarito, New Mexico. To the Navajo, Hubbell was not only a merchant but also a good friend and teacher who translated letters, settled family quarrels, explained government policy, and helped the sick. During the 1886 smallpox epidemic in the area, he turned his home into a hospital and personally ministered to the sick and dying. Hubbell died in 1930 and is buried not far from the trading post.

Today the Hubbell Trading Post operates much as it did more than a century ago. At the visitor center, National Park Service exhibits illustrate the post's history, and Navajo men and women frequently demonstrate the crafts of making jewelry and rugs. You may also take a guided tour of Hubbell's house, which contains one of the finest personal collections of Native American artistry anywhere, including rugs and paintings. Tours are given six times daily in summer, four in winter. The affiliated shop, run by the Southwest Parks and Monuments Association, specializes in Navajo rugs (*see* Shopping, *below*). *On AZ 264, 1 mi west of Ganado,* ☎ *520/755–3475.* ☛ *Free.* ☉ *June–Sept., daily 8–6; Oct.–May, daily 8–5. Closed major holidays.*

About 20 miles west of the trading post on the north side of AZ 264 is

❽ **Steamboat Rock,** an immense, jutting peninsula of stone that resembles an early steamboat, complete with a geologically formed waterline.

At Steamboat Rock, you are only 5 miles from the eastern boundary

★ line of the Hopi reservation, where you can visit the **Hopi Mesas** (*see* Tour 3, *below*), staying overnight in Second Mesa, if you'd like. Or, after driving through the mesas on AZ 264, you can join Tour 4 (*see below*) at Tuba City, which also has lodging, 50 miles west of the Hopi village of Hotevilla.

Tour 3: The Hopi Mesas

From I–40, at the easternmost of three Winslow exits (62 miles east of Flagstaff), exit onto AZ 87 north. Drive 58 miles to the Hopi town of Second Mesa, where you will meet AZ 264.

❾ Turn east and drive 21 miles on AZ 264 to the **Keams Canyon Trading Post,** the main tourist attraction in the Keams Canyon area, established by Thomas Keam in 1875. Originally, it served only Native Americans of the area, but today the trading post also includes a modest motel, primitive campground, restaurant (*see* Keams Canyon *in* Dining and Lodging, *below*), and shopping center (*see* Shopping, *below*). An administrative center for the Bureau of Indian Affairs, Keams Canyon also has a number of government buildings.

The first 3 miles of the 8-mile canyon running toward the northeast can be seen by car. At Inscription Rock, about 2 miles down the road, early frontiersman Kit Carson engraved his name in stone. There are several picnic spots in the pretty, wooded canyon.

From Keams Canyon, head west on AZ 264 for a tour of Hopi villages, most of which are situated on the top of or at the base of a trio of mesas: First Mesa, Second Mesa, and Third Mesa. You'll need permission beforehand to visit Hopi villages. For information, call the **Hopi Tribe Office of Public Relations** (☎ 520/734–2441), which also provides phone numbers for village leaders or village community development offices.

⑩ On **First Mesa,** 15 miles west of Keams Canyon, you will initially approach **Polacca;** the older and more impressive villages of **Hano, Sichomovi,** and **Walpi** are situated at the top of the mesa. From Polacca, a paved road (off AZ 264) angles up to a parking lot near the village of Sichomovi. For permission to visit Hano, Sichomovi, and Walpi, or for information on the guided walking tours of these villages, call the **First Mesa Visitor's Center at Ponsli Hall** (☎ 520/737–2262). Guided tours can be arranged between 9 AM and 4 PM daily, except when ceremonies are being held; the tours are free, but a contribution is suggested.

All the older Hopi villages have structures built of rock and adobe mortar in a simple architectural style. **Hano** actually belongs to the Tewa, a Pueblo tribe that fled from the Spanish in 1696 and secured permission from the Hopi to build a new home on First Mesa. **Sichomovi** is built so close to Hano that only the residents know the actual boundary line. Constructed in the mid-1600s, this village is believed to have been built to ease overcrowding at Walpi, the highest point on the mesa.

For most outsiders, **Walpi** is usually the most impressive stop on the Hopi reservation, but it can be visited only if you are accompanied by a Hopi guide. Built on solid rock and surrounded by steep cliffs, Walpi stands against an immense expanse of distant earth and sky. At its narrowest point, the mesa measures only 15 feet across. Inhabited for more than 500 years, Walpi's cliff-edge houses seem to grow out of the nearby terrain. Today, only about 30 residents occupy this settlement, which has neither electricity nor running water. Important ceremonial dances frequently take place here.

⑪ **Second Mesa,** accessed by AZ 264, is 10 miles west of Polacca. The small villages of **Sipaulovi** and **Mishongnovi** are situated off a paved road that goes north from 264, about ⅓ mile east of the Hopi Cultural Center. Both communities lie on a projection of the Second Mesa; Mishongnovi, the easternmost settlement, was built in the late 1600s. If you'd like to visit Sipaulovi, the most recently established village, call the Sipaulovi Village Community Center (☎ 520/737–2570).

Shungopavi, the largest and oldest village on Second Mesa, may be reached by a paved road angling south off AZ 264, between the junction of AZ 87 and the Hopi Cultural Center. The famous Hopi snake dances (now closed to the public) are held here in August during even-numbered years. For permission to visit Shungopavi, call the village's **Community Development Office** (☎ 520/734–2262).

One of the livelier spots on Second Mesa is the **Hopi Cultural Center,** on the north side of AZ 264, west of the junction at AZ 87. A cluster of shops carry the work of the Hopi artisans who live in the area; the selection is very good and the prices are reasonable. In addition, the center features a pueblo-style museum, a good restaurant that serves American and Native American dishes, and a decent motel (*see* Dining and Lodging, *below*). The cultural center is not only a good spot for an overnight stop, being as it hails itself to be "at the Center of the Universe," but it is also one of the best places on the reservation from which to obtain information. *Restaurant and motel* ☎ *520/734–2401; Museum* ☎ *520/734–6650.* ☛ *Museum: $3 adults, $1 children under 13.* ☉ *Mid-May–Oct., weekdays 8–5, weekends 9–4; Nov.–mid-May, weekdays 8–5, closed weekends.*

Located 1½ miles east of the Hopi Cultural Center is **Tsakurshovi,** a small, friendly shop brimming with everything you'd expect to find and more. The Hopis sometimes come here to buy kachina dolls and other ceremonial objects such as bundles of sweetgrass and sage, rustling baskets of deer hooves to make rattles with, and ceremonial belts adorned with seashells. *Box 234, Second Mesa, AZ 86043,* ☎ *520/734–2478.*

 If you drive 8 miles to the west of the Hopi Cultural Center on AZ 264, you'll approach **Kykotsmovi** at the eastern base of **Third Mesa.** Hopi from Old Oraibi (*see below*) descended from the mesa and built this village in a canyon with a perennial spring; the community is known for its greenery and its peach orchards. The town also serves as the home of the **Hopi Tribal Headquarters Chairman's Office** and the **Office of Public Relations** (☎ 520/734–2441), another good source of information regarding ceremonies and dances.

Old Oraibi, a few miles west and on top of Third Mesa, is widely believed to be the oldest continually inhabited community in the United States, dating from around AD 1150. It was also the site of a rare, bloodless conflict between two groups of the Hopi people; in 1906, a dispute, settled uniquely by a "push of war," a pushing contest, sent the losers off to establish Hotevilla (*see below*). Oraibi is a dusty spot, and as an act of courtesy, tourists are asked to park their cars outside and approach the village on foot.

As you continue to drive west on AZ 264, you'll pass more crafts shops and art galleries. The Third Mesa villages are known for their baskets, kachina dolls, weaving, and jewelry.

Hotevilla and **Bacavi** are about 4 miles west of Oraibi, and their inhabitants are descended from the former residents of that village. The men of Hotevilla continue to plant crops along the mesa slopes, and in warmer months these gardens on the cliffs are lovely to behold.

 Beyond Hotevilla, AZ 264 descends from Third Mesa, and you will soon exit the Hopi reservation and cross Navajo land. About 30 miles west of Hotevilla, you'll pass **Coal Canyon,** where Indians have long mined coal from the dark seam just below the rim. This canyon of colorful mudstone, dark lines of coal, and bleached white rock has an eerie, ghostlike appearance, especially by the light of the moon.

 Another 20 miles to the west is **Moenkopi,** the last Hopi outpost, just before Tuba City at the junction of AZ 264 and U.S. 160. Established as a farming community, it was also settled by the descendants of former Oraibi residents. Across U.S. 160, **Tuba City** is the administrative center for the western portion of the Navajo Nation, with about 12,000 permanent residents. In addition to a motel, hostel, and a few restaurants, this small town has a hospital, bank, and historic trading post. Founded in the early 1880s and recently restored, the octagonal **Tuba City Trading Post** (Main St., ☎ 520/283–5441) carries authentic Indian rugs, pottery, baskets, and jewelry; it also sells groceries.

 From Tuba City, take U.S. 160 west. About 5½ miles from the city, between mileposts 316 and 317, you'll see a small sign for **Dinosaur Tracks.** More than 200 million years ago, dilophosaurus, carnivorous bipedal reptiles more than 10 feet tall left their imprints in soft mud that subsequently turned to sandstone. There's no charge for a look.

 Four miles west of the Dinosaur Tracks on U.S. 160, you'll come to the junction with U.S. 89. This is one of the most colorful regions of the Painted Desert, with amphitheaters of maroon, orange, and red rocks facing west; it's especially glorious at sunset. If you turn left on U.S. 89 and drive 16 miles south, you will arrive at the **Cameron Trading Post** (☎ 520/679–2231). Established in 1916, this is one of the few remaining authentic trading posts in the Southwest. (*See* Shopping *in* Chapter 2, The Grand Canyon and Northwest Arizona, for details.)

To see the Hopi Mesas at a reasonable pace, it's a good idea to take at least one overnight on this tour, either at the Hopi Cultural Center on Second Mesa in the heart of the reservation or, if you're planning to head north into Navajo country, at a hotel in Tuba City (*see* Dining and Lodging, *below*) From the trading post, Flagstaff is 52 miles south.

Tour 4: Navajo Nation North

⑰ Twenty-two miles northeast of Tuba City on U.S. 160 is the tiny community of **Red Lake.** Off to the left of the highway is a geologic phenomenon known as **Elephant Feet.** These massive eroded sandstone buttes make a good photo stop.

⑱ You might enjoy a short side trip into real Navajo backcountry to look at **White Mesa Natural Bridge,** about 17 miles north of Red Lake on Indian Highway 21, a graded dirt road. The payoff is a view of a massive arch of white sandstone that extends from the edge of White Mesa. Return by the same route to Red Lake.

About 30 miles north of Red Lake on U.S. 160, you'll come to the turnoff for Navajo National Monument (*see below*).

⑲ For now, continue northeast from this turnoff and take note of the plateau to the right, the long **Black Mesa,** which will remain in view for about the next 15 miles. Above the prominent escarpments of this land formation, mining operations—a major source of revenue for the Navajo Nation—delve into the more than 20 billion tons of coal deposited there.

⑳ Turn more directly north from U.S. 160 onto U.S. 163; you'll soon approach **Kayenta,** a small town with a few grocery stores, two motels, ★ and a hospital. Kayenta is near the magnificent **Monument Valley,** which stretches to the northeast into Utah. At a base altitude of approximately 5,500 feet, this sprawling expanse was also populated by the ancestral Pueblo people and has been home to generations of Navajo who have farmed and herded livestock in this arid country. The soaring red buttes, eroded mesas, deep canyons, and naturally sculpted rock formations of Monument Valley are easy to enjoy by driving through and pausing from time to time at roadside stops. Many Westerns were filmed here, including *She Wore a Yellow Ribbon, How the West Was Won,* and John Ford's *Stagecoach.*

㉑ Within this vast area lies the 30,000-acre **Monument Valley Navajo Tribal Park.** The visitor center is 3½ miles off U.S. 163 and about 24 miles north of Kayenta. The park offers a scenic 17-mile self-guided tour on a rough but passable dirt road. You'll pass the memorable Mittens and Totem Pole formations, among others. Drive slowly, and be sure to walk from North Window around the end of Cly Butte for wonderful views (15 minutes round trip).

You may also consider taking one of the many guided tours offered by operators in and around the visitor center; most take visitors in enclosed vans and charge about $15 for 2½ hours. An Indian crafts shop and exhibits devoted to both ancient and modern Indian history within the area are also at the visitor's center. The park has a 100-site campground, which closes from early October through April. If you are visiting the area in winter, when there are fewer visitors, the rocks can have a beautiful covering of snow. Be sure to call ahead for road conditions. *Visitor center* ☎ *801/727–3287.* ☛ *Park: $2.50 adults, $1 se-*

nior citizens 60 and older, children under 5 free. ⊙ *Visitor center: May–Sept., daily 7–7; Oct.–Apr., daily 8–5. Closed major holidays.*

Monument Valley's scenic route, U.S. 163, continues from Arizona into Utah, where the land is crossed, east to west, by a stretch of the San Juan River known as the **Goosenecks**—so named for the type of twists and curves it takes at the bottom of a wildly carved canyon. Set in a lonely, untrafficked domain, this barren, erosion-blasted gorge has a stark beauty that is nearly as awesome as that of the Grand Canyon. The scenic overlook for the Goosenecks is reached by turning west from U.S. 163 onto UT 261, 4 miles north of the small community of **Mexican Hat** (named for the sombrerolike rock formation you'll see on the hills to your right as you drive north), then proceeding on UT 261 for 1 mile to a directional sign at the road's junction with UT 316. Turn left onto UT 316 and proceed 4 miles to the vista-point parking lot. If you visit during the week, you're likely to find yourself alone there, or perhaps joined by one or two Navajo women selling crafts.

After a stop at the Goosenecks vista point, backtrack along U.S. 163 and then take Indian Highway 42 a half mile west to **Goulding's Trading Post.** Established in 1924 by Harry Goulding and his wife, this remote outlet was used as a headquarters by director John Ford when he filmed the Western classic *Stagecoach.* Because of the numerous Westerns that have been shot in the area, the trading post, motel, and restaurant have gained a measure of international fame. In the old trading-post building, a museum displays prehistoric and modern Indian artifacts as well as memorabilia of the Goulding family. The lodge here is an ideal place for an overnight stay, but call in advance for reservations. You can also rest overnight in or near Kayenta, where there are three motels (*see* Dining and Lodging, *below*).

Take Indian Highway 42 back to the junction with U.S. 163, and proceed south until you reach U.S. 160. Continue south, turning right on AZ 564 and traveling 9 miles to **Navajo National Monument.** Here two unoccupied 13th-century cliff pueblos, **Keet Seel** and **Betatakin,** stand under the overhang of soaring orange and ocher cliffs. The largest ancient dwellings in Arizona, these pueblos were also built by ancestral Pueblo peoples. The two large stone-and-mortar complexes were obviously built for permanent occupancy, yet the people lived in them for less than half a century before they departed. Betatakin (Navajo for "ledge house") consists of a well-preserved, 135-room dwelling situated in a large alcove. Keet Seel (Navajo for "broken pottery") is also in good condition in a serene setting, with 160 rooms and five kivas.

For an impressive view of Betatakin, walk to the rim overlook about a half mile from the visitor center. You can also hike to Betatakin on tours with ranger guides, offered between early May and mid-October (5 miles round-trip from the visitor center). The trips leave once a day in early May, most of September, and early October, and twice a day from Memorial Day to Labor Day (weather permitting) at 9 AM and noon. They are limited to groups of 25. No reservations are accepted; groups form on a first-come, first-served basis.

Explorations of Keet Seel, which lies at an elevation of 7,000 feet and is 17 miles (round-trip) from the visitor center, are even more restricted: Only 20 people are allowed to visit per day, and only between Memorial Day and Labor Day, when a ranger is present at the site. A permit—which also allows campers to stay overnight near the ruins—is required. Those interested in horseback trips can make arrangements at the visitor center to rent horses and guides from a Navajo family.

Trips to Keet Seel are very popular, and places can be reserved up to (but not beyond) two months in advance; call 520/672–2367 or 520/672–2366 to reserve a visitor's permit (and, if you like, a horse) as soon you know the date you're coming.

The visitor center houses a small museum, exhibits of prehistoric pottery, and a crafts shop. Free campground and picnic areas are nearby, and rangers sometimes present campfire programs in summer. No food, gasoline, or lodging is available at the monument. *Navajo National Monument, HC71 Box 3, Tonalea 86044,* ☏ *520/672–2366.* ☛ *Free.* ⊙ *Memorial Day–Labor Day, daily 8–6; Dec.–Feb, daily 8–4:30; rest of yr, daily 8–5. Closed major holidays.*

You may want to follow this tour with a visit to Page (which has restaurants and lodging), Lake Powell, Glen Canyon Dam, and Rainbow Bridge (*see* Tour 5, *below*). To reach Page from Navajo National Monument, return to U.S. 160 and travel south for 12 miles, then take AZ 98 for 66 miles. If you haven't been to Canyon de Chelly (*see* Tour 2, *above*), stop at Navajo National Monument before you go on to Monument Valley. Then, from Kayenta (which also has dining and lodging), it is 103 miles to Chinle via U.S. 160 east and U.S. 191 south.

Tour 5: Glen Canyon Dam and Lake Powell

From Flagstaff, Page and nearby Glen Canyon Dam and Lake Powell are 136 miles north on U.S. 89. For much of this trip, on the right of the highway, you'll find a multihued geography almost identical to that of the Painted Desert contained within Petrified Forest National Park (*see* Tour 1, *above*). Farther north the landscape gives way to the immense Echo Cliffs, orange sandstone formations rising 1,000 feet and more above the highway in places. At Bitter Springs, the road ascends the cliffs and provides a spectacular view of the 9,000-square-mile expanse of the Arizona Strip to the west, and the sheer, 3,000-foot Vermilion Cliffs to the northwest.

㉕ **Page** was born out of the construction of Glen Canyon Dam in 1957. Prior to that, the broad mesa on which it lies was essentially barren land. Initially a construction camp, Page became a tourist stop after Lake Powell formed behind the dam. The town has gradually grown to its present population of about 7,000—the largest community in far-northern Arizona.

Most of the motels, restaurants, and strip shopping centers in Page can be found along Lake Powell Boulevard, the name given to U.S. 89 as it loops through the town's business district in a roughly northwest direction. At the corner of Navajo Drive is the **John Wesley Powell Memorial Museum,** a small building honoring the work of explorer John Wesley Powell, who, between 1869 and 1872, led the first expeditions down the Green River and the rapids-choked Colorado through the Grand Canyon. The one-armed Civil War hero mapped, explored, and kept detailed records of his trips, naming the Grand Canyon and many other geographic points of interest in northern Arizona. The displays—drawings and photographs of the expedition, area fossils, minerals, and Native American crafts—are rather unimpressive, but the museum serves as an information center for the area and a place to book river and lake trips and scenic flights. It also has a good selection of regional books and maps. *6 N. Lake Powell Blvd.,* ☏ *520/645–9496.* ☛ *Requested donation: $1 adults, 50¢ children.* ⊙ *May–Oct., Mon.–Sat. 8–6:30, Sun. 10–6:30; Nov. and Mar., weekdays 9–5; Apr., weekdays 8–6. Closed Dec.–Feb.*

㉖ Once you leave the Page business district, the **Glen Canyon Dam** and Lake Powell behind it immediately become visible. Completed in September 1963, the construction of this concrete-arch dam and its power plant was an engineering feat that rivaled the building of Hoover Dam. Nearly 5 million cubic feet of concrete were required. The dam's crest is 1,560 feet across and rises 710 feet from bedrock and 583 feet above the waters of the Colorado River. Lake Powell is 560 feet deep at the dam at full pool elevation.

Just off the highway at the north end of the bridge is the **Carl Hayden Visitor Center,** a museumlike facility dedicated to telling the story of the creation of Glen Canyon Dam and Lake Powell. Among the several exhibits is a giant, three-dimensional topographic map of Lake Powell country. The center's huge reception and observation room, with floor-to-ceiling glass, provides panoramic views of the dam, the wildly sculpted cliffs that border Lake Powell, and the immense sandstone buttes that protrude, islandlike, from the lake's emerald waters. Between May and October, free guided tours of the dam are offered daily between 8 AM and 4 PM every hour on the half hour. The rest of the year, visitors can take a 40-minute self-guided tour through the dam complex. *Glen Canyon Dam,* ☎ *520/645–2511 or 520/645–8404.* ☛ *Free.* ☺ *Memorial Day–Labor Day, daily 7–7; Labor Day–Memorial Day, daily 8–5. Closed Dec. 25 and Jan. 1.*

★ **Lake Powell,** with more than 1,900 miles of shoreline, is the heart of the huge (1,255,400-acre) Glen Canyon National Recreation Area. Created by the barrier of Glen Canyon Dam and fed by the mighty Colorado and five other rivers, the jade-green lake extends through eroded canyon country that is nearly devoid of vegetation and so rugged that it was the last major area of the United States to be mapped. The waters of Lake Powell are confined by immense red cliffs that twist off from the main body of the lake into 96 major canyons and countless inlets and coves—so many, in fact, that no single person claims to have explored all of them. In a number of places, huge sandstone buttes jut from the water. Seeing the stark, stunning geography of Lake Powell often makes tourists feel as if they are visiting another planet.

The most popular destination on the lake, which stretches 180 miles
㉗ through northern Arizona and southern Utah, is **Wahweap,** a vacation village 5 miles north of the Glen Canyon Dam on U.S. 89. Most recreational activity in the region takes place around here, where everything needed for a lakeside holiday is available: fishing, boat rentals, dinner cruises, and much more. Visitors can easily rent boats and a wide variety of water-sports equipment (*see* Sports and the Outdoors, *below*). Stop at **Wahweap Lodge** (*see* Dining and Lodging, *below*) for an excellent view of the lake area. In addition to Wahweap, three other full-service marinas operate year-round on the perimeter of Lake Powell. **Bullfrog** (☎ 801/684–2233) and, across from it, **Halls Crossing** (☎ 801/684–2261) are around mid-lake, while **Hite Marina** (☎ 801/684–2278), the smallest, is the farthest north, just off UT 95. A fifth marina 40 miles north of Wahweap, Dangling Rope, has limited services and can be reached only by boat.

Summer is a busy time in the Lake Powell area, and reservations for accommodations are essential. Travelers seeking a quieter vacation should plan a visit during late October through early May, when there are fewer people and lower prices. Skies in the Lake Powell area are blue nearly all year, and only about 8 inches of rain falls annually. Summer temperatures range from the 60s to the 90s (sometimes they rise to more than 100°F). Many fall and spring days are balmy, with daytime temperatures often in the 70s and 80s, but it is possible for chilly weather to set in. In winter, the risk of a cold spell increases, but all-weather houseboats and tour boats make year-round cruising possible.

★ ㉘ The best way to appreciate the beauty of Lake Powell is by boat. If you don't have access to one, the five-hour excursion cruise to **Rainbow Bridge National Monument** is the way to go. Along the 52-mile route (one-way from Wahweap Marina), you're treated to ever-changing, beautiful and bizarre scenery, including huge monoliths that look like people turned into stone and a butte that resembles a dinosaur. You might also see eagles perched on ragged outcrops of rock. Finally, after gliding through a deep and twisting canyon waterway, the boat docks near Rainbow Bridge, the massive 290-foot red sandstone arch that straddles a cove of the lake. The world's largest natural stone bridge, it can be reached only by water or by an arduous hike from a remote point on the Navajo reservation (*see* Sports and the Outdoors, *below*).

The excursion boats, which leave Wahweap daily, are two-tier craft with sundecks upstairs and interior seating with windows downstairs. Experienced pilots provide commentary throughout the trip. Pack a lunch or take snacks; no food is sold on the boats, though coffee and water are provided. And be sure to bring your camera.

Other cruises are offered at the Wahweap Marina, including an all-day trip that stops at Rainbow Bridge and then proceeds farther into the Utah portion of the lake. (*See* Boating *and* Cruises *in* Sports and the Outdoors, *below,* for information on prices and reservations.)

Off the Beaten Track

Most of the 25,000 square miles of the Navajo reservation and other areas of northeastern Arizona *are* off the beaten track. Many visitors to the northeast generally stay on paved roads, but this vast, sparsely populated region is crisscrossed with dirt roads. If you don't have the equipment for wilderness travel—including a four-wheel-drive vehicle, water, food, tools, and bedrolls—and do not have backcountry experience, we recommend that you stay off dirt roads unless they are signed and graded, and the skies are clear. Flash floods are life-threatening dangers (*see* Driving Precautions *in* The Gold Guide's Smart Travel Tips A to Z).

Antelope Canyon. You'll probably recognize it from one of many photographs: Red sandstone rising majestically in a corkscrew formation, dramatically illuminated by a chink of light streaming in from above. And, in fact, you're likely to see assorted shutterbugs standing patiently next to tripods, waiting hours for just the right shot. A highlight of any trip to the Lake Powell area, Antelope Canyon is on the Navajo reservation, about 3 miles from Page. If you don't have a four-wheel-drive vehicle (or the time to wait for the rather erratic—and limited—hours that the gate to the site is open), book a tour from Page (*see* Guided Tours *in* The Northeast Essentials, *below*).

Chuska Mountains. These impressive mountains in Navajo high country are covered with sprawling stands of ponderosa pine. To explore this part of the reservation, take Indian Highway 64 from the Canyon de Chelly visitor center to the community of Tsaile (23 miles). Although there are no established hiking trails in the mountains, logging roads provide good access. A backcountry use permit can be obtained at the Parks and Recreation Department (Box 9000, 86515, ☎ 520/871–6647), next to the Navajo Nation Zoo in Window Rock. Here Navajo medicine men worked in conjunction with architects to design Tsaile's six story

Navajo Community College (☏ 520/724–3311). Because all important Navajo activities traditionally take place in a circle (a hogan is essentially circular), the campus was laid out in the round with all of the buildings within its perimeter. The college's **Hatathli Museum** is devoted to Native American culture. ☏ 520/724–3311. ☛ *Donations accepted.* ⊘ *Weekdays 8:30–noon and 1–4; groups by appointment.*

Two miles northeast of Tsaile, turn left on Indian Highway 12 and continue 26 miles to Round Rock, where Indian Highway 12 meets U.S. 191. During your drive, the high country will rise off to the right. Dirt roads traverse the mountains, but they are often unsuitable for passenger cars. At U.S. 191, turn left and head back south to Chinle if you are following Tour 3, *above.*

Four Corners Monument. A simple concrete slab inlaid into the ground marks the only point in the United States where four states meet: Arizona, New Mexico, Colorado, and Utah. Most visitors—in summer, nearly 2,000 a day—stay only a few minutes to record the spot on film; you'll see many people posed awkwardly, with an arm or a leg in each state. *Off U.S. 160, 7 mi northwest of the U.S. 160–NM 502 junction (near Teec Nos Pos). The monument is a 75-mi drive from Kayenta, near Monument Valley.*

What to See and Do with Children

Although northeastern Arizona is an extremely popular area for families on vacation, the region has no attractions designed specifically for children. However, many youngsters will be fascinated by the area's scenic beauty, as well as its Native American history and present day culture. Kids will particularly enjoy the Navajo Nation Zoological Park in Window Rock (*see* Tour 2, *above*). At the Petrified Forest (*see* Tour 1, *above*), Canyon de Chelly (*see* Tour 2, *above*), and Navajo National Monument (*see* Tour 4, *above*), they'll have plenty of space for running around, climbing and exploring. Children may be bored on some of the longer lake excursions, but many motels in the Lake Powell area (*see* Tour 5, *above*) have swimming pools, and there are numerous water-related recreational activities for children.

Younger children may get restless during some of the long and lonely stretches on the Indian reservations, so it's a good idea to bring along toys and books for the car.

SPORTS AND THE OUTDOORS

Bicycling

For biking enthusiasts, the news is good and bad. If you carry a bike on your car, as many cyclists do these days, you will find endless miles of paved roads, and most of the time, traffic is very light. The bad news is that the mostly two-lane highways do not have paved shoulders, and local motorists and tourists alike are unaccustomed to encountering cyclists. As a result, you should practice extreme caution when riding. For safe bike rides, the roads at Canyon de Chelly National Monument, Navajo National Monument, Monument Valley Navajo Tribal Park, and Kinlichee Navajo Tribal Park are your best bets. There are no bicycle-rental companies in Navajo–Hopi country.

Boating

Lake Powell. The boating opportunities on Lake Powell are almost limitless. If you have your own boat, docks and launching ramps are available at State Line Marina, 1½ miles north of Wahweap Lodge. In addition, there are four full-service marinas at the lake at which to rent small or excursion boats, including houseboats, and water-sports equipment, including ski packages, water sleds, and motorized wave cutters: **Wahweap** (☎ 520/278–8888), **Bullfrog** (☎ 801/684–2233), **Halls Crossing** (☎ 801/684–2261), and **Hite Marina** (☎ 801/684–2278). Wahweap, 5 miles north of Page on U.S. 89, is the largest, with 850 slips and the most facilities. Houseboats range widely in size and price; one that sleeps six (in three double beds) may cost $675 for three nights. New houseboats are being added to the fleet, and many are being upgraded—some boats now have air-conditioning, TVs, VCRs, microwaves, and other amenities. Houseboats should be reserved well in advance. Small boats, too, vary in size and price. An 18-foot powerboat for eight passengers runs about $185 per day. Most of these prices drop after the summer months. A variety of boat-tour and lodging packages are also available. For detailed information on all the Lake Powell options and prices, contact ARA Leisure Services (Box 56909, Phoenix 85079, ☎ 800/528–6154, FAX 520/331–5258).

Camping and RV Parks

Although Navajo–Hopi country stretches thousands of square miles across an open and sparsely populated region, visitors are allowed to camp only in posted authorized areas. Most campgrounds are primitive, in many cases nothing more than open, level areas where sleeping bags can be laid out or RVs can be parked; outside the Lake Powell area, only Monument Valley has developed camping facilities. If you plan to stay in national monument and park areas, camping permission can be obtained on-site; for other camping situations, contact the **Navajo Parks and Recreation Department** (Box 308, Window Rock 86515, ☎ 520/871–6647) to find out whether you need a permit. (*See* Dining and Lodging, *below,* for some of the recommended campsites in the area.)

CAUTION: Be careful not to camp in low-lying areas, which are subject to extremely dangerous flash floods in sudden summer rains (*see* Lodging *in* The Gold Guide's Smart Travel Tips for more information).

Cruises

LAKE POWELL

A variety of excursions on double-decker scenic cruisers piloted by experienced guides leave from the dock of Lake Powell's Wahweap Lodge (off U.S. 89, 5 mi north of Page, ☎ 520/645–2433 or 800/528–6154). The most popular is the one to Rainbow Bridge National Monument, a 290-foot arch that spans an isolated cove 50 miles from Wahweap. Half-day cruises cost $51.30 adults, $27.30 children; full-days are $64.65 adults, $34.50 children. A 2½-hour sunset dinner cruise also departs from Wahweap. A buffet-style dinner is served on the fully glassed lower deck of the 95-foot Canyon King Paddlewheeler, an 1800s riverboat. The meal includes prime rib with fresh garden vegetables and a baked potato, a salad, and dessert; cocktails are available at an extra charge. The cost of the dinner cruise is $41.20 for both children and adults; adults who wish to take the cruise without eating pay $19.65, children $13.10.

Guided, piloted, 4½-hour **rafting excursions** cover a portion of the Colorado River that is relatively calm, with no white-water rapids. The scenery through Glen Canyon Dam is spectacular as the rafts glide beneath multicolored sandstone cliffs that are frequently adorned with Indian petroglyphs. The point of departure is the Wilderness River Adventures office in Page (50 S. Lake Powell Blvd., ☎ 520/645–3279 or 800/528–6154); transportation is furnished to the launch site and back from Lees Ferry, where the raft trip ends. The cost is $38.70 adults, $31 children under 12.

Fishing

The region has scattered lakes, most of them remote and small, that contain game fish. Two of the more popular and accessible lakes are in the eastern portion of the Navajo reservation in the vicinity of Canyon de Chelly: **Wheatfields Lake,** on Indian Highway 12 about 11 miles south of the community of Tsaile, and **Many Farms Lake,** near the community of Many Farms, on U.S. 191. Permits are always required for fishing on the reservation. Contact the **Navajo Fish and Wildlife Office** (Box 1480, Window Rock 86515, ☎ 520/871–6451 or 520/871–6452).

Lake Powell and the area below Glen Canyon Dam are excellent fishing sites. Lake Powell hosts 16 varieties of fish, including largemouth bass, black crappie, striped bass, bluegill, green sunfish, carp, smallmouth bass, threadfin, shad, walleye, rainbow trout, channel catfish, brown trout, and northern pike, while the Colorado River below Glen Canyon Dam is known for its large trout. Keep in mind that Lake Powell stretches through both Arizona and Utah, and an appropriate permit is required depending on where you fish; *see* Sports *in* The Gold Guide's Important Contacts for more information on fishing permits. Fishing licenses are available at the Wahweap Marina (off U.S. 89, 5 mi north of Page) and at Stix Market in Page (5 S. Lake Powell Blvd., ☎ 520/645–2891). If you want a fishing guide for the lake or the Colorado River at Lees Ferry, about 15 miles below the Glen Canyon Dam en route to the North Rim of the Grand Canyon, contact Ed Strasburg (Box 2699, Page 86040, ☎ 520/645–9489).

Hiking

There are many excellent places to hike at the national monuments, tribal parks, and other points of interest in this vast area, but the following merit special mention.

In **Canyon de Chelly,** some of the best hiking is up the streambed between the soaring orange sandstone cliffs, with the remains of the old Pueblo communities frequently in view. Guides, required for all but the White Horse Ruin Trail, currently charge about $10 per hour with a three-hour minimum for groups of up to four people for day hikes. For overnights, there's a $20 surcharge for the guide and usually a $30 charge for permission to stay on private land where the guide will take you; groups of up to 15 people can be accommodated. From Memorial Day through Labor Day, free three-hour ranger-led hikes leave from the visitor center at 9 AM (*see* Tour 2, *above*). Also during the summer, four-hour hikes costing $10 per person leave from the visitor center in the morning and afternoon; rates for two-hour evening hikes are $5 per person. Some of the hikes are a bit strenuous and precipitous, without clearly defined or gently graded trails. Visitors with health problems or a fear of heights should ask guides about the difficulty of the hike they're considering.

In addition to casual hikes along rim areas where the ruins of Betatakin can be viewed, in spring and summer **Navajo National Monument** offers a guided 5-mile (round-trip) hike to Betatakin once a day between early May and mid-October, twice a day from Memorial Day through Labor Day; visitors may also obtain permits to hike 17 miles (round-trip) on their own to the Keet Seel ruins from Memorial Day to Labor Day. (*See* Tour 4, *above*, for details.)

Seasoned hikers in good physical condition might want to try either of the two trails leading to **Rainbow Bridge,** the 290-foot sandstone arch in a remote cove on Lake Powell; both trails are about 26–28 miles round-trip. Take Indian Highway 16 north toward the Utah state border. When you come to a fork in the road, take either direction for about 5 miles and you'll come to a trailhead leading to Rainbow Bridge. Excursion boats pull in at the dock at the arch, but no supplies are sold there. For a back-country hiking permit, contact the **Navajo Parks and Recreation Department** (Box 308, Window Rock 86515, ☎ 520/871–6647). Note, too, that the trails are often poorly marked and ill maintained in this wilderness area. The **Glen Canyon Natural History Association** (Box 581, Page 86040, ☎ 520/645–3532) sells good topographical maps of the region as well as useful publications on hiking here.

CAUTION: Be sure to bring plenty of water with you when hiking and drink often. Dehydration can become a life-threatening condition. (*See* Hiking *in* The Gold Guide's Smart Travel Tips for more information.)

Horseback Riding

Justin's Horse Rental (Box 881, Chinle 86503, ☎ 520/674–5678), near the South Rim Drive entrance of Canyon de Chelly, offers trips into the canyon for $8 per hour for each horse plus $8 per hour for a guide.

Native American guides conduct horseback tours to Keet Seel at Navajo National Monument daily from Memorial Day weekend through Labor Day weekend; rates are approximately $55 per day. Reservations should be made two months in advance; there's often a waiting list. Contact **Virginia Austin** (c/o Navajo National Monument, HC-71 Box 3, Tonalea, AZ 86044, ☎ 520/672–2366 or 520/672–2367) for details.

If you've always wanted to ride off into the sunset at Monument Valley, get in touch with **Ed Black's Horseback Riding Tours** (Box 155, Mexican Hat, UT 84531, ☎ 800/551–4039). Prices for trail rides, which can be as short as 1½ hours or as long as five days, range from $20 to $65 (per overnight). Rides leave from the corral, a half mile north of the Monument Valley Visitor Center.

Rainbow Trails & Tours (Box 7218, Shonto, AZ 86054, ☎ 520/672–2397) runs pack trips in Lake Powell country from May through September. Tailored to individual interests and skills, Navajo-guided rides include a day trip to Rainbow Bridge and an overnight with tepee accommodations at Desha Canyon near Navajo Mountain. Rates are $75 per person per day, including meals. Shorter trail rides in the Lake Powell area are available in Page from **Rope & Saddle Promotions** (Vermilion Downs on Haul Road, ☎ 520/645–2752 or 520/645–2077); the fee is $20 for the first hour for adults and $10 for each additional hour, $10 for the first hour for children and $5 for each additional hour.

SHOPPING

Groceries, over-the-counter medicine, gasoline, and other supplies can be purchased in all of the major communities and trading posts on the Navajo and Hopi reservations, including Page, Window Rock, Fort Defiance, Ganado, Chinle, Hopi Second Mesa, Keams Canyon, Tuba City, Kayenta, Goulding's Trading Post, and Cameron Trading Post. Some of the smaller communities offer limited supplies; in general, don't count on a wide selection. Plan your gas stops for the locations cited.

Beyond the necessities for travel, most visitors here are interested in pottery, turquoise and sterling-silver jewelry, handwoven baskets, beautiful and often expensive Navajo wool rugs, and other examples of Native American crafts. In addition to the work of Hopi and Navajo artisans, many of the trading posts also carry the work of New Mexico's tribes, including exquisite inlaid Zuni jewelry and the world-acclaimed pottery of the Pueblo people. Many vendors have roadside stands that resemble Navajo shade arbors. Most products offered on the Hopi and Navajo reservations are authentic, but the possibility of imitations still exists. The trading posts are usually reliable.

Telephone lines—and thus connections with credit-card verification sources—are often iffy at the Hopi Mesas. It's a good idea to carry cash or traveler's checks to make purchases here or anywhere else outside of the trading posts.

Outlets of **Navajo Arts and Crafts Enterprises,** in Window Rock (off AZ 264, next to Navajo Nation Inn, ☎ 520/871–4090 or 520/871–4095) and Cameron (on U.S. 89 at the junction with AZ 64, ☎ 520/679–2244) stock fine authentic Navajo products. The nearby **Cameron Trading Post** has a large selection of goods from a variety of tribes; *see* Shopping *in* Chapter 2, The Grand Canyon and Northwest Arizona, for details. The **Hopi Cultural Center** (off AZ 264, Hopi Second Mesa, ☎ 520/734–2463) has a collection of shops that feature the work of local artists and artisans. Just to the west, the **Hopi Arts and Crafts/Silvercrafts Cooperative Guild** (no ☎) hosts many craftspeople selling their wares; you might even see some silversmiths at work here. **Keams Canyon Arts and Crafts** (Keams Canyon, ☎ 520/738–2295) also sells Hopi wares. The gift shop at **Navajo National Monument** (☎ 520/672–2366) has an excellent selection of jewelry. **Hubbell Trading Post** (off AZ 264, 1 mi west of Ganado, ☎ 520/755–3254) is famous for its "Ganado red" Navajo rugs; the quality is outstanding but prices are accordingly high. Be forewarned, though: It's hard to resist these beautiful designs and colors. The **swap meet** held every Friday from 8 AM on in Tuba City (on Main St., behind the community center and next to the baseball field) has good prices on jewelry, rugs, pottery, and other arts and crafts; there are also food concessions and booths selling herbs.

Although you may feel more comfortable shopping at an established store, you may find exactly what you want, at a good price, at a reservation roadside vendor. If you would like some tips on quality, the **Navajoland Tourism Office** (*see* Important Addresses and Numbers *in* The Northeast Essentials, *below*) has printed material on the subject.

In the Lake Powell area, **Page Factory Stores** (644 N. Navajo Dr. at Lake Powell Blvd., ☎ 520/645–5975) has discount outlets for London Fog, Benetton, and Polo Ralph Lauren. On South Lake Powell Blvd., just east of Hwy. 89, **Corral West Ranchwear** (Gateway Park mall, ☎ 520/645–9391) carries a good selection of cowboy and cowgirl duds.

DINING AND LODGING

Dining

Northeastern Arizona may offer few restaurants for fine dining, but there are opportunities to taste very good Native American food. For the most part, dress is casual, seating is on a first-come, first-served basis, and prices are reasonable. Only in the Page/Lake Powell area at the height of the summer season do we advise making reservations.

Because northeastern Arizona is a vast area and few communities offer eating establishments, visitors should keep in mind that the following major locations have restaurants: Cameron, Tuba City, Page, Kayenta, Goulding's Trading Post/Monument Valley, Hopi Second Mesa, Keams Canyon, Chinle, Ganado, Window Rock, Fort Defiance, Holbrook, and Winslow. Some serve Native American and Mexican dishes; most serve standard American fare. In some of the smaller reservation communities, only fast food may be available.

Restaurants are open daily unless otherwise noted.

CATEGORY	COST*
$$$$	over $25
$$$	$15–$25
$$	$10–$15
$	under $10

per person, excluding drinks, service, and sales tax (9.5% in Page), except on the Hopi and Navajo reservations, where no tax is charged

Lodging

Northeastern Arizona is a large territory with few people and long distances between communities. When you travel here, a top priority is making sure that you have a place to lay your head at the end of the day. Half the battle is knowing which of the scattered communities have motels. During summer months, it is especially wise to make reservations. Fortunately, most motels throughout the northeast are clean, comfortable, and well maintained.

Because of a demand for accommodations in the area, bed-and-breakfasts have begun to proliferate in Page in the last few years. Zoning restrictions currently prevent them from being anything other than informal homestays, but that is likely to change soon. Among the recommended B&Bs are **A Place Above the Cliff** (Box 2456, Page 86040, ☎ 520/645–3162), and the **American Bed & Breakfast** (Box 213, Page 86040, ☎ 520/645–9752). A brochure listing other members of the new Page/Lake Powell Bed & Breakfast Association is available from the Page/Lake Powell Chamber of Commerce (110 S. Lake Powell Blvd., Box 727, Page 86040, ☎ 520/645–2741).

Unless otherwise indicated, all the establishments listed have air-conditioning, private baths, telephones, and TVs in their rooms.

CATEGORY	COST*
$$$	over $80
$$	$50–$80
$	under $50

All prices are for a standard double room at summer rates (rates may be lower at other times), excluding hotel tax: 10.5% in the Page area, 8% on the Navajo reservation. No hotel tax is charged on the Hopi reservation.

Cameron

Dining and Lodging

Cameron Trading Post and Motel. This is a good place to stop if you're driving from the Hopi Mesas to the Grand Canyon. (*See* Dining and Lodging *in* Chapter 2, The Grand Canyon and Northwest Arizona, for details.)

Camping

Cameron RV Park (on U.S. 89, 26 mi southwest of Tuba City, ☎ 520/679–2231 or 800/338–7385) is adjacent to the Cameron Trading Post, with its restaurant, grocery store, even a butcher shop and post office. The fee with hookup is $14 per day. The park is open all year.

Canyon de Chelly/Chinle/Tsaile

Dining and Lodging

$$$ Holiday Inn Canyon de Chelly. This name-brand near Canyon de Chelly is less generic than you might expect: The territorial-style, Navajo-staffed complex stands on the site of a former trading post and incorporates part of the historic structure. Rooms, on the other hand, are predictably pastel and contemporary. The lobby restaurant, low-key by most standards, is the most upscale eatery in town, serving well-prepared specialties like fresh Navajo mountain trout dusted in blue corn meal and sauteed with piñon nuts. Fish and vegetarian entrées, steaks, and burgers are also available. Closed at lunchtime, the hotel restaurant offers to pack a box picnic for its guests. ⊡ *BIA Rte. 7, Box 1889, Chinle 86503, ☎ 520/674–5000 or 800/234–6835, FAX 520/674–8264. 108 rooms. Restaurant, pool. AE, D, DC, MC, V.*

$$$ Thunderbird Lodge. Set in an ideal spot at the mouth of Canyon de Chelly, this pleasant establishment has stone and adobe units that match the architecture of the site's original 1896 trading post. Some rooms feature roughly hewn beamed ceilings, rustic wooden furniture, and Navajo decor. The staff is friendly and knowledgeable about the locale. The manicured lawns and large, sheltering cottonwood trees help create a resortlike atmosphere. A cafeteria offers an inexpensive American menu of soups, salads, sandwiches, and complete meals, including charbroiled steaks, prepared by an all-Navajo staff. ⊡ *Box 548 (½ mi south of Canyon de Chelly visitor center), Chinle 86503, ☎ 520/674–5841. 72 rooms. Cafeteria. AE, D, DC, MC, V.*

$$ Coyote Pass Hospitality. You're not likely to encounter a more unusual lodging than this roving B&B run by the Coyote Pass clan of the Navajo Nation. It's not for everyone: You sleep on a mattress on the dirt floor of a hogan (its location depends on the season, but most are near Canyon de Chelly), use an outhouse, and eat a traditional Navajo breakfast prepared on a wood-burning stove. If you don't mind roughing it a bit, this is a rare opportunity to immerse yourself in Native American culture in beautiful surroundings. Guided hikes, nature programs, and other meals are optional extras. ⊡ *Contact Will Tsosie, Jr., Box 91, Tsaile 86556, ☎ 520/724–3383 or 520/674–9655. Rates per night: $75 1 person, $10 each additional person; call for tour and additional meal rates.*

Lodging

$$ Canyon de Chelly Motel. This two-story, Western-style motel, about 3 miles from Canyon de Chelly, has modern, cheerful rooms with light oak furnishings and Native American–print bedspreads and drapes. All rooms have cable TV and coffeemakers. The Junction Restaurant operates from the motel premises and serves inexpensive American-style food. ⊡ *Box 295 (on Rte. 7, ¼ mi east of U.S. 191), Chinle 86503, ☎ 520/674–5875, 520/674–5288, or 800/327–0354. 102 rooms. Restaurant, indoor pool. AE, D, DC, MC, V.*

Camping

Cottonwood Campground (Canyon de Chelly National Monument, near visitor center, Chinle, ☎ 520/674–5500) offers free, first-come, first-served camping at 52 RV sites (maximum length 35 feet; no hookups) and 95 tent sites on grounds with cottonwood trees and a picnic area. The campground is open all year, with water and flush toilets available April–September.

Holbrook–Winslow

Lodging

$ Wigwam Motel. Classic Route 66 kitsch, the Wigwam consists of 15 bright white cement wigwams where you can sleep inexpensively in a surreal environment. ▣ *811 West Hopi Dr., Holbrook, AZ 86025,* ☎ *520/524–3048.*

Dining

$–$$ Butterfield Stage Coach Restaurant. Easily identifiable by the stagecoach perched on its roof (a landmark from old Route 66 days), the Stage Coach serves predictable but reliable steak-and-roast-beef fare. It also has a salad bar and children's menu. ✕ *609 Hopi Drive,* ☎ *520/524– 3447.* ⊘ *11* AM*–10* PM *in summer, 4–10* PM *in winter.*

Camping

Homolovi State Park Campgrounds. The 52 sites and electric hook-ups are open year-round. Water and showers are available mid-April to mid-October. Prices are $8 per night for non-hookup, $13 for hookup. *1.3 miles from I–40 off AZ 87,* ☎ *520/289–4106.*

Hopi Reservation–Second Mesa

Dining

$ Tunosvongya Restaurant. Also known as the Hopi Cultural Center Restaurant, this clean, comfortable establishment operated by Native Americans provides the opportunity to sample traditional dishes, including Indian tacos, Hopi blue-corn pancakes, fry bread (not unlike a soft pizza crust), and *nok qui vi,* Hopi lamb stew. ✕ *AZ 264 on Second Mesa,* ☎ *520/734–2401. DC, MC, V.*

Lodging

$$ Hopi Cultural Center Motel. The only accommodation in the area, this no-frills pueblo-style lodging set high atop a Hopi mesa offers basic but clean rooms with telephones. One drawback: There's not always a night manager on the premises; guests are given a phone number to reach someone in case there are any problems. ▣ *Box 67 (on AZ 264, at Hopi Cultural Center), Second Mesa 86043,* ☎ *520/734–2401,* FAX *520/734–2435 (Attn: Hopi Cultural Center). 33 units. Restaurant. AE, DC, MC, V.*

Camping

Hopi Cultural Center Campground. There's no charge to stay at the modest camping and picnic area on the west side of the Hopi Cultural Center. There are no water hookups, but campers can use rest rooms in the cultural center.

Kayenta

Dining and Lodging

$$ Anasazi Inn at Tsegi. This unpretentious roadside motel, convenient to both Navajo National Monument and Monument Valley, offers clean, comfortable accommodations and striking views of Tsegi Canyon from its rear-facing rooms. Its restaurant, which features tasty Navajo fry-bread sandwiches and tacos, is one of the best in the area. ▣ *Box 1543 (on U.S. 160, 10 mi west of Kayenta), Kayenta 86033,* ☎ *and fax 520/697–3793. 56 units. Restaurant. AE, D, DC, MC, V.*

Lodging

$$ Holiday Inn. Except for the contemporary Southwestern-style decor, this accommodation about a half mile from Monument Valley provides what you would expect from the Holiday Inn chain. It has one of the few swimming pools in the western section of the region. Children under 19 stay in their parents' room free. ⊡ *Box 307 (south of junction of U.S. 160 and U.S. 163), Kayenta 86033,* ☎ *520/697–3221 or 800/465– 4329,* ℻ *520/697–3349. 160 rooms. Restaurant, pool, travel services. AE, D, DC, MC, V.*

$$ **Wetherill Inn Motel.** Named for John Wetherill, a frontier rancher, trader, and explorer who discovered many of the major prehistoric Native American ruins in Arizona, this clean, cheerful, two-story motel without frills has Southwestern decor and a well-stocked gift shop. ⊡ *Box 175 (on U.S. 163), Kayenta 86033,* ☎ *520/697–3231. 54 rooms. AE, D, DC, MC, V.*

Keams Canyon

Dining

$ **Keams Canyon Restaurant.** At this typical rural roadside dining spot, functionally furnished with Formica tabletops, you can choose from American dishes and a few Native American items, including Navajo tacos, made with Indian fry bread heaped with ground beef, chili, beans, lettuce, and grated cheese. (Note: The inexpensive motel in the same complex cannot be recommended.) ✕ *Keams Canyon Shopping Center (near AZ 264),* ☎ *520/738–2296 and 520/738–2297. MC, V.* ☉ *Weekdays 7 AM–8 PM, weekends until 6 PM.*

Monument Valley

Dining and Lodging

$$$ **Goulding's Lodge.** Built near the base of an immense red sandstone butte
★ with spectacular views of Monument Valley from all the rooms, this comfortable motel often serves as headquarters for the location crews of filmmakers. The lodge has handsome pueblo-style buildings stuccoed in a deep reddish-brown that makes them appear to be a part of the surrounding red-rock formations. The cozy rooms are furnished in contemporary style, with Southwestern colors and Navajo-design bedspreads. The on-premises Stagecoach restaurant, serving good standard American fare, is decorated with memorabilia from movies shot in the area; service is excellent, and large windows provide a splendid view across the valley. ⊡ *Box 1 (2 mi west of U.S. 163, just north of Utah border), Monument Valley, UT 84536,* ☎ *801/727–3231 or 800/874–0902. 62 rooms. Restaurant, pool, travel services. AE, D, DC, MC, V.*

Camping

Goulding's Good Sam Campground (off U.S. 163, near Goulding's Trading Post, 27 mi north of Kayenta, ☎ 801/727–3231, ext. 425) has tents and RV sites. The fee is $14 with no hookups, $22 with hookups (plus tax). ☉ *Mar. 15–Oct. 15.*

Mitten View Campground (Monument Valley Navajo Tribal Park, near visitor center, off U.S. 163, 25 mi north of Kayenta, ☎ 801/727–3287) has sites with a table, a grill, and a deck. Water is available, but no hookups; the fee is $5 per site, with hot showers extra. More sites are open in summer, but 10 or 15 are open year-round.

Navajo National Monument

Camping

Navajo National Monument (reached by turnoff on U.S. 160, 21 mi south of Kayenta, ☎ 520/672–2366) has a campground with RV and tent sites, water, and rest rooms, but no hookups. Camping here is free and is available May–October.

Page/Lake Powell

Dining

$$–$$$ Rainbow Room in Wahweap Lodge. You can't beat the beautiful setting of this attractive semicircular restaurant with panoramic views of Lake Powell and a colony of houseboats bobbing offshore. An extensive menu features Southwestern, standard American, and some Continental fare, accompanied by a good wine selection. Specialties include Southwest chicken breast marinated in a honey-and-jalapeño-pepper sauce, and coho salmon with a Dijon-mustard cream sauce. ✕ *Wahweap Lodge (on U.S. 89, 5 mi north of Page),* ☎ *520/645–2433 or 800/528–6154. Reservations accepted in summer. AE, D, DC, MC, V.*

$$ Salsa Brava. This cheerful Mexican restaurant, with upholstered booths, lots of windows, and beamed ceilings, emphasizes charbroiled rather than fried preparations and uses vegetable oil instead of lard. Good versions of the standard burritos, tamales, and enchiladas are available along with more unusual fare such as *carnitas* (slow-cooked pork), chicken with mole sauce, and fish tacos. There's an outdoor patio and a dark and clubby bar. ✕ *635 Elm St., Page,* ☎ *520/645–9058. MC, V.*

Lodging

$$$ Wahweap Lodge. On a promontory above Lake Powell, Wahweap Lodge
★ serves as the center for recreational activities in the area. This attractively landscaped property offers accommodations with oak furnishings and balconies or patios; many of the rooms have a lake view (rates are a bit higher for these). The brightly colored, Southwestern-style suites in the newest building are particularly attractive. Guests can enjoy two pools, a cocktail lounge, a marina, and the Rainbow Room (*see above*) for dining. Off-season rates are very reasonable. ⌂ *Box 1597 (on U.S. 89, 5 mi north of Page), Page 86040,* ☎ *520/645–2433 or 800/528–6154. 350 rooms. Boating, waterskiing, fishing, travel services. AE, D, DC, MC, V.*

$$–$$$ Inn at Lake Powell. It's neither an inn nor on Lake Powell, but never mind: This modern, well-run motel on a high bluff at the northern end of Page has large rooms with queen-size beds and Southwestern-print bedspreads. And, at a slightly higher room rate, you can get views of Lake Powell and Glen Canyon Dam. ⌂ *Box C (716 Rim View Dr.), Page 86040,* ☎ *520/645–2466 or 800/826–2718. 103 rooms. Restaurant, bar, pool, hot tub, meeting rooms. AE, D, DC, MC, V.*

$$ Weston's Empire House. Built in 1962, this classic 1950s-style motel on Page's main street recently renovated its comfortable rooms, which have individual air-conditioning and heating units. The smoky Western bar has a huge jukebox and a big-screen TV. ⌂ *Box 1747, 107 S. Lake Powell Blvd., Page 86040,* ☎ *520/645–2406 or 800/551–9005,* ℻ *520/645–2647. 69 rooms. Restaurant, bar, lounge, pool. MC, V.*

Camping

Page–Lake Powell Campground (849 Hwy. 98, ☎ 520/645–3374) has more than 70 full-hookup RV sites ($18 per night, $2 extra for cable-TV hookup), and eight tent sites ($15). A coin-op laundry, an indoor swimming pool, and two sets of men's and women's bathrooms and showers are available for no extra charge to both tenters and RVers. The campground is open year-round, and accepts reservations.

Wahweap RV Park (5 mi north of Page on U.S. 89 near shore of Lake Powell, ☎ 520/645–1004 or 800/528–6154) offers 120 full-service sites with full hookups, showers, and a laundromat; the fee is $21.50. It's open year-round and reservations are accepted. The adjacent **Wahweap Campground** (☎ 520/645–1059) has 180 sites, some near the marina. The fee for campsites with drinking water is $8.50; campers can use the coin-op laundry and showers ($2 extra) at the RV park. Open from April 1 to October 31, the campground operates on a first-come, first-served basis.

Tuba City

Dining

$ **Pancho's Family Restaurant.** The main fare here is Mexican, but the menu also features American and Navajo dishes. Mexican entrées are abundant and traditionally prepared, with chicken enchiladas and beef tamales as good as any you'll find south of the border. The large dining room looks like a Western coffee shop but has beamed wooden ceilings and incorporates such Native American touches as handmade pottery chandeliers and Navajo rugs on the walls. ✕ *Main St., adjacent to Tuba City Motel and Trading Post,* ☎ *520/283–5260. AE, D, DC, MC, V.*

$ **Tuba City Truck Stop Cafe.** Homecooking is the language of this small, conveniently located fast-service restaurant. Try the delicious Navajo vegetarian tacos. ✕ *Junction of U.S. 160 and AZ 264,* ☎ *520/283–4975.*

Lodging

$$ **Tuba City Motel.** In the largest community in the western part of Navajo–Hopi country, this property is conveniently situated near Pancho's Family Restaurant (*see* Dining, *above*), a trading post, and shops for essentials, gifts, and souvenirs. The spacious, well-maintained rooms are fine for an overnight stopover before or after a visit to the Hopi Mesas. ⌂ *Box 247 (at AZ 264–U.S. 160 junction), Tuba City 86045,* ☎ *520/283–4545 or 800/644–8383,* ℻ *520/283–4144. 80 rooms. AE, D, DC, MC, V.*

$–$$ **Grey Hills Inn.** Students at Grey Hills High School run this unusual lodging, a former dorm that offers large, clean accommodations. The beds are comfortable, and eclectic decor and kitschy paintings add character to the otherwise plain rooms. Bathrooms and showers are down the hall, and it's hard to find your way to the inn's entrance in the large high-school complex at night, but the rates are reasonable, especially for Youth Hostel members. ⌂ *Box 160 (off U.S. 160, ½ mi north of junction with AZ 264), Tuba City 86045,* ☎ *520/283–6271, ext. 141 or 520/283–6273 (on weekends or after school hrs). 32 rooms. No credit cards.*

Window Rock

Dining and Lodging

$$ **Navajo Nation Inn.** Indian officials in town on government business frequently stay in this motel in the Navajo Nation's tribal capital. The exterior is typical of contemporary roadside motels, but the rooms have been pleasantly decorated with Spanish Colonial furniture and Navajo art. The inexpensive restaurant serves standard American as well as Navajo entrées; the mutton stew is hearty, and the tasty fry-bread taco could easily feed two. ⌂ *48 W. Hwy 264, Box 2340, Window Rock 86515,* ☎ *520/871–4108 or 800/662–6189*

(reservations only), FAX *520/871–5466. 56 units. Restaurant, meeting rooms. AE, DC, MC, V.*

Camping
Summit Campground (off AZ 264, 9 mi west of Window Rock, ☎ 520/871–6645) has picnic tables but no water. The campground is open year-round and may charge a fee of $1 per person.

Tse Bonito Tribal Park (near AZ 264, Window Rock, ☎ 520/871–6645), set among sandstone monoliths, is a historically significant site: The Navajo camped here before being forced on the Long Walk to Fort Summer. The campground has shaded picnic tables and nearby rest rooms but no water. A fee of $2 per person may be charged. ☉ *Year-round except Dec. 25 and Jan. 1.*

NIGHTLIFE

Aside from sitting by a campfire, nightlife in northeastern Arizona is minimal. The Page/Lake Powell area offers the most options. The cocktail lounge at **Wahweap Lodge** (on U.S. 89, 5 mi north of Page, ☎ 520/645–2433) on the shore of Lake Powell and the **sunset dinner cruise** that departs from the dock at Wahweap Lodge (*see* Dining and Lodging, *above*) are two possibilities. Page also has a movie house, **Mesa Theater** (42 S. Lake Powell Blvd., ☎ 520/645–9565); a combination bowling alley/off-track betting parlor/comedy club/bistro called **Canyon Bowl** (24 N. Lake Powell Blvd. ☎ 520/645–2682); and **Ken's Old West** (718 Vista Rd., ☎ 520/645–5160), a country-and-western music and dancing spot where you can also get a pretty good steak or barbecued chicken dinner. In addition, there's an inexpensive first-run movie theater in Tuba City.

Keep in mind that no alcoholic beverages are sold on the Navajo and Hopi reservations, and possession or consumption of alcohol is against the law in these areas.

THE NORTHEAST ESSENTIALS

Arriving and Departing
By Plane
No major airlines fly directly into the reservations. To get closer to the northeastern part of the state, travelers will need to make flight connections in Phoenix to travel either on to Flagstaff, on I–40 near the southwestern corner of the Navajo reservation, or to the community of Page, on U.S. 89 near Lake Powell and the northern border of Arizona. At the end of your flight, you'll need to rent a car for the rest of the journey (*see* Rental Cars *in* Getting Around, *below*).

AIRPORTS AND AIRLINES
Sky Harbor International Airport (☎ 520/273–3300) in Phoenix is the primary hub for air travel coming into Arizona from points out of state. **Flagstaff Pullium Airport** (☎ 520/556–1234) and **Page Municipal Airport** (☎ 520/645–2494) are both small but modern. **Skywest** (☎ 800/453–9417) has daily flights from Phoenix to Page. (*See* Phoenix Essentials *in* Chapter 5, *and* Flagstaff Essentials *in* Chapter 4, for information on airlines that service Phoenix and Flagstaff.)

By Train
Amtrak (☎ 800/872–7245) provides daily service into Arizona from both the east and the west. It makes scheduled stops in Flagstaff,

which is a good jumping-off point for a car trip into the area. No passenger train enters the interior of the Navajo or Hopi reservation.

By Bus
Greyhound Lines (☎ 800/231–2222) has numerous Arizona destinations, but there is no service into the reservations. If you're coming from out of state and wish to tour northeastern Arizona, take a bus to Phoenix or Flagstaff and then rent a car.

Getting Around

By Car
If you are arriving from southern California or southern Arizona, Flagstaff is the best jumping-off point into northeastern Arizona (*see* Chapter 4, North-Central Arizona and Flagstaff). If you are traveling from Utah or Nevada, you might choose to come in from Utah on U.S. 89, starting your tour at Page, Arizona. For those driving south from Colorado, logical entry points are Farmington and Shiprock, New Mexico, via U.S. 64 (what looks like a more direct route to Canyon de Chelly through Red Rock ends up crossing an unimproved road). Gallup, New Mexico, to the east, is also a convenient starting point for exploring the area.

CAUTION: When driving off of major highways in low-lying areas, watch for rain clouds. Flash floods from sudden summer rains can be deadly (*see* Driving Precautions *in* The Gold Guide's Smart Travel Tips for more information).

ROAD MAPS
Because a tour of Navajo–Hopi country involves driving long distances among widely scattered communities, a detailed, recently published road map is absolutely essential. A wrong turn in this lonely country could send you many miles out of your way. Gas stations carry adequate state maps, but two other maps are particularly recommended: the Automobile Association of America's guide to Navajo–Hopi country or the excellent map of the northeastern region prepared by the **Navajoland Tourism Department** (*see* Visitor Information *in* Important Addresses and Numbers, *below*).

ROAD SERVICE AND WEATHER
It isn't easy to find a place to service your car here; we recommend that you make sure your car is inspected and serviced before your trip. Also, seek weather information if you see ominous rain clouds in summer or signs of snow in winter. Never drive into dips or low-lying road areas during a heavy rainstorm; they could be flooded or could flood suddenly. (For road service locations and emergency and weather information, *see* Important Addresses and Numbers *and* Weather, *below*.) If you heed these simple precautions, car travel through the region will be as safe as travel anywhere else. Paved highways in the interior are well maintained and are patrolled by police officers.

RENTAL CARS
Rental cars in heavily touristed Arizona are plentiful and usually available, but it's still smart to reserve a car in advance of your arrival. Major companies serving Phoenix and Flagstaff include **Avis** (☎ 800/331–1212), **Budget** (☎ 800/527–0700), **Hertz** (☎ 800/654–3131), and **National** (☎ 800/227–7368). Avis and Budget also offer rentals at the Page Municipal Airport. Weekly rates for a compact with unlimited mileage are most reasonable in Flagstaff (about $140 without any discounts), slightly higher in Phoenix (about $150), and much higher in Page (about $225).

By Bus

The **Navajo Transit System** (Drawer 1330, Window Rock 86515, ☎ 520/729–5449, 520/729–5457 or, at Navajo Nation Inn, ☎ 520/871–4108) offers regular service on fixed routes throughout the Navajo reservation as well as charter service; write ahead for schedules. The buses are modern, in good condition, and generally on time. However, this method of travel, across vast areas where towns and bus stops are many miles apart, may be too slow for some visitors.

Guided Tours

Except during winter months, the **Navajo Transit System** (*see above*) offers tours departing from Window Rock, the tribal capital. Destinations include Canyon de Chelly, the Painted Desert, and the Petrified Forest. **Nava-Hopi Tours, Inc.** (☎ 520/774–5003 or 800/892–8687), an affiliate of Gray Line, schedules tours into the area from Flagstaff. **Crawley's Monument Valley Tours** (☎ 520/697–3463) leaves from the small town of Kayenta, and **Goulding's Monument Valley Tours** (☎ 801/727–3231) departs from Goulding's Lodge (*see* Lodging, *above*). Half- and full-day truck and Jeep tours into Canyon de Chelly on the Navajo reservation depart from nearby **Thunderbird Lodge** (☎ 520/674–5841); the half-day tours leave twice daily (when there is a minimum of six passengers) throughout the year, while full-day tours are available only from April to October. The newspaper published by the Navajoland Tourism Department (*see* Important Addresses and Numbers, *below*) has a listing of operators offering Jeep and horseback tours on the Navajo reservation.

Unless you have a four-wheel-drive vehicle or don't mind hiking 8 miles (round-trip) through sand, you'll want to take a guided tour to Corkscrew Canyon, one of the most arresting sights in the Page/Lake Powell area (*see* Off the Beaten Path *in* Exploring the Northeast, *above*). If **Duck Tours'** (☎ 520/645–8581; tickets also available at the Page Chamber of Commerce, ☎ 520/645–2741, and the John Wesley Powell Museum ☎ 520/645–9496) owner Lee Woods is your guide, you're in for a fascinating introduction to the area.

Weather

With elevations in the area generally between 4,000 and 7,000 feet, summer temperatures average about 87°F but can climb beyond 100°F. Winter daytime temperatures range from the 30s to the 60s but can drop to zero or below at night. While the area gets less than 10 inches of rainfall in an average year, fierce summer thunderstorms can instantly flood low-lying areas. (*See* Driving Precautions *in* The Gold Guide's Smart Travel Tips for more information.) Sometimes in winter, heavy snows virtually stop all traffic on dirt back roads.

KTNN radio (AM 660) provides periodic weather information. This station serves Hopi and Navajo reservations from studios in Window Rock. Some programming is in Navajo, but there are news and weather reports in English. You might also telephone Canyon de Chelly (☎ 520/674–5500) or the Navajo or Hopi tribal police (*see* Emergencies *in* Important Numbers and Addresses, *below*) for weather updates.

Time

Unlike the rest of Arizona (including the Hopi reservation), the Navajo reservation observes daylight saving time. Thus for half the year—April to October—it's an hour later on the Navajo reservation than everywhere else in the state.

Banks

Norwest has branch offices with automated teller machines (ATMs) in Window Rock and Tuba City on the Navajo reservation. Adjacent to the reservation, Flagstaff, Page, Winslow, and Holbrook have banks and ATMs.

Important Addresses and Numbers

Emergencies

POLICE

Navajo tribal police: Chinle (☎ 520/674–5291), **Tuba City** (☎ 520/283–5242, **Window Rock** (☎ 520/871–6113 or 871–6116); **Hopi tribal police: Hopi Mesas** (☎ 520/738–2233).

HOSPITALS/MEDICAL CLINICS

Medical care in Navajo–Hopi country is not as easily accessible as in heavily populated urban areas. People with chronic medical conditions or those in frail health may wish to avoid a trip into Arizona's sparsely populated northeast. Hospital emergency care is generally not more than 60 minutes' driving time from any location on a paved highway.

Sage Memorial Hospital (☎ 520/755–3411), a public hospital located in Ganado, on the Navajo reservation, offers medical and dental services. **Monument Valley Hospital** (☎ 801/727–3241) in Utah (near Goulding's Trading Post off U.S. 163 at the Arizona–Utah border) has medical and dental services. Emergency care through the U.S. Public Health Service Indian Hospitals is available in the reservation communities of Fort Defiance (☎ 520/729–5741), Chinle (☎ 520/674–5281), Tuba City (☎ 520/283–6211), and Keams Canyon (☎ 520/738–2211). Another option in a medical emergency is to contact the Navajo or Hopi tribal police (*see* Police, *above*).

Page Hospital (N. Navajo and Vista Aves., ☎ 520/645–2424) has emergency-room service.

PHARMACIES

There are no pharmacies on the Navajo or Hopi reservations; for emergency medical supplies, go to the private or public hospitals noted in the Hospital/Medical Clinics section, *above*.

In Page, **Safeway** (Page Plaza, ☎ 520/645–5714 or 520/645–5068) is open weekdays 9–9, Saturday 10–6, and Sunday 10–4.

Road Service

Fed Mart Automotive (AZ 264 near Window Rock, ☎ 520/871–4764), **Tuba City Motors** (corner of Birch and Oak Sts., Tuba City, ☎ 520/283–5315 during the day, 520/283–5300 at night), **Kayenta Discount Auto Parts** (Kayenta on Hwy. 160, ☎ 520/697–3200), **Onsae Auto Repair** (Second Mesa, across from the Hopi Cultural Center, Hopi Mesas, ☎ 520/734–2211).

Visitor Information

For more information regarding Navajo–Hopi country, contact the **Navajoland Tourism Department** (Box 663, Window Rock 86515, ☎ 520/871–6659, 520/871–7371, or 520/871–6436) and the **Hopi Tribe Office of Public Relations** (Box 123, Kykotsmovi 86039, ☎ 520/734–2441); both publish tourist-oriented newspapers. The **Native American Tourism Center** (4130 N. Goldwater Blvd., Scottsdale 85251, ☎ 520/945–

0771) sells a map of Arizona reservations including a list of annual festivals and offers tourism brochures and a calendar of Indian events on and off the reservations. In addition, the center can help you contact any of the 14 tribal councils in the state. The **Page/Lake Powell Chamber of Commerce** (106 S. Lake Powell Blvd., Box 727, Page 86040, ☎ 520/645–2741) and the **National Park Service/Glen Canyon Recreation Area** (Box 1507, Page 86040, ☎ 520/645–8200) are both excellent sources for Lake Powell vacation information and prices.

•

4 North-Central Arizona and Flagstaff

Jerome and Prescott are two of the state's most popular towns, for their wild west history and their place in yet another wondrous locale. Sedona's red rocks, recognizable settings in numerous Hollywood westerns, are as captivating as they are easy to hike. Flagstaff has become more of a destination in its own right, with historical buildings, an increasing number of good restaurants, and nightlife. Outside the city, Wupatki and Walnut Canyon National Monuments and Sunset Crater are windows onto the world of a thousand years past.

RICH IN NATURAL attractions, north-central Arizona draws visitors to the striking red-rock formations of Sedona, to the limestone hills and desert scrub of the Verde Valley, and, just north of Flagstaff, to the San Francisco volcanic field, which has the highest peaks in the state as well as ancient lava flows and cinder cones. Sedona sits at the southern end of Oak Creek Canyon, where the Colorado Plateau meets the Sonora Desert to the south. Highway 89A, which traverses this wooded canyon en route to Flagstaff, is one of the most scenic drives in the state.

By Edie Jarolim

The area is also rich in artifacts from its earliest inhabitants: Several national and state parks—among them Walnut Canyon, Wupatki, Montezuma Castle, and Tuzigoot National Monuments—hold well-preserved evidence of the architectural accomplishments of Native American Sinagua and other ancestral Puebloans who made their homes in the Verde Valley and in the region near the San Francisco peaks. Nor will anyone interested in exploring the West's wild and woolly days be disappointed: Prescott's many Victorian houses attest to the attempt to bring "civilization" to Arizona's territorial capital; the preserved fort at Camp Verde gives an excellent feel for rugged frontier life; and funky old Jerome is living testament to Arizona's former mining madness.

The towns of Verde Valley—Cornville, Clarkdale, Cottonwood—are as sleepy as their names suggest. A visit to the historic sites in the region will take you through a part of America that seems to have changed little since the 1950s. Sedona couldn't provide a greater contrast, with its numerous shops, sophisticated restaurants, upscale accommodations, and New Age entrepreneurs. Prescott's temperate climate, along with its historic hotels, bed-and-breakfasts, and antiques shops, has long attracted weekending Phoenicians and is beginning to lure out-of-staters as well.

Flagstaff, the largest city in north-central Arizona and long considered a jumping-off point for tours of the region, is becoming recognized as an appealing destination in its own right, offering some of the best skiing in the state at reasonable prices, lots of opportunities to explore Arizona history and Native American culture, and pursuits for those with astronomical interests.

NORTH-CENTRAL ARIZONA

Exploring the Verde Valley and Prescott

About 100 miles north of Phoenix, as you round a curve approaching exit 285 of I–17, the valley of the Verde River suddenly unfolds in a stunning panorama of grayish-white cliffs, tinted red in the distance and dotted with desert scrub, cottonwood, and pine. With the exception of bustling Sedona at its northern edge, the valley is rather sleepy, but for hundreds of years it was home to many active Native American communities, especially those of the southern Sinagua people. In the second half of the 19th century the discovery of silver and gold in the Black Hills, which border the valley on the southwest, gave rise to such boomtowns as Jerome—and to military installations such as Fort Verde, set up to protect the white settlers and wealth-seekers from the Native American tribes they displaced. Mineral wealth was also the impetus behind the establishment of Prescott, across the Mingus Mountains from Verde

Valley, as a territorial capital by President Lincoln and other Unionists who wanted to keep the riches out of Confederate hands.

Numbers in the margin correspond to points of interest on the North-Central Arizona map.

❶ If you get off I–17 at any of the three Camp Verde exits, signs will direct you to **Fort Verde State Historic Park,** set on 10 acres overlooking the Verde Valley. Established in 1871–73 as the third of three military posts designed to protect miners and their suppliers from Tonto Apache and Yavapai raids, this fort oversaw the movement of nearly 1,500 Indians to the San Carlos and Fort Apache reservations. A museum details the history of the area's military installations, and three furnished officers' quarters show the day-to-day living conditions of the top brass; even on the frontier, the married men lived far more comfortably than their bachelor counterparts. *Box 397, Camp Verde, 86322, ☎ 520/567–3275. ☛ $2 adults, $1 children 13–17. ☉ Daily 8–4:30. Closed Dec. 25.*

★ ❷ Returning to Camp Verde's Main Street, you'll see a sign for the Montezuma Castle Road; it's about 3 miles from here to **Montezuma Castle National Monument** (from I–17, take exit 289 and follow signs for 3 miles). Mistakenly named by early explorers who believed it had been built by the Aztecs, this five-story, 20-room cliff dwelling of the southern Sinagua Indians is one of the best-preserved prehistoric ruins in North America—and one of the most accessible. An easy, paved trail (⅓ mile round-trip) leads to the structure and to the adjacent Castle A, a badly deteriorated six-story apartment with about 45 rooms. Visitors are not permitted to enter the ruins, but the viewing area is very close by. *Box 219, Camp Verde 86322, ☎ 520/567–3322. ☛ $2 adults 17 and over. ☉ 8–5 in winter, 8–6 in spring, 8–7 in summer.*

❸ Somewhat less accessible but equally striking is the **Montezuma Well** unit of the national monument, 4 miles from Exit 293 of I–17. Although there are some Sinagua and Hohokam ruins here, the limestone sinkhole with a limpid blue-green pool lying in the middle of the desert is the site's main attraction. This sink—55 feet deep and 365 feet across— is all that's left of an ancient subterranean cavern; the water remains at a constant 76°F year-round. It's a short hike up here, but the serene setting and the views of the Verde Valley amply reward the effort. *☎ 520/ 567–4521. ☛ Free. ☉ Same hrs as Montezuma Castle.*

❹ Not as well preserved as Montezuma's Castle but more impressive in scope is **Tuzigoot National Monument,** another complex of ruins of the Sinagua people, who lived on this land overlooking the Verde Valley from about AD 1000 to AD 1400. Items used for food preparation, as well as jewelry, weapons, and farming tools excavated from the site, are displayed in the visitor center, where there is also a reconstructed room from the pueblo. The site, near the town of Clarkdale, is off Highway 89A; take AZ 260 east from Camp Verde, or drive west from Sedona. *Box 68, Clarkdale 86324, ☎ 520/634–5564. ☛ $2 adults, senior citizens and children under 17 free. ☉ Memorial Day–Labor Day, daily 8–7; Labor Day–Feb., daily 8–5; Mar.–May, daily 8–6 (call ahead in Apr. and May to check; schedule is affected by Easter holidays).*

TIME OUT Two restaurants in Cornville, roughly between Camp Verde and Clarkdale, are worth a detour. The **Manzanita Restaurant & Lounge** (11425 E. Cornville Rd., ☎ 520/634–8851) serves reasonably priced Continental fare in a lace-curtained dining room; you can lunch on bratwurst with sauerkraut and spaetzle for $6.95, including soup or salad, or enjoy a dinner of roast half-duckling with orange sauce for $12.95. **Page Springs**

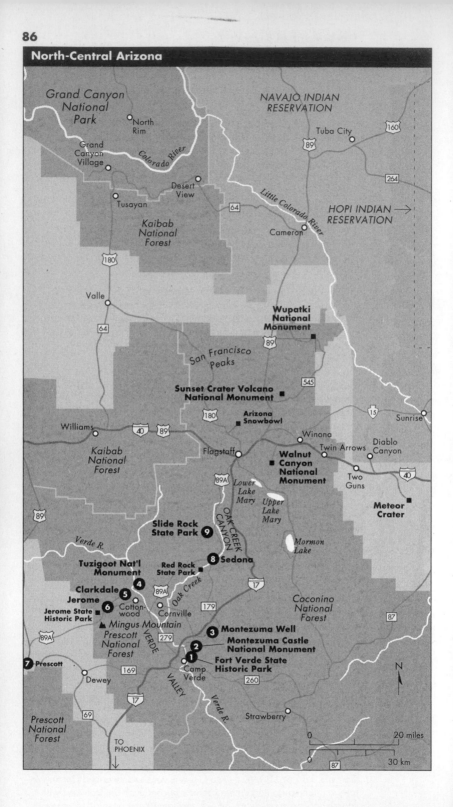

North-Central Arizona

Grand Canyon National Park

North Rim

Grand Canyon Village

Desert View

Tusayan

Kaibab National Forest

NAVAJO INDIAN RESERVATION

Tuba City

160

264

Little Colorado River

HOPI INDIAN RESERVATION →

Cameron

64

180

Valle

64

San Francisco Peaks

Wupatki National Monument

89

545

Sunset Crater Volcano National Monument

180

Arizona Snowbowl

15

Sunrise

Williams

40 89

Kaibab National Forest

Flagstaff

89A

Lower Lake Mary

Upper Lake Mary

Walnut Canyon National Monument

Winona

Twin Arrows

Diablo Canyon

Two Guns

40

89

Meteor Crater

Verde R.

Slide Rock State Park 9

OAK CREEK CANYON

Mormon Lake

Tuzigoot Nat'l Monument

Red Rock State Park

8 Sedona

Clarkdale 5
Jerome

4

Oak Creek

Jerome State Historic Park

6 Cotton-wood

Cornville

89A

179

17

Coconino National Forest

87

Mingus Mountain

Prescott National Forest

VERDE

279

3 Montezuma Well

2 Montezuma Castle National Monument

89A

7 Prescott

Dewey

169

1 Fort Verde State Historic Park

Camp Verde

260

17

VALLEY

Verde R.

69

Prescott National Forest

Strawberry

TO PHOENIX ↓

0   20 miles

30 km

87

N

Bar & Restaurant (Page Springs Rd., ☏ 520/634–9954), in two rustic, wood-panel rooms, both overlooking Oak Creek, has more of what you might expect to find out West: great chili, burgers, and steaks.

❺ There's little to see in **Clarkdale** itself, but the sleepy town was once home to the smeltery for the copper mines in nearby Jerome. The original settlement is said to have arisen from an encampment of prostitutes and hard-core gamblers who were tossed out of a rowdy mining camp in one of its periodic purges of sinners. These days, Clarkdale draws a somewhat more sedate group of train buffs who come to catch the

★ Verde River Canyon Excursion Train. Knowledgeable announcers regale riders on this scenic 22-mile route with the colorful history of the area, pointing out natural attractions along the way—say, a bald eagle's nest in the side of a cliff. A cowboy balladeer entertains passengers on the return trip. This trip, which takes about four hours, is especially popular in fall-foliage season and in the spring when the desert wildflowers bloom; make reservations well in advance. The train sells snacks, drinks, and sandwiches. For an additional fee you can ride the comfy, living-room-like first-class cars, where hot hors d'oeuvres, coffee, and champagne are included in the price. *Arizona Central Railroad, 300 N. Broadway, Clarkdale 86324, ☏ 520/639–0010. ☛ Round-trip rides: $34.95 adults, $30.95 senior citizens, $19.95 children 12 and under. First class: $52.95. ☉ Trains run Wed.–Sun. except in Apr., May, Oct., and Nov., when they run Wed.–Mon. Call for times.*

Jerome

★ ❻ From Clarkdale, it's 4 miles up the mountain to **Jerome,** once known as the Billion Dollar Copper Camp. The road winds along this side of the mountain, but the grades are not very steep. After the last mines closed in 1953, a booming population of 15,000 dwindled to a low of 50 determined souls, earning Jerome the "ghost town" designation it still holds. The town saw a slight revival during the mid-1960s, when hippies moved in and turned it into a funky art colony of sorts. Some 400 people currently reside here full-time, but tourists keep the place alive. Worth a visit for its historic interest as well as for its scenery, Jerome is literally built into the side of Cleopatra Hill, and from here you can see Sedona's red rocks, Flagstaff's San Francisco Peaks, and even eastern Arizona's Mogollon Rim country (*see* Tour 5: The White Mountains *in* Chapter 5, Phoenix and Central Arizona).

Jerome is about a mile above sea level, but structures within town sit at elevations that vary by as much as 1,500 feet, depending on whether they're perched on Cleopatra Hill or at its foot. Blasting at the mines regularly shook buildings off their foundations, and the town's jail slid across a road and down a hillside, where it can still be seen today. That's not all that was unsteady about Jerome. In 1903 a reporter from a New York newspaper called Jerome "the wickedest town in America" because of its abundance of drinking and gaming establishments; town records from 1880 list 24 saloons. Whether due to divine retribution or simply to drunken accidents, the town was burned down several times—some historians say five, others two or three. The mine's financial backers were a bit more respectable: Eugene Jerome, for whom the town was named, was first cousin to Jenny Jerome, Winston Churchill's mother.

Of the three mining museums in town, the most inclusive is part of **Jerome State Historic Park.** Just outside town, signs on Highway 89A will direct you to the turnoff for the park, reached by a short, precipitous road. The museum occupies the mansion of Jerome's mining king, Dr. James "Rawhide Jimmy" Douglas, Jr., who purchased Little Daisy

Mine in 1912; the house was built in 1917 at the height of Little Daisy's success. (Rawhide Jimmy's first mining fortune was made in southern Arizona; *see* Exploring Southeast Arizona *in* Chapter 6, Tucson and Southern Arizona.) Take a look at some of the tools and heavy equipment once used to grind ore. A video details the history of Jerome. The bawdy parts—relating, for example, to the one-time brothel, the House of Joy—have been left out, but you can read between the lines for some sense of the town's wild mining days. Views from the mansion and its surrounding grounds are spectacular. *State Park Rd.,* ☎ *520/634–5381.* ☛ *$2 adults, $1 children 12–17.* ☉ *Daily 8–5.*

The other worthwhile museum, the **Mine Museum,** is downtown. Staffed by the Jerome Historical Society, the museum's collection of mining stock certificates alone is worth the (small) price of admission—the amount of money that changed hands in this town 100 years ago boggles the mind. *Main St.,* ☎ *520/634–5477.* ☛ *50¢.* ☉ *Daily 9–4:30 (5:30 in high season).*

Jerome, like Sedona on a smaller, less expensive scale, is a scenic shopper's haven. Artsy boutiques and galleries carrying local and imported goods line the streets in the tiny downtown area (*see* Shopping, *below*).

TIME OUT   Ask where to have lunch and nearly every shop owner in town will direct you to the **Flatiron Cafe** (416 Main St., ☎ 520/634-3023), a tiny eatery at the fork in the road. The menu includes a choice of sophisticated sandwiches such as black bean hummus with feta cheese, and an array of coffee drinks.

Prescott

The 34-mile drive southwest down a mountainous section of Highway **❼** 89A from Jerome to **Prescott** is gorgeous (if somewhat harrowing in bad weather), filled with twists and turns through Prescott National Forest. If you're coming from Phoenix and taking AZ 69 from I–17 at Cordes Junction (a total of 96 miles), the route crosses the Mogollon Rim, overlooking the Verde Valley, and is scenic but less precipitous.

In a forested bowl at some 5,300 feet about sea level, Prescott is a prime summer refuge for Phoenix-area dwellers. It was proclaimed the first capital of Arizona Territory in 1864 by President Lincoln and settled by Yankees to ensure that gold-rich northern Arizona would be a Union resource. (Tucson and southern Arizona were strongly pro-Confederacy). It is believed that ancestors of the Yavapai Indians, whose reservation is today on the outskirts of town, were the area's original inhabitants, but early Territorial settlers thought that ruins in the area were of Aztec origin. You can see the results of this notion—inspired by the *History and Conquest of Mexico,* a popular book by historian William Hickling Prescott, for whom the town was named—in such street names as Montezuma, Cortez, and Alarcon. Despite a devastating downtown fire in 1900, Prescott remains the Southwest's richest store of late-19th-century New England–style architecture (some have called it the "West's most Eastern town"). With two institutions of higher education, Yavapai College and the innovative Prescott College, Prescott could be called a college town, but it doesn't really feel like one, perhaps because its transient youthful population is balanced by the many retirees drawn here by a temperate climate and low cost of living.

The city's main drag is Gurley Street, named after John Addison Gurley, who was slated to be the first governor; he died days before he was to move to Arizona Territory. **Courthouse Plaza,** between Cortez and Montezuma streets, is the heart of the city: Here the 1916 Yavapai County Courthouse stands, guarded by an equestrian bronze of turn-of-the-century journalist and lawmaker Bucky O'Neill, who died while charging San Juan Hill with Teddy Roosevelt. At the south end of the plaza, across from the courthouse's main entrance, the **Chamber of Commerce** (117 W. Goodwin St., 86303, ☎ 520/445–2000 or 800/266–7534) is a good place to get your bearings; on Monday and Friday at 10 AM, knowledgeable volunteer guides offer free orientation tours of the town. Those interested in architecture should be sure to get a map of the town's Victorian neighborhoods, most within walking distance of the Chamber office. Many of the Queen Anne houses have been beautifully restored, and a number of them are now bed and breakfasts.

Flanking the plaza's west side, Montezuma Street, is **Whiskey Row,** named for a string of brawling pioneer taverns; it was once host to 20 saloons and houses of pleasure, but social activity is more subdued these days. Antiques and collectibles shops line both sides of Cortez Street just to the north of the courthouse. It's a good idea to stop at the first one you see and ask for the brochure that the local dealers group put together. It includes a clear map and description of 19 participating stores.

Lovers of the past won't want to miss the **Sharlot Hall Museum,** a remarkable complex devoted to the history of the area, just two blocks west of Courthouse Plaza. Along with the original Ponderosa pine log cabin that housed the Territorial governor and the museum named for pioneering historian and poet Sharlot Hall, the parklike setting holds three fully restored period homes, a working blacksmith shop, and a transportation museum. Territorial times are the focus, but natural history and artifacts of the area's prehistoric peoples are among the many fascinating displays. It's easy to spend half or all of a day in this place. *415 W. Gurley St.,* ☎ *520/445–3122.* ☛ *$2 donation requested for adults.* ☉ *Apr.–Oct., Mon.–Sat. 10–5, Sun. 1–5; Nov.–Mar., Tues.–Sat. 10–4, Sun. 1–5.*

Prescott is also home to the much respected **Phippen Museum of Western Art** about 5 miles north of the entrance to town. The gallery's permanent collection includes work by many prominent artists of the west along with the painting and bronze sculpture of George Phippen; the rotating shows are often excellent. *4701 Hwy. 89 N,* ☎ *520/778–1385.* ☛ *$2 adults, $1.50 senior citizens, $1 students.* ☉ *Mon. and Wed.–Sat. 10–4, Sun. 1–4; Jan. and Feb., Wed.–Mon. 1–4.*

The stone-and-log structure built in 1935 to house the **Smoki Museum** is almost as interesting as the Native American artifacts inside. A priceless array of baskets as well as pottery, rugs, and beadwork highlight this fine collection, dating from the Pre-Columbian period to the present. *147 N. Arizona St.,* ☎ *520/445–1230.* ☛ *Free.* ☉ *May–Sept., Mon., Tues., Thurs.–Sat. 10–4, Sun. 1–4; Oct., Fri–Sun. 10–4; Nov.–Apr., no regular hrs; exhibits may be seen by appointment.*

The little **Bead Museum** on Courthouse Plaza tells an intriguing story of international trade and intricate bead craft from 3,000 BC through today. Jewelry and books are sold at the adjoining museum store. *138-40 S. Montezuma St.,* ☎ *520/445–2431.* ☛ *Free.* ☉ *Mon.–Sat. 9:30–4:30.*

Sedona

❽ **Sedona,** at the north rim of the Verde Valley, is one of Arizona's natural wonders—a Monument Valley in miniature. Its canyons and sensuous red-rock buttes, Cathedral Rock, Bear Mountain, Courthouse

Rock, and Bell Rock, among others, will remain long in your mind. For the tourist trade, numerous galleries, shops, resorts, and restaurants have become an attraction of their own.

The former artists' colony is now home to some 15,000 residents, many retired, and many (alas) more interested in making money than in creating beauty. Expansion during the past 10 years has been rapid, and the lack of planning has taken its toll in unattractive malls, developments, and increased traffic and congestion, especially on weekends and during busy summer months when Phoenix residents, overcome by heat flee north to higher elevations.

That said, it's easy to see what draws so many visitors to Sedona. Deep red rocks reach up into an almost always clear blue sky—these colors both enhanced by inviting dark green pine forests. The wilderness—canyons, creeks, Indian ruins, and the ever-present dreamscape of towering red rock—is readily accessible on foot or on any number of Jeep tours. The rugged landscape once attracted surrealist Max Ernst, writer Zane Grey, and filmmakers, who shot more than 80 Westerns in the area in the 1940s and '50s. These days, Sedona—which seems likely to become the next Santa Fe—draws enterprising restaurateurs and gallery owners from the East and West coasts. The town has also become a center of interest to New Age followers, who believe that the area contains some of the Earth's more important vortices (energy centers). Several entrepreneurs have set up crystal shops or New Age bookshops here, catering both to the curious and to true devotees.

Exploring

There are innumerable trails crisscrossing the red rocks, and the area is thrilling and easy to walk and hike. Don't pass up the breathtaking experience of constantly changing perspectives as you move among the formations. For free detailed maps and advice, speak to the rangers at the **Sedona Ranger District** office (250 Brewer Rd., ☎ 520/282–4119), which is open weekdays 7:30–4:30. Ask here or at your hotel for directions to trailheads for Doe's Mountain, beautiful Loy Canyon, Margs Draw, Devil's Kitchen, Long Canyon, or the Sinagua ruins in the very popular Boynton Canyon. Nearby Red Rock State Park and Slide Rock State Park (*see below*), both within 10 miles of Sedona, also offer many trekking opportunities.

Driving around Sedona, or taking one of the ubiquitous Jeep tours (*see* Special-Interest Tours *in* North-Central Arizona Essentials, *below*), is another way to take in the splendor of the rocks. The drive out to the Enchantment Resort, in Boynton Canyon, is stunning. Even if you're not staying there, consider hiking the canyon or stopping for a scenic lunch or late-afternoon drink. The views from the Chapel of the Holy Cross (*see below*) are also outstanding. Weather permitting, the Schnebly Hill Scenic Drive is another ooh-and-ah–inspiring option, and the vistas of the town from Airport Mesa at sunset can't be beat. Many of the most picturesque spots in Sedona are considered energy centers; vortex maps of the area are available at most of Sedona's New Age stores.

TIME OUT   The tiny **Sedona Coffee House & Bakery** (293 N. Hwy. 89A, ☎ 520/282–2241) serves good home-baked bread, healthy sandwiches, and soups; most seating is outside. Nearby, you'll find the usual chili and nachos at the **Cowboy Club** (241 N. Hwy. 89A, ☎ 520/282–4200)—along with more unusual western fare, like snake bites (breaded and fried pieces of rattlesnake meat) and Navajo flat bread.

You needn't be religious to be inspired by the setting and the architecture of the **Chapel of the Holy Cross** (☎ 520/282–4069; look for the Chapel Road turnoff on AZ 179 about 2 miles south of the Hillside mall, then drive another mile to the top of the road). Built by Marguerite Brunwige Staude, a disciple of Frank Lloyd Wright, this striking modern landmark, with a huge cross on the facade, rises between two red-rock peaks. Vistas of the town and the surrounding area are spectacular. There are no regular services, but visitors are welcome to come in daily 9–5 for quiet meditation. A small gift shop sells religious articles and books.

A trail east of the chapel leads you, after a 20-minute walk over occasional loose rock surfaces, to a magical seat surrounded by voluptuous red-limestone walls, worlds away from the bustle around the chapel.

Although it's set in an area that was inhabited by Native Americans for centuries, the town of Sedona itself is very new—it wasn't incorporated until 1988—so there are few historical sights for visitors to peruse. The main activity in the town proper is shopping, mostly for Southwestern-style paintings, rugs, jewelry, and Native American artifacts. During warmer months it makes sense to visit air-conditioned shops at midday and save hiking and Jeep tours for very early morning or late afternoon, when the light is softer and the heat less oppressive.

Around Sedona

Two miles west of Sedona on Highway 89A, you'll come to the turnoff for the 286-acre **Red Rock State Park;** drive another 3 miles to enter one of the newest state parks in Arizona (opened in 1991), and one of the most beautiful. An ideal place to enjoy both the red-rock formations of the Sedona area and lovely Oak Creek, it's also a less crowded alternative to the popular Slide Rock State Park (*see below*). The 5 miles of interconnected park trails are well marked and provide beautiful vistas. One trail leads to the House of Apache Fire, an unfinished residence started in 1946 by the former owners of the land, Jack and Helen Fry. (He was president of TWA.) You can enter the house only on ranger-led tours, offered on Wednesday and Sunday. There are bird-watching excursions on Wednesday and Saturday, and a guided hike to Eagle's Nest scenic overlook, the highest point in the park, every Saturday. Nature walks are given daily, weather permitting. Call ahead for times, which change with the season. *HCO2, Box 886, Sedona 86336, ☎ 520/282–6907.* ☞ *$5 per car.* ☉ *Daily 8–5 winter, 8–6 rest of yr.*

Whether you want to swim, hike, picnic, or enjoy beautiful scenery framed through a car window, head north on U.S. 89A through the wooded ★ **Oak Creek Canyon.** This is the most attractive route to Flagstaff and the Grand Canyon. Although the forest is primarily evergreen, there are enough changing colors in the fall to make the view especially glorious then. The road winds through a steep-walled canyon, and visitors crane their necks for views of the dramatic rock formations above. Oak Creek, which runs along the bottom of the canyon, is lined with tent campgrounds, fishing camps, cabins, motels, and restaurants.

❾ Look for **Slide Rock State Park** on your left, 7 miles north of Sedona. It's a good place for a picnic and a hike back into the forest. On a hot day, you can plunge down a natural rock slide into a swimming hole—a delightful experience. (Bring an extra pair of jeans to wear on the slide.) About 3 miles farther north is the popular West Fork Trail, which follows a creek where you can cool off in summer. The only downside to this trip is the traffic, particularly on summer weekends. *Box 10358,*

Sedona 86339, ☎ 520/282–3034. ☛ $5 per car. ⓧ Daily 8–5 winter, 8–6 spring, 8–7 summer.

What to See and Do with Children

Anglers young and old will enjoy the sure catch at the **Rainbow Trout Farm.** For $1 you'll get a cane pole with a hook and bait. There's no charge if your catch is under 8 inches: it's $2.75 for anything from 8 to 9 inches, $3.75 for 10- to 11-inchers, $4.75 from 12 to 13 inches, and $5.75 for 14 inches and larger. The real bargain is that the staff will clean your fish for 50¢ each and pack them in ice for you. *3 mi north of Sedona on Hwy. 89A, ☎ 520/282–3379. ⓧ Weekdays 9–5, weekends 8–6; summer, daily 8–6, weather permitting.*

Youngsters will love the plunge down the **natural rock slide** into the water at Slide Rock State Park in Oak Creek Canyon (*see* Sedona and Environs, *above*).

All ages enjoy **Jeep tours** (*see* Special-Interest Tours *in* North-Central Arizona Essentials, *below*). And the **train from Clarkdale** (*see* Sedona and Environs, *above*) also keeps children entertained.

Sports and the Outdoors

Camping

There is a large number of campgrounds in the Sedona, Prescott, and Jerome area. For a full listing, consult the *Arizona Camping and Campgrounds Guide,* available from the **Arizona Office of Tourism** (*see* Important Contacts A to Z *in* The Gold Guide). Reservations for many of the campgrounds in the area are handled by **Mistix** (☎ 800/365–2267), but you'll need to know in advance which one you want to book—it's impossible to get hold of a human being to ask questions with Mistix.

Campgrounds close to **Sedona** often fill up in summer, especially those along Oak Creek in Oak Creek Canyon. Two good places to try are Manzanita and Banjo Bill. For information on the six Forest Service campgrounds in the area, call 520/282–4119. Campgrounds near **Prescott** and **Jerome** in the Prescott National Forest are generally less crowded; Potato Patch and Granite Basin are both scenic, and sleeping out on top of Mingus Mountain is unforgettable. Contact the Prescott National Forest (344 S. Cortez St., Prescott 86303, ☎ 520/771–4700) for information.

If you're camping in winter, remember that this area gets quite cold, with frequent snowstorms. In summer, night temperatures can dip to 40°F, while daytime temperatures can reach 90°F.

CAUTION: Be careful not to camp in low-lying areas, which are subject to extremely dangerous flash flooding in sudden summer rains (*see* Lodging *in* The Gold Guide's Smart Travel Tips for more information).

Golf

In addition to the many private clubs in the area, golfers will find semiprivate courses, which accept a limited number of nonmembers, as well as public courses. Just outside **Prescott,** the city-owned **Antelope Hills** (19 Clubhouse Dr., ☎ 520/445–0583 or 800/972–6818 in AZ) offers 36 holes on two courses, one of them another of Gary Panks' creations. The **Prescott Country Club Golf Course** (14 mi east of Prescott on Hwy. 69, ☎ 520/772–8984) is also open to the public. In the **Sedona** area, the **Oak Creek Country Club** (690 Bell Rock Blvd., Sedona, ☎ 520/284–1660) is a good semiprivate option. The public is also welcome at the

Sedona Golf Resort (7260 Hwy. 179, Oak Creek, ☎ 520/284–9355), where the 18-hole course was designed by Gary Panks.

Hiking

For information on the numerous trails in **Sedona,** contact the **Sedona Ranger District** office (250 Brewer Rd., ☎ 520/282–4119) for detailed hiking maps. The **Verde Ranger District** office of the **Prescott National Forest** (300 E. Hwy. 260, Camp Verde, ☎ 520/567–4121) is a good resource for places to hike—as well as to fish and boat—along the Verde River. (*See* Exploring Sedona, *above,* for some specific hiking options.)

CAUTION: Be sure to bring plenty of water with you when hiking and drink often. Dehydration can become a life-threatening condition. (*See* Hiking *in* The Gold Guide's Smart Travel Tips for more information.)

Horseback Riding

Some 5 miles northeast of **Prescott, Granite Mountain Stables** (HC 29, ☎ 520/771–9551) has daily guided rides as well as group specials such as hay wagon outings. In **Sedona, Kachina Riding Stable** (5 J La., Lower Red Rock Loop Rd., West Sedona, ☎ 520/282–7252) includes riding with an Oak Creek swim and a picnic lunch. Weight limit for riders is 240 pounds.

Shopping

Jerome

Shoppers in Jerome will find a variety of boutiques in houses perched precariously on the side of Cleopatra Hill. The town has its share of art galleries, but they're likely to be a bit more on the funky side than the ones you'll find in Sedona. An exception is the **Anderson-Mandette Art Studios** (Old Mingus High School, Bldg. C, ☎ 520/634–3438). Robin Anderson and Margo Mandette made the building their workplace in 1978; at almost 20,000 square feet, it is considered by many to be the largest private art studio and gallery in the United States. The gallery is open Tues.–Sun. 11–6; guided tours are available on request.

Shopping is easy in Jerome; all you need to do is stroll up and down Main Street. Your eyes may begin to glaze over after browsing one boutique after another, each offering tasteful Southwestern goods. A special store recently opened at the bottom of Main: **The Shaman** (☎ 520/ 639–3577) carries the ceremonial art of the Huichols, the oldest indigenous tribe in Mexico; the friendly Huichol owners are happy to explain the purpose of each of the exquisite pieces. Just up the road, **Aurum** (☎ 520/634–3330) focuses on lovely imported and locally made jewelry, much of it silver. Next door, you'll be drawn in by the bright patterns and attractively styled women's clothing of **Designs on You** (☎ 520/634–7879). Farther up the hill, **Sky Fire** (☎ 520/634–8081) has two floors of items to adorn your person and your house, ranging from greeting cards to a handcrafted wrought-iron vanity for $2,500. **Nellie Bly** (☎ 520/634–0255) offers a wide range of kaleidoscopes, walking sticks, and perfume bottles, in addition to a good selection of silver jewelry.

Prescott

As noted in the Exploring section, shops selling antiques and collectibles line Prescott's Cortez Street around the central Courthouse Plaza; you should be able to pick up a guide to hours, location, and wares of the many dealers around town at the first shop you enter. For one-stop antiques shopping, try the **Merchandise Mart Antique Mall** (205 N. Cortez St., ☎ 520/776–1727), which gathers a variety of retailers together in a 14,000-square foot space. **Deja Vu Antiques** (134 N. Cortez St., ☎ 520/445–6732) takes you back to more tasteful past with an old-time soda fountain. If it's illumination you're seeking, try **The Curiosity Shop** (127 N. Cortez, ☎ 520/778–6323), which specializes in lamps. The other streets adjoining the plaza, particularly Montezuma and Gurley streets, are lined with a nice variety of specialty and gift shops. Gurley Street is also host to **Bashford Courts** (130 Gurley St.), with three floors of interesting stores; among them are Diversity (Suite 304, ☎ 520/778–7738), which features unusual designs in jewelry and ceramics, and Sunburst (Suite 204, ☎ 520/445–7099), focusing on attractive Santa Fe–style furnishings.

Sedona

The so-called **Uptown shopping area** is cut in half by Highway 89A; the stores in this area tend to cater primarily to the tour-bus trade.

Native & Nature (248 N. Hwy. 89A, ☎ 520/282–7870) is outstanding for its regional books and Southwest artifacts; at the end of the strip, **North Wind** (450 N. Hwy. 89A, ☎ 520/282–6505) is a fine arts gallery that hosts some unusual Native American pieces.

For upscale shopping, drive less than a minute south to the attractive **Tlaquepaque** development (AZ 179, ☎ 520/282–4838), where more than 100 artists, most of them painters and sculptors, sell their works. Prices tend to be high here; when asked how to pronounce the name of this shopping complex, locals joke that it's "to-lock-your-pocket." **Isadora** (☎ 520/282–6232) has beautiful handwoven jackets and shawls, and **Carusetta** (☎ 520/282–7793) showcases gold, silver, lapis, and turquoise jewelry; **Estebans** (☎ 520/282–4686) focuses on ceramics, as well as Native American crafts. Some good bets for Southwestern art are **El Prado Galleries** (☎ 520/282–7390) and **Aguajito del Sol** (in the bell tower, ☎ 520/282–5258).

A half mile south of Tlaquepaque (take a right out of the parking lot), at the junction of AZ 179 and Schnebly Hill Road, a small strip of shops includes **Garland's Navajo Rugs** (☎ 520/282–4070), with its huge collection of new and antique carpets, as well as Native American kachina dolls, pottery, and baskets. Next door to Garland's, **Sedona Pottery** (☎ 520/282–1192) features unusual pieces, including life-size ceramic statues by shop owner Mary Margaret Sather.

The next cluster of shops you'll come to on the same side of the road is the **Hozho Center** (431 AZ 179, ☎ 520/282–1038), a small, upscale complex set in a beige Santa Fe–style building. The center's **Lanning Gallery** (☎ 520/282–6865) sells attractive Southwestern art and jewelry, while **James Ratliff Gallery** (☎ 520/282–1404) has many pieces by not-yet-established artists; well-heeled buyers can find lots of fun, functional pieces. Drive another minute or two south on AZ 179 and you'll come to the **Hillside Courtyard & Marketplace** (671 AZ 179, ☎ 520/282–4500). Among the 23 shops and galleries, **Soderberg/Stevenson** (☎ 520/282–3818) specializes in Western sculpture.

Inveterate bargain hunters will want to continue south on AZ 179 2 miles past Chapel of the Holy Cross to the village of Oak Creek. At the **Oak Creek Factory Stores** (6601 S. AZ 179, ☎ 520/284–2150), Corning/Revere, Mikasa, Anne Klein, Van Heusen, and many other manufacturers have factory outlets.

Dining and Lodging

When it comes to lodging in Sedona, there are stunning settings and outstanding amenities but few bargains. Prescott, in contrast, has a nice range of accommodations. If you have a penchant for staying in a historic place—or having gambling close to your room—it's the place to overnight. Prices in Sedona tend to remain pretty much the same year-round. In tiny Jerome, there aren't many hotel rooms. If you think you might want to spend the night there, be sure to call ahead.

Dining choices in Sedona are much more evenly balanced than lodging options. And although many Sedona eateries tend toward the upscale, a number of good, low-key places can be found. Note: A number of Sedona restaurants close for stretches in January and February. Call to make sure that a restaurant will be open before you go.

Dining

CATEGORY	COST*
$$$$	over $35
$$$	$25–$35
$$	$15–$25
$	under $15

per person, excluding drinks, service, and sales tax

Lodging

CATEGORY	COST*
$$$$	over $150
$$$	$110–$150
$$	$60–$110
$	under $60

All prices are for a standard double room in high (summer) season, excluding room tax.

Jerome

Dining

$$$ House of Joy. Situated in a former bordello, this now-respectable restaurant attracts patrons from all over the region—perhaps as much for its legendary setting as its food. Two small dining rooms are dimly lighted and strung with red lights, but the stuffed animals and dolls on display (and for sale) offset any air of luridness. Book a table several weeks in advance as this popular restaurant is open only on weekends and only for dinner. Classic Continental dishes such as chicken Kiev and veal cordon bleu are well prepared. The hot muffins, home-baked breads, and desserts, all of which vary from day to day, are tasty. ✕ *Hull Ave., just off Main St.,* ☎ *520/634–5339. No credit cards; personal checks accepted. Closed weekdays. No weekend lunch.*

Lodging
BED-AND-BREAKFAST

 # 8791 Conf #

$$ Ghost City Inn. This inn, opened in 1994, would be appealing wherever it was located. It's especially welcome in Jerome, considering the dearth of good lodging. Set in a converted 1898 home, it affords sweeping views of the Verde Valley and Sedona from an outdoor veranda. All rooms are beautifully decorated, most in Victorian style, but "Champagne and Propane" and "Satin and Spurs" offer contemporary Western touches. Such luxuries as afternoon tea and turn-down with chocolates are especially surprising in a formerly rough 'n' ready town. Full breakfast is served outside when weather permits. ⌂ *541*

(520) 634-4678

N. Main St., Box 382, Jerome 86331, ☎ and fax 520/63–GHOST. 4 rooms with bath, 2 rooms share bath. AE, D, MC, V.

INN

$ **Jerome Inn.** This creaky Victorian with character is left over from Jerome's heyday almost 100 years ago. The bar and restaurant downstairs can be noisy, especially on Saturday night. Walls are thin, and most rooms share a bath, but it's hard to beat the prices. Try to book the Montana room—it's one of the hotel's largest, and it offers a lovely view of the mountains and downtown as well as a firm mattress. ⊞ *Main St., Box 36, Jerome 86331, ☎ 520/634–5094. 7 rooms, 1 with private bath. Restaurant, library. DC, MC, V.*

Prescott

Dining

$$–$$$ **Murphy's.** Locals love this large, dark, bustling restaurant and wait forever for a table on weekends. But as interesting as the late 19th-century building may be, the food doesn't always justify the fuss. Still, you'll find decently prepared seafood and steaks here—prime rib is particularly popular—and a selection of 60 beers, including many interesting microbrews. ✕ *201 N. Cortez, ☎ 520/445–4044. Reservations accepted for 5 or more. AE, D, MC, V.*

$$–$$$ **The Peacock Room.** The Hassayampa Inn has a pretty Art Nou-
★ veau–style dining room with tapestried booths, dim lighting, and an impressive Continental menu to match. The attention to detail is unexpected outside a major city—astonishingly sweet shrimp, for example, is flown in from a preserve in Mexico. Veal sautéed in white wine with capers makes an excellent entrée, as does chicken Venezia with mushrooms and artichokes in creamed sherry sauce. Soup and large salad are included with dinner, which makes the dessert tray no less tempting. ✕ *122 Gurley St., ☎ 520/778–9434. AE, D, MC, V.*

Lodging
BED-AND-BREAKFAST

$$–$$$ **Hassayampa Inn.** Built in 1927 for early automobile travelers, the Hassayampa Inn oozes character (be sure to look up at the hand-painted ceiling in the lobby). Rooms are individually decorated, a number with original furnishings like oak headboards inset with tiles. A complimentary cocktail at the elegant lounge and free breakfast (anything you want from the morning menu of the excellent restaurant) gilds the lily of reasonable rates. One drawback: its location on the town's main square can make the inn very noisy on weekend nights. ⊞ *122 Gurley St., Prescott 86301, ☎ 520/778–9434 or 800/322–1927. 58 rooms, 10 suites. Restaurant, bar. AE, D, DC, MC, V.*

$$ **The Marks House.** Victoria still reigns at this bed and breakfast, once owned by the mayor of Territorial Prescott. It now belongs to Beth Maitland, star of the daytime soap *The Young and the Restless,* and is ably managed by her parents. Rooms are impeccably furnished with period antiques: the suite in the circular turret, overlooking Thumb Butte, is particularly impressive. Full breakfast is served in the formal dining room, at an hour that guests agree upon in advance. ⊞ *203 E. Union St., Prescott 86303, ☎ 520/778–4632. 2 rooms with private bath (1 adjoining), 2 suites. D, MC, V.*

$$ **Mt. Vernon Inn.** A seamless series of additions has made this 1900 Victorian residence on a quiet street four blocks from the center of Prescott an ideal destination for a variety of travelers. The beautifully restored main house hosts four light-filled, romantic rooms, one with a private entrance. Guests enjoy a buffet-style breakfast in the downstairs din-

ing room. Two attractive cottages are large enough for families, while a third is a private little aerie for two; all three have kitchens, so cottage guests must make their own breakfast. ▣ *204 North Mt. Vernon Ave., Prescott 86301,* ☎ *520/778–0886. 4 rooms with bath, 3 cottages. Phones in all rooms, TVs in cottages. AE, D, MC, V.*

HOTEL/CASINO

$$$ Prescott Resort Conference Center and Casino. Perched on a hill on the outskirts of town, this former Sheraton affords forever views of the mountain ranges surrounding Prescott. Many guests hardly notice, so riveted are they by the poker machines and slots in Arizona's only hotel casino. There are plenty of recreational facilities to occupy those who don't have a penchant for one-armed bandits. Attractive, if bland, Southwestern-style rooms all have wet bars, refrigerators, and coffeemakers. ▣ *1500 Hwy. 69, Prescott 86201,* ☎ *520/776–1666 or 800/967–4637,* FAX *520/776–8544. Restaurant, piano bar, indoor-outdoor pool, sauna, tennis courts, exercise room, racquetball, casino. AE, D, DC, MC, V.*

Sedona–Oak Creek Canyon

Dining

$$$$ L'Auberge de Sedona. This highly regarded French restaurant had been playing musical chefs for a while, but John Harrings has successfully reigned for the past few years. One of the most romantic dining spots in Arizona, L'Auberge is done in Pierre Deux Country-French style. The cuisine takes advantage of both classic and nouvelle styles, with light, subtle sauces, somewhat modest portions, and fresh ingredients. A six-course, fixed-price menu ($49) might include smoked Scottish salmon, wild game consommé with duck ravioli, and filet mignon with foie gras, wild mushrooms, and truffle sauce; an à la carte menu is also available. Ask for a table overlooking the stream, preferably in the smaller room near the entrance. ✕ *L'Auberge La.,* ☎ *520/282–1667. Reservations strongly advised. Jacket required. AE, D, DC, MC, V.*

$$$ Pietro's. A savvy entrepreneur from New York's garment district has managed to pull together the ingredients for a successful Sedona restaurant: good northern Italian cuisine, friendly, attentive staff, and a lively, casual atmosphere (which sometimes feels crowded). Shrimp *fra diavolo* and rigatoni Siciliano are among the popular dishes, as is an eggplant and ricotta appetizer. Desserts like amaretto cheesecake, tiramisù, and zabaglione will take care of whatever's left of your diet. ✕ *2445 W. Hwy. 89A,* ☎ *520/282–2525. Reservations advised. AE, D, MC, V.*

$$$ Sedona Swiss. It's hard to go wrong with a chef who's used to pleasing Swiss embassy diplomats in Washington—and this very *gemütlich* European restaurant doesn't go wrong. Breakfast pastry in the adjoining café is light and buttery, and such classic dinner entrées as beef Stroganoff or rack of lamb Provençale are delicately seasoned and well prepared. Lighter alternatives like pasta with fresh salmon are also available. A low-priced buffet lunch draws in the tour-bus crowd (the restaurant sits on a street just off the main Uptown drag), but in the evening the pretty chalet-style dining room is suitably sedate and romantic. French, Italian, and German are spoken here. ✕ *350 Jordan Rd.,* ☎ *520/282–7959. Reservations advised. MC, V. Closed Sun.*

$$$ Troy's. Don't be put off by shopping center surroundings: You'll be
★ in another world as soon as you step inside. The main room of this imaginative restaurant has been designed to replicate the courtyard of a Spanish hacienda, with a flowered trellis and billowy clouds. A red-tile-roof "villa" contains the cleverly disguised smoker's dining room. A basket of fresh baked bread, including focaccia, sets the

tone for the expertly prepared American/Continental dishes to follow. Chicken liver paté is a fine starter, and for entrées, roast tenderloin of beef glazed with molasses and black peppercorns, and New Zealand rack of lamb are both deserving favorites. ✕ *2370 E. Hwy. 89A, Park Sedona Plaza,* ☎ *520/282–3532. Reservations advised. No lunch on weekends. MC, V.*

$$–$$$ **Heartline Cafe.** Attention to detail—fresh flowers on the tables, house
★ salads without a leaf of iceberg—and outstanding, innovative cuisine make this attractive café stand out in a town that's beginning to form a yuppie-restaurant profile. The dinner menu has a Southwestern emphasis, as in oak-grilled salmon marinated in tequila and lime or chicken breast with black beans and salsa. There are also at least six appealing vegetarian selections. A temptingly priced sampler for two presents all of the luscious desserts on the menu. On nice days you may want to sit on a rosebush-lined terrace. ✕ *1610 W. Hwy. 89A,* ☎ *520/ 282–0785. Reservations advised. AE, D, MC, V. No lunch Sun.*

$$ **The Atrium.** With a chic new bistro menu and an attractive, plant-filled look, The Atrium is still going through some growing pains. Still, prices are reasonable enough to make it worth taking a chance. At dinnertime, such appetizers as sweet-potato ravioli might precede sautéed fresh rainbow trout or pan-roasted pork tenderloin with garlic mushroom ragout. Breakfast—like comforting hot Irish oatmeal or brioche French toast—is always a winner. ✕ *Tlaquepaque, AZ 179 at the bridge,* ☎ *520/282–5060. Reservations advised. MC, V.*

$$ **Rincon del Tlaquepaque.** This lovely Spanish-style restaurant nestled in the upscale Tlaquepaque mall serves Arizona-Mexican food and some Native American-inspired items such as Navajo pizza. Towering sycamores shade the outdoor patio, where diners can watch shoppers stroll through the flower-filled and stone-sidewalk shopping area. Try margaritas and chimichangas, tasty without being deep-fried. ✕ *Tlaquepaque, AZ 179 at the bridge,* ☎ *520/282–4648. Reservations advised. MC, V. Closed Mon. No dinner Sun.*

$–$$ **Shugrue's Restaurant Bakery & Bar.** A combination coffee shop and upscale restaurant (one room has vinyl booths, another pink tablecloths and a fireplace), Shugrue's in West Sedona attracts a loyal following of locals who come for safe food and large portions rather than for culinary adventure. Omelets, salads, and burgers are on the menu, along with Mexican fare and, at dinnertime, steaks and seafood. Shugrue's Hillside branch has a more ambitious, more expensive, and more inconsistent menu, as well as a lovely setting overlooking Sedona's red rocks. ✕ *2250 W. Hwy. 89A,* ☎ *520/282–2943; 671 AZ 179 (Hillside Shopping Center),* ☎ *520/282–5300. Reservations advised. Breakfast on weekends. AE, MC, V.*

$ **Mandarin House.** Its name notwithstanding, the Mandarin House serves everything from standard Cantonese to Szechuan and Hunan fare, with dishes ranging from the exotic (shark-fin salad) to the old standbys (egg foo yong). Well-priced lunch specials include crispy egg rolls made on the premises. Dark green tablecloths, carved chairs, and dark-wood furnishings lend this restaurant, just down the road from the Oak Creek Factory Stores, a certain elegance. ✕ *6486 Hwy. 179, Suite 114,* ☎ *520/284–9088. Reservations accepted. AE, D, MC, V.*

Lodging
BED-AND-BREAKFAST

$$$–$$$$ **Briar Patch Inn.** Set in a wonderfully verdant canyon with a rushing
★ creek, this B&B has accommodations to match. All the hewn-wood cabins (in Native American and Mexican styles) have kitchenettes; some offer decks overlooking Oak Creek, and many feature fireplaces. On

summer mornings you can sit outside and enjoy home-baked breads and fresh egg dishes while listening to classical music performed live. New Age and crafts workshops are held on the premises at various times. ⊞ *Off Hwy. 89A 3 mi north of Sedona, HC 30, Box 1002, Sedona 86336,* ☎ *520/282–2342,* 𝔽𝔸𝕏 *520/282–2399. 12 2-person cabins, 4 4-person cabins. Massage, fishing, library. MC, V.*

$$–$$$$ **Casa Sedona.** You can have all the modern amenities—Jacuzzi for two, air-conditioning and heating units—and still be able to commune with nature at this appealing B&B. A large redwood deck, where a full breakfast is served when the weather is fine, has stunning red-rock views, also enjoyed by all of the rooms. The rooms, which all have refrigerators and gas-run fireplaces, are done in an eclectic style with differing Southwestern themes; one is done in deep blues, burgundies, and tans with a Native American–print bedspread, another in shades of peach and sea green with a light oak closet. ⊞ *55 Hozoni Dr., Sedona 86336,* ☎ *520/282–2938 or 800/525–3756. 15 double rooms with bath. TV with VCR and music center in living room. D, MC, V.*

$$–$$$$ **The Lodge at Sedona.** A first-class operation—breakfast, for example, is prepared by a chef who graduated from New York's Culinary Institute—The Lodge still manages to feel intimate and friendly. Rooms in this rambling wood-and-stone house are individually decorated in every style from romantic Renaissance to cowboy kitsch; some have fireplaces, redwood decks, and/or Jacuzzi tubs. Of the five public areas where guests can mingle, perhaps the best is the lace-curtain breakfast nook, shaded by trees and looking out onto the red rocks in the distance. ⊞ *125 Kallof Pl., Sedona 86336,* ☎ *520/204–1942 or 800/619–4467. 11 rooms with bath, 2 suites. Library, meeting room. MC, V.*

RESORTS, HOTELS, AND INNS

$$$$ **Enchantment Resort.** Designed as a tennis resort, Enchantment has ex-
★ cellent sports facilities, but it's the stunning setting of Boynton Canyon that makes it unique. Southwest-pattern rooms are set in 56 pueblo-style casitas. Many have fireplaces and kitchenettes, and all have superb views. Fresh-squeezed orange juice and a newspaper are delivered to rooms each morning, and the Yavapai Room has more vistas and excellent Continental cuisine. One drawback: Although flashlights are provided, it's difficult to find one's way around the largely unlighted premises at night; of course, guests can call the front desk for golf-cart transport. ⊞ *525 Boynton Canyon Rd., Sedona 86336,* ☎ *520/282–2900 or 800/826–4180,* 𝔽𝔸𝕏 *520/282–9249. 162 rooms with bath. Restaurant, bar, kitchenettes, 5 outdoor pools, 12 tennis courts, pitch-and-putt golf course, aerobics, croquet, health club, hiking, bicycles, pro shop, children's program. AE, D, MC, V.*

$$$$ **Garland's Oak Creek Lodge.** In the heart of Oak Creek Canyon, this lodge was built in the 1930s and bought by its current owners, Gary and Mary Garland, in the 1960s. Sixteen comfortably furnished cabins, some including fireplaces and pullout beds for extra guests, share 17 acres of beautiful land (at an elevation of 5,000 feet) with an organic apple orchard. Accommodations look out over the canyon itself or the rugged cliffs surrounding it. The lodge is operated on a modified American plan, with excellent breakfasts and dinners included in the room price, along with afternoon tea. Garland's is often booked solid a year in advance—it's open only from April 1–November 15—but it's worth a phone call to check. ⊞ *Hwy. 89A, 8 mi north of Sedona (Box 152), 86339,* ☎ *520/282–3343. 16 cabins with bath. Restaurant, lake, tennis court, croquet, volleyball. MC, V.*

$$$$ **L'Auberge de Sedona Resort.** This resort consists of a central building and—the major attraction—a number of sweet, secluded cabins in a wooded setting along a stream. You may wake to the sound of friendly geese, used to gifts of food from generous guests, honking around in the morning. Phoenix couples flock to these romantic, Country French hideaways and dine in the first-class French restaurant (*see* Dining, *above*). There's a small heated pool for summertime swimming. ☎ *L'Auberge La. (Box B), Sedona 86336,* ☎ *520/282–1661 or 800/272–6777,* ℻ *520/282–2885. 69 rooms, 30 cottages, all with bath. 2 restaurants, pool, spa. AE, D, DC, MC, V.*

$$$$ **Los Abrigados.** This place really sparkles at Christmas when half a mil-
★ lion tiny lights illuminate the grounds, but it's a dazzler year-round. All the spacious suite accommodations, attractively decorated in earth tones, have microwaves, minibars, and coffeemakers, as well as two TVs; in addition, some have private spas and fireplaces. A state-of-the-art health club, offering such extras as massages and facials will help burn off the calories picked up at Joey Bistro, the resort's bustling new southern Italian restaurant. Steak & Sticks, opened in 1995, features billiards and backgammon along with its grill. Guests can also picnic at Oak Creek, which runs through the grounds of this 20-acre, tree-lined property. The shops of Tlaquepaque are right next door. ☎ *160 Portal La., Sedona 86336,* ☎ *520/282–1777 or 800/521–3131,* ℻ *520/282–2614. 175 suites. 3 restaurants, bar, grill, pool, 3 tennis courts, health club, volleyball, children's programs, baby-sitting. AE, D, DC, MC, V.*

$$–$$$ **Southwest Inn at Sedona.** This upscale motel in West Sedona is a new and reasonably priced alternative to the town's more pricey proper-ties. Rooms have a fresh Santa Fe look, with viga-style ceiling beams, art prints, light wood furnishings, and vibrant colors; all have gas fire-places as well as decks or patios (some with red rock vistas, others with uninspiring views of the parking lot). The inn is totally nonsmoking. Continental breakfast is included in the room rate. Sedona's new movie theater, Cinedona, is right next door. ☎ *3250 W. Hwy. 89A, West Se-dona 86336,* ☎ *520/282–3344 or 800/483–7422,* ℻ *520/282–0267. 28 rooms and suites with bath. Hot tub. AE, D, MC, V.*

$$ **Bell Rock Inn.** Just down the road from Oak Creek's factory-outlet stores, a few miles south of Sedona, this motel offers rooms nicely furnished in Southwestern pastels; many have red-rock views. Some 52 new units, many of them suites, were added in 1994. ☎ *6246 AZ 179, Oak Creek 86351,* ☎ *520/282–4161 or 800/881–7625,* ℻ *520/284–0192. 97 rooms and suites with bath. Restaurant, lounge, pool. AE, MC, V.*

$–$$ **Sky Ranch Lodge.** There may be no better vantage point in town from
★ which to view Sedona's red-rock canyons than the private patios or balconies at Sky Ranch Lodge, perched near the top of Airport Mesa. Some rooms have stone fireplaces, some have kitchenettes; all are well decorated in dark blues and beiges with ceramic tile trim. Paths on the grounds wind around fountains and, in summer, through colorful flower gardens. This is an excellent value choice. ☎ *Airport Rd., Box 2579, Sedona 86339,* ☎ *520/282–6400,* ℻ *520/282–7682. 92 rooms with bath, 2 cottages. Pool. MC, V.*

The Arts and Nightlife

The Arts

Jerome

Jerome's annual music festival has been canceled, but in 1995 the **Liar's Festival** was added to the **Chili Cookoff** on April Fool's Day. The an-nual **Jerome Home Tour** in May is also worth checking out. Contact the Jerome Chamber of Commerce (Box K, 86331, ☎ 520/634–2900) for details.

Prescott

The mainstay of culture in the community, the **Prescott Fine Arts Association** (208 N. Marina St., ☎ 520/445–3286) sponsors a wide range of musicals and dramas, a series of plays for children, and a variety of concerts. The association's gallery also offers rotating exhibits by local, regional, and national artists. The **Yavapai Symphony Association** (☎ 520/776–4255) hosts performances by the Phoenix and Flagstaff symphonies; call ahead for schedules and venues.

Prescott, which had its first organized cowboy competition in 1888, lays claim to having the world's oldest rodeo; the annual **Frontier Days** roundup, held on the July 4th weekend at the Yavapai County Fairgrounds, is duly revered (call 520/445–1891 for tickets and information). It's followed later in the month by the popular **Prescott Bluegrass Festival** (Watson Lake Park, ☎ 520/445–2000). In August, the **Cowboy Poets Gathering** (☎ 520/445–3122) at the Sharlot Hall Museum brings together campfire bards from around the country. December sees the **Christmas Parade and Courthouse Lighting** and the **Victorian Holiday Home Tour,** designed to evoke festivities of olden days; call the Chamber of Commerce (☎ 800/266–7534) for details.

Sedona

Find out about cultural events in Sedona at **The Book Loft** (175 AZ 179, just south of the "Y," ☎ 520/282–5173), which often hosts poetry readings, theatrical readings, book signings, and lectures. The Sedona **Jazz on the Rocks Festival** (☎ 520/282–1985), held every September, always attracts a sellout crowd that fills the town to capacity; at jazz-festival time it's even more important than usual to book ahead for rooms. The **Sedona Heritage Day Festival,** sponsored by the Sedona Historical Society (☎ 520/282–2186), is celebrated in early October; this family-oriented event includes pioneer storytellers, barbecue, and an appearance by the Forte Verde Cavalry. The **Sedona Arts Center** (Hwy. 89A and Art Barn Road, ☎ 520/282–3809) sponsors events ranging from classical concerts to plays; phone for information about upcoming programs.

Nightlife

Jerome

Fun-seeking Sedonans often head to Jerome on weekends for live music and a livelier scene at the **Spirit Room** (☎ 520/634–8809) on Main Street. Just down the block, **Paul & Jerry's Saloon** (☎ 520/634–2603) also attracts a rowdy crowd to its two pool tables and old wooden bar.

Prescott

In Prescott, Montezuma Street's Whiskey Row, just off the central Courthouse Plaza, is nowhere near as wild as it was in its historic heyday, but most of the bars have live music on the weekends; just walk up and down and poke your head in when you hear some sounds you like. Even if there's nothing happening, stop in at the **Palace** (100 block of Montezuma, no ☎) to see the beautiful mahogany bar brought over from Europe in the late 1800s. The venerable bar at **Lizzard** (120 N. Cortez St., ☎ 520/778–2244) was also shipped from overseas via the Colorado River. **Nolaz** (216 West Gurley St., ☎ 520/445–3765) often features good Cajun, bluegrass, or country-western bands. For a more refined atmosphere, head over to the Art Nouveau piano bar at the **Hassayampa Inn** (122 Gurley St., ☎ 520/778–9434); there's always someone tickling the ivories on the weekend. The main source of entertainment at the **Prescott Resort** (1500 Hwy. 69, ☎ 520/776–1666) is its casino, but the mellow tunes of a piano are an alternative to the clank of the slots on Friday and Saturday nights.

Sedona

Nightlife in Sedona, geared toward a resort crowd, tends to be a bit more sedate. **On the Rocks,** the bar and grill at Los Abrigados (160 Portal La., ☎ 520/282–1777), hosts bands nightly, mostly of the swing and jazz variety. **Enchantment Resort** (525 Boynton Canyon Rd., ☎ 520/282–2900) has an attractive bar where live piano music keeps the beautiful people entertained on Friday and Saturday night. **Cups Bistro & Gallery** (1670 W. Hwy. 89A, ☎ 520/282–2531), a comfy coffeehouse, often features live jazz or blues in the evenings during high season. The closest you'll come to a rollicking cowboy bar in town is **Rainbow's End** (3235 W. Hwy. 89A, ☎ 520/282–1593), a steak house with a large dance floor and live country-western bands on weekends.

North-Central Arizona Essentials

Arriving and Departing

By Plane

The tiny **Sedona Airport** (☎ 520/282–4487) has a very scenic location on Airport Mesa. It is serviced only by Scenic Airlines.

Scenic Airlines (235 Air Terminal Dr., Sedona, ☎ 520/282–7935 or 800/535–4448) has three daily round-trips between Phoenix and Sedona in winter, four in summer. The cost is $95 to $110 round-trip.

AIRPORT TO DOWNTOWN SEDONA

By Taxi. While no cabs wait at the airport, **Bob's Sedona Taxi** (☎ 520/282–1234) or **Bell Rock Taxi** (☎ 520/282–4222) will dispatch a car which should show up in about five minutes; there's a courtesy phone for both at the terminal. A ride to town will cost about $7 or $8, without tip.

By Rental Car. Budget (☎ 520/282–4602 or 800/527–0700) has an office at the Sedona Airport.

By Car

To get to Sedona and the Verde Valley from Phoenix, take I–17 north for 113 miles. Sedona is another 15 miles on AZ 179 (driving to Sedona should take about 2½ hours). The 27-mile drive from Flagstaff to Sedona on Highway 89A is breathtaking beginning at the top of Oak Creek Canyon as you wind down into town through stunning scenery.

CAUTION: When driving off major highways in low-lying areas, watch for rain clouds. Flash floods from sudden summer rains can be deadly (*see* Driving Precautions *in* The Gold Guide's Smart Travel Tips for more information).

By Train

There is no rail service into Prescott or Sedona.

By Bus

The **Sedona/Phoenix Shuttle Service** (Box 3342, West Sedona 86340, ☎ 520/282–2066 or 800/448–7988 in AZ) makes six trips daily between those cities; the fare is $30 one-way, $55 round-trip. The bus leaves from three terminals of Sky Harbor International Airport in Phoenix. Reservations are required.

Getting Around

Sedona stretches along Highway 89A, its main thoroughfare, which runs roughly east–west through town. Highway 89A is bisected by AZ 179. The more commercial section of Highway 89A east of AZ 179 is known as Uptown; locals tend to frequent the shops on the other side, called West Sedona. To the south of Highway 89A, AZ 179 is lined with upscale retailers for a couple of miles. There is no public transportation in Sedona; if you don't have your own wheels, you'll need to rent a car or Jeep or take a taxi (*see* Airport to Downtown Sedona, *above*).

By Jeep

If you want to explore the back roads of Sedona's red rocks on your own, you can rent a four-wheel-drive vehicle from **Sedona Jeep Rentals** (Sedona Airport, ☏ 520/282–2227) or **Sedona Vacation Rentals** (Oak Creek Terrace Resort, Hwy. 89A, ☏ 520/282–6061).

Opening and Closing Times

Sedona, is a resort that caters to retirees, so restaurants tend to close by 10 PM. Banking can be done at odd hours by way of automated teller machines (ATMs) located all over town. Some banks stay open until 6 PM on Friday. In summer, shops and attractions are open longer: 9–9 Monday through Saturday and noon–5 on Sunday.

Guided Tours

Orientation

Sedona Trolley (☏ 520/282–6826) offers two types of daily orientation tours, both departing from the main bus stop in Uptown and lasting less than an hour. One goes along AZ 179 to the Chapel of the Holy Cross, with stops at Tlaquepaque and some of the resorts; the other passes through West Sedona to Boynton Canyon (Enchantment Resort). Rates are $6 each, or $9 for both.

Special-Interest Tours

SEDONA

One of the most popular things to do in the Sedona area is to take a **Jeep tour;** several operators headquartered along Sedona's main Uptown drag offer a variety of excursions, some focusing on geology, some on astronomy, some on vortices, some on all three, and some generally hokey. **Time Expeditions** (Box 2936, Sedona 86339, ☏ 520/282–2137 or 800/999–2137) has particularly knowledgeable tour guides; the ubiquitous **Pink Jeep Tours** (Box 1447, Sedona 86339, ☏ 520/282–5000 or 800/8–SEDONA), as well as **Sedona Adventures** (Box 1476, Sedona 86339, ☏ 520/282–3500 or 800/888–9494) and **Sedona Red Rock Jeep Tours** (Box 10305, Sedona 86339, ☏ 520/282–6826 or 800/848–7728) are also reliable operators. Prices start at about $18 per person for one hour and go up to $45 per person for two hours. Car seats are available for youngsters; check with your operator before you book. Although all the excursions are safe, those who dislike heights or bumps should choose one that's easy on the nerves and spine.

Rahelio (10 Traumeri La., Sedona 86336, ☏ 520/282–6735) offers vortex tours, vision quests, a variety of mystical hikes, and adventures. Those interested in Native American culture and spirituality should contact **Anasazi Healing Tours** (Box 3448, West Sedona 86340, ☏ 520/204–1053); Steven Alish-TaSen is an excellent guide to the Hopi Mesas and other Native American sites.

A **hot-air-balloon tour** of Sedona provides a unique perspective of the red-rock landscape. Prices generally start at $135 per person for a one- to two-hour tour. Plan to spend about three or four hours on this venture, including driving time to the launch site and a champagne picnic. The only two companies with permits to fly over Sedona are **Northern Light Balloon Expeditions** (Box 1695, Sedona 86339, ☎ 520/282–2274 or 800/230–6222) and **Red Rock Balloon Adventures** (Box 2759, Sedona 86339, ☎ 520/284–0040 or 800/258–3754).

It's a rare visitor who won't snap a roll or two of film in beautiful Sedona; **Sedona Photo Tours** (Box 1650, Sedona 86339, ☎ 520/282–4320) will take you to all the prime spots and help you take your best shot. Rates are $35 per person for a basic two-hour tour; it's an additional $15 per hour for private tours.

Those interested in the photographs of others—and in art in general— might consider a tour of some of the galleries in town; contact **Sedona Art Tours** (Box 10578, Sedona 86339, ☎ 520/282–7686) for information.

Important Addresses and Numbers

Visitor Information

At the south end of the town's main plaza, the **Prescott Chamber of Commerce** (117 W. Goodwin St., 86303, ☎ 520/445–2000 or 800/266–7534) provides visitors with many useful maps and brochures, including the excellent "Historic Downtown Prescott: Walking Tour Guide" and "Prescott's Driving Tour Guide." It is open weekdays 9–5, weekends 10–4.

Some information about the Verde Valley is available from the Chamber of Commerce offices in **Jerome** (Box K, Jerome 86331, ☎ 520/634–2900), **Clarkdale** (Town Hall, Box 308, Clarkdale 86321, ☎ 520/634–8700), **Cottonwood** (1010 S. Main St., Cottonwood 86326, ☎ 520/634–7593), and **Camp Verde** (435 S. Main St., Camp Verde 86322, ☎ 520/567–9294).

The **Sedona–Oak Creek Canyon Chamber of Commerce,** at the corner of North Highway 89A and Forest Road (Box 478, Sedona 86339, ☎ 520/282–7722 or 800/288–7336), is staffed with knowledgeable residents who can guide you to points of special interest. It's open Monday to Saturday 9–5, Sunday 9–3.

Emergencies

Call 911 to reach the **fire department, police,** and **emergency medical services.**

HOSPITALS AND DOCTORS

The **Sedona Medical Center** has a doctor on call 24 hours. *75 Kallof Pl., ☎ 520/282–1285. Walk-in hrs weekdays 8–5, Sat. 9–2.*

LATE-NIGHT PHARMACIES

In Sedona, **Walgreen's** (180 Coffee Pot Dr., ☎ 520/282–2528) stays open until 9 PM Monday–Saturday, until 8 on Sunday; **Payless** (2350 W. Hwy. 89A, ☎ 520/282–9577) closes at 9 PM every day except Sunday, when it closes at 8.

FLAGSTAFF AND ENVIRONS

Few visitors slow down long enough to explore Flagstaff, a town of 42,000, known locally as "Flag." Most stop only to spend the night at one of the town's many motels before making the last leg of the trip to the Grand Canyon, 80 miles north. But the city, set against a lovely backdrop of pine forests and the snowcapped San Francisco Peaks, retains a frontier flavor downtown and is home to the excellent Museum of Northern Arizona, the Riordan mansion, the Lowell Observatory, and other interesting sights. Festivals celebrating summer often fill the streets with parades and its sidewalks with Native American art exhibits and crafts sales. Flag also makes a good base for day-trips north, east, and south in Arizona: to the Grand Canyon (*see* Chapter 2), to Native American ruins (*see below and* Tours 1, 3, and 4 *in* Chapter 3, The Northeast) and current-day Navajo and Hopi reservations (*see* Tours 2 and 3 *in* Chapter 3), and to Petrified Forest National Park and Painted Desert (*see* Tour 1 *in* Chapter 3).

Flagstaff has more fast-food outlets per permanent resident than most cities do, no doubt because of the incredible demand for it: Two major interstate highways crisscross the town; thousands of tourists drive through on the way to the Grand Canyon; other thousands, of students attending Northern Arizona University, reside here. And many Native Americans come in from nearby reservations. Of course, there are other much better restaurants downtown, and the city is packed with motels, although there are no major hotels or resorts. Traffic to the Grand Canyon is heavy all year, but in summer it skyrockets, increasing the number of overnight visitors. During that time of year, the streets are also filled with Phoenix residents seeking relief from the desert heat.

Phoenicians also come to Flagstaff in winter to ski at the Arizona Snowbowl, a small ski area about 15 miles northeast of town among the San Francisco Peaks. Accommodation rates are low at this time of year, making winter visits an excellent option for downhill and cross-country enthusiasts. At any time of the year, temperatures in Flagstaff are approximately 20°F cooler than in Phoenix. It's wise to reserve a room ahead of time in Flagstaff, and during the summer months, it's essential.

Exploring

Central Flagstaff

Numbers in the margin correspond to points of interest on the Flagstaff map.

The **downtown historic district** offers a glimpse of Flagstaff in its prime, with some excellent examples of late Victorian and early Art Deco architecture. Allowed to become somewhat seedy over the years, downtown is currently undergoing a major restoration under the auspices of the national Main Street organization. A walking-tour map of the area, prepared by the Arizona Historical Society, is available at the **Visitors Center** (*see* Important Addresses and Numbers *in* Flagstaff Essentials, *below*), now in the Tudor Revival–style Santa Fe Depot and an excellent place to begin the tour. Highlights include the Monte Vista Hotel (*see* Lodging, *below*) and the gabled-roof Orpheum Theatre. You may notice a lot of structures that bear the name Babbitt, after one of Flagstaff's wealthiest founding families. Former Arizona governor and current Secretary of the Interior Bruce Babbitt is just the latest member of the family to wield power and influence. This is also the part of town in which the most interesting shops are concentrated (*see* Shopping, *below*); it's fun to stroll around the area and poke around in stores selling everything from sporting goods to Native American crafts.

TIME OUT Chili-pepper strings, a neon cactus, and a pastel mural all add to the upbeat atmosphere at **Café Olé** (119 S. San Francisco St., ☎ 520/774-8272), a small, family-run restaurant. Vegetarian green-chile-and-cheese tamales and the best guacamole in town are among the Mexican specialties here. Part art gallery, part bakery, and totally hip, **Café Express** (16 N. San Francisco St., ☎ 520/774–0541) serves up heaping portions of tasty food that's good for you: Mediterranean salads, tempeh burgers, pita pizzas, and (maybe not-so-healthy) chocolate-chip cookies.

② To reach **Lowell Observatory,** less than 2 miles from downtown, drive west on Route 66 (which resumes its former name, Santa Fe Avenue, before it merges into Mars Hill Road). This scientific institution was founded in 1894 by Boston businessman, author, and scientist Percival Lowell, who studied the planet Mars from here. His predictions of the existence of a ninth planet led to the discovery of Pluto at Lowell in 1930 by Clyde Tombaugh. V.M. Slipher's observations here between 1912 and 1920 led to the theory of the expanding universe.

The 6,500-square-foot Steele Visitor Center, opened in 1994, hosts exhibits, a lecture hall, and a gift shop; a "Tools of the Astronomer" display explains what professional stargazers do. During the day, the staff welcomes guests and offers slide lectures and tours. There are several interactive exhibits (simple, but interesting) for children, who will especially enjoy the Pluto Walk, a scaled-down version of our solar system that is designed for exploring.

On different evenings every month except January, weather permitting, the public is invited to peer through the 24-inch Clark telescope; viewings through the Pluto telescope have also been initiated recently. The greatest number of viewings (four a week) are offered from June through August; call ahead for a schedule. The observatory dome is open and unheated—any change in temperature would affect the telescope lens—so dress for an outdoor rather than an indoor activity. *1400 W. Mars Hill Rd., ☎ 520/774–2096. ☞ $2.50 adults, $1 children 5–17. ☉ Visitor center and night viewing hrs change seasonally; call ahead.*

③ A unique artifact of Flagstaff's logging heyday, **Riordan State Historic Park,** near Northern Arizona University, is a must-see. Its centerpiece is a mansion built in 1904 for Michael and Timothy Riordan, lumber-baron brothers who married two sisters. The 13,300-square-foot, 40-room log-and-stone structure—designed by Charles Whittlesley, who was also responsible for the El Tovar Hotel at the Grand Canyon—contains a good deal of furniture by Gustav Stickley, father of the American Arts and Crafts design movement. Fascinating details abound; one room holds "Paul Bunyan's shoes," a two-foot-long pair of boots made by Timothy in his workshop. Everything on display—from books to family photos and clothes—is original to the house, half of which was occupied by members of the family until 1986. The mansion may be explored on a guided tour only. Special evening tours given during Halloween week are very popular; they're limited to groups of 20, so book at least a month in advance if you want to be spooked. *1300 Riordan Ranch St., ☎ 520/779–4395. ☞ $3 adults, $2 children 12–17. ☉ Mid-May–mid-Sept. daily 8–5, with tours at 9, 10, 11, 1, 2, 3, and 4; mid-Sept.–mid-May, daily 11–5, with tours at noon, 1, 2, 3, and 4. Closed Dec. 24–25.*

④ Riordan State Park lies near **Northern Arizona University.** Go two blocks south on Milton Road, then make a left onto University Drive. After about a half mile, turn right on San Francisco Street and continue to the university's **observatory.** The observatory and 24-inch telescope were built in 1952 by Dr. Arthur Adel, who had been a scientist at Lowell Observatory until he joined the college faculty as a professor of mathematics. His work on infrared astronomy pioneered research

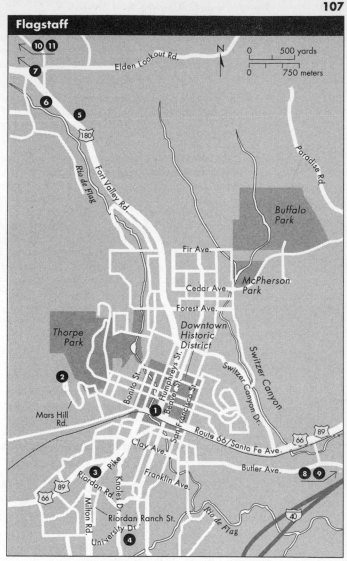

Flagstaff

into molecules that absorb light passing through the Earth's atmosphere. Today's studies of our planet's shrinking ozone layer rely on some of Dr. Adel's early work. Visitors to the observatory—which houses one of the largest telescopes that the public is allowed to move and manipulate—are usually hosted by friendly students and faculty members of the university's Department of Physics and Astronomy.

Public viewings take place every clear Friday night from 7 PM to 10 PM. Tours for individuals and small groups can be arranged any day except Friday by calling at least 24 hours in advance. *Northern Arizona Campus Observatory, Dept. of Physics and Astronomy, S. San Francisco St.,* ☎ *520/523–7170.* ☛ *Free.*

Flagstaff Museums and the Arizona Snowbowl
In a wooded residential section at the northwest end of town, the Pioneer Historical Museum, Coconino Center for the Arts, and the Mu-

seum of Northern Arizona give visitors an introduction to the natural and cultural history of the area. They're all on the way to the Arizona Snowbowl, which is worth visiting even in the summertime, when a ski lift to the top of the San Francisco Peaks affords marvelous views of the area.

From downtown, drive north on Humphreys Street, which turns into U.S. 180 after veering a block to the left. Once you're on U.S. 180, you'll soon see a large brown sign on the right-hand side of the road for the Pioneer Historical Museum and the Coconino Center for the Arts.

 The first building as you enter the Fort Valley Park complex is the **Pioneer Historical Museum,** operated by the Arizona Historical Society in a volcanic rock building constructed in 1908—Coconino County's first hospital for the poor. You can still see one of the depressingly small patients' rooms, an old iron lung, and a reconstructed doctor's office, but most of the displays touch on more cheerful aspects of Flagstaff history—for example, road signs and children's toys. The museum hosts a folk-crafts festival on the Fourth of July, where you can watch traditional tradespeople, such as blacksmiths, weavers, spinners, quilters, and candle makers, at work. Their crafts, and those of other local artisans, are sold in the museum's gift shop, a tiny space filled with teddy bears, dolls, hand-dipped candles, and hand-stitched quilts. *2340 N. Fort Valley Rd.,* ☎ *520/774–6272.* ☛ *Suggested donation: $1 per individual, $3 per family.* ✹ *Mon.–Sat. 9–5.*

Walk a few hundred feet up a gentle hill to reach the **Coconino Center for the Arts,** a nonprofit community center that puts on two major annual arts-and-crafts festivals (*see* The Arts and Nightlife, *below*) and hosts exhibits, performing arts events, and educational programs throughout the year. A gallery features the work of local artists, from photographers to sculptors and lithographers, on a rotating basis; write or phone for a calendar of events. Warning: The gift shop, filled with handcrafted jewelry, pottery, and posters by featured artists, can be detrimental to your pocketbook. All proceeds go to the center, though, so you're shopping for a worthy cause—and there's no tax on your purchases. *2300 N. Fort Valley Rd., Box 296, Flagstaff 86002,* ☎ *520/779–6921.* ☛ *Free.* ✹ *Apr.–Sept., Tues.–Sun. 10–5; Oct.–Mar., Tues.–Sat. 10–5. Closed Easter, Thanksgiving, and Dec. 24–early Jan.*

When you leave the complex, turn right out of the parking lot and drive **6** 1 mile northwest on U.S. 180; on your left you'll see the **Museum of Northern Arizona,** a large stone building shaded with trees. Founded in 1928, the museum is now respected worldwide for its research and for its collections centering on the natural and cultural history of the Colorado Plateau; only 1% of its vast holdings on the archaeology, ethnology, geology, biology, and fine arts of the region is on display at any given time. Among the permanent exhibitions are an extensive collection of Navajo rugs as well as an authentic Hopi kiva (men's ceremonial chamber). Every summer, the museum hosts exhibits and sales by Native American artists, whose wares are also sold in the museum gift shop (*see* The Arts *in* Arts and Nightlife, *below*).

Two interesting outdoor features are a life-zone exhibit, which shows the changing vegetation in the area from the bottom of the Grand Canyon to the highest peak in Flagstaff (the equivalent of a trip from Mexico to Canada), and a nature trail that heads down across a small stream into a canyon and up into an aspen grove (open only in summer).

Two galleries—one devoted to the biology and the other to the geology of the area—opened in 1992. The latter includes a cast of the dilophosaurus; this medium-size carnivorous dinosaur, unique to northern Arizona, roamed the area back when much of it was swampland.

The museum is not particularly child-oriented, but both of the above galleries include some hands-on displays. Docent-led tours are available for individuals or groups, but appointments must be made at least two weeks in advance. In addition, the museum's education department sponsors excellent tours of the area and some as far away as New Mexico and California (*see* Guided Tours *in* North-Central Arizona Essentials, *below*). *3001 N. Fort Valley Rd.,* ☎ *520/774–5213.* ☞ *$4 adults, $3 senior citizens over 55, $2 children and students with ID.* ☉ *Daily 9–5. Closed major holidays.*

❼ Five miles farther along the same road is the turnoff for the **Arizona Snowbowl.** The Fort Valley Lodge to the right is a good place to stop for groceries and clean rest rooms, as well as for information about skiing and other recreational opportunities at the Snowbowl; it's open in the daytime only. If there's a crowd visiting the ski area or a recent heavy snow that makes travel difficult, park here and ride the shuttle to the top; it runs continuously and costs $4 per person round-trip.

After you leave U.S. 180, it's another 7 paved miles on Snowbowl Road to the **Arizona Snowbowl Skyride,** which takes you through the Coconino National Forest to a height of 11,500 feet in 25 minutes. From this vantage point, you can see up to 70 miles; views include the North Rim of the Grand Canyon. There's a lodge nearby with a restaurant and bar. ☎ *520/779–1951.* ☞ *$9 adults, $6.50 senior citizens, $5 children 6–12. Group discounts are available.* ☉ *The ride operates daily mid-June–Labor Day, weekends only (weather permitting) Labor Day–mid-Oct. Operating hrs and prices may change; call ahead.*

There is plenty of **hiking** here in Arizona's alpine tundra, where more than 80 species of plants grow on the upper elevations of the San Francisco Peaks. The habitat is fragile, so hikers are asked to stay on established trails (and there are lots of them).

The Humphreys Peak Trail is 9 miles round-trip, with a vertical climb of 3,843 feet to the summit of Arizona's highest mountain (12,643 feet). Those who don't want a long hike will be well rewarded if they do just the first mile of the 8-mile-long Kachina Trail; completely flat, this route is surrounded by huge stands of aspen and offers fantastic vistas. It's particularly worthwhile in fall, when changing leaves paint the landscape shades of yellow, russet, and amber. All trails are well marked and maintained by the **Coconino National Forest** (☎ 520/527–3600). The altitude here will make even the hardiest hikers breathe a little harder, so individuals with cardiac or respiratory problems should be cautious of overexertion.

In winter the Arizona Snowbowl offers an average of 250 inches of snow and 32 **downhill skiing** trails of varying difficulty (30% beginner, 40% intermediate, and 30% advanced). Enthusiasts who favor the challenging slopes of Colorado's Rockies might find the Snowbowl a bit disappointing. There are a couple of good bump runs, but it's better for skiers of beginning or moderate ability. Senior citizens ages 65 and over pay only $10, and children ages 7 and under ski for free; all-day lift tickets for adults are $30. Half-day discounts are available, and group-lesson packages (including two hours of instruction, an all-day lift ticket, and equipment rental) are a good buy at $46.

Many Flagstaff motels offer ski packages, including transportation to the Snowbowl. Write or call the **Arizona Snowbowl Ski Area** (Box 40,

Flagstaff 86002, ☎ 520/779–1951 or 800/828–7285) for more information. For the current snow report, call 520/779–4577.

East of Flagstaff

The sites below are marked on the Flagstaff and North-Central Arizona maps.

The area east of Flagstaff is often neglected by visitors to the region because, regardless of its beauty or historical significance, it gets overshadowed by the Grand Canyon. But traveling east has its unique rewards. If you don't have enough time to do everything, take a quick drive to Walnut Canyon—only about 15 minutes out of town—and stay in this lovely spot for as long as you can.

★ ⑧ **Walnut Canyon National Monument** (7½ mi east of Flagstaff at exit 204 off I–40, then 3 mi south) consists of a group of spectacular cliff-dwelling homes constructed by the Sinagua people who lived and farmed in and around the canyon starting around AD 700. The more than 300 dwellings here were built between 1125 and 1250 and left, like those at so many settlements in Arizona and New Mexico, around 1300. The Sinagua traded far and wide with other Native Americans, including people at Wupatki (*see* San Francisco Volcanic Field, *below*). Even Macaw feathers, which would have come from tribes in what is now Mexico, have been excavated in the canyon. The area wasn't explored by Europeans until 1883, when early Flagstaff settlers shamelessly looted the site for pots and "treasure." Woodrow Wilson declared the site a national monument in 1915, which began a 30-year process of stabilizing the ruins.

Walnut Canyon is a fascinating place to visit, in part because of the opportunity to enter the dwellings and feel ancient life at close range. A number of the Sinagua homes are in near-perfect condition, in spite of all the looting, because of the dry, hot climate and the protection of overhanging cliffs. You can reach them by descending 185 feet on the mile-long, stepped Island Trail, which starts at the visitor center. As you follow the trail, stop occasionally to look across the canyon for other dwellings not accessible on the path.

Island Trail takes about an hour to complete at a normal pace. The entrance to the trail closes one hour before the park does. Those with health concerns should opt for the easier Rim Trail (a half-mile route that most people complete in about a half hour) that has overlooks from which dwellings can be viewed as well as an excavated, reconstructed pit house. Attractive picnic areas dot the grounds and line the roads leading to the park. Park service guides conduct tours on Wednesday, Saturday, and Sunday from Memorial Day through Labor Day. Visitors are permitted to enter about two dozen ruins. *Walnut Canyon Rd.*, ☎ 520/526–3367. ☛ *$2 per person entering by foot or bicycle, $4 per vehicle.* ☉ *Daily 8–5; hrs extended during summer months.*

⑨ To reach **Meteor Crater** from Walnut Canyon, drive about 33 miles farther east on I–40; get off at Exit 233, then go 6 miles south on Meteor Crater Road. This natural phenomenon, set in a privately owned and run park, is impressive if for no other reason than its sheer size. A hole in the ground 600 feet deep, nearly a mile across, and more than 3 miles in circumference, Meteor Crater is large enough to accommodate the Washington Monument or 20 football fields. It was created when a meteorite came hurtling through space at a speed of 43,000 miles per hour and crashed here some 49,000 years ago. The area looks so much like the surface of the moon that NASA made it one of the official training sites for the Project Apollo astronauts.

Visitors can't descend into the crater because of the efforts of its owners to maintain its condition—scientists consider this to be the best-preserved crater on Earth—but guided rim tours, given every hour on the hour, weather permitting, afford visitors a bird's-eye view of the hole. Two short, rather corny films, which play every half hour, detail the history of the crater and of astronaut training here. A small snack bar sells soft drinks, coffee, and sandwiches. Rock hounds will enjoy the Lapidary Shop, filled with raw specimens from the area as well as with jewelry made from native stones. *Meteor Crater Rd., ☎ 520/289– 2362. For information, write or call administrative offices, 603 N. Beaver St., Suite C, Flagstaff 86001, ☎ 520/774–8350. ✏ $7 adults, $6 senior citizens, $2 children 6–17. ☉ May 16–Sept. 14, daily 6–6; Sept. 15–May 15, daily 8–5.*

San Francisco Volcanic Field

North of Flagstaff, the San Francisco Volcanic Field encompasses 2,000 square miles of fascinating geological phenomena—ancient volcanoes, cinder cones, and valleys carved by water and ice, and the San Francisco Peaks themselves, some of which soar to almost 13,000 feet—as well as some of the most extensive Native American ruins in the Southwest. If you have any time at all, don't miss Sunset Crater and Wupatki. These national monuments are not only extremely interesting but can be explored in relative solitude during a large part of the year. The area is short on services, so fill up on gas and consider taking along a picnic. There are plenty of lovely spots for lunch along the way. A good source for hiking and camping information in this area is the Peaks Ranger Station (5075 N. U.S. 89, ☎ 520/526–0866). If you do camp, do not pitch your tent in a low-lying area, where dangerous flash floods can literally wipe you out (*see* Lodging *in* The Gold Guide's Smart Travel Tips for more information).

★ ⑩ To get to **Sunset Crater Volcano National Monument,** take Santa Fe Avenue east of Flagstaff to U.S. 89, and drive north for about 12 miles. Turn right onto the road marked Sunset Crater—it's another 2 miles from here to the visitor center.

Sunset Crater, a cinder cone that rises some 1,000 feet into the air, was an active volcano 900 years ago. The final eruption contained iron and sulfur, which gives the rim of the crater its glow and thus its name, Sunset. You can walk around the base, but you can't descend into the huge, fragile cone. If you take the Lava Flow Trail, a half-hour, mile-long, self-guided walk, you'll have a good view of the evidence of the volcano's fiery power: lava formations and holes in the rock where volcanic gases vented to the surface. Three smaller cones to the southeast were formed at the same time and along the same fissure.

If you're interested in hiking a volcano, head to **Lenox Crater,** about a mile east of the visitor center. It's 280 feet to the top of the cinder cone. Wear closed, sturdy shoes if you plan to do this; the cinder is soft and crumbly, without vegetation. From **O'Leary Peak,** 5 miles from the visitor center on Forest Route 545A, there are great views of the San Francisco Peaks, the Painted Desert, and beyond; the road is unpaved and rutted, however, so it's advisable to take only high-clearance vehicles. In addition, there's a gate, about halfway along the route, that's usually closed—in which case, it's a steep 2½-mile hike to the top. *Rte. 3, Box 149, ☎ 520/556–7042. ✏ $4 per car, $2 to enter on foot or by nonmotorized vehicle; admission includes Wupatki National Monu-*

ment (see below). ☉ *Memorial Day–Labor Day, daily 8–6; rest of yr, daily 8–6.*

★ Drive 20 miles north of the Sunset Crater visitor center along the unmarked Sunset Loop Road to get to the entrance of **Wupatki National Monument.** En route, parts of the Painted Desert are visible in the distance. The immediately surrounding landscape is starkly beautiful, with little vegetation. In summer, rangers give interpretive lectures on the history of the region.

Some 2,700 identified sites contain archaeological evidence of Native American settlement in this area. Families from the Sinagua and other ancestral Puebloans are believed to have lived together in harmony here, farming and trading with one another and with those who passed through their "city." The eruption of Sunset Crater, 20 miles away, may have caused migration to this area—and may have disrupted the settlement more than once around 1064. The earliest inhabitants are believed to have settled here around AD 600, leaving the pueblo by about 1300.

The site for which the national monument was named, the **Wupatki** (meaning tall house in Hopi), was originally three stories high, built above a large, unexplored system of underground fissures. The structure had almost 100 rooms and a large, open ball court—evidence in itself of southwestern trade with Mesoamerican tribes for whom ball games were a central ritual. Next to the ball court is a blowhole, a geologic phenomenon in which air is forced upward by underground pressure; scientists speculate that early inhabitants may have attached some spiritual significance to the many blowholes in the region.

Other ruins to visit at the national monument are **Wukoki, Lomaki,** and the **Citadel,** a pueblo that sits on a knoll above a limestone sink. Although the largest remnants of Native American settlements at Wupatki National Monument are open to the public, other sites are off-limits to casual visitors. Permits are available from the park service for limited access beyond the open areas, but rules regarding entering closed sites are strictly enforced. If you are interested in an in-depth tour of the area, consider taking a ranger-led overnight hike to the **Crack-in-the-Rock Ruin.** The 14-mile trek (round-trip) covers areas marked by ancient petroglyphs and dotted with well-preserved ruins. Anyone who is interested should contact the rangers for details. There are a limited number of trips, conducted in April and October; it's best to call in February and August if you'd like to take part in the lottery for one of the 100 available places on these hikes. The cost is $25. *HC 33, Box 444A, Flagstaff 86004,* ☎ *520/556–7040.* ☛ *$4 per vehicle; $2 to enter by foot, bicycle, motorcycle, or nonmotorized vehicle;* ☛ *collected at Sunset Crater.* ☉ *Daily 8–5; hrs may be extended in summer.*

Between the Wupatki and Citadel ruins, the **Doney Mountain** affords 360° views of the Painted Desert and the San Francisco Volcanic Fields. It's a perfect spot for a sunset picnic.

What to See and Do with Children

Small children should enjoy the **Grand Canyon Deer Farm,** 25 miles west of Flagstaff on I-40, at Exit 171 (8 miles east of Williams). Visitors can pet and feed the deer, including the tiny fawns born every June and July. There are also pygmy goats, llamas, and other animals to pet. *100 Deer Farm Rd., Williams 86046,* ☎ *520/635–4073.* ☛ *$4.75 adults, $3.50 senior citizens, $2.50 children 3–13.* ☉ *Mar.–May, daily 9–dusk;*

June–Aug., daily 8–dusk; Sept.–Oct., daily 9–dusk; Nov.–Feb., daily 10–5 in good weather. Closed Thanksgiving, Dec. 1.

School-age children will be impressed by **Meteor Crater** (*see* Exploring, *above*).

Shopping

Flagstaff's prime shopping area is downtown. Even if you're not looking for anything in particular, it's fun to stroll along San Francisco Street and Route 66 where most of the interesting shops—many in historic buildings—are concentrated. For fine arts and crafts—everything from ceramics and stained glass to weaving and painting—visit the **Artists Gallery** (17 N. San Francisco St., ☎ 520/773–0985), a cooperative that carries the work of more than 30 local artists. Locals go to **Four Winds Traders** (118 W. Santa Fe Ave., ☎ 520/774–1067) for good buys on both pawned and new Native American jewelry. **Winter Sun Trading Company** (107 N. San Francisco St., ☎ 520/774–2884) carries a full range of medicinal herbs, along with jewelry and crafts, in a soothing New Age atmosphere. **McGaugh's Newsstand** (24 N. San Francisco St., ☎ 520/774–2131) is the place to come for international newspapers and books on any topic you can think of; even nonsmokers will enjoy the aroma of the pipe tobacco sold in the back. A bit north of the town center, the **Carriage House** (413 N. San Francisco St., ☎ 520/774–1337) is a collection of 19 antiques shops that offer old clothes, furniture, fine china, and jewelry; **Down Under** (☎ 520/774–6677), a pretty tearoom with an Aussie accent, has the space next door. The **Coconino Arts Center** gift shop (*see* Flagstaff Museums and the Arizona Snowbowl, *above*) carries high-quality art posters and crafts.

Don't worry if you've come to town without all your hiking supplies. You can pick up any sporting-goods items you might be missing at **The Edge** (12 E. Aspen Ave., ☎ 520/774–4775). The **Flagstaff Mall** (4650 N. U.S. 89, ☎ 520/526–4827) is just east of town off Exit 201 of I–40. Small by most standards, this mall has the greatest number of department and specialty stores in the area, including Dillards, Sears, and JCPenney. It's a good place for travelers who need camping gear, car-repair items, or warm clothing for the area's cool nights.

Sports and the Outdoors

Biking

A map of the Urban Trails System, available at the Flagstaff Visitors Center (*see* Flagstaff Essentials, *below*), details biking and hiking options in the area.

Camping

For a full listing of campgrounds around Flagstaff, consult the *Arizona Camping and Campgrounds Guide,* available from the **Arizona Office of Tourism** (*see* Important Contacts A to Z *in* The Gold Guide). Reservations for many of the campgrounds in the area are handled by **Mistix** (☎ 800/365–2267), but, again, choose a campground before you call in order to make the most of the automated phone system.

In **Coconino National Forest** near Flagstaff (ranger's ☎ 520/527–3600), the campgrounds near Mormon Lake and Lake Mary—including Pinegrove, Lakeview, Forked Pine, Double Springs, and Dairy Springs—are popular to the point of overcrowding in summer.

If you're camping in winter, remember that this area gets quite cold, with frequent snowstorms. In summer, temperatures can dip to 40°F at night and climb to 90°F in daytime.

CAUTION: Be careful not to camp in low-lying areas, which are subject to extremely dangerous flash flooding in sudden summer rains (*see* Lodging *in* The Gold Guide's Smart Travel Tips for more information).

Golf

In addition to many private clubs in the area, golfers will find semiprivate courses, which accept a limited number of nonmembers, as well as public courses. The best club open to the public in the Flagstaff vicinity is the Elden Hill Course at the **Continental Country Club** (2380 N. Oakmont Dr., ☏ 520/526–5125).

Hiking

In the Coconino National Forest at **Arizona Snowbowl,** there are numerous trails short and long in the state's highest alpine area (*see* Exploring, *above*). Just north of Flagstaff, but still in town, the **Peaks Ranger Station** (5075 N. U.S. 89, ☏ 520/527–3630) has excellent hiking and recreational guides. And for general hiking maps and camping tips, contact the **U.S. Forest Service** (2323 Greenlaw La., Flagstaff 86002, ☏ 520/527–3600).

CAUTION: Be sure to bring plenty of water with you when hiking and drink often. Dehydration can become a life-threatening condition. (*See* Hiking *in* The Gold Guide's Smart Travel Tips for more information.)

Horseback Riding

Spring, summer, and fall are the best times of the year to ride in this area. The wranglers at **Hitchin' Post Stables** (448 Lake Mary Rd., ☏ 520/774–1719 or 520/774–7131) lead rides into Walnut Canyon and have horseback or horse-drawn wagon rides with sunset barbecues.

Skiing

The ski season usually starts in mid-November and ends in mid-April. A good option for downhill skiers is the **Arizona Snowbowl** (*see* Exploring, *above*). Cross-country skiers can find well-groomed trails near Flagstaff at the **Mormon Lake Ski Center** (28 mi southeast of Flagstaff by way of Lake Mary Rd., Mormon Lake, ☏ 520/354–2240) and **Flagstaff Nordic Center** (14 mi northwest of Flagstaff via Hwy. 180 North, ☏ 520/779–1951), operated by Arizona Snowbowl.

Dining and Lodging

You'll find many comfortable motels in Flagstaff (all the familiar U.S. chains are represented here) but no real luxury. Prices are highest in summer. As for dining, there are interesting and occasionally unique restaurants where you will find very pleasant, and in some cases elegant, meals. By city ordinance, all restaurants in Flagstaff forbid smoking.

Price categories are the same as those in North-Central Arizona Dining, *above*.

Dining

$$–$$$ **Chez Marc Bistro.** This classic French restaurant, run by the Cannes-born former head chef of L'Auberge de Sedona resort, is set in a 1911 mansion built by the influential Babbitt family. In three pretty Country French–style dining rooms you can enjoy such entrées as blackened *ahi* tuna atop pink and green lentils or roast quail with elephant garlic and lobster mushrooms. The setting is romantic and the food gen-

erally good, but service can be unsophisticated. ✗ *503 Humphreys St.*,
☎ *520/774–1343. AE, D, DC, MC, V. Closed Wed. No lunch during
low season.*

$$–$$$ **Cottage Place.** Another unexpectedly elegant spot in a town known for
hearty food and drive-through service, this cozy restaurant in a 50-year-
old cottage has intimate dining rooms decorated in traditional style,
with fresh flowers and candles. New owners have managed to keep
locals who were loyal to the old regime happy with a menu that strays
only slightly from Continental to include some classic American dishes,
such as charbroiled lamb chops. Try their artichoke chicken breast or
sautéed scallops in phyllo crust. Dinner includes both soup and salad,
but save room for desserts like fresh apple pie. ✗ *126 W. Cottage Ave.*,
☎ *520/774–8431. AE, MC, V. Closed Mon. No lunch.*

$$ **Brix Grill & Wine Bar.** Tucked away in a nondescript strip mall near
★   the university, Brix is probably the most interesting new restaurant in
town. Innovative Southwestern cuisine and a nice selection of wines
by the glass are served in an appropriately pared-down (but comfort-
able) room. Entrées, which change daily, might include grilled polenta
with hazelnut pesto and mozzarella, or rack of New Zealand lamb with
rosemary and red-wine sauce; everything, including the excellent breads
and desserts, is prepared on the premises. The owners also have a deli,
wine shop, and coffee bar next door. ✗ *801 S. Milton Rd.*, ☎ *520/779–
5117. AE, DC, MC, V.*

$$ **Horsemen Lodge & Restaurant.** Three miles north of Flagstaff Mall,
in a ranch-style stone building decorated with hunting trophies (the
furry kind that stare at you during dinner), this restaurant is very
"Flagstaff," reflecting the blend of Native American and frontier cultures that shaped the area. The knotty-pine beams and huge stone fireplace make this a perfect place to spend a snowy evening. Traditional
American fare is prepared without pretense for hearty appetites. ✗ *8500
N. U.S. 89*, ☎ *520/526–2655. MC, V. Closed Sun. May–Oct., Sun.
and Mon. Nov.–Apr. No lunch.*

$$ **Sakura Restaurant.** The oddness of finding a good sushi bar in Flagstaff
★   is doubled by the fact that the only other entrées at Sakura are pre-
pared *teppan* (Japanese grill) style. If your dining companion doesn't
like raw fish, you'll be eating yours at a large table accompanied by a
grill chef's pyrotechnics. That said, the fish, flown in every other day
from the West Coast, is excellent; spicy sushi-style tuna salad will
knock your socks off; and even if you haven't set foot in a Benihana
in years, you'll probably enjoy well-seasoned, large portions of steak
or seafood with vegetables being flipped in front of you. ✗ *1175 W.
Hwy. 66*, ☎ *520/773–9118. AE, D, DC, MC, V. No lunch Sun.*

$–$$ **Buster's Restaurant.** At lunchtime, families and students from nearby
Arizona State University (ASU) frequent the comfortable booths and
tables of this popular restaurant. The menu includes fresh seafood, homemade soups, salads, giant burgers, and mesquite-grilled steaks. Try the
lahvosh appetizer—a giant cracker heaped with a choice of toppings
ranging from smoked salmon to mushrooms—or Caesar salad with
grilled Cajun chicken. Upscale single professionals and skiers crowd
the bar at night. ✗ *1800 S. Milton Rd.*, ☎ *520/774–5155. AE, D, DC,
MC, V.*

$–$$ **Pasto.** This downtown Italian restaurant proved so popular with a young
crowd that, little more than a year after it opened, it took over another
historic building next door. The expanded digs are still intimate, and
the food is as good and plentiful as before. Spaghetti with meatballs
and marinara sauce standards appear on the menu along with more
innovative fare like artichoke orzo, and there's a nice selection of beer,

soft drinks, wine, and coffee. A courtyard in the back, tucked away among higher buildings, has a romantic urban feel. ✗ *19 E. Aspen St.,* ☎ *520/779–1937. MC, V.*

$ Café Espress. A wholesome, natural food, all-day restaurant, Café Espress serves a largely vegetarian menu (red meat is excluded). Hearty stir-fried vegetables, pasta dishes, daily soups, tasty fish or chicken specials, delicious homemade deserts, and a friendly atmosphere (work of local artists hangs on the walls) all come at prices that will make you feel good, too. ✗ *16 N. San Francisco St.,* ☎ *520/774–0541. MC, V.* ⊘ *Mon.–Thurs. 7 AM–10 PM, Fri.–Sat 7 AM–11 PM.*

$ Kachina Cafe. Tables in this family-style Mexican restaurant are Formica and chairs are vinyl, but the food is well-prepared, spicy, and served in copious portions. Their combination plates are a real bargain: you can get an enchilada, taco, and tostada with beans and rice, a *sopapilla* (fried dough coated with powdered sugar), plus coffee for $6. There are terrific breakfast specials too, and the variety of Mexican and American beer is unusually large. ✗ *2220 E. Route 66,* ☎ *520/556–0363; and Kachina Downtown, 522 E. Route 66,* ☎ *520/779–1944. MC, V. Closed Tues. and Wed.; downtown location open daily.*

$ Macy's. Students, skiers, new and aging hippies, and just about everyone who likes good coffee jams into Macy's for the best cup in town. Beans are roasted on the premises in a huge red machine that dominates one wall of this bustling spot. Coffee—including espresso and cappuccino—is the focus, but good fresh pasta, soup, and salads are also offered for lunch and early dinner. ✗ *14 S. Beaver St.,* ☎ *520/774–2243. No credit cards.* ⊘ *Sun.–Wed. 6 AM–7 PM, Thurs.–Sat. 6 AM–8 PM.*

$ Salsa Brava. This cheerful Mexican restaurant, with light-wood booths and bold, colorful designs, eschews heavy Sonoran-style fare in favor of the grilled dishes found in Guadalajara (determined artery-cloggers will still find enough cheese-smothered items on the menu). The fish tacos are particularly popular, and this place has the only salsa bar in town. One annoyance: After the first bowl, additional tortilla chips cost extra. ✗ *1800 S. Milton Rd.,* ☎ *520/774–1083. AE, MC, V.*

$ Stromboli's. Nicer-than-average decor raises Stromboli's above pizza
★ joint status, but the pizza oven is still the biggest draw. Many come for the huge calzones, which, as with pizza, you can have with any of 25 fresh, tempting ingredients. Of course, you may prefer pasta, like linguine with basil pesto cream sauce. If you're very hungry, consider the delicious spinach dip appetizer, which comes with tortilla chips, odd as that may seem in an Italian place. Reservations aren't accepted, but there is a call-ahead waiting list. ✗ *1435 S. Milton,* ☎ *520/773–1960. AE, D, MC, V.*

Lodging

BED-AND-BREAKFAST

$$–$$$ Inn at Four Ten. B&Bs are a nice alternative to the chain motels in
★ Flagstaff, and this one offers a quiet but convenient downtown setting. All of the accommodations in this beautifully restored 1907 structure are spacious suites with private baths; some offer private entrances, minikitchens, and fireplaces. The new owners have done extensive remodeling and added such luxurious touches as Jacuzzi baths in two rooms. The full breakfasts are delicious as well as health-conscious; in the afternoon, the hosts bring out fresh-baked cookies. There's no smoking inside. ⊡ *410 N. Leroux St., Flagstaff 86001,* ☎ *520/774–0088 or 800/774–2008. 8 suites (1 accessible to travelers with disabilities). AE, MC, V.*

HOTELS AND MOTELS

$$ AmeriSuites. Look elsewhere if you want character, but if you're seeking mod-cons in a pleasant, convenient setting, you can't go wrong here. Rooms with two phones, a well-lighted desk, free local phone calls—this new property was designed for business travelers, but leisure goers won't mind a 26-inch stereo TV/VCR or sink, minifridge, and microwave. A morning newspaper and nice Continental buffet are included in the room rate. ⊡ *2455 S. Beulah Blvd., Flagstaff 86001, ☎ 520/774–8042 or 800/833–1516,* ℻ *520/774–5524. Hot tub, guest laundry. AE, D, DC, MC, V.*

$$ Best Western Woodlands Plaza Hotel. This upscale link in the Best Western chain is the glitziest accommodation in town—which isn't saying much in Flagstaff. A brass-and-marble lobby, although tasteful, is somehow oddly eclectic. But the hotel is conveniently located near downtown and major outbound roads; rooms are large, comfortable, and nicely furnished in Southwestern pastels; and there are two good restaurants on the premises, including Sakura (*see* Dining, *above*). ⊡ *1175 W. Rte. 66, Flagstaff 86001, ☎ 520/773–8888 or 800/528–1234,* ℻ *520/773–0597. 183 rooms with bath. Bar, fitness center, pool, indoor-outdoor spa. AE, D, DC, MC, V.*

$$ Howard Johnson's. Just off I–40, this three-story motel is typical Howard Johnson's. But guest rooms are in an attractive ski-lodge-style building, and some suites have fireplaces. There is a small, heated indoor pool, a 24-hour coffee shop, and a courtesy van that transports guests to the airport, train, or bus station. VCRs and movies are available for rental. ⊡ *2200 E. Butler Ave., 86004, ☎ 520/779–6944 or 800/654–2000,* ℻ *520/779–6944, ext. 341. 100 rooms with bath. Restaurant, lounge, hot tub, sauna, recreation room. AE, D, DC, MC, V.*

$$ Little America of Flagstaff. This is the biggest motel in town, and a de-
★   servedly popular place. It's far enough from the tracks to allow visitors to sleep undisturbed as trains roar through town, the grounds are surrounded by evergreen forests, and it's one of the few places in Flagstaff that offers room service. Rooms are surprisingly plush: All have brass chandeliers, comfortable sitting areas with French Provincial–style furniture, phones in bathrooms, and large stereo TVs; king rooms also have small refrigerators. ⊡ *Box 3900, 2515 E. Butler Ave., Flagstaff 86004, ☎ 520/779–2741 or 800/352–4386,* ℻ *520/779–7983. 248 rooms with bath. Restaurant, bar, coffee shop, kitchenettes, fitness center, hiking, laundry service. AE, D, DC, MC, V.*

$–$$ Monte Vista Hotel. Over the years many Hollywood stars have stayed at this historic downtown hotel built in 1926—so the guest rooms come by the glamorous names attached to them honestly. The restored Southwestern-deco lobby, with its shoe-shine stand and curved archways, is appealing, and rates are low, but rooms and hallways are somewhat dark, and the men buying racing forms who hang out at the front desk make this an iffy choice for female travelers. Bunk bed rooms at $15 per person are available. ⊡ *100 N. San Francisco St., Flagstaff 86001, ☎ 520/779–6971 or 800/545–3068,* ℻ *520/779–2904. 45 rooms with bath. Restaurant, bar. AE, D, DC, MC, V.*

The Arts and Nightlife

The Arts

Between the **Flagstaff Symphony Orchestra** (☎ 520/774–5107), **Theatrikos Community Theater** (11 W. Beaver St., ☎ 520/774–1662), and Northern Arizona University's **School of Performing Arts** (☎ 520/523–3731), there's bound to be something cultural going on in Flagstaff when you visit. This is especially true in summer: During the month of July, the **Flagstaff Festival of the Arts** (Box 1607, Flagstaff 86002, ☎ 520/774–7750 or 800/266–7740) fills the air with the sounds of music. Events include sunset jazz dinners and chamber music brunches; many of the symphony and pops performers are world renowned.

Other annual events that reflect the area's culture and crafts include the **All Indian Powwow** (☎ 520/526–6593) and **Festival of Native American Arts** (☎ 520/779–6921), both held in the summer; call ahead for details on dates and events. **Festival in the Pines,** sponsored annually during the first weekend of August by the Mill Avenue Merchants' Association (☎ 520/967–4877), features an arts-and-crafts fair. The **Coconino Center for the Arts** (2300 N. Fort Valley Rd., ☎ 520/779–6921) hosts a **Festival of Native American Arts** each summer from late June through mid-August; the center also sponsors the **Trappings of the American West** from mid-May to early June, which focuses on cowboy art—everything from painting and sculpture to cowboy poetry readings. Sales shows of artwork by Zuni, Hopi, and Navajo tribes are held at the **Museum of Northern Arizona** (3001 N. Fort Valley Rd., ☎ 520/774–5211), a judged event that runs from late May through early August. Flagstaff's observatories help make September's **Festival of Science** (☎ 800/842–7293) a stellar attraction.

Nightlife

A university town, Flagstaff has a number of places where the college crowd gathers after dark. The misleadingly named **Museum Club** (3404 E. Route 66, ☎ 520/526–9434) is a tourist-friendly cowboy honky-tonk, housed in an old barnlike structure with a dance floor; there's usually a country-swing band. For live entertainment nightly—everything from bluegrass to jazz and rock—in a sociable atmosphere, try the **Main Street Bar and Grill** (14 S. San Francisco St., ☎ 520/774–1519); the food's good, too, so come early for dinner. **Charly's** (23 N. Leroux St., ☎ 520/779–1919), in the lobby of the historic Weatherford Hotel, attracts a loyal local following to its late-night jazz and blues bands. **Monsoon's** (22 E. Rte. 66, ☎ 520/774–7929), which books good alternative and reggae bands, gets the most interesting crowds in town, from mohawks to dreadlocks. **The Depot** (26 S. San Francisco St., ☎ 520/773–9550) inspires dancing fools to move to either live or DJ sounds. The **Beaver Street Brewery and Whistlestop Café** (11 S. Beaver St., ☎ 520/779–0079) gets things hopping (as it were) with its fine microbrews.

Flagstaff Essentials

Arriving and Departing

By Plane

Air travelers arrive at the refurbished **Flagstaff Pullium Airport** (☎ 520/556–1234), 3 miles south of town off I–17 at exit 337.

America West Express/Mesa (☎ 800/235–9292) has frequent daily flights into Flagstaff from Phoenix. If you plan to rent a car, the most cost-effective plan might be to fly into Phoenix, which has more flight options, and rent a car there. The drive from Phoenix to Flagstaff is a scenic one, climbing almost 5,000 feet in 134 miles.

AIRPORT TO DOWNTOWN

By Taxi. A taxi ride from the airport to the downtown area should cost about $9 to $11. Cabs are not regulated; some, but not all, have meters. It's wise to agree on a rate before you leave with a driver for your destination. **My Chauffeur Taxi and Tours** (☎ 520/526–1442) and **A Friendly Cab** (☎ 520/774–4444) are two reliable options.

By Bus. There is no public bus from the airport to downtown. Some hotels have shuttles; inquire when making reservations.

By Rental Car. Agencies represented at the airport include **Avis** (☎ 520/774–8421 or 800/331–1212), **Budget** (☎ 520/779–0306 or 800/527–0700), and **Hertz** (☎ 520/774–4452 or 800/654–3131). Ask about a rate that allows you unlimited mileage, as you're likely to drive several hundred miles while you're in this part of the state.

To get downtown from the airport, follow signs to I–17 (the airport is just off the highway). Turn right (north) on I–17, and in about 3 miles exit at the downtown turnoff.

By Car
Flagstaff lies at the intersection of I–40 (east–west) and I–17 (running south from Flagstaff). Phoenix is 134 miles south via I–17 (also known in Phoenix as Black Canyon Freeway) north. A four-lane divided highway, I–17 has several steep inclines and descents (you'll see a number of runaway-truck ramps). In winter, snowstorms occasionally restrict travel to vehicles with snow chains.

CAUTION: When driving off major highways in low-lying areas, watch for rain clouds. Flash floods from sudden summer rains can be deadly (*see* Driving Precautions *in* The Gold Guide's Smart Travel Tips for more information).

By Train
Flagstaff is a railroad town: The tracks that spawned the city's growth are still active today. **Amtrak** (☎ 520/774–8679 or 800/872–7245) comes into the downtown station at 1 East Route 66 twice daily.

By Bus
In Flagstaff, the **Greyhound Lines** station is downtown at 399 South Malpais Lane (☎ 520/774–4573 or 800/231–2222). There are daily connections to Phoenix, but none to Sedona. Buses also serve San Francisco, Los Angeles, Las Vegas, and other cities. **Nava-Hopi** buses also depart daily to the Grand Canyon and offer sightseeing trips to Sedona (*see* Special-Interest Tours, *below*).

Getting Around

Flagstaff is a compact town, much of it situated along the railroad tracks. Just north of, and roughly parallel to, the tracks is the busy street that was called Santa Fe Avenue for many years. In 1992 it officially resumed its famous original name, Route 66.

Not all signs in town have been changed yet, however, and many maps—and most locals—still refer to Santa Fe Avenue, so the change may cause confusion for some time. I–40 lies south of the tracks and also runs east–west. The main north–south thoroughfare is I–17, which turns into Milton Road, Humphreys Street, and then U.S. 180 as you drive north through town.

Because Flagstaff is the gateway to the Grand Canyon, most people on the road here are from out of town; keep that in mind when you ask for directions.

By Car

It makes sense to rent a car at the airport if you fly into Flagstaff (*see* Airport to Downtown, *above*).

By Bus

Pine Country Transit (☎ 520/779–6624) offers clean and reliable service throughout the city for 75¢. Senior citizens, riders with disabilities, and children 7–17 pay 60¢ a ride. Three bus lines run weekdays from 6:15 AM to 7:10 PM; only one bus line, on a more limited schedule, operates Saturday and holidays, and there is no service on Sunday. Passengers with disabilities should check with the office to find out which buses can accommodate wheelchairs.

Opening and Closing Times

Flagstaff is a town of travelers and students, so restaurants tend to stay open late, some of them 24 hours. Banking can be done at odd hours by way of automated teller machines (ATMs) located all over town. Some banks stay open until 6 PM on Friday. In summer, shops and attractions are open longer: from 9 to 9 Monday through Saturday and from noon to 5 on Sunday.

Guided Tours

Orientation

For self-guided tour maps of Flagstaff itself, stop at the **Flagstaff Visitors Center** (*see* Visitor Information, *below*); if you're going to spend any time in town, it's well worth taking the route outlined in the "Historic Downtown Walking Tour" pamphlet.

Special-Interest Tours

The Gray Line of Flagstaff, operated by **Nava-Hopi Tours** (Box 339, 114 W. Route 66, Flagstaff 86002, ☎ 520/774–5003 or 800/892–8687), runs bus trips from its downtown bus station to the **Grand Canyon** ($38 round-trip, including park entry fee). A tour of **Sedona** costs $36 per person (plus a $2 entry fee for Montezuma Castle; there are no dropoffs—that is, all passengers must return to Flagstaff on the same bus that evening. The company also offers a variety of package tours, such as the one to the **Hopi Indian Reservation** ($62 round-trip, including lunch). All require reservations, which are taken until two hours before departure. Free hotel and motel pickups are included in the price.

The Ventures program, run by the education department of the **Museum of Northern Arizona** (3001 N. Fort Valley Rd., Flagstaff 86001, ☎ 520/774–5213), offers tours of the area led by local scientists, artists, and historians. Trips might include rafting excursions down the San Juan and lower Verde rivers, hikes into the Grand Canyon or Arizona Strip Country, or bus tours into Albuquerque or Santa Fe. Prices start at $300 and go up to $1,300, with most tours in the $300 to $600 range.

Alpine Air Service (Box 252, Flagstaff 86002, ☎ 520/779–5178) plane tours of the area's attractions leave from Flagstaff Pullium Airport. The cost for the pilot and plane, which carries three passengers, is $90 an hour plus tax. FAA regulations prevent tour companies, including this one, from flying over the Grand Canyon.

Important Addresses and Numbers

Visitor Information

One of the busiest tourist information offices in the country, the **Flagstaff Visitors Center** (1 East Rte. 66, ☎ 520/774–9541 or 800/842–

7293) is open every day of the year, except December 25. From May 1 to September 30, hours are Monday through Saturday, 8 AM–7 PM, Sunday 8 AM–5 PM; the office closes one hour earlier Monday through Saturday the rest of the year, but the Sunday schedule remains the same. In 1994 the center moved downtown into the refurbished historic train depot, which it shares with Amtrak.

For hiking maps and camping tips, contact the **U.S. Forest Service** (2323 Greenlaw La., Flagstaff 86002, ☎ 520/527–3600).

Emergencies

Call 911 to reach the **fire department, police,** and **emergency medical services.**

HOSPITALS AND DOCTORS

At an altitude of nearly 7,000 feet, Flagstaff has "thin" air; heart and respiratory patients may experience difficulty here, particularly upon exertion.

Flagstaff Medical Center, a full-service hospital, has a 24-hour emergency room downtown (1200 N. Beaver St., ☎ 520/779–3366), about nine blocks north of Route 66. The facility also provides referrals to local doctors and dentists.

LATE-NIGHT PHARMACIES

The pharmacy at the **Flagstaff Medical Center** (*see above*) is open 24 hours. **Walgreen's** (1500 E. Cedar Ave., ☎ 520/773–1011), a few blocks north of downtown, is open Monday through Saturday 9 AM–10 PM, Sunday 9 AM–8 PM; the pharmacy at **Smith's Food and Drug** (201 Switzer Canyon Dr., cnr. Route 66, ☎ 520/774–3389) is open Monday through Saturday 9–9, Sunday 10 AM–4 PM.

5 Phoenix and Central Arizona

The ever-widening Phoenix metropolitan area provides a tremendous variety of activities for almost all interests—from hiking in superb parks on some of the country's most-traveled (and appreciated) trails to golfing on championship courses, and from dining at the restaurants where Southwestern cuisine was born to the last word in pampering at world-class resorts—and watching bucking broncos at a rodeo, of course! The White Mountains are a nearby escape, with Old West towns, the stunning Salt River Canyon, and more great hiking.

By Mark Hein

IN CENTRAL ARIZONA, one of the world's great deserts meets one of its great mountain ranges, providing a stunning variety of natural environments for visitors to enjoy in a relatively small area. Central Arizona also combines some of the oldest human dwellings in the Western Hemisphere with the homes of contemporary Native American tribes and America's newest, fastest-growing, major urban center: metropolitan Phoenix.

At the heart of central Arizona lies the Valley of the Sun, named for its 330-plus days of sunshine each year. This 1,000-square-mile valley is the northern tip of the Sonoran Desert, a surprisingly fertile, rolling expanse of prehistoric seabed that stretches from central Arizona deep into northwestern Mexico.

The valley is studded with cacti and creosote bushes, crusted with hard-baked clay and rock, and scorched by summer temperatures that can stay above 100°F for weeks at a time. But its dry skin responds magically to the touch of rainwater. Spring is a miracle of poppies strewn among the flower-crowned saguaro cacti, of ruby, ivory, and golden blossoms bursting from the dry spikes of the ocotillo and the thorny beaver-tail pads of the nopal. And, as the Hohokam discovered 2,300 years ago, this miracle can be augmented by human hands. Having migrated north from northwestern Mexico, they cultivated cotton, corn, and beans in tilled, rowed, and irrigated fields for about 1,700 years. The Hohokam, like northern Puebloans in the 14th and 15th centuries, moved out of the area as a result of the combination of droughts, longer winters, and other causes. They are believed to be ancestors of the present-day Pimans: the Pima and Tohonó O'odham.

From the time the Hohokam left until the American Civil War, the once-fertile Salt River valley lay forgotten, used only by occasional small bands of Pima and Maricopa peoples. Then in 1865, the U.S. Army established Fort McDowell in the mountains to the east, where the Verde River flows into the Salt. To feed the men and the horses stationed there, Jack Swilling, a former Confederate army officer, had the idea of reopening the Hohokam canals in 1867. Within a year, fields bright with barley and pumpkins earned the area the name of Punkinsville. But by 1870, when the town site was plotted, the 300 inhabitants had decided that their new city would rise "like a phoenix" from the ashes of a vanished civilization.

Phoenix indeed grew steadily. Within 20 years, it had become large enough—at about 3,000 people—to wrest the title of territorial capital from Prescott. It gained a high school in 1895, and by statehood in 1912 the area, irrigated by the brand-new Roosevelt Dam and Salt River Project, had a burgeoning cotton industry. Copper and cattle were mined and raised elsewhere but were banked and traded in Phoenix, and the cattle were slaughtered and packed here in the largest stockyards outside Chicago.

Meanwhile climate, so long a crippling liability, became an asset. Desert air was the prescribed therapy for respiratory ills rampant in the sooty, factory-filled East; Scottsdale began in 1901 as "30-odd tents and a half dozen adobe houses" put up by health-seekers. By 1930, visitors seeking warm winter recreation rather than a cure filled the elegant San Marcos Hotel in Chandler and the new Arizona Biltmore, first of the many luxury resorts for which the area is known worldwide today.

When low-cost air-conditioning made its summer heat manageable, the Sun Belt boom began. From 1950 to 1990, the Phoenix urban area more than quadrupled in population, catapulting real estate and home-building into two of the state's biggest industries. Cities planted around Phoenix have become its suburbs, and fields that for decades grew cotton and citrus now grow microchips and homes. Glendale and Peoria on the west side, and Tempe, Mesa, Chandler, and Gilbert on the east, make up the nation's third-largest silicon valley.

The Valley of the Sun is ringed by mountains. Squaw Peak is situated within Phoenix, just north of downtown, and Camelback Mountain and the Papago Peaks are landmarks between Phoenix and Scottsdale. South of the city, not five miles from downtown, rise the much less lofty peaks of South Mountain Park. This 12-mile-wide chain of dry mountains divides the valley from the rest of the Sonora Desert. All of these mountain areas provide the city with wonderful and locally popular outdoor activities.

Past Tempe and Mesa to the east, the barren peaks of the Superstition Mountains—named for their eerie way of seeming just a few miles away and luring unwary prospectors to a dusty death—are the first of a series of mountains that stretch all the way into New Mexico. To the west, past Glendale and Tolleson, the formidable, barren-seeming White Tank Mountains separate the valley from the empty lands that slope steadily downward toward the Colorado River and the Mojave Desert of California.

But north of Phoenix, behind the dusty Hieroglyphic Mountains (misnamed for Hohokam petroglyphs found there), rises the gigantic Mogollon Rim. This shelf of land, almost as wide as Arizona, was thrust 2,000 to 5,000 feet into the air back in the Mesozoic age; it got its name for posing an overwhelming *mogollon* (obstruction) to Spanish-speaking explorers probing northward. These slopes are green with pine trees, and the alpine meadows are lush with grasses and aspen. Here, after gold was found in the early 1860s, President Lincoln sent the Arizona Territory's first governor to found the capital at Prescott (*see* Exploring the Verde Valley and Prescott *in* Chapter 4) and secure mineral riches for the Union.

Today, the northern mountains serve as a cool, green refuge for valley dwellers. The bumpy wagon roads up the Black Canyon toward Prescott and Flagstaff were key summer escape routes 100 years ago, and their dramatically engineered successor, the four-lane, split-level I–17, leads tens of thousands on exodus every weekend from May to September.

Phoenix and central Arizona are places in which to take it easy, go slowly, and dress informally. As old desert hands say, you don't begin to see the desert until you've looked at it long enough to see its colors; and you aren't ready to get up and move until you've seen the sun go down.

Note: If you are interested in visiting southwestern Arizona, towns like Ajo, Yuma, and Why, or sights at Organ Pipe Cactus National Monument, *see* the last section of Chapter 6, Tucson and Southern Arizona.

EXPLORING

Tour 1: A Walking Tour of Downtown Phoenix

Numbers in the margin correspond to points of interest on the Phoenix: Tours 1 and 2 map.

A stroll through the renovated east end of downtown gives you a look at Phoenix's past and present, as well as a peek at its future. In moderate weather, it's a pleasant walking day; from late May to mid-October, it's best to break it up over two days. And be sure to take advantage of the 25¢ DASH (Downtown Area Shuttle)—*see* Getting Around by Bus *in* Phoenix and Central Arizona Essentials, *below.*

You'll notice a number of Time Out options here and in the tours that follow—in the warm months, it's best to allow a half hour sitting out of the sun, sipping a tall, cool drink (not alcohol; it speeds dehydration) for every hour of walking or shopping.

★ ❶ Begin your tour at **Heritage Square,** from 5th to 7th streets between Monroe and Adams, a city-owned block of turn-of-the-century homes in a parklike setting. Renovations underway in the area in 1995 should be complete by spring 1996. (There's ample parking in adjacent lots, and it's free if you get your ticket stamped by a merchant along the walking tour.)

To the east, across 7th Street, you'll see the ornate brick bulk of Monroe School; built in 1914, it now houses part of the U.S. Department of Defense Analysis. Just south of it are the graceful, modern copper-roof condos of Renaissance Square, a pioneering urban project built on city-donated land.

The queen of Heritage Square itself is the **Rosson House,** an 1895 gingerbread Victorian in the Eastlake style (made famous in San Francisco). Built by a physician who served a brief term as mayor, it is the sole survivor of the fewer than two dozen Victorians erected in Phoenix. It was bought and restored by the city in 1974. A 30-minute tour of this classic is worth the modest admission price. *6th and Monroe Sts.,* ☎ *602/262–5071.* ☛ *$3 adults, $2 senior citizens and students, $1 children 6–12.* ⊙ *Wed.–Sat. 10–3:30, Sun. noon–3:30.*

On the south side of the square, along Adams Street, stand four houses built between 1899 and 1901 on sites bought from the Rossons. The Midwestern-style **Stevens House** holds the **Arizona Doll and Toy Museum** (602 E. Adams St., ☎ 602/253–9337); next to it, in the California-style **Stevens-Haustgen House,** is the temporary home of the **Phoenix Museum of History** (604 E. Adams St., ☎ 602/253–1271). The fourth dwelling is the **Silva House,** a mail-order 1900 bungalow restored by the Salt River Project (one of the valley's two major power companies and its largest irrigator) that includes a room devoted to Phoenix history and one with rotating displays on water and electricity in the valley. Two houses on the south side of Adams Street are still being restored.

TIME OUT Just north of the third house in the row, the Bouvier-Teeter house, you'll find the charming **Carriage House Bakery** (618 E. Adams St., ☎ 602/495–1997, open Mon.–Sat. 10–4, Sun. 12–4). This sandwich shop and bakery is a throwback to the early 1900s and has treats like homemade lemonade, cinnamon rolls, and picnic baskets. For $5 you can get a lunch in a brown paper sack that includes a sandwich, chips, cookie, fruit, and drink.

★ ❷ **The Mercado** (542 E. Monroe St., ☎ 602/256–6322), a bright-colored, neo-Aztec fantasy built in 1990, occupies two blocks immediately north of Heritage Square, just across Monroe Street, from 5th to 7th streets. Spend some time at the **Museo Chicano** on the second story. It supports the work of modern Hispano-American artists in the United States and Mexico, and its exhibits portray the range of Hispanic cul-

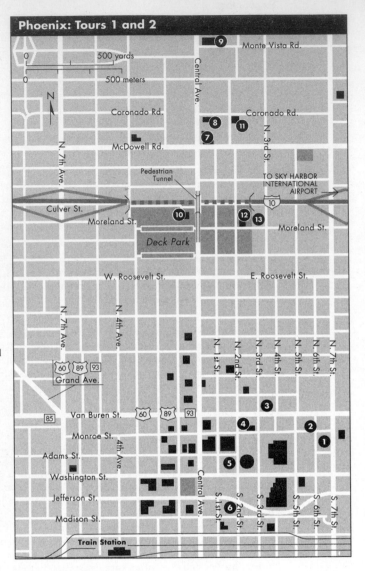

ture, classic and modern. Its gift shop also offers some terrific bargains. *641 E. Van Buren St., ☎ 602/257–5536.* ✒ *$2 adults, $1 senior citizens and students.* ⊗ *Wed.–Sat. 10–3.*

From The Mercado, cross 5th and Van Buren streets. On your right, you'll see the imposing buildings of old Phoenix Union High School, Greek Revival–style buildings that served as the city's first secondary school in 1900 and were abandoned three-quarters of a century later. With their shells preserved and their interiors remodeled, they are now home to several city and county offices.

★ ❸ On the northwest corner of the intersection, you'll see two glass-clad office towers with a lane of royal palms between them. Follow the palm trees: They lead to the **Arizona Center's** dramatic sunken garden and fountains (see how many giant bronze frogs you can find). Opened in

1991, this multi-use complex provides downtown's premier spot for cool, shaded outdoor sitting and wandering, even in the heat of summer.

On the other side of the ponds stands the curved, double-deck open structure of the city's newest downtown shopping mall. There are a variety of chain and specialty stores, from men's and women's clothing to Southwestern art and '50s collectibles, and a host of clever cart merchants. And there's usually live music (including top valley jazz artists) in the courtyard. In addition to hosting several good eateries, Arizona Center is the home of the state's biggest sports bar—would you believe eight restaurant-size spaces spread over two stories, indoors and out?

TIME OUT The most restful refreshment spot in the center is **Amalfi** (455 N. 3rd St., ☎ 602/257–0605), a real Italian sidewalk café that does Caesar salads, great sandwiches and desserts, as well as Italian sodas and steamed coffees.

Leaving the Arizona Center at Amalfi, head south to 3rd and Van Buren streets. You can catch the 25¢ DASH shuttle here, or you can stroll a block south to Monroe, with the mission-style adobe of **St. Mary's Basilica** on your left, then a block west to the dramatic modern facades of
❹ the **Herberger Theater Center** (on your right) and **Symphony Hall** (on your left) facing each other across the fountain- and sculpture-dotted Phoenix Civic Plaza courtyard. The two structures have jointly undergone a $31 million renovation. Walk one more block south along 2nd Street, past the Hyatt Regency Phoenix to Adams, to the next stop.

Here, amid the splendor and dignity of downtown, is a building with
❺ children's paintings all over its windows. It's the **Arizona Museum of Science and Technology,** a hands-on exploratorium for children of every age. Permanent displays include exercises in gravity, centrifugal force, and optical illusions. *80 N. 2nd St.,* ☎ *602/256–9388.* ☛ *$4.50 adults, $3.50 senior citizens and children 4–12.* ⊙ *Mon.–Sat. 9–5, Sun. noon–5.*

Finally, if you're really an indefatigable walker and an avid sports fan, another two blocks down 2nd Street will take you to the site of the
❻ **America West Phoenix Suns Arena** (2nd and Jefferson Sts., ☎ 602/379–2000). This multifacility sports palace is almost a mall in itself, with cafés, an athletic club, and shops, in addition to the basketball-and-hockey stadium and team offices. It's an interesting tour even when there's no game on.

From the arena (or from Symphony Hall, across from the science museum, if you skip the arena), you can catch the DASH northbound for The Mercado and walk back to your car.

Tour 2: Cultural Center Walking Tour

The heart of Phoenix's new downtown cultural center is the rolling greensward of **Deck Park.** Begun in 1991 atop the I–10 tunnel under Central Avenue, it spreads a mile from 3rd Avenue on the west to 3rd Street on the east, and a quarter mile from Portland Street north to Culver. Completed in 1993, it is the city's second-largest downtown park (the largest is half-century-old Encanto Park, 2 miles northwest).

Gathered around Deck Park, mostly to the north, are museums, theaters, an art center, and the central library. Seeing all of them makes a comfortable day tour in moderate weather; in the warm months, it is too much for one day. Bus 0 runs up and down Central Avenue every 10 minutes on weekdays (at half-fare from 9 to 3) and every 20 minutes on weekends.

⑦ Start at the **Phoenix Central Library** (12 E. McDowell Rd., ☎ 602/262–4636), on the northeast corner of McDowell Road and Central Avenue. It's easy to find, and its palm-lined parking area has no time limit.

Immediately north of the library, in the same complex and sharing a
⑧ courtyard, is the **Phoenix Art Museum.** It is particularly noteworthy for its clothing and costume collection, fine Asian art, 19th-century European paintings and drawings, and the American West collection, featuring painters from Frederic Remington to Georgia O'Keeffe. *1625 N. Central Ave.,* ☎ *602/257–1222.* ☛ *$4 adults, $3 senior citizens, $1.50 students, children under 6 free; free to all Wed.; tours free.* ☉ *Tues. and Thurs.–Sat. 10–5, Wed. 10–9, Sun. noon–5.*

Two blocks north, cross Monte Vista and turn right 100 yards to the
★ **⑨** **Heard Museum.** In 1928 Dwight and Maie Heard donated their classic Arizona adobe home and their impressive Southwestern art collection to found what has become the nation's leading museum of Native American art and culture. Orient yourself with the multimedia show, then see the award-winning "Native Peoples of the Southwest" display; don't miss the kachina doll room (anchored by the Barry Goldwater collection). Modern Native American arts, interactive art-making exhibits for children, and live demonstrations by artisans are always on hand. In the spring, you may catch the annual Native American Arts & Crafts Show; call ahead because its dates vary. *22 E. Monte Vista Rd.,* ☎ *602/252–8840.* ☛ *$5 adults, $4 students and senior citizens, $3 teens 13–18, $1 children 4–12, Native Americans free; free to all Wed. after 5.* ☉ *Mon.–Sat. 9:30–5, Wed. 9:30–9, Sun. noon–5.*

If your day hasn't unaccountably disappeared in the museums, go back to Central Avenue, cross the street, and catch Bus 0 heading south. (Or walk, if it's below 90°F and you're hardy.)

At Culver Street, a long block south of McDowell Road, is the northern edge of Deck Park. The stately brick home with the gabled roof
⑩ on the southwest corner is the **Ellis–Shackelford House** (1242 N. Central Ave., ☎ 602/261–8699). One of Phoenix's first mansions, it was long the home of the Arizona Historical Society Museum (now in Papago Park, near the Phoenix Zoo). It houses the Phoenix Historic Preservation Office and, in back, the restored railcars of the **Phoenix Street Railway** (☎ 602/254–0307 to arrange a visit).

TIME OUT Halfway back to McDowell Road are two places that offer both rest and nourishment. At the **Spaghetti Company** (1418 N. Central Ave., ☎ 602/257-0380) you can have lunch, spinach salad and wine, any of countless pasta dishes or other dinners, any day of the week. Across the street at **The Blue Fin** (1401 N. Central Ave., ☎ 602/254-3171), the atmosphere is quick and informal, and the Japanese fast food is light and pleasant.

Now you have a choice: You can head back to the library complex and
⑪ visit the **Phoenix Theatre** (25 E. Coronado Rd., ☎ 602/254–2151), just east of the museum and north of the library. Here the city's leading community theater group and its adjunct, the PT Cookie Company, present plays and musicals for adults and children; you might end your day by catching a show.

Or, if you're not ready to head back, go into Deck Park at the Ellis–Shackelford House, through the pedestrian tunnel under Central Avenue (with I–10 roaring beneath your feet), and walk 2½ blocks east to the **City**
⑫ **Arts Center** (3rd and Moreland Sts., ☎ 602/262–6583). In the **Phoenix Visual Arts Building,** valley professional and amateur artists do class

(13) and studio work in graphics, ceramics, sculpture, photography, and other media; check for current exhibits and sales. Adjacent is the **Phoenix Performing Arts Building,** a venue for small, experimental dance and theater groups. A performance here is a fine way to spend an evening after a day spent walking the city's cultural paths.

Tour 3: Scottsdale Walking Tour

Numbers in the margin correspond to points of interest on the Scottsdale map.

Historic sites, nationally known art galleries, and lots of clever boutiques fill downtown Scottsdale, easily turning a walking tour into several hours if you browse. Historic Old Town Scottsdale features the look of the Old West, while fashionable 5th Avenue is known for shopping. Cross onto Main Street and enter a world frequented by the international art set; discover more galleries and interior-design shops along Marshall Way and Craftsman Court. This tour offers an overview of the area; *see* Shopping, *below,* for some specific recommendations.

While your tour can easily be completed on foot, a trolley (cost: $2 in summer, free rest of year) runs through the entire downtown area; the Ollie Trolley tours all of Scottsdale and charges $3 for an all-day pass. For information about both, call 602/941–2957. Also look for horse-drawn Wagonmasters (☎ 602/423–1449), which provide romantic transportation throughout Old Town Scottsdale.

Begin your tour by parking in the free public lot on the northwest corner of 2nd Street and Wells Fargo Avenue east of Scottsdale Road. A portion of the garage is signed for a three-hour limit; go to upper levels that don't carry time restraints, as enforcement is strict.

1 Head north on the brick-paved sidewalks leading to **Scottsdale Mall.** This tree-shaded setting has plenty of benches and grassy areas for restful contemplation. To your right, paths lead to a sculpture- and fountain-filled plaza around Scottsdale's **city hall, public library,** and **Center for the Arts** (7380 E. 2nd St., ☎ 602/994–ARTS). The center presents a full schedule of concerts, and exhibits are changed frequently. Its gift shop, **The ArtSpot,** has unusual jewelry as well as posters and art books.

2 After circling the plaza, head west to the **Scottsdale Chamber of Commerce** (7343 Scottsdale Mall, ☎ 602/945–8481), which is open seven days a week. Inside, maps, guidebooks, brochures, and helpful tips are abundant. Ask for the walking-tour map of Old Town Scottsdale to note historic sites as you go. Next door in the redbrick building is the **Scottsdale Historical Museum** (7333 Scottsdale Mall, ☎ 602/945–4499), open Wednesday through Saturday. The building, built in 1910, was Scottsdale's first schoolhouse.

3 Continue west into **Old Town Scottsdale** on Main Street. Billed as "The West's Most Western Town," this area features rustic storefronts and wooden sidewalks; it's touristy, but it's also the genuine item, giving visitors a taste of life here 80 years ago. Stores carry kitsch souvenirs, but you'll also find some nicer jewelry, pots, and Mexican imports.

Head north on Brown Avenue and turn left on 1st Avenue to continue sightseeing in Old Town Scottsdale.

TIME OUT The southeast corner of 1st Avenue and Scottsdale Road marks a landmark of sorts: the candy pink-and-white **Sugar Bowl Ice Cream Parlor** (4005 N. Scottsdale Rd., ☎ 602/946–0051), run by a local family since 1958 and frequented from its beginning by Paradise Valley car-

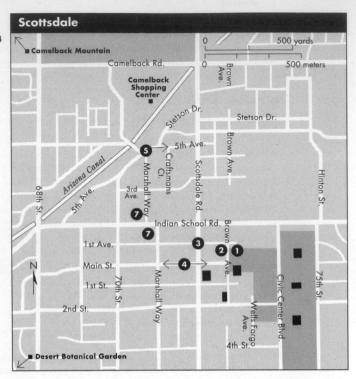

toonist Bill Keane (the menu carries his "Family Circus" work). Although sandwiches, soups, and salads are available, you'll miss the point if you don't indulge in the gooey sundaes, floats, and parfaits.

For an entirely different milieu, walk south on Scottsdale Road and turn right onto **Main Street.** This block is literally filled with art galleries showing artwork of a variety of styles, including contemporary, Western realism, Native American, and traditional. With very few exceptions, casual visitors are made welcome in the galleries, although children may be bored. Another option for viewing the galleries is the seasonal **Art Walk** (☎ 602/990–3939), held from 7 to 9 PM each Thursday, October through May. The street takes on a party atmosphere during the evening hours when everyone is browsing.

Continue on Main Street across Marshall Way for several antiques shops, where specialties include elegant porcelains and china, fine antique jewelry, and Oriental rugs.

TIME OUT For a cool drink or light meal after daytime gallery-hopping, try **Arcadia Farms** (7014 E. 1st Ave., ☎ 602/941–5665), where such eclectic sandwiches as rosemary-seasoned *focaccia* with chicken, roasted eggplant, and feta cheese are brought out to diners on a tree-shaded patio. Desserts are exceptional, so leave room. ☼ *Mon.–Sat. 8 am–3 pm. Lunch reservations recommended.*

If you walk north on 70th Street and cross Indian School Road, you'll discover another niche of galleries, upscale gift and jewelry stores, and several specialty boutiques. Farther north on Marshall Way across 3rd Avenue, the street is filled with more art galleries and creative stores with a Southwestern flair.

5 When you reach the fountain with the prancing horses, you're on **5th Avenue,** a 40-year-old stretch that is a shopping tradition in Phoenix. Whether you're seeking cacti or casual clothing, fine art or handmade Native American jewelry, you'll find it here.

Off 5th Avenue, Stetson Drive has a few interesting stores carrying original Native American artifacts, as well as books on Arizona and the Southwest; here you'll find **O'Brien's Art Emporium** (7122 E. Stetson Dr., ☎ 602/945–1082), the oldest art gallery in Arizona.

Tour 4: Casa Grande Ruins National Monument and Florence

Numbers in the margin correspond to points of interest on the Around Phoenix map.

An hour's drive south of Phoenix takes visitors back to prehistoric times and the site of Arizona's first known civilization, as well as one of its major pioneer western towns. The Casa Grande Ruins National Monument, 1 mile north of Coolidge, captures some vivid reminders of the Hohokam Indians who began farming in this area more than 1,500 years ago. Florence, one of central Arizona's first cities, is rich in examples of Territorial architecture.

Start your tour by heading southeast on I–10 leaving Phoenix. You'll pass Exit 160, which leads to the former **Williams Air Force Base,** once the site of the largest pilot-training facility in NATO, but now closed. The same exit is the closest freeway access to **Compadre Stadium,** spring-training home of the Milwaukee Brewers each February and March.

1 Soon you'll see a sign noting that you've entered the **Gila River Indian Reservation.** On the right, Exit 162A indicates **Firebird International Raceway** (20000 S. Maricopa Rd., ☎ 602/268–0200), site of the Arizona National drag-racing finals each February and local Friday-night races; **Firebird Lake** (20000 S. Maricopa Rd., ☎ 602/268–0200), a boat-racing site where the World Hydroplane Finals are held each April; and **Compton Terrace** (20000 S. Maricopa Rd., ☎ 602/796–0511), one of the valley's largest outdoor concert venues.

The landscape changes to desert scrub, and the sun can become intense, so make use of sunscreen, hats, and drinking water. Large, strangely shaped saguaro cacti next begin to dominate the landscape, covering
2 a hillside as you cross the **Gila River.**

TIME OUT Thirty-seven miles south of Phoenix off I–10 is a wheelchair-accessible **rest area** with covered picnic tables. It's the last available stop until you reach your destination 20 miles later.

Take Exit 185 east off I–10 and follow the signs a short way to AZ 387. It's a two-lane road flanked by saguaros, and the spring landscape features brilliant red-tipped ocotillo cacti and yellow and purple wild-flowers. Halfway into this 7-mile stretch, you'll climb a rise and see the Gila River valley spread out below. Four miles later, turn right onto AZ 87 and head 7½ miles to the ruins.

★ 3 The **Casa Grande Ruins National Monument,** established in 1918, provides a close look at a structure first seen by European explorers in the 17th century. Allow an hour to inspect the site, longer if park rangers are giving a talk at the interpretive ramada or leading a tour.

Start at the visitor center, where a small museum features artifacts and information on the Hohokam, who lived here and farmed irrigated cot-

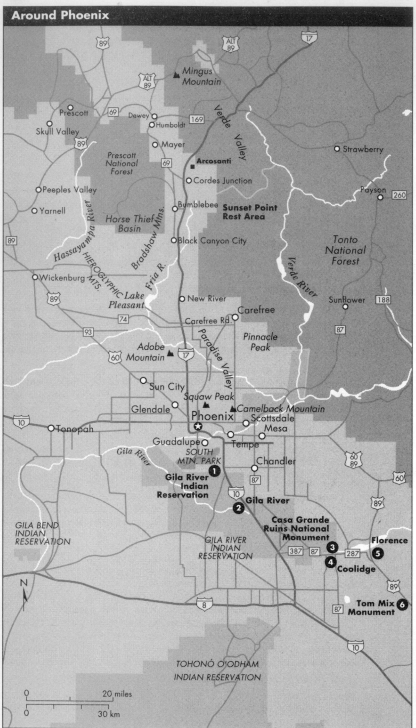

ton fields until they vanished mysteriously in about AD 1450. Step outside and begin your self-guided tour with an inspection of the 35-foot-tall Casa Grande (Big House), built around 1350 and still close to its original size. It's covered by a modern roof for protection from the sun and wind. Neighboring structures are much smaller, and only a bit of the 7-foot wall around the compound is still in evidence. The original purpose of Casa Grande still puzzles archaeologists; some think it was an ancient astronomical observatory.

Cross the parking lot by the covered picnic grounds and climb the platform for a view of an unexcavated ball court, said to date from the 1100s. Although only a few prehistoric sites can be viewed, more than 60 are included in the monument area.

A small gift shop in the lobby of the visitor center sells books about early Native American civilizations and other aspects of Arizona history. *1 mi north of Coolidge on AZ 87, ☎ 602/723–3172. ☛ $2 adults, senior citizens and children under 16 free. ⊙ Daily 7–6.*

4 If traipsing among the ruins has given you an appetite, it's a short trip to **Coolidge,** 1 mile south on AZ 87, where you'll find fast-food hamburgers, chicken, and pizza. A public park with a children's playground is at 4th and Central avenues.

5 Take AZ 287 another 9 miles east from the monument to **Florence,** an old Western town distinguished by an American Victorian courthouse and more than 150 other sites listed on the National Register of Historic Places. An annual walking tour of historic Florence is held on the first Saturday in February.

The **Pinal County Visitor Center** (912 N. Pinal St., ☎ 602/868–4331) answers questions and provides brochures weekdays 9–4 September through May, and 10–2 June through August. Two attractions are the **Pinal County Historical Museum** (715 S. Main St., ☎ 602/868–4382), which displays furnishings from early 1900s homes and Native American crafts and tools, and the **McFarland Historical State Park,** where the 1878-era Pinal County Courthouse (Main and Ruggles Sts., ☎ 602/868–5216) houses memorabilia of former Governor and U.S. Senator Ernest W. McFarland.

Several attractive shops and restaurants are found on Florence's Main Street, including the turn-of-the-century **Florence General Store** (110 N. Main St., ☎ 602/868–5748) and **Old Pueblo Restaurant** (505 S. Main St., ☎ 602/868–4784), serving good Mexican food.

TIME OUT At **Jim-Bob's Auld Tyme Ice Cream Parlor** (289 N. Main St., ☎ 602/ 868-9392), ice cream and hard-packed frozen yogurt are made on the circa-1886 adobe-wall premises.

6 Fans of Western-movie hero Tom Mix may want to drive 18 miles south on U.S. 89 to the **Tom Mix Monument,** at the site of his fatal automobile accident in 1940. Pack some soft drinks; it's low desert (in fact, a showplace of dry-land vegetation), and no refreshments are on hand.

From Florence, retrace your route to Phoenix via AZ 287, 87, and 387 to link up with I–10 north and the 40-minute drive back to the Valley of the Sun.

Tour 5: The White Mountains

Numbers in the margin correspond to points of interest on The White Mountains map.

The drive into eastern Arizona's White Mountains offers a representative tour of the state's many climates and striking vistas. This trip can be completed as either of two loops, depending on which scenery sounds most appealing. Most of the year, it can be done in a long day, but the beauty of the mountains and meadows makes at least one overnight stay worthwhile. If you're going in the winter or early spring, you may need chains—and take ski clothes and equipment and stay for a couple of days.

❶ From Phoenix, take I–10 and then U.S. 60 (the Superstition Freeway) east through the suburbs of Tempe, Mesa, and Apache Junction. The massive escarpment of the **Superstition Mountains** heaves into view and slides by to the north, as the Phoenix metro area gives way to cactus-and creosote-dotted desert. The Superstitions are supposedly home to the legendary **Lost Dutchman Mine,** the location—not to mention the existence—of which has been hotly debated since pioneer days.

❷ About 8 miles southeast of Apache Junction off U.S. 60, the Peralta Trail Road (about 3 miles past King's Ranch Road) is an almost 8-mile, rough gravel road to the Peralta Trail. The 4-mile round-trip trail winds 1,400 feet up a small valley for a spectacular view of **Weaver's Needle,** a monolithic rock formation that is one of Arizona's more famous sights. Allow a few hours for the rugged hike, bring plenty of water and a snack or lunch, and don't hike it in the middle of the day in summer.

At Florence Junction, four lanes drop to two and the highway starts to rise steadily into the foothills of the Mescal Mountains.

❸ Be sure to stop at the **Boyce Thompson Southwestern Arboretum,** about a dozen miles beyond Florence Junction. Its compact, informative walking tour takes in exhibits of Arizona's exotic desert flora, and it's a shady spot to break for a picnic lunch (*see* What to See and Do with Children, *below*).

A few miles farther, **Superior** is the first of several modest mining towns and the launching point for a dramatic winding ascent through the Mescals to a 4,195-foot pass that affords panoramic views of this copper-rich range and its huge, dormant, open-pit mines. Collectors will want to watch for antiques shops through these hills, but be forewarned that quality varies considerably. A quick descent will take you into **Miami** and **Claypool,** once-thriving boom towns that have carried on quietly since major-corporation mining ground to a halt in the 1970s. Working-class buildings are dwarfed by the mountainous piles of copper tailings to the north.

❹ Dotted with majestic cypress trees, **Globe,** in the southern reaches of Tonto National Forest, is the last and most cosmopolitan of area mining towns. Have a bite and fill the gas tank if necessary, because it's the last appreciable town for about 90 miles of mostly mountainous country. **Jerry's Restaurant** (933 E. Ash St., Globe, ☏ 602/425–5282) is a humble café with standard American and Mexican eats at reasonable prices.

❺ After Globe, follow U.S. 60 north (don't continue east on U.S. 70), and the terrain immediately changes to the Tonto's ponderosa pine forests as the highway begins climbing through rolling hills. The highlight of this stretch is the magnificent **Salt River Canyon** about 40 miles past Globe. After entering the San Carlos Indian Reservation, U.S. 60 drops from the Natanes Plateau into a vast gorge, making a series of hairpin turns, to cross the Salt River and then climb out again along the

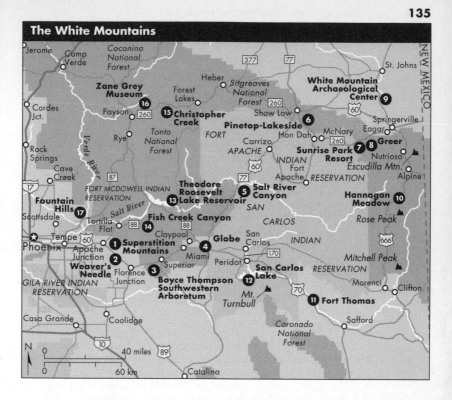

The White Mountains

canyon's northern cliffs. This is a truly spectacular chasm, unfairly overlooked in a state full of world-famous gorges.

TIME OUT Stop before crossing the bridge to stretch your legs and wander along the banks of the Salt, enjoying its rock-strewn rapids. On hot Arizona days you can slip your shoes off and dip your feet into the chilly water for a cool respite.

The road out of the Salt River Canyon offers several breathtaking overlooks worth stopping to enjoy. The highway continues to climb to the **Mogollon Rim**—a huge geologic upthrust that bisects Arizona from northwest to southeast—and its cool upland pinewoods. **Show Low,** in the Apache Sitgreaves National Forest, is a crossing point for east–west traffic along the rim and traffic headed for Holbrook and points north.

At Show Low, turn right onto AZ 260, and soon you'll find yourself in the newer tourist/retirement community of **Pinetop–Lakeside** (the two towns joined in 1984 but still have separate post offices). It's a lengthy succession of shopping malls, restaurants, and motels, more numerous than appealing. But the slowly curving highway through these twin towns is usually dotted on the weekends with fruit-and-vegetable stands purveying modestly priced, wonderfully fresh Arizona produce.

If you plan to stay the night, there is a good mix of hostelries worth considering, among them **Bartram's Bed and Breakfast** (Rte. 1, Box 1014, Lakeside 85929, ☎ 800/257–0211); **Coldstream B&B** (Box 2988, Pinetop 85935, ☎ 602/369–0115); and the cottages (with boats available) at **Spring Hill on Rainbow Lake** (Box 1040, Lakeside 85929, ☎ 602/368–8688).

After Pinetop–Lakeside, the road dips into the Fort Apache Indian Reservation. At the tiny crossroads town of **Hon Dah,** AZ 260 swings east again. **McNary** is next, a ramshackle Native American community built among the pines—but slow down if you see a tent and a sign advertising Indian fry bread. Try this doughy fried dish with honey or other fillings for a taste of Native American cuisine.

Already more than a mile above sea level, the highway continues its gradual but steady climb after McNary into the White Mountains, leaving the reservation for the Apache National Forest. Get a breath of the thin, pine-scented air; it tends to be cool even in the middle of a summer day.

At AZ 273 winter and early spring visitors will want to turn right to
❼ **Sunrise Park Resort,** the state's largest ski area, with five day lodges, 11 lifts, and 65 trails on three mountains rising to 11,000 feet. Operated by the White Mountain Apaches, the resort is one of the most successful Native American business enterprises in the United States. The recently remodeled **Sunrise Ski Lodge** offers modern accommodations and solid American dining at reasonable prices. The tribe also operates a modest outdoor-sports center, which rents a variety of equipment, from cross-country skis to mountain bikes. *Sunrise Park Resort, Greer 85927,* ☎ *800/772–SNOW or 602/735–7676 for skiing reports.* ☯ *Year-round.*

Down AZ 260 another five minutes is the turnoff summer and fall tourists
❽ won't want to miss—AZ 373 for **Greer,** a tiny, charming community built around a meadow and trout ponds. Here are numerous lodges and resorts of varying quality and price. **Greer Lodge** offers huge and hearty meals, with cozy overnight accommodations in a rustic log cabin; the friendly help keeps a fire stoked and roaring through the cool alpine evenings. *Greer Lodge, Box 244, Greer 85927,* ☎ *602/735– 7515.* ☯ *Year-round.*

This area of gently sloping national forest land is dotted with meadows, lakes, and small reservoirs and dominated by 11,590-foot Baldy Peak. It's a wonderland for outdoor activities: hunting, fishing, horseback riding, hiking, boating, camping. Much of it remains under the control of the Apache nation, so visitors must take care to respect the land as they do and to honor their wishes.

Another 10 minutes east on AZ 260 are the twin towns of **Springerville** and **Eagar,** in Round Valley. The region, hard against the New Mexico border, brims with Old West lore. This is where William Bonney (aka Billy the Kid) herded livestock before turning outlaw. Many of the towns were founded by Mormon pioneers and there is a big Mormon church between the two towns, but they are dominated by their high school's domed stadium, testament to the residents' love of sports and to the sometimes harsh winter weather.

For a pleasant stop and a step back 1,000 years, head north on AZ
❾ 666 about 12 miles from Springerville to the **White Mountain Archaeological Center.** At Raven Site Ruin, on a former cattle ranch, James and Carol Cunkle lead amateurs, students, and professionals in unearthing evidence of a pottery-making Native American culture that flourished from about AD 1000 to 1450. Half-day hikes visit nearby petroglyphs; day-long programs add hands-on training in ruin-sifting. Longer stays include accommodations at a restored 19th-century bunkhouse. The tiny museum is a marvel. *White Mountain Archaeological Center, HC 30, Box 30, St. Johns 85936,* ☎ *602/333–5857.*

☛ *$3.50 adults, $2.50 senior citizens and children 12–17; admission includes 1-hr guided tour.* ⊗ *May 1–Oct. 15, daily 10–5.*

Springerville is a decision point: Should you head south or west on the return trip to Phoenix? At Springerville, AZ 260 joins U.S. 60, which continues east into New Mexico, and the so-called "Devil's Highway" (AZ 666), surely one of the world's curviest roads, coming down from the Painted Desert.

 If you decide to head south from Springerville on AZ 666, this lonely highway passes through **Nutrioso** under 10,912-foot Escudilla Mountain and eventually rises to **Hannagan Meadow,** one of Arizona's most splendid camping areas. Lush and isolated, it provides a home to elk, deer, and range cattle. Don't miss the splendid overlooks on the way.

TIME OUT Waiting by the roadside in the middle of the meadow is the log-built **Hannagan Meadow Lodge,** where you can enjoy a meal or a month in a setting of unparalleled peace and beauty, with people who have true appreciation for life outside the city, but not without amenities. *Hannagan Meadow Lodge, HC61 Box 335, Alpine 85920, ☎ 602/339–4370.*

From Hannagan Meadow, the road south twists and turns as it descends into a huge wilderness devoid, for the most part, of humans, and passes under Rose and Mitchell peaks (there is camping near the latter).

Eventually passing through the mining towns of **Morenci** and **Clifton,** AZ 666 then swings back west, links up with U.S. 70, and provides a fairly straight shot through **Safford** and across rather uninteresting desert to Globe. As you near **Fort Thomas,** keep your eyes peeled—$28,000 in gold pieces, meant to pay the soldiers there, was stolen back in May 1889 and still hasn't been found. About 12 miles farther along, on your left, you'll see towering 8,282-foot Mt. Turnbull, then the spreading expanse of **San Carlos Lake,** a reservoir behind Coolidge Dam. (Dedicating it in 1927, Will Rogers observed, "If that was my lake, I'd mow it.") At Peridot, if you turn north on AZ 170, 4 miles brings you to the town of San Carlos: It used to be Rice, until the dam put the original San Carlos underwater.

Once you reach Globe, you can retrace your original route back along U.S. 60 to Phoenix. Or if you prefer, **The Apache Trail** (AZ 88) departs from Claypool to the north, passing several ranches en route to the massive **Theodore Roosevelt Lake reservoir,** a favorite aquatic recreational area flanked by the desolate Mazatzal and Sierra Anchas mountain ranges. The Apache Trail eventually winds its way back to Apache Junction via the magnificent, bronze-hued **Fish Creek Canyon.**

TIME OUT Close to the end of the Apache Trail are the old-time restaurant, bar, and country store at **Tortilla Flat.** This is a fun place to stop for a well-earned rest and refreshment—miner- and cowboy-style grub, of course—before heading back the last 20 miles to civilization. *1 Main St., Tortilla Flat 85290 ☎ 602/984–1776.* ⊗ *Year-round weekdays 9–6, weekends 8–7.*

Back at Springerville, your other homeward option is to follow U.S. 60 west along the forested Mogollon Rim, enjoying its thrilling overlooks. From Show Low, take AZ 260 west along the Rim through a variety of small retirement and ranching communities. After **Forest Lakes,** the road dives off the Rim, hugging sheer cliffs for a 2,000-foot drop to the broad, verdant **Tonto Basin.**

⑮ Below the rim, in the Tonto Basin, is **Christopher Creek,** a primitive community with a humble but decent restaurant, the **Creekside Steak House & Tavern** (HCR Box 146, Payson, ☎ 602/478–4389). The **Christopher Creek Lodge,** 23 miles east of Payson (Star Route Box 119, Payson 85541, ☎ 602/478–4300) offers no-frills log-cabin accommodations.

West of Christopher Creek a huge forest fire charred much of the terrain several summers ago, destroying (along with millions of trees) the antiques-filled **Zane Grey Cabin,** once the home of the novelist whose popular tales—many of which were made into films—colorfully documented the rough-and-tumble life of this corner of the Old West. Now Mel and Beth Counseller recall his life and career a dozen miles down the road with photographs, videos, art, and new mementos at the ⑯ modest **Zane Grey Museum.** *408 W. Main St., Suite 8, Payson 85547,* ☎ *602/474–6243.* ☉ *Year-round, daily 9–5.*

You're back to civilization in **Payson,** a bustling vacation town with an interesting, unpretentious municipal golf course and a good supply of antiques shops. Turn south on U.S. 87 for the last hour-long dash across the ridges of the Mazatzals.

Descending into a saguaro-studded basin, you reach the Salt River again, this time on the Fort McDowell Mohave–Apache Reservation, whose residents have outlasted the fort where the U.S. Army based its northern campaign against the Apaches. When you see the 140-foot spray ⑰ of the **Fountain Hills** fountain, get ready to turn right at Shea Boulevard and head back, via Scottsdale, into Phoenix.

What to See and Do with Children

Aimed at children of elementary-school age, the **Arizona Museum for Youth** displays fine arts in a manner accessible to youngsters. Hands-on exhibits allow children to make crafts or participate as they go through the museum. A tour takes about 1–1½ hours. *35 N. Robson St., Mesa,* ☎ *602/644–2468.* ☛ *$2.* ☉ *Tues.–Fri. 1–5, Sat. 10–5, Sun. 1–5.*

Arizona Museum of Science and Technology (*see* Tour 1, *above*).

About an hour east of Phoenix on U.S. 60, the **Boyce Thompson Southwestern Arboretum** is one of the treasures of the Sonoran Desert. From the visitor center, well-marked, self-guided trails traverse 35 acres, winding through all of the desert's varied habitats—from gravelly open desert to lush creekside glades—rich with native flora and wildlife. The **Smith Interpretive Center,** a National Historic Site, houses displays on such topics as geology and mining plus two greenhouses with cacti and other succulents. The arboretum is a wonderful place to stop for a picnic on your way to the mining towns of Superior and Miami, 55 miles east of Phoenix. *Box AB, Superior 85273,* ☎ *602/689–2811.* ☛ *$4 adults, $2 children 5–12.* ☉ *Daily 8–5. Closed Dec. 25.*

Great Arizona Puppet Theatre mounts a yearlong cycle of inventive puppet productions, mostly original, in a converted church; it also offers classes in puppet making and operation. *3302 N. 7th St., Phoenix 85011,* ☎ *602/277–1275).* ☛ *$4; group rates also available.*

At the **Hall of Flame,** retired firefighters lead tours past more than 100 restored fire engines and more than 3,000 helmets, badges, and other fire fighting–related articles. *6101 E. Van Buren St. (in Papago Park),* ☎ *602/275–3473.* ☛ *$4 adults, $1.50 children 6–17.* ☉ *Mon.–Sat. 9–5, Sun. 12–4.*

Model-train displays, stores with railway memorabilia and items for the train hobbyist, and a restored Pullman car fill the popular **McCormick Railroad Park.** For $1, children can ride the miniature train or the 1929 merry-go-round. *7301 E. Indian Bend Rd., Scottsdale,* ☎ *602/994–2312.* ☛ *Free. Call for hrs.*

At the foot of South Mountain, **Mystery Castle,** hand-built out of found desert rocks, is chock-full of oddities that will fascinate everyone in the family. There are 18 rooms with 13 fireplaces, 90 bottle-glass portholes, a downstairs grotto, and a roll-away bed with a mining railcar as its frame. *800 E. Mineral Rd. (at south end of 7th St.)* ☎ *602/268–1581.* ☛ *$3 adults, $1 children 5–15.* ☯ *Tues.–Sun. 11–4.*

Phoenix Children's Theatre (1202 N. 3rd St., ☎ 602/265–4142) stages a full season, usually adaptations of fairy tales and children's books, at the city's Performing Arts Building.

At the **Phoenix Zoo,** a new 21,000-square-foot Baboon Kingdom exhibit brings together more than 1,300 animals, grouped by continent of origin. Indian and African elephants (including one that produces artwork sold in galleries!) and a rare Sumatran tiger are among the attractions. A 30-minute narrated tour on the safari train costs $1.50 and gives a good overview of the park. *5810 E. Van Buren St. (in Papago Park off Galvin Parkway),* ☎ *602/273–7771.* ☛ *$7 adults, $6 senior citizens, $3.50 children 4–12.* ☯ *Daily 9–5, May 1–Labor Day 7–4. Closed Dec. 25.*

Original and reconstructed buildings from all over Arizona set the stage for the **Pioneer Arizona Living History Museum.** Guides in the blacksmith shop, print shop, schoolhouse, and homes demonstrate 19th-century craft. *Pioneer Rd. exit off I-17,* ☎ *602/993–0212.* ☛ *$5.* ☯ *Wed.–Sun. 9–5. Closed mid-June–Oct. 1.*

The false fronts on **Rawhide**'s dusty Main Street house saloons, gift shops, old-time photo studios, and craftspeople, as well as opportunities to take a stagecoach ride or to pan for gold. Hayrides travel a short distance into the desert for a cookout under the stars on weekends. *23023 N. Scottsdale Rd., Scottsdale,* ☎ *602/563–1880. Separate charges for shops, restaurants, attractions.* ☯ *Mon.–Thurs, 5–10 PM, Fri.–Sun. 11–10.*

Similar to Rawhide, but a better deal because the price of entry is all-inclusive, **Rockin' R Ranch** includes a petting zoo, a reenactment of a wild shoot-out, and—the main attraction—a nightly cookout with a Western stage show. Browse the shops until the chow—beef, beans, and biscuits—is served, followed by music and entertainment. Reservations are required. *6136 E. Baseline Rd., Mesa,* ☎ *602/832–1539.* ☛ *$16.95 adults, $9.50 children 3–12; includes meal and show. Call for hrs.*

The **Sunrise Preschool** (642 E. Monroe St., ☎ 602/253–0381) at the east end of The Mercado (*see* Tour 1, *above*) offers high-quality child care with drop-in rates, 24 hours a day.

Off the Beaten Path

The following places, Arcosanti and Wickenburg, make interesting half-day or day trips from Phoenix. You also might consider them as stopovers on the way to or from Flagstaff, Prescott, or Sedona (*see* Chapter 4, North-Central Arizona and Flagstaff).

About 52 miles north of Phoenix on I-17, you'll find one of the world's architectural wonders—**Arcosanti.** Located near the exit for Cordes Junction (AZ 69), a mile down a partly paved road northeast from the gas stations and cafés, this evolving community was masterminded by Italian architect Paolo Soleri. It is now being built by its residents as a totally energy-independent town. It looks almost like a huge playground or contemporary-art theme park, with desert-rock retaining walls and festive, cast forms. But it's full of ideas for dramatic design and ecologically sensitive living. It's worth taking an hour out for a tour, eating at the café, and bringing home one of the hand-cast wind-bells. *I–17 at Cordes Junction, Mayer 86333, ☎ 602/632–7135. ☉ Daily 9–5; tours ($5) hourly 10–4.*

If you're interested, travel a few miles northwest on AZ 69 in the Valley of Big Bug Creek (you can see its course by looking for the willows south of the road) to **Mayer,** a provisioning center for the gold hunters who scoured the area in the last century. The tall stack of its long-silent smelter peers over a hill, and some enchanting historic buildings still stand on Main Street, a mile or so off the road.

And if you do continue from here to Prescott, consider stopping in at **Young's Farm** (AZ 169 just outside of Dewey, ☎ 602/632–7272). This family-run, 49-year-old farm with a 25-year-old store has become a beloved purveyor of potpies and pumpkins, sweet corn and cider, hayrides, and honey, and fresh bread. The Farm Kitchen coffee-shop and bakery is open daily, 6 AM to 4 PM.

To visit **Wickenburg,** follow I–17 north for about 15 minutes to the Carefree Road (AZ 74) exit. Thirty miles west, it reaches AZ 89/93, from which point it is another 10 miles to Wickenburg, home of dude ranches and tall tales. This city is named for Henry Wickenburg, whose nearby Vulture Mine was the richest gold strike in the Arizona Territory. On the main drag are the **Hassayampa Bridge,** the nearby **Jail Tree** (where prisoners were chained, the desert heat sometimes finishing them off before their sentences were served), and the **Gold Nugget** (222 E. Wickenburg Way, ☎ 602/684–2858), a Western-style eating place perfect for easy refueling. Half a block north on Valentine Street is **Anita's Cocina** (57 N. Valentine St., ☎ 602/684–5777), which offers authentic Mexican fare. If you are interested in lore of the American West, the 20,000 square-foot **Desert Caballeros Western Museum** (21 N. Frontier St., ☎ 602/684–7075) makes a fine stop. If you opt for a longer stay in Wickenburg, there are plenty of dude ranches to accommodate you (*see* Lodging, *below*). From town, Prescott is about 59 miles north on AZ 89.

SHOPPING

Since its resorts began multiplying in the 1930s and 1940s, Phoenix has acquired a healthy share of high-style clothiers and leisure-wear boutiques. But well before that, Western clothes were dominant here—jeans and boots, cotton shirts and dresses, 10-gallon hats and bola ties (the state's official neckwear). They still are.

In the past decade, Sun Belt awareness has brought a tide of interest in Southwestern furnishing styles as well, from the pastels of the desert mountains and skies to handmade lodgepole furniture of the pueblo and rancho. These—as well as Mexican tiles and tinware, wrought iron and copper work, courtyard fountains and paper flowers—have never died out here. Always an essential part of the way southwesterners shape their homes, work spaces, and public places, these crafts have flourished in the current revival.

At the same time, the drivers of many a wagon train in the past century and many a U-Haul in this one have headed west and ended up unloading here. As a result, the shops and auctions of Phoenix and its suburbs contain an unexpectedly wide array of antiques and collectibles.

On the scene long before any of these, of course, were the arts of the Southwest's true natives—Navajo weavers, sand painters, and silversmiths; Hopi weavers and kachina-doll carvers, Pima and Tohonó O'odham (Papago) basket makers and potters, and many more.

Inspired by the region's rich cultural traditions, contemporary artists have flourished here as well, making Phoenix—and in particular, Scottsdale, a city with more art galleries than gas stations—one of the Southwest's largest art centers (alongside Santa Fe, New Mexico).

Most of the valley's power shopping is concentrated in central Phoenix and downtown Scottsdale. But auctions and antiques shops cluster in odd places—and as treasure hunters know, you've always got to have an eye open.

Markets and Auctions
Guadalupe Farmer's Market (9210 S. Avenida del Yaqui, Guadalupe, ☎ 602/730–1945) has all the fresh ingredients of Mexican cuisine that you'd find in a rural Mexican market—tomatillos, many varieties of chili peppers (fresh and dried), fresh-ground *masa* (cornmeal) for tortillas, cumin and cilantro, and on and on.

Mercado Mexico (8212 S. Avenida del Yaqui, Guadalupe, ☎ 602/831–5925), about six blocks north, sells childhood treats Mexican adults remember fondly, from *cajetas* (goat's milk candy) to cocoa blocks and sweet powders in paper tubes. The rest of the shop is shelf after shelf of ceramic, paper, tin, and lacquerware, at unbeatable prices.

John Brunk & Sons Auctions (4001 N. 7th St., ☎ 602/264–3204) moves a barnful of cast-off furnishings, appliances, tools—and often several decent antiques or collectibles—twice each Wednesday, at 9 AM and from 7 PM until the last lot is gone. **Ron Brunk Inc. Auction** has a warehouse auction Sunday at noon in the western valley, not far from Sun City (10109 Grand Ave., ☎ 602/933–7748). **Hudson & Associates** (3602 N. 35th Ave., ☎ 602/269–8662) gavels off a diverse gathering of goods starting at 6 PM each Friday, as does **Ware's Auction** (38th Ave. at Indian School Rd., ☎ 602/278–0489) at 6 PM Monday.

Barrett & Jackson Classic Car Auction (5530 E. Washington St., ☎ 602/273–0791) is a nationally recognized dealer in rare and antique autos, and the annual January mega-auction draws collectors from around the world.

Southwestern Arts and Crafts
The **Heard Museum** (22 E. Monte Vista Rd., ☎ 602/252–8848) sells the finest selection of Southwestern Native American arts and crafts in the valley—both traditional and modern—at its gift shop. The museum is also the ideal place for learning about whatever medium or art form interests you and to see Native American artists and artisans at work almost every day.

Herman Atkinson's Indian Trading Post (3957 N. Brown Ave., Scottsdale, ☎ 602/949–9750) is another fine—but eclectic—source for Native American and especially Mexican work, from silver to lacquer goods to boots and paper flowers. Mixed in is a good deal of inexpensive (but often pretty good) tourist ware, and even an intriguing roomful of African carvings.

Godber's Jewelry (7542 E. Main St., Scottsdale, ☎ 602/949–1133) is one of the oldest, most reliable Native American-jewelry outlets in central Arizona. Begun 60 years ago by a reservation trading-post family, it's a fine place for learning the many styles of Southwestern jewelry and discovering your own preferences.

Gilbert Ortega (7229 E. Main St., Scottsdale, ☎ 602/947–2805) began as a reliable trader, then mushroomed into an industry with nine Scottsdale locations (including two at The Borgata), four in Phoenix, and one each in Tempe, Sun City, and Carefree. Only a fairly experienced Native American–jewelry buyer should shop here.

Folklórico (7216 E. Main St., Scottsdale, ☎ 602/947–0758) is a fine purveyor of Southwestern folk arts and crafts.

Finally, don't forget the gift shop at the **Museo Chicano** (1242 E. Washington, ☎ 602/257–5536, open Tues.–Fri., 10 AM–3 PM).

Malls

The open-air **Park Central Mall** (Central Ave. and Earll Dr., ☎ 602/264–5575) is the oldest and closest to downtown, amid the high rises of Central Avenue. Anchored by a **Dillard's** department store (3033 N. 3rd Ave., ☎ 602/277–0564) that sells all the seasonal clearance items from the other stores in the Dillard's chain, Park Central also has the popular **Limited Express** (55 Park Central Mall, ☎ 602/266–3450); the **Miracle Mile Deli** (9 Park Central Mall, ☎ 602/277–4783), a traditional favorite with downtown shoppers; and **Leonard's Luggage** (Park Central Mall, ☎ 602/264–3591), the valley's oldest purveyor of luxury leather goods and accessories.

Metrocenter (I–17 and Peoria Ave., ☎ 602/997–2641), on the west side of Phoenix, is an enclosed double-deck mall, the state's largest. The adjacent **Castles N Coasters** (9445 N. Metro Pkwy. E, ☎ 602/997–7575), a miniature-golf park and video-game palace, and the in-mall **Metro Midway** (13615 N. 35th Ave., ☎ 602/395–9915), an array of rides and games, make Metro the valley's best mall for teens and younger children. Inside, its anchor department stores include **Robinson's** (9700 N. Metro Pkwy. E, ☎ 602/943–2351). Metrocenter has nearly every store Park Central has and many more, but in a Muzakfilled, disinfected, deodorized environment that might as easily be in St. Louis or Seattle or Secaucus.

Fiesta Mall (AZ 360 and Alma School Rd., Mesa, ☎ 602/833–5450) and the new **Superstition Springs Mall,** a dozen miles farther east (AZ 360 and Superstition Springs Rd., Mesa, ☎ 602/832–0212), provide slightly smaller copies, without the youth attractions, for the eastern valley—though the latter does boast a handsome indoor carousel and a pleasant outdoor cactus garden to stroll in. The somewhat older but just expanded **Paradise Valley Mall** (Cactus and Tatum Rds., ☎ 602/996–8840) does likewise for northeastern Phoenix.

Scottsdale Fashion Square (Scottsdale and Camelback Rds., Scottsdale, ☎ 602/990–7800) is a definite step up. Besides Robinson's and Dillard's, it is anchored by **Bullock's** (6900 E. Camelback Rd., Scottsdale, ☎ 602/994–3111), and its mix of stores runs more to specialty shops; children will want everything in the **Disney Store** (7014 E. Camelback Rd., Scottsdale, ☎ 602/423–5008) and **Warner Bros. Studio Store** (7014 E. Camelback Rd., Scottsdale, ☎ 602/423–1663).

Biltmore Fashion Park (24th St. and Camelback Rd., ☎ 602/955–8400), about 8 miles west in Phoenix, is yet another step up. **Broadway Southwest** (2410 E. Camelback Rd., ☎ 602/468–2100) and **Saks Fifth Avenue** (2500 E. Camelback Rd., ☎ 602/955–8000) are its anchors, and designer boutiques are its stock-in-trade—**Banana Republic** (2582 E. Camelback Rd., ☎ 602/955–9108), **Via Vento** (2542 E. Camelback Rd., ☎ 602/956–6661), **Gucci** (2504 E. Camelback Rd., ☎ 602/957–8710), and **Polo by Ralph Lauren** (2580 E. Camelback Rd., ☎ 602/952–0155) are among them. Grown-up toy shops include **The Sharper Image** (2596 E. Camelback Rd., ☎ 602/956–8077) and **Williams-Sonoma** (2450 E. Camelback Rd., ☎ 602/957–0430). **Borders Books and Music** (2402 E. Camelback Rd., ☎ 602/957–6660) is a great family place, complete with coffee shop; the new outpost of **Planet Hollywood** (2402 E. Camelback Rd., ☎ 602/954–7827) seasons its menu with the hope of spotting one or more of its movie-star owners. Biltmore Fashion Park also has more fine eating in a small radius than anywhere else in Arizona; *see* the reviews of **RoxSand, Steamers, Oscar Taylor's,** and **Christopher's** *in* Dining, *below.*

The Borgata (6166 N. Scottsdale Rd., ☎ 602/998–1822), a re-creation of a medieval Italian walled village, may slip into pretentiousness, but it offers a pleasant enough selection of boutiques and galleries. **Dos Cabezas** (☎ 602/991–7004) has won a well-deserved following as a creative source of Southwestern interior and apparel design.

SPORTS AND THE OUTDOORS

Participant Sports

When participating in outdoor sports in Phoenix, be aware that the desert heat imposes its particular restraints on activities. From May 1 to October 1, do not jog or hike from one hour after sunrise until a half hour before sunset. During those times, the air is so hot and dry that your body will lose moisture—and burn calories—at a dangerous, potentially lethal rate. Don't head out to desert areas at night, however, to jog or hike in the summer; that's when rattlesnakes and scorpions are out hunting. Hikers and bicyclists should wear lightweight but opaque clothes, strong sunscreen (rated 15 or higher), high UV-rated sunglasses, a hat or visor, and should carry a water supply of one quart per person for each hour of activity, even in winter.

Bicycling

Although the relatively level terrain is great, the desert climate makes special demands on cyclists: *See* the advice on hours and clothing, *above.* Be sure to have a helmet and a mirror when riding in the streets: There are few adequate bike lanes in the valley.

Scottsdale's Indian Bend Wash (along Hayden Rd., from Shea Blvd. south to Indian School Rd.) has bikeable paths winding among its golf courses and ponds. **Pinnacle Peak,** about 25 miles northeast of downtown Phoenix, is a popular place to take bikes for the ride north to Carefree and Cave Creek, or east and south over the mountain pass and down to the Verde River, toward Fountain Hills. **Cave Creek** and **Carefree,** in the foothills about 30 miles northeast of Phoenix, offer pleasant riding with a wide range of stopover options. **South Mountain Park** (*see* Hiking, *below*) is the prime site for mountain bikers, with its 40-plus miles of trails—some of them with challenging ascents, and all of them quiet and scenic.

For rentals, contact **Landis Cyclery** (712 W. Indian School Rd., ☎ 602/264–5681; 2180 E. Southern Ave., Tempe, ☎ 602/839–9383; 10417 N. Scottsdale Rd., Scottsdale, ☎ 602/948–9280) or **Tempe Bicycle** (330 W. University Dr., Tempe, ☎ 602/966–6896).

To get in touch with fellow bike enthusiasts and find out about regular and special-event rides, contact the **Arizona Bicycle Club** (Gene or Sylvia Berlatsky, ☎ 602/264–5478), the state's largest group.

Golf

The Valley of the Sun is the valley of year-round golf par excellence. More than 100 courses, from par-3 to PGA championship links, are available (some lighted at night), and the PGA's Southwest section headquarters here. For a detailed listing, contact the **Arizona Golf Association** (*see* Sports *in* The Gold Guide's Important Contacts A to Z).

One of the newer, upscale courses, **Ahwatukee Country Club** (12432 S. 48th St., ☎ 602/893–1161), set along the edge of South Mountain Park, is semiprivate but also has a public driving range. The **Arizona Biltmore** (24th St. and Missouri Ave., ☎ 602/955–9655), the granddaddy of Phoenix golf courses, offers two 18-hole PGA championship courses, lessons, and clinics. Two low-price public courses, both in scenic city settings, are **Encanto Park** (2705 N. 15th Ave., ☎ 602/253–3963) and **Papago Golf Course** (5595 E. Moreland St., ☎ 602/275–8428). If you're in the Superstition Mountains area, try the desert course at **Gold Canyon Golf Club** (6100 S. Kings Ranch Rd., Apache Junction, ☎ 602/982–9449). The best course in the Sun Cities, **Hillcrest Golf Club** (20002 N. Star Ridge, Sun City West, ☎ 602/584–1000), is a PGA Senior Tour site. Take the children along to **PGA Tour Family Golf Center** (8111 E. McDonald Dr., Scottsdale, ☎ 602/991–0018), which combines goofy golf, a driving range, and lessons at all levels. For big, sweeping views of the city, **Thunderbird Country Club** (701 E. Thunderbird Trail, Phoenix, ☎ 602/243–1262) has 18 holes of championship-rated play on the north slopes of South Mountain. **Tournament Players Club at Scottsdale** (17020 N. Hayden Rd., Scottsdale, ☎ 602/585–3600), a 36-hole course created by Tom Weiskopf and Jay Morrish, is the site of the PGA Phoenix Open.

Health Clubs

The Arizona Athletic Club (1425 W. 14th St., Tempe, ☎ 602/894–2281), near the airport at the border between Tempe and Scottsdale, is the valley's largest facility. It offers nonmember visitors a day rate of less than $15.

Jazzercise (☎ 602/893–1557) has 20 franchised sites in the valley, where people who are already on a program can keep on course while on vacation.

Life Centers of Arizona (4041 N. Central Ave., ☎ 602/265–5472), in central Phoenix, is geared to the working man and woman, so it offers nonmembers both reasonable day rates ($5–$15) and a variety of quick workout options.

Naturally Women (2827 W. Peoria Ave., ☎ 602/678–4000; 3320 S. Price Rd., Tempe, ☎ 602/838–8800; 7750 E. McDowell Rd., ☎ 602/947–8300) focuses on women, from its health profiles to its diet and exercise programs; it offers one free visitor's day, then a day rate of about $10 afterward.

Hiking

The valley boasts some of the best desert mountain hiking in the world—the **Phoenix Mountain Preserve System** (☎ 602/495–0022), in the mountains that surround the city, even has its own park rangers who can help you select and plan your hikes. Phoenix's hiking trails are some of the most heavily-used in the world—and for good reason. Call for information and group hiking reservations.

Squaw Peak (2701 E. Squaw Peak Dr., just north of Lincoln, ☎ 602/ 262–7901) is a favorite two-hour hike that ascends the landmark mountain from a well-equipped park in the North Mountains Preserve. Children can handle this one if adults take it slowly. The rangers also lead a fine, easy hike through the park, introducing desert geology, flora, and fauna.

Camelback Mountain (north of Camelback Rd. on 48th St., ☎ 602/256– 3220), another landmark hike, has no park, and the trails are more difficult. This is for intermediate to experienced hikers.

The soft sandstone **Papago Peaks** (Van Buren St. and Galvin Pkwy., ☎ 602/256–3220) were sacred sites for the Tohonó O'odham tribe and probably the Hohokam before them. The peaks contain accessible caves, some petroglyphs, and splendid views of much of the valley. This is another good spot for family hikes. The Phoenix Zoo, the Desert Botanical Garden, and the new Arizona Historical Society Museum are all within the area.

South Mountain Park (10919 S. Central Ave., ☎ 602/495–0222) is the jewel of the city's Mountain Park Preserves. At 16,000 acres, it is the nation's largest city park, and its mountains and arroyos contain more than 40 miles of marked and maintained trails—all multiuse, for hiking, horseback riding, and mountain biking. It also has three auto-accessible lookout points, with 65-mile sightlines. The rangers can help you plan hikes to see some of the 200 petroglyph sites located so far.

CAUTION: Be sure to bring plenty of water with you when hiking and drink often. Dehydration can become a life-threatening condition. (*See* Hiking *in* The Gold Guide's Smart Travel Tips for more information.)

Horseback Riding

More than two dozen stables and equestrian tour outfitters in the valley attest to the saddle's enduring importance in Arizona—even in this auto-dominated metropolis.

All Western Stables (10220 S. Central Ave., ☎ 602/276–5862), one of several stables at the entrance to South Mountain Park, offers rentals, guided rides, hayrides, and at the end of the trail, steak fries.

The **Hole-in-the-Wall Stables** (7777 Pointe Pkwy., ☎ 602/431–0817) is near large areas of the Phoenix Mountain Preserve System and has guided solo and group, hourly and overnight options.

Adjacent to the Phoenix North Mountains Preserve, **North Side Stables** (25251 N. 19th Ave., ☎ 602/581–0103) offers everything from pony rides to pack trips—even stagecoach rentals.

Old MacDonald's Ranch (26540 N. Scottsdale Rd., Scottsdale, ☎ 602/ 585–0239) provides guided trail rides, hayrides, and catered cookouts.

Superstition Stables (Windsong and Meridian Rds., Apache Junction, ☎ 602/982–6353) is licensed to lead tours throughout the entire Superstition Mountains area for more experienced riders; easier rides are also available.

Hot-Air Ballooning

Another unusual sport that has soared in the desert air is hot-air ballooning. The following are a few of the three dozen companies that offer uplifting experiences; all use pilots who are certified by the Federal Aviation Administration: **An Aeronautical Adventure** (☎ 602/991–4260) has daily flights and will sell you a balloon if the bug really bites. **Hot Air Expeditions** (☎ 602/788–5555 or 800/831–7610) features a champagne flight and free pickup and return at local resorts. **Naturally High** (☎ 602/252–6766) offers not only ascents with trained pilots, among them recent state champions, but also training for aspiring crew members.

Jogging

Phoenix's unique 200-mile network of canals provides a naturally cooled (and often landscaped) scenic track throughout the metro area. Two other popular jogging areas are Phoenix's **Encanto Park,** 3 miles northwest of Civic Plaza, and Scottsdale's **Indian Bend Wash,** which runs for more than 5 miles along Hayden Road—both have lagoons and tree-shaded greens.

Tennis

At **Hole-in-the-Wall Racquet Club** (7677 N. 16th St., Pointe Hilton at Squaw Peak Resort, ☎ 602/997–2626), eight paved courts are available for same-day reservation at $15 per hour; at the affiliated **Watering Hole Racquet Club** (11111 N. 7th St., Pointe Hilton at Tapatio Cliffs Resort, ☎ 602/997–7237) the 15 courts are hard and lighted for night games. **Mountain View Tennis Center** (1104 E. Grovers St., ☎ 602/788–6088), just north of Bell Road, is a Phoenix city facility with 20 lighted courts that can be reserved for $3 for 90 minutes of singles. For the same price you can play at **Phoenix Tennis Center** (6330 N. 21st Ave., ☎ 602/249–3712), another city facility with 22 lighted hard courts. **The Pointe Hilton at South Mountain Tennis Club** (7777 S. Pointe Pkwy., ☎ 602/438–9000) has 10 lighted hard courts for $15 per hour.

Tubing

In a region not known for water, one indigenous aquatic sport has developed. Tubing—riding an inner tube down calm water and mild rapids—has become a very popular tradition on the Salt and Verde rivers. Outfitters that rent tubes include **Saguaro Lake Ranch Tube & Raft Rental** (13020 N. Bush Hwy., Mesa, ☎ 602/984–2194), right on the way into the McDowell Mountains, where the river action is (they also offer bed-and-breakfast accommodations), and **Salt River Recreation Tube Rental & Shuttle** (Bush Hwy., Mesa, ☎ 602/984–3305), conveniently located and offering transportation to and from your starting point.

Spectator Sports

Auto Racing

Phoenix International Raceway (7602 S. 115th Ave., Avondale 85323, ☎ 602/252–3833), the valley's NASCAR track, is the site of a Winston Cup 500 each October and the Indy car Slick 50 race each April.

Balloon Racing

The **Thunderbird Hot-Air-Balloon Classic** (☎ 602/978–7208) has grown into a schedule of festivities surrounding the national invitational balloon race, held each November.

Baseball

See Pleasures & Pastimes *in* Chapter 1, Destination: Arizona, for information on **Cactus League** spring training.

Basketball

The **Phoenix Suns** (2nd and Jefferson Sts., ☎ 602/379–SUNS) have been NBA playoff regulars for several years. Their new America West Phoenix Suns Arena is almost as exciting as their game.

Golf

The **Phoenix Open** (☎ 602/585–4334), played each January at the Tournament Players Club in Scottsdale, is a $1 million event on the PGA Tour. In March, the women compete for the purse in **Standard Register PING Tournament** (☎ 602/942–0000), held at the Moon Valley Country Club.

Rodeos

The **Parada del Sol,** held each year by the Scottsdale Jaycees (3515 N. 75th St., Scottsdale, ☎ 602/990–3179), includes a rodeo, a lavish parade famed for its silver-studded tack, and a 400-mile daredevil ride from Holbrook down the Mogollon Rim to Phoenix by the Hashknife Riders.

The **Rodeo of Rodeos,** sponsored by the Phoenix Jaycees (4133 N. 7th St., ☎ 602/263–8671), has one of the Southwest's oldest and best parades.

The **World's Oldest Rodeo** (Box 2037, Prescott 86302, ☎ 800/358–1888), held each July as part of Frontier Days, gives the Phoenix rodeos a run for their money.

DINING

Phoenix's culinary traditions arose from a unique blend of Old West and New West cultures. In the mid-19th century, the north-Mexican rancho cooking that had been in Arizona for 150 years was joined by the Anglo-European food of American settlers. Arizona Territory was also an outpost of the West's cattle-ranching boom, and the railroads brought a significant early influx of Chinese settlers.

By the mid-20th century, the valley was rich in Mexican food, mostly in the style of the adjoining Mexican state of Sonora; steak houses from cowboy to fancy (Phoenix was a major stockyard center until the 1970s); and Chinese restaurants, mostly Cantonese. There was plenty of family eating, heartburn, and *agita.* When Phoenicians wanted to get fussy, men put on bola ties and women donned silver-and-turquoise jewelry, and they paid someone to pour "Continental" sauces on their steaks.

Then, during the 1970s, things took off. Southeast Asian refugees brought spicy Oriental dishes that were instantly welcome in a city used to salsa and sweet-and-sour. Immigrants from Central America and the Middle East brought more variations on familiar themes, as well as new approaches. Soon, "Southwestern international" was born—and by the late '80s, it had taken hold of America's culinary imagination. Arizona being what it is, along with this vibrant and inventive cuisine, Phoenix has plenty of good old meat-and-potatoes and diner fare (*see* the American section, *below*).

Few restaurants require men to wear jackets and ties (in any situation, a bola tie will always suffice). The *guayabera* (Mexican wedding shirt) is also an appropriate warm-weather option in all but the fanciest places. Similarly, pants or a simple dress are welcome almost everywhere for women. Only the fanciest places expect a dress or pantsuit. (Restaurants are open daily, unless otherwise noted.)

CATEGORY	COST*
$$$$	over $40
$$$	$20–$40
$$	$10–$20
$	under $10

per person, excluding drinks, service, and sales tax (6%–7%)

American

$$$ **Ruth's Chris Steakhouse.** Most meat fanciers agree that steak seldom gets better handling than at this New Orleans–based chain. Amid brass, wood, and glass (and great views at the Scottsdale location), you can get thick, juicy lamb or pork chops, but planks of beef are this restaurant's business. Calorie- and cardiac-watchers, beware: Portions are massive, and everything—even the broiled shrimp—comes swimming in the house butter bath. ✕ *2201 E. Camelback Rd.,* ☎ *602/957–9600; 7001 N. Scottsdale Rd., Scottsdale,* ☎ *602/991–5988. Reservations required. AE, MC, V.*

$$$ **Steamers.** Watching the chefs at work in the open kitchen is one of the attractions of this bright, spacious seafood house. Another is attentive, knowledgeable service staff. Yet another is a wonderful array of New England–style standards like chowder and halibut and lobster. Don't stray into the fancy nouvelle part of the menu, simplicity is the strong point here. ✕ *2576 E. Camelback Rd.,* ☎ *602/956–3631. Reservations advised. AE, MC, V.*

$$$ **Top of the Market.** This smaller, slightly more expensive annex above
★   the noisy, popular Fish Market has the atmosphere of a San Francisco wharf restaurant. And its menu—everything from charbroiled orange roughy to whole Dungeness crab to handmade pastas—is skillfully handled and imaginatively seasoned. Try flan or strawberries for dessert. ✕ *1720 E. Camelback Rd.,* ☎ *602/277–3474. Reservations required. AE, DC, MC, V.*

$$ **American Grill.** Leather, brass, ferns, and etched-glass—a large bar at the entry and a lounge with cozy tables and soft, live jazz—all recreate a classic San Francisco pub. But the action is in the glassed-in exhibition kitchen and the booths, where varieties of American Cajun and Southwestern cuisine are prepared and consumed. N'awlins barbecued shrimp is a fine appetizer, and chowder in a bowl of sourdough bread can't be beat—powerful desserts, too. ✕ *1233 S. Alma School Rd., Mesa,* ☎ *602/844–1918. Reservations advised. AE, D, DC, MC, V.*

$$ **Durant's.** This downtown standby in black leather and red wallpaper hasn't changed since the '50s, and neither has its popularity (who can argue with prices that are also out-of-date?). With a crowded bar and open booths, Durant's is one of Phoenix's prime see-and-be-seen places. On the menu, steaks and chops are prominent, but check out steamed clams or chicken livers. (It does have a front door, but everyone enters through the kitchen from the parking lot.) ✕ *2611 N. Central Ave.,* ☎ *602/264–5967. Reservations advised for dinner. AE, D, DC, MC, V.*

$$ **Landmark.** After 50 years as a Mormon church and a brief turn as a
★   college, this massive brick Victorian became a restaurant. Expect to wait a half hour downstairs in the small lounge, surrounded by historical photos. Upstairs, you start at the huge salad bar of well-made Americana, from iceberg and garden marinade to seafood salad and thick, rich soups. A sauerbraten-sauce pot roast with heavenly mashed potatoes leads the entrées. After all of that, Landmark pie is a must for fudge lovers. ✕ *809 W. Main St., Mesa,* ☎ *602/962–4652. No reservations. AE, DC, MC, V.*

$$ Oscar Taylor's. Another favorite with the meat-and-potatoes crowd, this 1920s Chicago-style steak house combines a cozy atmosphere, brisk service, and beautiful cuts of meat. The prime rib is a house specialty, and the ribs are, too. ✗ *2420 E. Camelback Rd.,* ☎ *602/956–5705. Reservations advised. AE, DC, MC, V.*

$$ Rose's. Comfortably elegant in blue and burgundy and conveniently located on the northern edge of downtown, the restaurant at the Best Western Executive Park hotel is a quiet, tony haven of American–Continental cuisine with some nice Southwestern edges. Regional pasta dishes are a house specialty, as is chicken quesadilla. ✗ *1100 N. Central Ave.,* ☎ *602/252–2100. Reservations required. AE, D, DC, MC, V.*

$$ Rustler's Rooste. ★ This Johnny-come-lately among the valley's Western restaurants is the biggest and nearest to town—and the most fun. It's at the east end of South Mountain Park just off I-10 (take the Baseline exit west), in the theme-park atmosphere of the Pointe Hilton on South Mountain, Arizona's largest resort. Decorated in a playful miner-cowpoke style, complete with a slide from the bar down to the dining rooms, it offers excellent steaks, juicy barbecued pork ribs and chicken, and homemade ice cream. The Cowboy Stuff Platter ($16) puts a sample of almost everything the restaurant serves (except rattlesnake) on your plate. ✗ *7777 S. Pointe Pkwy.,* ☎ *602/431–6474. Reservations advised. AE, D, DC, MC, V.*

$$ The Stockyards. ★ When Arizona had cattle barons, they cut their deals and steaks here. The feedlots and barons are gone, but the restaurant remains, a landmark just a half mile east of Sky Harbor Airport. Its ornate Victorian interior retains the original brass-trim bar and three salons—the black-leather Cattleman's Room, the gold-papered Gold Coast Room, and the mural-wall Rose Room. Beef on the menu has been handled with respect, from massive prime rib and steaks to succulent calves' liver and calf fries (Rocky Mountain oysters). ✗ *5001 E. Washington St.,* ☎ *602/273–7378. Reservations advised. AE, DC, MC, V.*

$$ T-Bone Steakhouse. Drive south on 19th Avenue past the end of the pavement and there, on the slopes of South Mountain, is a big outdoor barbecue in a parking lot. Inside the rustic wooden building are wooden benches at oilcloth-covered tables. Steak and chicken come to you, and you're swept into vistas of the desert sunset or the valley lit up at night. Salad and beans, giant slices of toast, and fresh hot baked potatoes are always on hand. Friday and Saturday, amateur Western musicians take the microphone. ✗ *10037 S. 19th Ave.,* ☎ *602/276–0945. Reservations required for 8 or more. AE, MC, V.*

$ Bev's Kitchen. ★ Some folks call it country, some call it soul food, and some just call it home. Whatever you call it, you may have to wait in line to enjoy it. This handsome downtown diner (which started its life beside an auto lot on the south side) has gracious staff and great food—hand-pounded chicken-fried steak, crumbling moist catfish, lively hot links, and potatoes and greens and corn and cabbage and yams done by people who love their vegetables (boiled down some, of course). Your reward for finishing all that is a slice of one of Bev's pies. ✗ *7 W. Monroe St.,* ☎ *602/252–1455 and 4621 S. Central Ave.,* ☎ *243–2788. No reservations. AE, D, DC, MC, V.*

$ Ed Debevic's. This brash, noisy place adjacent to the Camelback Marriott is a nostalgic, half-accurate, but wholly entertaining, revision of the '50s. With red-leather dinettes, gum-snapping waitresses, and a working jukebox playing Elvis, Tessy Brewer, and dozens more, it has terrific burgers, malts, fries, and blue-plate specials like chili or meat loaf and gravy. With prodding, "Edna" and the girls (and the waiters, led by a guest-kissing nerd) will provide tableside diversions. Forty-plus

150

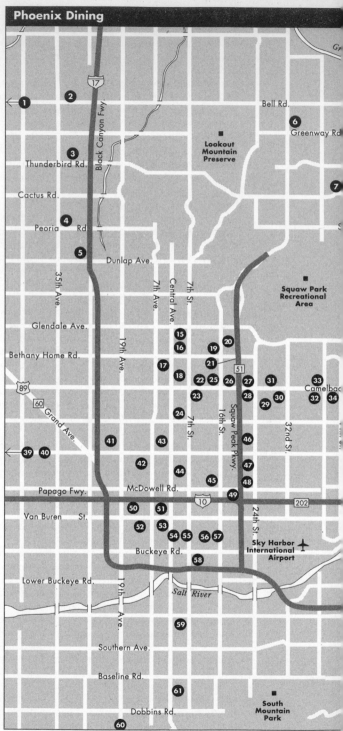

Phoenix Dining

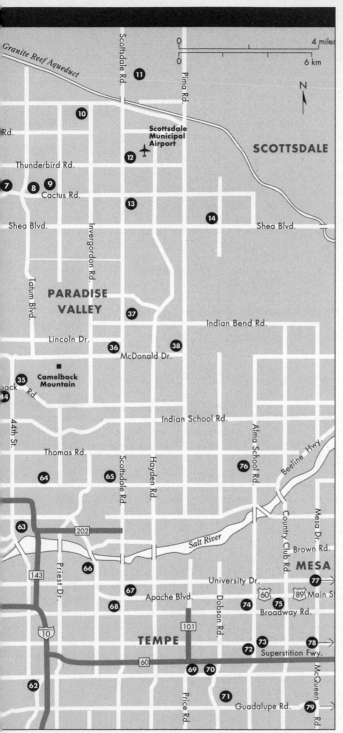

diners blush to remember, but children love it. ✗ *2102 E. Highland Ave.,* ☎ *602/956–2760. Reservations advised on weekends. AE, D, DC, MC, V.*

$ **The Eggery/The Good Egg.** Cute decor (airy and Southwestern at Eggery outlets, cluttered country at Good Eggs) and a lengthy menu mark this cheerful, comfy breakfast-brunch chain. Besides an array of cleverly named egg creations, from scrambler skillets to frittatas, as well as pancakes and waffles, there are welcome light options like yogurt, granola, and fruit dishes. Service is brisk and friendly, children are welcome, and there's no rush despite the crowds. ✗ *5109 N. 44th St.,* ☎ *602/840–5734; 4326 E. Cactus Rd. (at Paradise Valley Mall),* ☎ *602/953–2342; 2957 W. Bell Rd. (northwest),* ☎ *602/993–2797; 2 E. Camelback Rd.,* ☎ *602/263–8554; 906 E. Camelback Rd,* ☎ *602/274–5393; 6149 N. Scottsdale Rd., Scottsdale,* ☎ *602/991–5416; 14046 N. Scottsdale Rd., Scottsdale,* ☎ *602/483–1090. AE, MC, V.*

$ **Texaz Grill.** Tucked in an uptown corner mall, this noisy and crowded spot cluttered with Texas and country-western items does simple, effective things with steak (including classic chicken-fried) and serves up some of the best mashed potatoes you've had since you were a youngster. On steak, ask them to hold the lemon butter; the meat's better by itself. ✗ *6003 N. 16th St.,* ☎ *602/248–STAR. Reservations accepted for 6 or more. AE, MC, V.*

$ **Mrs. White's Golden Rule Café.** This little downtown, down-home lunch spot brings smiles to those who love liver and boiled cabbage, as well as fanciers of standard American fare such as fried chicken, corn on the cob, and yams. Food is cooked with a light, loving touch; service is friendly, prices are low, and the payin' is honor system. ✗ *808 E. Jefferson St.,* ☎ *602/262–9256. No reservations. No credit cards. No dinner.*

$ **Unique Foods & Services.** For snappy barbecue and soul classics done simply and with authority, this downtown café across the street from the restored Booker T. Washington School (now home to the *New Times* alternative newspaper) is the place to be. Breakfasts are hearty. Hot links and ribs are memorable at lunch and dinner, and delicate catfish and fried chicken demonstrate chef Barbara Karim's concern for healthful, flavor-rich cooking. Greens and gumbo are cooked with love, and don't forget about bean pie—good local jazz, too. ✗ *1153 E. Jefferson St.,* ☎ *602/257–0701. No reservations. V, MC.*

Chinese

$$ **China Doll.** The venerable ancestor of valley Cantonese restaurants still is *the* place for family and association banquets and Chinese New Year feasts. Dinners—including ginger fish, for which you select your own tilapia, swimming in the lobby tank—are reliably executed classics. The dim sum is among the best in town. ✗ *3336 N. 7th Ave.,* ☎ *602/264–0538. Reservations advised. AE, DC, MC, V.*

$$ **China Gate.** Seldom do chain restaurants rise so high or remain so con-
★ sistent in quality—not to mention the breadth of cuisines, from Mongolian to Cantonese, Beijing to spicy Szechuan. Mandarin ribs are a special experience, as is a combination of shrimp and sea cucumber. Decor is striking, and the layout emphasizes privacy amid open space. ✗ *3033 W. Peoria Ave., Phoenix,* ☎ *602/944–1982; 7820 E. McDowell Rd., Scottsdale,* ☎ *602/946–0720; 2050 W. Guadalupe Rd., Mesa,* ☎ *602/ 897–0607. Reservations advised. AE, D, DC, MC, V.*

$ **Golden Gate.** Owner and hostess Sue Kao maintains a friendly touch with diners at this charming restaurant serving delicious Mandarin and Szechuan cuisine. Highly recommended are garlic chicken, three kings chicken, Golden Gate shrimp, and moo shu pork. ✕ *2640 W. Baseline Rd., Mesa,* ☎ *602/897–1335. Reservations advised. MC, V.*

$ **Golden Moon Palace.** A modest place in the somewhat seedy area just north of the state capitol mall, Golden Moon is one of Phoenix's old standards. Half of the restaurant is simply decorated with red-leather booths and lanterns; the other half is a banquet room where local families celebrate and entertain guests. Egg rolls are sweet and stuffed with fresh veggies, garlic chicken is a masterpiece, and fried rice is a meal in itself. Service is genteel and attentive. ✕ *1408 W. Van Buren St.,* ☎ *602/ 254–9229. Reservations advised. AE, D, DC, MC, V. Closes 9 PM.*

$ **Gourmet of Hong Kong.** Get ready for the bustling sounds and incomparable flavors of Hong Kong, squeezed into a tiny downtown restaurant. Staff and owners rush in and out of a narrow, steamy, open kitchen to take your order and serve you, and take-out diners stand between tables, eagerly waiting (sounds like Chinatown). The house plate is a succulent, satisfying sampler, and hot-sour chicken wings, king duck, lobster, and garlic pork are delightful (tastes like it, too). ✕ *1438 E. McDowell Rd.,* ☎ *602/253–4859. Reservations advised. MC, V.*

$ **Lucky Restaurant.** Lucky for you—that is, if you look past the unpromising exterior, skip the buffet, and try something from the menu or the chalkboard (a little nerve and you'll have a rewarding adventure). If beef with bitter melons is available, don't miss it. Soft-shell crabs (in season) in black-bean sauce are unforgettable, too. ✕ *3317 N. 19th Ave.,* ☎ *602/274–9477. No reservations. No credit cards.*

Deli

$–$$ **Chompie's.** In a north Phoenix corner mall not far from Paradise Val-
★ ley Mall you'll find a cheerful New York deli. Big breakfasts—from blintzes to home fries to hefty omelets—give way to piled-high sandwiches on fresh-baked bread and rolls at lunchtime (all with pickles, the way it's meant to be). Not only do they make their own bagels, but the huge bakery case is a trip to the old country with a stunning array of traditional European treats and American inventions. Take a number! ✕ *3202 E. Greenway Rd.,* ☎ *602/971–8010. Reservations advised for 6 or more. MC, V.*

$ **Munch a Bagel.** Just north of Camelback, on one of the main morn-
★ ing routes into downtown, sits one of Phoenix's most popular reasons to leave home early or get to work a little late. A quick breakfast special of eggs, onion-tossed potatoes and a fresh bagel is worth stopping for. So is a more leisurely lingering over huge omelets (try No. 3 with tongue or pastrami) and a frothy cappuccino or café latté. Any deli sandwich you order for lunch is guaranteed to send you home with a smile and a doggie bag. ✕ *5114 N. 7th St.,* ☎ *602/264–1975. Reservations advised for 6 or more. AE, D, DC, MC, V.*

French

$$$$ **Christopher's.** Christopher Gross, one of the valley's leading chef-en-
★ trepreneurs, has re-created a bistro nearly worthy of the Champs-Elysées and, adjacent to it, an elegant, monogrammed-linen-and-silver, modern restaurant. They share an open kitchen. Classic fish, veal, and chicken are flawlessly prepared and presented—with surprising Southwestern touches. ✕ *2398 E. Camelback Rd.,* ☎ *602/957–3214. Reservations required. AE, DC, MC, V.*

$$$ **Voltaire.** The valley's most consistent classical French cuisine makes its home in a residential Scottsdale neighborhood. Nothing nouvelle here—there may not be a recipe that's less than 100 years old. But when you have the urge to cap off a drive through the desert with escargot, onion soup *gratinée,* and perfectly handled lamb, this is the place. And

how could one miss crêpes suzette, cherries jubilee, or exquisite crème caramel? ✕ *8340 E. McDonald Dr., Scottsdale,* ☎ *602/948–1005. Reservations required. AE, MC, V. Closed Sun.*

German

$$ Zur Kate. Though on the outside you may find yourself in a corner mall on a busy Mesa thoroughfare, inside you'll enter a friendly, family inn in Bavaria. Steins and Tyrolean caps belonging to regulars line the walls. Soups are good and hearty, sauerbraten, *kassler ripchen* (smoked pork loin), dumplings, and tiny spätzle dumplings are wonderful—not to mention wurst and fresh apple strudel. Music and gemütlich service complete the pleasures. ✕ *4815 E. Main St., Mesa,* ☎ *602/830–4244. MC, V. Closed Sun.*

Greek

$$ Greekfest. Greek cooking meets haute cuisine in this tasteful Athenian
★ taverna with wine racked along whitewashed walls. Classic dishes are handled exquisitely. Greekfest offers a quietly festive evening with feather-light spanakopita appetizers, sweet, succulent lamb, fresh, tart dolmades stuffed to bursting, and sour-light avgolemono as both soup and sauce. Baklava anyone? ✕ *1940 E. Camelback Rd.,* ☎ *602/265–2990. Reservations advised. DC, MC, V.*

$$ Greektown. At this warm family operation cheered by posters and murals, Papa greets, Mama cooks, and Son seats. A combo appetizer samples the Greek islands, and lamb stew and seafood are good bets. When it's time for dessert, there are honey, nuts, and phyllo dough aplenty—and Mama's rice pudding. Wash it down with sweet, cocoay coffee. ✕ *539 E. Glendale Ave.,* ☎ *602/279–9677. Reservations advised. AE, MC, V.*

Indian

$$ Indian Delhi Palace. Midway between downtown and Tempe, right across from Motorola's semiconductor plant, you'll step through the door of a double storefront right into India. Attentive service and delightful flavors enhance the illusion. Sip tea and nibble home-baked *naan* and *kalcha* breads while perusing the lengthy menu. Tandoori chicken and yogurt lamb are two of many wonderful dishes, but the best bet is the inclusive dinner. A lunch buffet is another fun way to tour India's kitchens. ✕ *5050 E. McDowell Rd.,* ☎ *602/244–8181. No reservations. MC, V.*

Italian

$–$$$ Giuseppe's. In a tiny, noisy storefront in a corner mall, the Carotenuto
★ family has hidden treasures: Savory pasta and homemade sauces, exquisitely creamy stuffed eggplant and zucchini, drop-off-the-bone ribs and rich, moist meatballs—and desserts from *tiramisù* to hard-shelled ice cream *tartuffo*. All this and checkered tablecloths, too. (Bring your own wine.) ✕ *2824 E. Indian School Rd.,* ☎ *602/381–1237. Reservations advised for 5 or more. AE, MC, V. Closed Sun.*

$ Chianti. This charming little poster-hung restaurant stays crowded, but the unusually alert service neither forgets nor flusters you. Antipasto salad is a crisp overture of clear, tangy flavors, and pasta is well handled and sauced. Espresso or cappuccino, with gelato, perhaps, or spumoni, close a delightful meal. ✕ *3943 E. Camelback Rd.,* ☎ *602/957–9840. Reservations advised. AE, MC, V.*

$ The Olive Garden. Plant-filled rooms, cleverly cut into private nooks on various levels, create a pleasing atmosphere. The food does more justice to the range of Italian cuisine than you would expect from a chain—from garlicky bread sticks to fine pesto and very creditable sauces (Alfredo and marinara are both consistently successful). A good place to go beyond spaghetti and pizza, and a nonthreatening "grown-up" setting for the young. ✗ *10223 N. Metro Pkwy. E (at Metrocenter Mall),* ☎ *602/943–4573; 9805 W. Bell Rd., Sun City,* ☎ *602/977–8378; 1261 W. Southern Ave. (at Fiesta Mall), Mesa,* ☎ *602/890–0440; 4868 E. Cactus Rd., Scottsdale,* ☎ *602/494–4327. 6201 E. Southern Ave., Mesa,* ☎ *602/807–0207; 2626 N. 75th Ave., Phoenix,* ☎ *602/849–6533. No reservations. DC, MC, V.*

Japanese

$$ Shogun. ★ In this small converted tavern, the cheerful staff offers the best all-around Japanese experience in the valley, starting with an outstanding sushi bar. At the tables there are both finely turned standards such as teriyaki and tempura and adventures into less familiar areas like fish marinated in rice wine. Children are welcome here, too. ✗ *12615 N. Tatum Blvd.,* ☎ *602/953–3264. Reservations advised. DC, MC, V.*

$$ Yamakasa. Simple and serene in decor and service, this family-run restaurant offers excellent sushi and a tempura- and teriyaki-style menu. Calm consistency makes this a refreshing place in which to enjoy an unhurried evening in the shadow of Fuji. ✗ *9301 E. Shea Blvd., Scottsdale,* ☎ *602/860–5605. Reservations advised. AE, DC, MC, V.*

Korean

$ Korean Garden. Another example of east-Asian simplicity, this friendly, well-staffed, place provides both familiar fare, such as *bulgoki* (grilled, marinated beef strips), and exotic treats such as *bibim bab* (a bowl of assorted vegetables and beef, with hot sauce, topped with a fried egg) and *jap chae* (pan-fried clear noodles with vegetables and beef). And each of the many kinds of *kimchi* (hot, marinated chopped cabbage) is a fiery treat. ✗ *1324 S. Rural Rd., Tempe,* ☎ *602/967–1133. MC, V.*

Mexican and Latin American

$$$–$$$$ La Hacienda. ★ About 20 miles northeast of downtown in the Scottsdale Princess Resort, this tile-roofed hacienda shows what happens when Sonoran food is elevated to haute cuisine. Dishes range from an enchilada stuffed with crab to the tableside drama of *cochinillo asado* (roast stuffed suckling pig), from chili relleno filled with pork loin and nuts to the sea-sweet *cabrilla rellena de salpicón* (crab-stuffed bass in lime mayonnaise). ✗ *7575 E. Princess Dr. (1 mi north of Bell Rd.), Scottsdale,* ☎ *602/585–4848. Reservations required. AE, DC, MC, V.*

$$–$$$$ La Pila. ★ For more than a decade, chef Norman Fierros has been elaborating his "Nueva Mexicana" fantasies, based on fresh Sonoran peasant dishes and inventive seasonings and presentations. Fans have followed him happily. At his latest restaurant, tucked amid ferns and fountains (*pilas*) beneath a midtown high-rise, he creates flowerlike six-inch tortilla chips for warm-hearted brown *chipotle* salsa, shrimp-and-lime ceviche so light it floats, tender grilled chicken morsels in a fiery mole sauce (quench it in custardlike rice), and his signature fish tacos with cilantro pesto. If you're coming for lunch, skip breakfast; if you're coming for dinner, fast all day. ✗ *2020 N. Central Ave.,* ☎ *602/252– 7007. Reservations advised for 5 or more. MC, V. Sun. only brunch.*

$$ Havana Café. ★ At this clean, cozy café in black and gray, you'll likely have to wait. So try Arriba, the tapas bar upstairs, for Spanish-style snacks and sherry. Cuban cuisine, surprisingly, shows more European than Latin American influence. Pork becomes a moist, marinated, garlic-laden roast, and tamales are moist and sweet, with meat mixed throughout the *masa* (cornmeal), not wrapped in it. Mexican hot sauces are unheard of, and *papas fritas* (french fries) are much in evidence. Don't miss their desserts—and have a cup of espresso at hand. ✕ *4225 E. Camelback Rd.,* ☎ *602/952–1991 and 6425 E. Bell,* ☎ *602/991–1496. AE, MC, V.*

\$\$ **Macayo.** This family-run chain has been a valley standby for half a century, and its six colorful outlets provide well-prepared Sonoran dishes amid folk-art decor. With tacos, tostadas, tamales (especially the sweet green corn), chilis relleno, *huevos rancheros* (fried eggs rancho style, atop corn tortillas and slathered with fresh salsa), refried beans, and creamy flan or honey-filled *sopapillas* (puffy tortillas) for dessert, it's a great place for introducing children to Mexican food. ✕ *4001 N. Central Ave.,* ☎ *602/264–6141; 7829 W. Thomas Rd.,* ☎ *602/873–0313; 1909 W. Thunderbird Rd.,* ☎ *602/866–7034; 11107 N. Scottsdale Rd., Scottsdale,* ☎ *602/596–1181; 300 S. Ash Ave., Tempe,* ☎ *602/966–6677; 1920 S. Dobson Rd., Mesa,* ☎ *602/820–0237. Reservations advised for dinner. AE, D, DC, MC, V.*

\$\$ **Richardson's.** Loose-cushioned, Santa Fe adobe booths surround a small, lively sports bar, and the open kitchen turns out that fiery fugue of flavors known as New Mexican style. Green chile stew is to die for—or from, if you're not used to the spicy heat. *Carne adovada* (pork roast in red chile sauce) and angel-hair pasta made of red chilies are scrumptious, Chimayo chicken (stuffed with spinach, dried tomatoes, poblano chilies and Asiago cheese) is also memorable. ✕ *1582 E. Bethany Home Rd.,* ☎ *602/265–5886. Reservations advised for 4 or more. AE, DC, MC, V.*

\$\$ **Such Is Life.** In an intimate corner of a small office building, chef-owner
★   Moises Treves creates a cuisine worthy of Guadalajara's famed Tapatío district. Squeeze in and start with *nopal polanco,* broiled prickly pear cactus, no thorns; move on to black bean soup; then choose a signature salad or an entrée: fillets done in peppers or chipotle sauce; stunning garlic shrimp; chicken Maya, shredded in anise-hinted *achiote* sauce, or *poblano,* a cocoa-chili sauce; or meltingly tender pork any of three ways. ✕ *3602 N. 24th St.,* ☎ *602/955–7822. Reservations advised. AE, D, DC, MC, V.*

\$ **Adrian's.** This modest, creek-rock building with wrought-iron grilles and a tiny outdoor patio transports you in food and decor south of Sonora to the coastal towns of Sinaloa on the Sea of Cortés (Anglos call it the Gulf of California). Many dishes are similar to Sonoran rancho fare, and Adrian prepares them well, especially pork with *nopalitos* (sliced cactus pads); but local Hispanic families keep coming for such treats as *Vuelve a la Vida* (Return to Life)—a cocktail of shrimp, abalone, oyster, and crab—or garlic-broiled whole pike over which you squeeze tiny, sweet Mexican limes. ✕ *2234 E. McDowell Rd.,* ☎ *602/ 273–7957. No reservations. No credit cards.*

\$ **Bahía San Carlos.** In the shadow of the Squaw Peak Parkway, just down the street from Adrian's, is that restaurant's best competitor in the *mariscos* (seafood) category. This popular, noisy little place is hung with huge posters of Mexico's palm-shaded beaches. Tostadas piled with sweet-tangy *salpicón* (lime-soaked, seasoned, shredded crab) make a splendid appetizer; *Caldo Siete Mares* (Seven Seas Soup) is a wonderful sampler of fish, squid, shrimp, crab, and more. ✕ *19th St. and McDowell Rd.,* ☎ *602/340–0892. No reservations. No credit cards.*

\$ **Los Dos Molinos.** One location is a standard storefront in Mesa, the other is a large white hostelry in south Phoenix. Both house pure, hot, New Mexico–style cooking—Victoria Chávez and her daughters turn out delicious *barbacoa* (spicy rancho barbecue), multitextured *chilaquiles* (layered tortillas, cheeses, and homemade chili sauce), and other delights with a humor as lively as the seasonings. It keeps the handful of tables and booths full. Beware: The hot sauce can rip your lips off. ✘ *260 S. Alma School Rd., Mesa,* ☎ *602/835–5356; 8646 S. Central Ave.,* ☎ *602/243–9113. No reservations. No credit cards. Both closed Sun.; S. Central location closed Mon.*

$ **Eliana's.** Salvadoran food is an interesting variation on the staple themes of Latin American fare, and this family-run storefront has plenty of heart and hearty food. You know tacos and burritos, now meet *papusas,* crisp crosses between tortillas and puffy pita pockets, stuffed with meat, cheese, and sauces. From tamales, it's a short but tasty leap to these veggie-filled varieties with soft, creamy masa wrappings. And *sopas* (soups) are an adventure. ✘ *1627 N. 24th St.,* ☎ *602/225–2925. No reservations. No credit cards.*

$ **Matador.** This downtown tradition, across from the Hyatt Regency Phoenix in a tastefully Mayan-modern setting, is a fine way to meet Mexican and Sonoran cuisine. Dishes are reliable, authentic, well-spiced, and they range from the familiar (tacos, enchiladas, quesadillas) to the adventurous (*menudo,* or tripe soup, *burros de lengua,* or beef-tongue burritos). It's also a perennially popular breakfast spot for civic leaders and many others. ✘ *125 E. Adams St.,* ☎ *602/254–7563. Reservations advised for large parties. AE, D, DC, MC, V.*

Middle Eastern

$$ **Mediterranean House.** On a dozen white-clothed tables in a corner-★ mall storefront, a Korean family serves an array of fine Mediterranean standards. An appetizer platter introduces hummus and *baba ghanoush* (eggplant dip) with pita triangles for dipping, falafel balls (herbed, deep-fried hummus). Don't miss lemon-garlic Egyptian chicken rolled in sesame flour, creamy herbed Moroccan chicken in yogurt sauce, ambrosial Olympic chicken in a secret marinade with black-olive sauce, or one of the half dozen vegetarian main dishes (like fettuccine in creamed spinach). ✘ *1588 E. Bethany Home Rd.,* ☎ *602/248–8460. Closed Sun.*

$ **Byblos.** This Lebanese standby in Tempe is not heavy on ambience, but care is taken with the food, and the staff usually dines at one of the tables, inquiring regularly as to how you're doing. Hummus and falafel are reliable, but save room for main courses, easily sampled with a mixed grill, which includes three kinds of shish kebab. ✘ *3332 S. Mill Ave., Tempe,* ☎ *602/894–1945. No reservations. AE, MC, V. Closed Mon.*

$ **Samyra's Lebanese Cuisine.** In this modest, out-of-the-way spot 2 miles south of downtown, Samyra Sopp has been cooking and serving friendly Lebanese lunches for 16 years. Scoop hummus *bitahini* (hummus-and-sesame paste) and baba ghanoush onto chunks of fresh-baked bread, then dig into tangy *yabrak* (lamb and rice rolled in grape leaves) or, if she has made any, some *koosa* (lamb-stuffed squash) or *fasoulia* (a lamb-lima bean stew). Delicate strains of Arabic music lull you along to honeyed baklava for dessert. ✘ *713 E. Mohave St.,* ☎ *602/ 252–9644. Reservations advised for 6 or more. No credit cards.* ☉ *Weekdays 11–2.*

Southwestern International

$$$$ **Vincent's on Camelback.** Vincent Guerithault is acknowledged to be ★ among the West's master chefs extraordinaire—this is where people come to experience his art. One of the handful of Southwestern cuisine's originators, he married his classical country-French training to Mexican traditions to create duck tamales, crab cakes in avocado salsa, lobster with smoky chipotle chili pasta, and so on. Racks of lamb with spicy jalapeño jelly and symphonic pâté are here, too, as are a heart-smart menu and an intelligent wine list. Desserts are simply lus-

cious. ✕ *3930 E. Camelback Rd.,* ☎ *602/224–0225. Reservations advised. AE, DC, MC, V.*

$$$ **Compass Room.** Spectacular views have always made the Hyatt Re-
★ gency Phoenix's rotating rooftop restaurant an attraction. Since 1989,
chef Mark Ching has given it food to match. In fact, it's become one
of the most exciting galleries for Southwestern culinary art. Consider
a dinner of smoky eggplant soup, calamari salad, and seared medal-
lions of beef with whole grain mustard over braised wild mushrooms.
And Cajun croutons are remarkable—crusty fried oysters in a red-pep-
per mayonnaise—as a side or in the Caesar salad. While the room ro-
tates another 90 degrees, try one of Ching's cobblers or chocolate pâté.
✕ *122 N. 2nd St.,* ☎ *602/252–1234. Reservations required. Jacket
and tie. AE, D, DC, MC, V.*

$$$ **Eddie's Grill.** Its look and location are upscale—a modern office com-
★ plex 4 miles north of downtown, black-trim art deco furniture, fine
handmade ceramics. Its cuisine, as eclectic as the decor, makes this one
of Phoenix's hottest half dozen. Chef-owner Eddie Matney's "Ameriter-
ranean" is a playful, shifting blend of Southwestern and North African
style. Try Mo' Rockin' Shrimp in *chermoula* sauce (lime juice, olive
oil, four kinds of pepper, cilantro, and mustard) or toasted seafood wan-
ton served with raspberry jalapeño sauce. There's a Southwestern
Tower of mixed greens and margarita chicken with peppers and jack-
cheese dressing, layered in corn tortillas, and steak wrapped in herbed
mashed potatoes. How Eddie loves to feed you! ✕ *4747 N. 7th St.,*
☎ *602/241–1188. Reservations advised. AE, MC, V.*

$$$ **RoxSand.** RoxSand Suarez and Spyros Scocos have woven together Greek,
★ Asian, Continental, and Caribbean influences (among others) creating
a unique trans-Continental cuisine that adds zest to its Biltmore Fash-
ion Park mall location. Be on the lookout for sea-scallop salad, air-dried
duck-and-rice tamales, and an ever-changing array of handmade desserts.
It is a nice compliment to customers that solo snackers are as welcome
as a hungry foursome. ✕ *2594 E. Camelback Rd.,* ☎ *602/381–0444.
Reservations advised. AE, DC, MC, V.*

$$–$$$ **Christo's.** The sign says "Ristorante," and northern Italian food here
is nicely done, but Christo and Connie Panagiotakapoulos have in fact
scoured the Mediterranean for their cuisine of pasta, lamb dishes,
calamari, and other tasty regional specialties. Decor and ambience are
contemporary, and service is adroit. ✕ *6327 N. 7th St.,* ☎ *602/264–
1784. Reservations advised. AE, MC, V. Closed Sun.*

$$ **Goldie's 1895 House.** This charming downtown Victorian would fit
right in on California's Mendocino coast. There's always soft music
(live jazz, classical guitar) and an art gallery and museum that change
shows regularly. Standard dishes get subtle extra touches—a hot turkey
sandwich on sourdough under light dill sauce, or baked orange roughy
in Parmesan-scallion butter—and there are surprises like roast duck
in pomegranate sauce. There's also a new high-health menu. Plan
ahead if you intend to come here: The hours are as compact as the rooms.
✕ *362 N. 2nd Ave.,* ☎ *602/254–0338. Reservations advised. AE, DC,
MC, V. Lunch weekdays 11–2; dinner Mon.–Thurs. 5–9, Fri.–Sat. 5–
10, Sun. 4–10. The Attic Dinner Theater performs 7:30 PM Thurs.–Sun.*

$$ **Timothy's.** In this cozy cottage north of Camelback Road, chef-owner
Tim Johnson offers a double treat—French-influenced Southwestern
cuisine and live jazz. He does jambalaya, steak au poivre, and veal;
like the music, the food gets hottest when the voices blend, as in
salmon in phyllo dough with chili hollandaise. It may not be quiet, but
service is brisk and dinner is served until midnight. ✕ *6335 N. 16th
St.,* ☎ *602/277–7634. Reservations advised. AE, D, DC, MC, V.*

Spanish

$$$$ **Marquesa.** Two soft-hued, intimate rooms at the Scottsdale Princess
★ are accented with huge glass jars of jewel-like vegetables and fruits and
graceful giant clay olive-oil urns. Here, Catalan food gets an exciting
Southwestern interpretation, and stunning presentations match the
flavors—paella and saffron rice; pimentos stuffed with crab; a rich chowder of mussels, scallops, and spicy chorizo sausage; and huge shrimp
in almond sauce, to name a few. Service is gracious, wines well chosen, desserts inspired. ✕ *7575 E. Princess Dr., Scottsdale,* ☎ *602/585–
4848. Reservations required. AE, DC, MC, V.*

Thai

$$ **Mint Thai.** A tiny, graceful place that has managed to remain remark-
★ able, Mint Thai offers the broadest menu of the valley's Thai restau-
rants—and if you find a dish not prepared with delicacy and power,
you'll be a first. Soups range from the subtly simple *tom ka gai* (hot-
sour in coconut milk) to the spectacular *Thai suki* (a beef-pork-chicken-
squid-shrimp extravaganza). Curries are gentle, with deep flavors,
rama beef in peanut sauce is amazing, and you've never had sweet-and-
sour like this before. Even their Thai tea stands out. ✕ *1111 N. Gilbert
Rd., Gilbert,* ☎ *602/497–5366. Reservations advised weekends. AE,
MC, V.*

$ **Char's.** This austerely simple restaurant gave birth to Phoenix's brood
of Thai houses. Meals are carefully prepared and courteously served,
from the snappy skewered-chicken *satay* appetizer to *tom yum gai* (hot-
sour soup) and *yum yai* salad (chicken and shrimp with peanut dress-
ing) to a noodle-rich *pad Thai* or a belly-warming curry. Tell your server
if you'd like the pepper meter set low—Thai people like it hot. ✕ *927
E. University Dr., Tempe,* ☎ *602/967–6013. Reservations advised for
large groups. AE, MC, V.*

LODGING

Metropolitan Phoenix has a considerable array of lodging options, from
world-class resorts and dude ranches to roadside motels, from luxury
and executive hotels to no-frills business suites and family-style oper-
ations where you can do your own cooking.

Resorts are usually far from the heart of town—too far to be conve-
nient if your interests are in Phoenix proper. The exceptions: the his-
toric Arizona Biltmore, unthinkably far out when it was built and now
handily close in; the gigantic Pointe Hilton on South Mountain, less
than 3 miles from the airport; and its two sister Pointe resorts, each
within 7 miles of downtown. Most of the others are in Scottsdale, a
self-contained, very tourist-friendly suburb; a few are scattered 20 to
30 miles out of town. And the dude ranches cluster around Wicken-
burg, 60 miles northwest.

Business and family hotels are closer to town—and to the average va-
cation budget. Until 20 years ago, families drove in from the west on
Grand Avenue or from the east on Van Buren Street and pulled into
any of dozens of courtyard motels with mission-style adobe facades.
That is no longer a safe option, as the neighborhood is seedy; but aside
from the airport, no single hotel district has emerged, so offerings are
scattered throughout Phoenix and its suburbs.

Travelers flee snow and ice to bask in the Valley of the Sun. As a re-
sult, winter is the high season, peaking in January through March, and
summer is giveaway time, when weekend packages at the fanciest re-
sorts cost less than a winter night at a mid-range hotel.

The rise of suite hotels in recent years—with kitchenettes for in-room meal preparation—is rapidly making room service obsolete in all but luxury or resort-class hotels. In its place, such complimentary services as a made-to-order breakfast, poolside or lounge happy hour, and a morning newspaper are becoming standard. Where room service is not noted below, expect some combination of these.

CATEGORY	COST*
$$$$	over $160
$$$	$110–$160
$$	$60–$110
$	under $60

All prices are for a standard double room, excluding 6.5% state tax, 1% city tax, and 15% service charge.

Central Phoenix

$$$$ Hyatt Regency Phoenix. This landmark faces Civic Plaza like a giant kachina figure, its disk-shape rotating restaurant atop 24 floors of dark sandstone. Desert- and Indian-style decor dominate, blended together with Hyatt's trademark atrium design and sky-view elevators. Shops, meeting rooms, and an on-site branch of the visitors bureau attest to the focus on conventions, which crowd the hotel in spring. Rooms are comfortable, utilitarian, and modestly sized; there are balcony rooms on floors 3–7, poolside rooms on 3 (the atrium roof blocks east views on 8–10). The Theater Terrace Café's Southwestern food and themed seasonal menus are a cut above standard hotel fare; the rooftop Compass Room's meals match its splendid views (*see* Southwestern International *in* Dining, *above*). ☎ *122 N. 2nd St., 85004,* ☎ *602/252–1234 or 800/233–1234,* ᶠᴬˣ *602/254–9472. 711 rooms. 2 restaurants, bar, pool, health club, meeting rooms, concierge, parking. AE, D, DC, MC, V.*

$$$ Embassy Suites. Just 5 miles from downtown, this 19-year-old, four-story open-courtyard hotel was overhauled in 1990. Lush palms and olive trees hide bubbling fountains and a huge sunken pool, while four glass-wall elevators lift you to your floor. Free breakfast and evening social hour are shared in the spacious clubhouse at café tables, by a large sunken fireplace/conversation pit and in front of a wide-screen TV off in a corner. Suites are compact but dramatic, with emerald carpets and drapes, Santa Fe geometric wallpaper and bedspreads. The tiny kitchenette has a microwave, sink, and minifridge. The Squaw Peak Cafe offers dinner from 5 to 10 with wonderful views. ☎ *2333 E. Thomas Rd., 85016,* ☎ *602/957–1910 or 800/EMBASSY,* ᶠᴬˣ *602/955– 2861. 183 suites. Restaurant, pool, sauna, meeting rooms, airport shuttle, parking. AE, D, DC, MC, V.*

$$$ Hilton Suites. A model of excellent design within tight limits, this 11-
★ story atrium opened in 1990. A more luxurious version of the frequent-traveler suites concept, it sits off Central Avenue, 2 miles north of downtown amid the Phoenix plaza cluster of office towers. The marble-floor, pillared lobby with giant urns opens into the atrium, with fountains, palms, and the lantern-lighted sidewalk cafe. Modern fauvist art hangs on the walls; thematic colors are sand and bright teal blue, and Navajo-inspired motifs mark carpets and borders. Suites continue the bold design, with bleached wood furniture and rough-cut custom metal chandeliers. Each large bathroom opens to both living room and bedroom, which have two windows apiece (one that opens), and every couch is a sofa bed. Each room also has a microwave (the gift shop sells snacks and rents VCR movies). This practical and popular property is likely to become a classic. ☎ *10 E. Thomas Rd., 85012,* ☎ *602/222–1111 or 800/HILTONS,* ᶠᴬˣ *602/265–4841. 226 suites.*

Restaurant, bar, pool, sauna, exercise room, parking. AE, D, DC, MC, V.

$$$ Holiday Inn Crowne Plaza. After a huge fire decades ago, total rebuilding, and a series of owners, the historic Adams Hotel is just a memory. In its place stands a 19-story modern shell cleverly crafted for the desert, with sand-colored walls, arcaded sidewalks, and scooped arches shading each window. A 1994 renovation brought the tired inside back to life, healing several years of neglect. Soft green carpeted halls lead to compact rooms in desert shades, with rose and stone-blue carpeting; tables, desks, and lamps are marble, glass, and bronze and patinated copper. The young staff is gracious, and the scale and services are those of a major hotel, including the revitalized shops and restaurants. ☎ *111 N. Central Ave., 85004, ☎ 602/257–1525 or 800/465–4329, FAX 602/253–9755. 534 rooms. 2 restaurants, bar, pool, health club, sauna, jogging, meeting rooms, concierge, travel services, parking. AE, D, DC, MC, V.*

$$ Best Western Executive Park. One of downtown's hidden jewels, this
★ small eight-story facility sits on Central Avenue at the new Deck Park (beneath which I–10 passes under the heart of the city). Simple and elegant, the rooms are brightened by peach-and-sand color walls and prints by Southwestern masters. Moderate-size rooms have comfortable beds and large, well-lighted desks, compact brass-trim bathrooms with coffeemakers, and (above the second floor) commanding city views. The eighth-floor suites are dramatic, with ample balconies and sitting rooms; off the drape-swathed bedroom is a vast dressing room with Roman tub, plus a standard bathroom with shower. Rose's restaurant does a nice array of American–Continental dishes, with Southwestern accents. The Heard Museum, Phoenix Art Museum, and main library are within walking distance. This hotel has charm, a great location— and great prices. ☎ *1100 N. Central Ave., 85004, ☎ 602/252–2100 or 800/528–1234, FAX 602/340–1989. 107 rooms. Restaurant, bar, pool, sauna, health club, meeting rooms, parking. AE, D, DC, MC, V.*

$$ Travelodge Suites. A mile east of the Embassy Suites is an older, cozier, and cheaper version of the open-courtyard suite hotel. Under its red-tile roofs are apartment-style suites dating from the mid-1960s, with orange-and-brown outside trim and discreet but stylish furnishings (rose carpets with a light Japanese floral motif for wall art, drapes, and bedspreads) and half-kitchens, complete with refrigerator, utensils, and dishes. Front suites hear 32nd Street's traffic; 24 second-story suites have balconies overlooking the pool and densely landscaped garden. An 8-by-10 nook serves daily breakfast, a second dispenses poolside happy hour, and a third houses the four-station exercise room. ☎ *3101 N. 32nd St., 85018, ☎ 602/956–4900 or 800/950–1688, FAX 602/957–6122. 76 suites. Pool, exercise room, meeting rooms, airport shuttle, parking. AE, D, DC, MC, V.*

$$ Lexington Hotel. Only 3 miles from downtown, in a nest of midtown corporate-headquarters buildings, this is Phoenix's best bet for sports lovers. Carved out of the poolside conference wing of the old Del Webb Towne House in 1987 (the former hotel became an office tower), the Lexington now houses a sports bar (noisy and crowded), 11 racquetball courts (a national tournament site), an aerobics room, a 40-station machine workout center, a full indoor basketball court, and a large outdoor waterfall pool. The ambience is bright, modern, and informal. Rooms range in size from moderate (in the cabana wing first-floor rooms have poolside patios) to very small (tower wing) and were completely redecorated in early 1993. In the locker rooms, no amenity is spared. And the restaurant serves hefty, home-cooked meals. This is where visiting pro teams—and fans—like to stay. ☎ *100 W. Clarendon Ave.,*

162

Phoenix Lodging

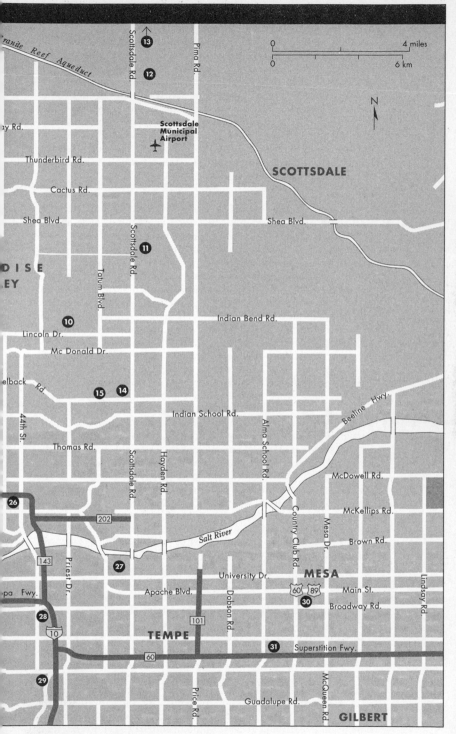

85013, ☎ 602/279–9811; ℻ 602/631–9358. 180 rooms. Restaurant, bar, pool, sauna, health club, parking. AE, D, DC, MC, V.

$$ San Carlos Hotel. Phoenix's second-oldest hotel is being reborn. Built in 1927, it was a popular downtown hub and landmark for decades; now, its seven stories are dwarfed by the valley Bank Center and other skyscrapers. A 1990 refurbishment put deep blue carpeting in the halls and added new wallpaper, drapes, and spreads in the 120 snug rooms and suites (whose 3-inch concrete walls ensure quiet). Fixtures—from the pedestal sinks and old-fashioned toilets to the Austrian crystal chandeliers in the lobby—echo '30s and '40s high style. 🗓 *202 N. Central Ave., 85004, ☎ 602/253–4121 or 800/528–5446; ℻ 602/653–6668. 111 rooms. Restaurant, deli, pub, pool, meeting rooms, parking. AE, D, DC, MC, V.*

Airport

$$–$$$$ The Buttes. Two miles east of Sky Harbor, nestled in desert buttes at
★   I–10 and AZ 360, is Phoenix's best hotel buy. Built in 1986 and re-decorated in 1993, it joins dramatic architecture (the lobby's back wall is the volcanic rock itself), classic Southwest design (pine and saguaro-rib furniture, original works by major regional artists), and stunning valley views. Rooms are moderate in size and comfortable, with a compact bath and half-closet; decor includes desert colors and live cactus. "Radial" rooms are largest, with the widest views; inside rooms face the huge free-form pool in its rock amphitheater, with waterfall, Jacuzzis, and cantina. Concierge-floor amenities are well worth the nominal added fee. The elegant Top of the Rock restaurant and the quiet luxury of the dawn-to-midnight Market Café are definite pluses. 🗓 *2000 Westcourt Way, Tempe 85282, ☎ 602/225–9000 or 800/843–1986, ℻ 602/438–8622. 353 rooms. 2 restaurants, 3 bars, sauna, pool, 5 tennis courts, health club, hiking, jogging, concierge floor, meeting rooms, parking. AE, D, DC, MC, V.*

$$–$$$$ Doubletree Suites. In the Gateway Center, just a mile north of the airport, this striking hotel is the best of a dozen choices for the traveler who wants to get off the plane and into a comfortable room. Past the lobby full of modernist regional art lies a honeycomb of six-story towers, linked by mazes of walkways and richly landscaped gardens. The over-size rooms are rose, blue-gray, and Navajo white with comfy furniture. The kitchenettes have microwaves. Topper's, a pleasantly intimate restaurant, offers a relaxed wine bar. Business and sports facilities are extensive; the casual elegance and easy access attract visiting celebrities. 🗓 *320 N. 44th St., Phoenix 85008, ☎ 602/225–0500 or 800/800–3098, ℻ 602/225–0957. 242 suites. Restaurant, bar, pool, sauna, 2 tennis courts, health club, meeting rooms, airport shuttle, parking. AE, D, DC, MC, V.*

$$–$$$$ The Pointe Hilton on South Mountain. While this Spanish-Mediter-
★   ranean oasis is the Southwest's largest resort, it's also one of the nicest. Part of its charm lies in its location: it sits next to South Mountain Park, a 16,000-acre desert preserve that offers hiking, mountain biking and horseback riding. You're also only 15 minutes from downtown Phoenix and the East Valley. The suites are lavish and comfortable: marble counters, whitewash timbers, high ceilings and teal and peach accents. Also on site is a premiere four-story sports center and four separate restaurants. Landscaped walkways and roads link everything together on the 750-acre property. Carts and drivers are on 24-hour call. Golf, tennis, riding, and several pools are among the amenities. The Hilton also runs two identically-themed resorts in the area: The Pointe Hilton at Squaw Peak (☎ 602/997-2626, North Phoenix); and The Pointe Hilton Tapatio Cliffs (☎ 602/866-7500). 🗓 *7777 S. Pointe Parkway, Phoenix*

85044, ☎ *602/438-9000 or 800/876-4683,* FAX *602/431-6535. 638 suites. 4 restaurants, 3 lobby lounges, lake, 6 pools, saunas, 10 tennis courts, 18-hole golf course, health club, hiking, horseback riding, jogging, meeting rooms, parking. AE, D, DC, MC, V.*

$ Ambassador Inn. The scenic enclosed courtyard with flowers, fountain, and bubbling stream sets the tone for this 170-room property 4 miles north of Sky Harbor International Airport. The blue-and-brown traditionally styled rooms have refrigerators and electric stove tops. A small weight room with exercise bikes as well as a cheerful pink coffee shop and a brass-trim bar are on the premises. Less than a mile away are shopping, golf, tennis, and an indoor ice rink. Rates are adjusted for room location, with those nearest the pool costing more than those on the street side, but all are bargains. ⊞ *4727 E. Thomas Rd., Phoenix 85018,* ☎ *602/840-7500 or 800/624-6759,* FAX *602/840-5078. 170 rooms. Restaurant, bar, pool, spa, exercise room, meeting room, airport shuttle, parking. AE, D, DC, MC, V.*

$ Comfort Inn Airport. The location isn't scenic but it's convenient: This Spanish-style motel is 4 miles from downtown Phoenix and 2 miles north of Sky Harbor International Airport. A red-tile roof and Mexican-tile accents give character to the premises; where rich greenery surrounds the pool. The 49 traditional rooms are dark and small but include a table and two chairs. There's no restaurant, but Bill Johnson's Big Apple three blocks west has good biscuits, grits, and barbecue. ⊞ *4120 E. Van Buren St., Phoenix 85008,* ☎ *602/275-5746 or 800/228-5150. 49 rooms. Pool, parking. AE, D, DC, MC, V.*

Biltmore–Scottsdale

$$$$ Arizona Biltmore. The grande dame of Arizona resorts is as lively and lovely as ever. Designed by Frank Lloyd Wright's colleague Albert Chase McArthur, it has been a masterpiece among world-class resorts since it opened in 1929. The lobby has stained-glass skylights and wrought-iron pilasters. Rooms feature natural colors, Frank Lloyd Wright-inspired furnishings, and tan and off-white marble baths. Outdoors there are lush flower gardens and stunning views. Restaurants— all very good—range from casual to late-night elegant, with a soda fountain open till 10. ⊞ *24th St. and Missouri Ave., Phoenix 85016,* ☎ *602/955-6600 or 800/950-0086,* FAX *602/381-7600. 502 rooms. 3 restaurants, 3 lounges, 5 pools, 12 tennis courts, 2 18-hole golf courses, health club, jogging, biking, concierge, parking. AE, D, DC, MC, V.*

$$$$ The Boulders. A dozen miles north of The Princess on Scottsdale Road, the valley's most dramatic luxury resort hides among hill-size granite boulders in the foothills town of Carefree. Opened in 1984, The Boulders offers adobe casitas (and patio homes for long-term rental) in a graceful desert landscape; golf courses stretch like carpeting between the giant stones, and a stunning main lodge by the architect Robert Bacon blends beautifully with its surroundings. Remodeled in 1994, the casitas are compact but comfortable, with curving, pueblo-style half-walls and shelves; each has a patio with a view, miniature kiva fireplace, stocked wet bar, and a spacious bath and dressing area with a deep tub and adobe vanity. The dining facilities include The Latilla, creative American and Sonoran cuisine; The Boulder Club, Italian; the Palo Verde, Southwestern international; the Cantina del Pedregal, Mexican fare; and the deli-style Bakery Cafe. The nearby el Pedregal center, a dramatic twin to the resort, has shopping and more eating options; and Carefree multiplies these many times over. ⊞ *34631 N. Tom Darlington Dr., Carefree 85377,* ☎ *602/488-9009 or 800/553-1717,* FAX *602/488-4118. 160 casitas, 31 patio homes. 2 pools, spa, 6* *tennis courts, 2 18-hole golf courses, exercise room, hiking, horseback riding, jogging, meeting rooms, parking. AE, D, DC, MC, V.*

$$$$ **Marriott's Camelback Inn.** Begun in the mid-1930s as a posh "by invitation only" resort, the Camelback Inn was bought and expanded in the late '60s by J. W. Marriott, who recouped his investment by selling the 423 casitas and suites as condos in 1970–72. (Owners are guaranteed four weeks a year.) The inn "Where Time Stands Still," as its adobe clock-tower entrance still proclaims, is an oasis of comfortable predictability in the gorgeous valley between Camelback and Mummy Mountains. The lobby, a classic of early Southwestern design, is a high point. So is the young, helpful staff and the airy, calm, and clean 25,000-square-foot spa. The casita rooms, redecorated in 1994–95, are big on windows and amenities but small in size. The Camelback is undergoing a major five-year renovation plan, with an intention to enhance room decor, executive facilities, pools, and the spa. ☎ *5402 E. Lincoln Dr., Scottsdale 85253, ☎ 602/948–1700 or 800/24–CAMEL, ℻ 602/951–8469. 400 rooms, 23 suites. 5 restaurants, 2 lounges, 3 pools, spa, 10 tennis courts, 2 18-hole golf courses, hiking, horseback riding, meeting rooms, parking. AE, D, DC, MC, V.*

$$$$ **The Phoenician.** Before the Arizona financier Charles Keating was otherwise distracted, he and his wife devoted a lot of time to this resort. You may question the suitability of the lobby's French-provincial decor and authentic Dutch master paintings for a desert locale, but there's no question that a great deal of attention was paid to details. It's the highest-priced property in town, and in order to keep the superb service working for you, remember to have tips ready for service people when appropriate, and use valet parking. Then you can relax and enjoy all that the Phoenician has to offer. ☎ *6000 E. Camelback Rd., Scottsdale 85251, ☎ 602/941–8200 or 800/888–8234. 442 rooms, 107 casitas, 31 suites. 4 restaurants, 7 pools, barbershop, beauty salon, sauna, steam room, golf course, 11 tennis courts, health club, archery, badminton, basketball, croquet, jogging, volleyball, children's programs. AE, D, DC, MC, V.*

$$$$ **Scottsdale Princess.** The most tasteful of the Scottsdale resorts, the ★ Princess can accommodate large groups—such as those who come to play in the PGA Tour Phoenix Open, held here every year—without seeming crowded. Rooms in the red-tile-roof main building and the casitas, spread out over 450 beautifully landscaped acres, are furnished in Spanish style, with large, carved pieces, but sand-color rugs and bedspreads contribute to an overall airy effect; each casita has three telephones, an oversize tub, and such extras as an iron and an ironing board. The Marquesa Restaurant (*see* Dining, *above*) has been consistently rated one of the best in the state. ☎ *7575 E. Princess Dr., Scottsdale 85255, ☎ 602/585–4848 or 800/344–4758, ℻ 602/585–0091. 400 rooms in main building, 125 casitas, 75 villas. 5 restaurants, bar, 3 pools, spa, steam room, 9 tennis courts, 2 18-hole golf courses, health club, racquetball, squash, pro shops, nightclub. AE, D, DC, MC, V.*

$$$–$$$$ **Hyatt Regency Scottsdale at Gainey Ranch.** A fun place for families, ★ with its complex of pools, fountains, water slides, and lagoons plied by gondolas, this resort has a bit of a Disneyland ambience. At night the palm trees are lit up in bright shades of green and orange, and the public areas tend to be crowded. Rooms, which are comfortably, if predictably, furnished in contemporary style, offer all the expected amenities. A standout is The Golden Swan Restaurant, serving Southwestern cooking at its best—light and wonderfully tasty. Three 9-hole courses offer golfers a choice of terrains—dunes, arroyo, or lakes—depending on whether you fancy sand traps or water traps. ☎ *7500 E. Doubletree Ranch Rd., Scottsdale 85258, ☎ 602/991–3388 or 800/233–1234,*

FAX 602/483–5550. *493 rooms. 3 restaurants, 2 lounges, 10 pools, 9 tennis courts, 3 9-hole golf courses, health club, concierge floor, parking. AE, D, DC, MC, V.*

$$$–$$$$ **Ritz-Carlton.** Like an 11-story false front, this sand-color neo-Federal
★ mid-rise facing Biltmore Fashion Square mall hides a graceful, well-appointed luxury hotel that pampers the traveler. Built in 1988, it has large public rooms decorated with 18th- and 19th-century European paintings and handsomely displayed china collections. Rooms are moderately spacious with an armoire closeting a TV and refrigerator (stocked), a small closet with a safe, and a marble bath well supplied with amenities. Because the hotel is business-oriented, rates go down on the weekend. The compact, elegant health club and the daily high tea are highlights, and a modestly named The Restaurant is among the valley's best at Southwest-flavored Continental. ⊞ *2401 E. Camelback Rd., Phoenix 85016,* ☎ *602/468–0700 or 800/241–3333,* FAX *602/468–9883. 267 rooms, 14 suites. 2 restaurants, 2 bars, pool, 2 saunas, tennis court, health club, concierge, concierge floor, business services, parking. AE, D, DC, MC, V.*

$$ **Camelback Courtyard by Marriott.** This four-story hostelry, which opened in 1990, delivers compact elegance in its public areas and no-frills comfort in its rooms and suites. A medium-size lap pool and whirlpool fill the courtyard, landscaped with granite boulders and palms. Standard doubles are handsomely carpeted and draped while suites are done in gray with rose accents. The considerable savings are achieved by dropping such "hotel" features as 24-hour room service (it's available from 5 to 10 PM) and relying on the attached Town and Country mall for gift and grooming shops, travel services, and the like. ⊞ *2101 E. Camelback Rd., Phoenix 85016,* ☎ *602/955–5200 or 800/321–2211,* FAX *602/955–1101. 144 rooms, 11 suites. Restaurant, bar, pool, spa, health club, parking. AE, D, DC, MC, V.*

$ **Motel 6 Scottsdale.** The best bargain in Scottsdale lodging is easy to miss, but it's worth hunting for the sign along Camelback Road. Just steps away from the newly renovated Scottsdale Fashion Square and Camelview Plaza, this motel is also close to the specialty shops of 5th Avenue and Scottsdale's Civic Plaza. Amenities aren't a priority here, but the price is remarkable considering the stylish and much more expensive resorts found close by. Rooms are small and spare with brown carpets and print bedspreads, but the well-landscaped pool offers a pleasant outdoor respite under the palms. ⊞ *6848 E. Camelback Rd., Scottsdale 85251,* ☎ *602/946–2280,* FAX *602/949–7583. 122 rooms. Pool, hot tub, parking. AE, D, DC, MC, V.*

East Valley

$$–$$$ **Hilton Pavilion.** The Pavilion's ambience is defined by etched glass and brass, tropical greenery, and art deco–style furniture; the staff is young and eager to help. Rooms are moderately spacious and darkly earth-toned, with small baths and closets and a large lighted table; corner suites and the top two floors have unstocked minibars and the best views. This eight-floor atrium hotel is in the heart of the East valley, just off AZ 360. The east valley's largest shopping mall, Fiesta Mall, is almost next door, and downtown Phoenix is 18 miles away. ⊞ *1011 W. Holmes Ave., Mesa 85210,* ☎ *602/833–5555 or 800/445–8667,* FAX *602/649–1886. 263 rooms, 57 suites. Restaurant, 2 bars, pool, parking. AE, D, DC, MC, V.*

$$–$$$ **Radisson Tempe.** Set snugly between the Arizona State University campus and Old Town Tempe, this informal courtyard hotel is handy to the East valley and downtown Phoenix. The tone is set by the spacious adobe-and-verdigris lobby and the young, polo-shirted staff. Many vis-

itors come for ASU sports and the pro-football Cardinals (the stadium is virtually next door); Tempe's Chamber of Commerce is headquartered here. Rooms are bright, simple Southwestern, and comfortable. The hotel has a pleasant, quiet sports bar, and a creditable restaurant (The Arches); guests also have Old Town Tempe's wide array of restaurants, shops, and clubs at their feet. ⌕ *60 E. 5th St., Tempe 85281,* ☎ *602/894–1400 or 800/547–8705; FAX 602/968–7677. 303 rooms. Restaurant, bar, pool, sauna, 3 tennis courts, exercise room, meeting rooms, parking. AE, D, DC, MC, V.*

$ **Mesa Travelodge.** Rooms are newly refurbished at this small, plain motel three blocks west of Mesa's downtown center: New blue carpet, cream wallpaper, and bedspreads and art prints in Southwestern motifs, brighten the 38 rooms overlooking a small pool. The motel's busy corner spot can mean continual street noise, but low prices help compensate. ⌕ *22 S. Country Club Rd., Mesa 85210,* ☎ *602/964–5694 or 800/578–7878, FAX 602/964–5697. 39 rooms. Pool, parking. AE, D, DC, MC, V.*

West Valley and Metrocenter

$$$ **Crescent Hotel.** This eight-story, terraced white concrete hostelry across I–17 from Metrocenter, the state's largest shopping mall, was built in 1987 by financier Charles Keating. In 1989 it was taken over by the federal government, and it was purchased by Sheraton in May, 1994. They appear to have made the Crescent a viable upscale hotel. The decor is Southwestern—vast public rooms with massive stone arches and concrete columns, terra-cotta tile floors and bleached-wood paneling, with rose carpets in the hallways. The sizable rooms have deep-rose carpeting, mauve bedspreads and drapes, and pale-tone furnishings. The full-size pool and tennis courts, and the compact health club are all well appointed. Charlie's restaurant is pricey and uneven, but there are ample eating options nearby. ⌕ *2620 W. Dunlap Ave., Phoenix 85021,* ☎ *602/943–8200 or 800/423–4126, FAX 602/371–2856. 342 rooms, 12 suites. Restaurant, bar, pool, 2 saunas, tennis court, putting green, health club, squash, volleyball, concierge, concierge floor, business services, parking. AE, D, DC, MC, V.*

$$$ **Hotel Westcourt.** This undistinguished-looking brown block sits on the outer circle of the huge Metrocenter shopping mall, but in a small space it packs 284 rooms around a large central pool. Modest-size rooms (identical to those in its stunning sister hotel, The Buttes) are done in muted Southwestern colors, with bentwood chairs, small refrigerators, and compact baths. The concierge floor charges only a minimal additional fee; lobby-suite sitting rooms overlook the atrium; poolside junior suites (carved from regular-size rooms) are like elegant little cabanas. Breakfast and luncheon buffets are available in Trumps Bar and Grill, as is menu service through the evening. Other dining options abound within a short walk. ⌕ *10220 N. Metro Pkwy. E, Phoenix 85051,* ☎ *602/997–5900 or 800/858–1033, FAX 602/997–1034. 269 rooms, 15 suites. Restaurant, bar, pool, sauna, tennis court, health club, concierge, concierge floor, business services, parking. AE, D, DC, MC, V.*

Wickenburg

$$$$ **Rancho de los Caballeros.** Now more of a luxury resort than a dusty dude ranch, this 20,000-acre spread began with 320 acres in 1947 and gradually evolved to include an exclusive housing development, a championship golf course, and a 5,000-square-foot conference center. Trail rides are still a popular feature here, and the annual weeklong Desert Caballeros Trail Ride, starting downtown, is a major event among southwestern horse folk. In the huge main lodge, the original *sala* (liv-

ing room) has been remodeled; surrounding the copper fireplace now is bright, neo-Mexican decor, and adjacent are game rooms. The American-plan (15% tips included) meals are provided in the bright dining room (breakfast and dinner, restaurant style) and poolside from a half dozen buffet carts. Rooms—from the original brick Sun Terrace duplexes to the recently built Bradshaw Suites (with optional kitchenette and sitting room)—are spacious and done in low-key Southwestern decor; the baths do not have luxury amenities. The Rancho also has skeet and trap shooting for those who are interested. ⌧ *1551 S. Vulture Mine Rd., 85390,* ☎ *602/684–5484,* Ⅸ *602/684–2267. 73 rooms. Pool, 18-hole golf course, 4 tennis courts, horseback riding, parking. Closed mid-May to mid-Oct. No credit cards.*

$$$ **Flying E Ranch.** This vast spread, on a breeze-swept rise with a 400-square-mile view, typifies the modern dude ranch. About 4 miles west of town to the site of the Wickenburg Massacre and then a mile back from the highway, the 21,000-acre ranch was established in 1946. Most of the rooms have grand views, the original knotty pine walls and white-washed pine and leather furniture; bathrooms are clean and modern. Minifridges and wet bars are unstocked, as is the lounge (which does have mixers for the sundown cocktail hour); bring your own spirits. But the staff's spirits are high and infectious; city slickers adore the morning, lunch, and evening cookout rides and the occasional "dudeos," in which Flying E greenhorns ride and rope against dudes from other spreads; and the weekly barn dance is not to be missed. American-plan meals are family style on gingham-check oilcloth over trestle tables, with Western music playing in the background. Rides cost extra. ⌧ *Box EEE, 85358,* ☎ *602/684–2690 or 602/684–2173,* Ⅸ *602/684–5304. 7 rooms. Pool, lounge, exercise room, tennis court, basketball, horseback riding, parking. No credit cards. Closed Nov. 1–May 1.*

$$$ **Kay El Bar Ranch.** Tucked into a hollow beside the Hassayampa River just 3 miles north of town, this is what dude ranches used to be—homey, comfy, and away from it all, with more horses than people, but not too many of either. This National Historic Site, opened as a dude ranch in 1925, was revived in 1980 by two sisters from the East, Jane Nash and Jan Martin. Immense, old salt cedars tower over fat saguaros and some of the biggest mesquite trees in Arizona, all shading the 8-room lodge; the two-bedroom, two-bath cottage (built in 1914); and the brightly decorated cookhouse, where eating is family style. Rooms are compact and clean, with small, modern bathrooms, and decor is down-home Western. The American-plan rates include three hearty meals a day (some outdoors by the corral) and horseback rides. ⌧ *Box 2480, Wickenburg 85358,* ☎ *602/684–7593. 8 rooms, 1 cottage. Bar, pool, golf privileges, horseback riding, volleyball, library, parking. MC, V. Closed May–mid-Oct.*

THE ARTS AND NIGHTLIFE

The Arts

Phoenix performing-arts groups have grown rapidly in number and sophistication, especially in the past two decades. Completion of the downtown **Symphony Hall** (225 E. Adams St., ☎ 602/262–7272) and **Herberger Theater Center** (222 E. Monroe St., ☎ 602/252–TIXS), which face each other across the Civic Plaza mall, has given many groups a state-of-the-art permanent home amid spiffy surroundings; the developing "cultural district" just 2 miles north, around Deck Park, houses several more.

The most comprehensive ticket agencies are **Dillard's** (13 locations including all Dillard's department stores and Phoenix Civic Plaza, ☎ 602/678–2222) and the **Arizona State University ticket office** (Gammage Center, Tempe, ☎ 602/965–3434).

Theater

Actors Theatre of Phoenix (815 N. 1st Ave., Suite 3W, ☎ 602/254–3475) is the resident theater troupe at the Herberger. The theater presents a full season of drama, comedy, and musical productions.

Arizona Theatre Company (Herberger Theater Center, 222 E. Monroe St., ☎ 602/256–6995), Arizona's only full Equity company, splits its season between Tucson and Phoenix, where it performs at the Herberger. Its playbill usually includes four popular plays and two lesser-known works.

Black Theater Troupe (333 E. Portland St., ☎ 602/258–8128) performs at its own house, the Helen K. Mason Center, a half block from the city's Performing Arts Building on Deck Park. It presents original and contemporary dramas and musical revues, as well as adventurous adaptations, such as its recent version of *Steel Magnolias*.

DINNER THEATER

Copper State Dinner Theatre (6727 N. 47th Ave., Glendale, ☎ 602/937–1671), the valley's oldest dinner troupe, stages light comedy at Max's, a West valley sports bar.

Murder Ink (4110 N. Goldwater Blvd., Scottsdale, ☎ 602/423–8737 or 800/255–4440) presents audience-participation whodunits at Slim & Curly's Steakhouse (Mesa), Avanti (Scottsdale), and Beefeater's (Scottsdale).

Classical Music

Arizona Opera (Symphony Hall, 225 E. Adams St., ☎ 602/266–7464), one of the nation's most highly respected regional companies, stages a four-opera season, primarily classical, in Tucson and Phoenix.

Phoenix Symphony Orchestra (3707 N. 7th St., ☎ 602/264–6363), the resident company at Symphony Hall, has reached the first rank of American regional symphonies. Its rich season includes orchestral works from classical and contemporary literature, a chamber series, composer festivals, and outdoor pops concerts.

Dance

A. Ludwig Co. (☎ 602/965–3914), the valley's foremost modern dance troupe, includes the choreography of founder-director Ann Ludwig of the Arizona State University faculty in its repertoire of contemporary works.

Ballet Arizona (3645 E. Indian School Rd., ☎ 602/381–0184), the state's professional ballet company, presents full seasons of classical and contemporary works (including commissioned pieces for the company) in both Tucson and Phoenix, where it performs as the resident dance company at the Herberger Theater Center, Symphony Hall and Gammage Auditorium.

Film

Harkins Theaters, a locally owned chain, is the only one in the valley that shows anything but mass-market movies. Its **Cine Capri** (2323 E. Camelback Rd., ☎ 602/956–4200), a classic wide-screen, superstereo theater from the '60s, occasionally offers giant-screen revivals such as *Dr. Zhivago* and *Spartacus*. At **Camelview 5** (70th St. and Camelback

Rd., ☎ 602/423–9900), one screen usually shows a major foreign release or domestic art film.

Galleries

The gallery scene in Phoenix and Scottsdale is so extensive that your best bet is to consult the Friday and Sunday listings in *The Arizona Republic* or the Marquee section in Saturday's *Phoenix Gazette*. Southwestern art—from traditional to avant-garde Native American, from the Cowboy Artists of America to performance art—is varied and abundant. Photography also enjoys a strong tradition in Arizona.

Nightlife

Downtown Phoenix used to close up at sunset—until the advent of the Arizona Center. The heart of town at last has nightclubs, restaurants, and upscale bars that compete with livelier resorts and clubs in Scottsdale, along Camelback Road in north-central Phoenix, and elsewhere around the valley.

Among music and dancing styles, country-western has the longest tradition here; jazz, surprisingly, runs a close second. Rock clubs and hotel lounges are also numerous and varied. At its major and minor venues, the valley attracts a steady stream of pop and rock acts; for concert tickets, try **Dillard's** (13 valley locations, ☎ 602/678–2222).

The best listings and reviews are in the weekly *New Times* tabloid newspaper, distributed Wednesday; the Friday and Sunday Life & Leisure sections of *The Arizona Republic;* and the Marquee section of Saturday's *Phoenix Gazette*.

Country and Western

Cheyenne Cattle Co. (455 N. 3rd St., ☎ 602/253–6225), in the Arizona Center downtown, is one of the best in town.

At **Mr. Lucky's** (3660 W. Grand Ave., ☎ 602/246–0686), the granddaddy of Phoenix western clubs, you can dance the two-step all night (or learn it, if you haven't before).

Toolie's Country (4231 W. Thomas Rd., ☎ 602/272–3100) books the best national acts.

Rockin' Rodeo (7850 S. Priest, ☎ 602/496–0799) is the newest country-and-western spot in town.

Jazz

American Bar & Grill (1233 S. Alma School Rd., Mesa, ☎ 602/844–1918) books easy-listening artists for Wednesday–Saturday gigs that fit its San Francisco–style lounges. (Good neo–New Orleans and Southwestern food are featured, too.)

At **Unique Foods and Services** (1153 E. Jefferson St., ☎ 602/257–0701), a fine jazz sextet accompanies the barbecue and greens Friday and Saturday nights till 11 PM (and via closed-circuit radio the rest of the week) in a smoke- and alcohol-free environment youngsters can enjoy.

Timothy's (6335 N. 16th St., ☎ 602/277–7634) is yet one more venerable venue that joins top jazz performances with fine French-influenced Southwestern cuisine.

Rock and Blues

A small club, **Anderson's Fifth Estate** (6820 E. 5th Ave., Scottsdale, ☎ 602/994–4168) mixes DJ nights, local bands, and occasional touring rock and country/folk acts.

Mason Jar (2303 E. Indian School Rd., ☎ 602/956–6271) hosts regular alternative rock nights and occasional blues and rock oldies.

Warsaw Wally's (2547 E. Indian School Rd., ☎ 602/955–0881) is the top valley blues club, but its poolroom draws rough trade.

Bars and Lounges
The Plaza Bar on the mezzanine of the Hyatt Regency Phoenix (122 N. 2nd St., ☎ 602/252–1234) offers a quiet getaway with a sparkling downtown view.

A lively (during happy hour, noisy) upscale crowd takes advantage of the city's most spectacular view at **Top of the Rock Bar,** the lounge in Top of the Rock restaurant (2000 W. Westcourt Way, Tempe, ☎ 602/ 225–9000) at The Buttes.

An elegant uptown spot, **Top of Central** (8525 N. Central Ave., ☎ 602/ 861–2437) has soft music and room for larger groups.

Comedy
The Improv (930 E. University Dr., Tempe, ☎ 602/921–9877), part of a national chain, books better-known talent.

Star Theater (7146 E. 6th Ave., ☎ 602/423–0120) features Oxymoron's Improvisational Troupe on Friday and Saturday nights.

Singles
With 57 TVs and seven giant screens, as well as an outdoor volleyball court, **America's Original Sports Bar** (455 N. 3rd St., ☎ 602/252–2112) in The Arizona Center is big and boisterous.

At the popular **Denim & Diamonds** (3905 E. Thomas Rd., ☎ 602/225– 0182), folks turn up dressed in anything from casual to glam for drinking and dancing.

In the Arizona Center, **Hooters** (455 N. 3rd St., ☎ 602/257–0000) draws crowds with its T-shirted, short-shorted waitresses, its beer and burgers and potato-skins menu, and its indoor-outdoor visibility.

Macayo's Depot Cantina (300 S. Ash Ave., Tempe, ☎ 602/966–6677) combines a lively "meet market," frequented by students from the nearby ASU campus, with a very creditable Mexican restaurant.

Studebaker's (103045 N. Scottsdale Rd., Scottsdale, ☎ 602/829– 8495) joins bar, buffet, and dancing with live DJs for a noisy place to meet friends Tuesday through Saturday nights.

PHOENIX AND CENTRAL ARIZONA ESSENTIALS

Arriving and Departing

By Plane
Most air travelers visiting Arizona fly into Sky Harbor International Airport (☎ 602/273–3300). Just 3 miles east of downtown Phoenix, it is surrounded by freeways linking it to almost every part of the metro area. Although it is one of the nation's half dozen busiest airports, it is also one of the most compact.

Sky Harbor has three commercial terminals, each with rental luggage carts, taxi stands, car-rental booths, ATM banking, and courtesy telephones. Terminals 3 and 4 (there is no longer a Terminal 1) also have several shops and restaurants, and 24-hour car-rental booths.

Answers & Apples passenger service desks at all three terminals (☎ 602/267–7994) offer fax, notary, and insurance services; the airport chaplain's office (☎ 602/244–1346) aids travelers in distress.

AIRLINES

Sky Harbor is the home airport of **America West** (☎ 800/235–9292) and a hub for **Southwest** (☎ 800/435–9792). Other airlines with frequent flights to Sky Harbor are **Alaska** (☎ 800/426–0333), **American** (☎ 800/433–7300), **Continental** (☎ 800/525–0280), **Delta** (☎ 800/221–1212), **TWA** (☎ 800/221–2000), **United** (☎ 800/241–6522), and **USAir** (☎ 800/428–4322).

For flights to the Grand Canyon, Page, Lake Powell, Lake Havasu, and other Arizona points, try **America West** (☎ 800/235–9292) and commuter **Skywest** (☎ 800/453–9417).

BETWEEN THE AIRPORT AND DOWNTOWN

It's easy to get to downtown Phoenix, and Tempe (3 miles away to the west and east, respectively) is one of Sky Harbor's strong points. It's also only 20 minutes by freeway from Glendale (to the west) and Mesa (to the east).

Unfortunately, two favorite tourist areas, Scottsdale (to the northeast) and Sun City (to the northwest) are harder to reach—each takes 30–45 minutes by car and requires using local roads for all or part of the trip.

Sky Harbor has limited bus service, ample taxi service, and very good shuttle service to points throughout the metro area. Very few hotels offer a complimentary limo or shuttle, but most resorts do. You should probably rent a car, either at the airport or wherever you are staying (most rental firms deliver).

The following companies have airport booths or free pickup from nearby lots: **Alamo** (☎ 800/327–9633), **Avis** (☎ 800/831–2847), **Budget** (☎ 800/527–0700), **Hertz** (☎ 800/654–3131), **Thrifty** (☎ 800/367–2277), and, if you care more about your wallet than about appearances, **Rent-A-Wreck** (☎ 602/254–1000).

By Bus. Phoenix Transit buses (☎ 602/253–5000) will get you directly from Terminal 2, 3, or 4 to the bus terminal downtown (1st and Washington Sts.) or to Tempe (Mill and University Aves.) in about 20 minutes and for $1. Senior citizens and children ages 6–12 pay half-fare; children 5 and under ride free.

The **Red Line** runs westbound to Phoenix every half hour from about 6 AM until after 9 PM weekdays (Saturday, you take Bus 13 and transfer at Central Avenue to Bus 0 north; there is no Sunday service). The Red Line runs eastbound to Tempe every half hour from 4 AM to 7 PM weekdays (no weekend service); in another 25 minutes, it takes you to downtown Mesa (Center and Main streets).

With free transfers, Phoenix Transit can take you from the airport to most other valley cities (Glendale, Sun City, Scottsdale, etc.), but the trip is likely to be slow unless you take an express line.

By Taxi. Only three firms—and one specializing in transporting handicapped travelers—are licensed to pick up at Sky Harbor's commercial terminals. All add a $1 surcharge for airport pickups, do not charge for luggage, and are available 24 hours a day. A trip to downtown Phoenix can range from $4 to $12, or $13.75 for a wheelchair-lift van. The fare to downtown Scottsdale averages about $15–$16.

AAA Cab (☎ 602/253–8294), **Checker/Yellow Cab** (☎ 602/252–5252), and **Courier Cab** (☎ 602/232–2222) all charge about $2 for the first mile and $1.30 per mile thereafter. **American HTS** (☎ 602/253–0911) offers wheelchair and stretcher service, the former at a $15 pickup fee ($20 evenings and weekends) and $1.25 per mile. All expect tips.

The blue vans of **Supershuttle** (☎ 602/244–9000) also cruise Sky Harbor, each taking up to seven passengers to their individual destinations, with no luggage fee or airport surcharge. Fares range from competitive with the cheapest taxi for a short run, such as downtown Phoenix or Tempe, to 25% or more below the best taxi fares on longer trips. You can reserve a Supershuttle back to the airport (call ahead to schedule pickup, and allow one hour at the airport before your flight). Wheelchair vans are also available. Drivers expect tips.

By Limousine. A few limousine firms are allowed to cruise Sky Harbor, and many more provide airport pickups by reservation. All of these are on 24-hour call. **La Limousine** (☎ 602/242–3094) charges $15–$50, depending on distance. **Classic Limousine** (☎ 602/252–LIMO) will take up to six riders (by reservation only) for $30–$50, depending on how far you're going. **Scottsdale Limousine** (☎ 602/946–8446) also requires reservations but offers a toll-free number (☎ 800/747–8234) and complimentary soft drinks; it costs from $40 to $70, plus tip.

By Car

If you're coming to Phoenix from the west, you'll probably come on I–10. This transcontinental superhighway's last link was joined in 1990 in a tunnel under downtown Phoenix. The trip from the Los Angeles basin, via Palm Springs, takes six to eight hours, depending on where you start and how many rest stops you make. I–40 enters the state in the northwest and runs along old Route 66. From Kingman, U.S. 93 traverses southeast to Phoenix. From San Diego, I–8 slices across low desert to Yuma and on toward the valley on what the Spanish called El Camino del Diablo (the Devil's Highway); at Gila Bend, take AZ 85 up to I–10. The trip takes a total of six to seven hours.

From the east, **I–10** takes you from El Paso, across southern New Mexico, and through Chiricahua Apache country into Tucson, then north to Phoenix (a total of about 9–11 hours). The northeastern route, **I–40** from Albuquerque, crosses Hopi and Navajo historic lands to Flagstaff, where I–17 takes you south to Phoenix—an eight-hour journey. For a scenic shortcut, take AZ 377 south at Holbrook, through Petrified Forest country to Heber and the pines of the Mogollon Rim; then take AZ 260 down the 2,000-foot drop to Payson and AZ 87 through saguaro cactus forests to Phoenix.

By Train

Amtrak (☎ 800/872–7245) has only one connection, the former Southern Pacific line between New Orleans and Los Angeles, that passes through Phoenix (eastbound, 8:08 AM Monday, Wednesday, and Saturday; westbound, 10:20 PM Tuesday, Thursday, and Sunday). It stops at the downtown terminal (4th Ave. and Harrison St., ☎ 602/253–0121) in what is now the industrial part of town, and you may have to phone for a taxi. The much more heavily used former Santa Fe line between Los Angeles and Chicago runs through Flagstaff, 150 miles north of the valley; Amtrak buses leaves Sky Harbor International Airport daily at various times.

By Bus
Greyhound Lines (☎ 602/271–7425 or 800/231–2222) has statewide and nationwide routes from its main terminal downtown (525 E. Washington St.).

Getting Around

To get around Phoenix, *you will need a car.* The metro area developed in the automobile era, and only a few downtowns (Phoenix, Scottsdale, Tempe) are pedestrian-friendly. There is no mass transit beyond a bus system that does not even run seven days a week.

By Car
Driving is easy in the Valley of the Sun: Rain and fog are rare, and snow gets major headlines. Most metro-area streets are well marked and well lighted, and the freeway system is making gradual progress in linking valley areas. Arizona requires seat belts on front-seat passengers and children 16 and under. (For car-rental firms, *see* Between the Airport and Downtown, *above.*)

Around downtown Phoenix, AZ 202 (Papago Freeway), AZ 143 (Hohokam Freeway), and I–10 (Maricopa Freeway) make an elongated east–west loop, embracing the state capitol area to the west and Tempe to the east. At mid-loop, AZ 51 (Squaw Peak Freeway) runs north into Paradise Valley. And from the loop's east end, I–10 runs south to Tucson, 100 miles away, while U.S. 60 (Superstition Freeway) branches east to Tempe and Mesa.

Driving in the valley presents one major challenge: Phoenix and all its suburbs are laid out on a single, 800-square-mile grid of horizontal and vertical streets. Even the freeways all run north–south and east–west. (Grand Avenue, running about 20 miles from downtown northwest to Sun City, is the *only* diagonal.) This makes places easy to find but means you must allow a lot of driving time to get from point A to point B, since you have to trace two legs of a right triangle to do it.

CAUTION: When driving off major highways in low-lying areas, watch for rain clouds. Flash floods from sudden summer rains can be deadly (*see* Driving Precautions *in* The Gold Guide's Smart Travel Tips for more information).

By Bus
Valley Metro (☎ 602/253–5000) is a good rudimentary bus system, with 19 express lines and 51 regular routes that reach most of the valley suburbs. But there are no 24-hour routes; only a skeletal few lines run between sundown and 10:30 PM or on Saturday; and there is no Sunday service. Fares are $1, with free transfers; senior citizens and children 6–18 pay half-fare, and children 5 and under ride free. The City of Phoenix also runs a 25¢ **Downtown Area Shuttle (DASH),** with purple minibuses circling the area between the renovated east end of downtown and the state capitol, on the west end, at 10-minute intervals. The system also serves major thoroughfares in several suburbs— Glendale, Scottsdale, Tempe, Mesa, and Chandler. The City of Tempe operates the **Free Local Area Shuttle (FLASH),** which serves the downtown Tempe and Arizona State University area. In addition, **Dial-A-Ride** services (☎ 602/253–4000) are available throughout the valley.

By Taxi
Taxi fares are unregulated in Phoenix, except at the airport. (For a listing of leading firms and their fares, *see* Between the Airport and Downtown, *above.*) The 800-square-mile metro area is so large that one-way

fares of $30–$50 are not uncommon; you might want to ask what the damages will be before you get in. Except within a compact area, such as central Phoenix, travel by taxi is not recommended.

Guided Tours

Reservations for tours are a must all year, with seats often filling up quickly in the busy season, October–April. All tours provide pickup services at area resorts, but some offer lower prices if you drive to the tour's point of origin.

Orientation Tours

Gray Line Tours (Box 21126, Phoenix 85036, ☎ 602/495–9100 or 800/732–0327) offers a seasonal, three-hour narrated drive through Phoenix and Scottsdale for $27, touring downtown Phoenix, the Arizona Biltmore hotel, Camelback Mountain, mansions in Paradise Valley, Arizona State University, Papago Park, and Scottsdale's 5th Avenue. For $30, **Vaughan's Southwest Custom Tours** (Box 31312, Phoenix 85046, ☎ 602/971–1381 or 800/513-1381) offers a four-hour trip for 11 or fewer passengers in custom vans, stopping at the Heard Museum, the Arizona Biltmore, and the state capitol building. Vaughan's will also take visitors east of Phoenix on the Apache Trail, a scenic route that passes through old mining towns and includes a narrated boat ride on **Dolly's Steamboat Cruises** at Canyon Lake. The cost is $55, with the tour available September through May, weather permitting.

Special-Interest Tours

If you prefer to see the desert country from a four-wheel-drive vehicle, you'll find plenty of options. For example, **Carefree Jeep Adventures** (Box 5423, Carefree 85377, ☎ 602/488–0023 or 800/294–JEEP) travels into the Tonto National Forest on old stage and mining roads, where you can see petroglyphs and rock carvings, taste the fruit of cholla cactus, and hold target practice with tin cans and .22 handguns. That three-hour journey costs $50–$70, as does a sunset tour; children 12 and under are half-price.

Arizona Scenic Tours (3116 E. Shea Blvd., Suite 165, Phoenix 85028, ☎ 602/971–3601) heads past Pinnacle Peak toward the Verde River on dirt desert roads. Two people can expect to pay $50 each (beverages included) for four hours, but the price drops to $45 per person if more than two make the trip.

For a longer trip into the Sonoran Desert north of the valley, **Explorer Desert Tours** (3310 W. Bell Rd., Phoenix 85023, ☎ 602/938–1302) takes group tours only, in 15-person vans to nature trails, gold mines, and a mountain steak house on the six-hour "Sundowner" tour, at $67 per person.

If you'd rather hike than ride, **The Open Road Tours** (748 E. Dunlap #2, Phoenix 85020, ☎ 602/997–6474 or 800/766–7117) takes hikers to the Squaw Peak Mountain Preserve or South Mountain Park for $35 per half day. Three- to five-day hikes can be arranged.

Cimarron Adventures and River Co. (7714 E. Catalina Dr., Scottsdale 85251, ☎ 602/994–1199) arranges half-day float trips and moonlight dinner cruises down the Salt, Verde, and Gila rivers. Day trips cost about $55 per person, with the night cruise about $70. Multiday wilderness tours are available on the Upper Gila River and the scenic Upper Verde River.

Want to tour Phoenix from above? Check out the many hot-air-balloon ascents. **Naturally High Balloon Co.** (4845 E. Desert View Dr.,

Phoenix 85044, ☎ 602/252–6766 or 800/23–TO–FLY) flies daily all year at $100–$110 per person, depending on the season. The cost includes either Continental breakfast or an afternoon snack and a champagne ceremony at the end of the 60-to 90-minute ride, with bubbly, balloon history, and a souvenir certificate. (*See* Hot-Air Ballooning *in* Sports and the Outdoors, *above*.)

At the Estrella Sailport, **Arizona Soaring Inc.** (Box 858, Maricopa 85239, ☎ 602/568–2318) offers sailplane rides in a basic trainer or high-performance plane for prices ranging from $48 to $90. The adventuresome can opt for a wild 15-minute acrobatic flight for $80.

If you prefer a less dizzying option, **Wagonmasters** (7319 E. Second St., Scottsdale 85251, ☎ 602/423–1449 or mobile phone 602/501–3239) leads 15-minute to one-hour horse-drawn-carriage tours around Old Scottsdale for $20–$70. They are also available for weddings, birthdays, and other special events.

One of the most interesting guided tours in town explores **Taliesin West** (12621 N. Frank Lloyd Wright Blvd., Scottsdale 85261, ☎ 602/860–2700), winter headquarters of the Frank Lloyd Wright Foundation. With its redwood-and-rock design set at the base of the McDowell Mountains, Wright's winter home typifies his concept of blending function with nature. Hour-long guided tours cost $10; a weekly three-hour tour goes behind the scenes and talks with Wright associates working and studying at the site. The cost is $25. A weekly night tour entitled "Night Lights on the Desert" runs from March through May and costs $25.

Walking Tour

A 45-minute self-guided walking tour of **Old Scottsdale** takes visitors to 14 historic sites in the area. Maps showing the route can be picked up in the **Scottsdale Chamber of Commerce** office (7343 E. Scottsdale Mall, Scottsdale 85251, ☎ 602/945–8481 or 800/877–1117) weekdays 8:30–5, Saturday 10–5, and Sunday 11–5.

Opening and Closing Times

Generally, banks are open Monday–Thursday 9–4, Friday 9–6. Selected banks have Saturday morning hours, and a few large grocery stores have bank windows that stay open until 9 PM.

Most enclosed shopping malls are open weekdays 10–9, Saturday 10–6, and Sunday noon–5; some of the major centers (*see* Shopping, *above*) are open later on weekends.

Many grocery stores are open 7 AM–9 PM, but several stores within major chains throughout the valley are open 24 hours.

Radio Stations

AM
KTAR 620: News, talk, sports; **KIDR 740:** Children; **KFYI 910:** News, talk; **KPHX 1480:** Spanish-language.

FM
KBAQ 89.5: Classical; **KJZZ 91.5:** Jazz, National Public Radio; **KKFR 92.3:** Top 40; **KUPD 97.9:** Rock; **KNIX 102.5:** Country; **KVVA 107.1:** Spanish-language.

Important Addresses and Numbers

Emergencies

For **police, fire, ambulance** or **highway** emergencies dial 911.

HOSPITALS

Samaritan Health Service (☎ 602/230–CARE) has four valley hospitals—Good Samaritan (downtown), Desert Samaritan (east), Maryvale Samaritan (southwest), and Thunderbird Samaritan (northwest)—and a west Valley urgent-care clinic; all share a 24-hour hot line. **Scottsdale Memorial Hospital** (☎ 602/481–4411) has three campuses in the northeastern valley. **Maricopa County Medical Center** (☎ 602/267–5011) has been rated one of the nation's best public hospitals.

DOCTORS

The **Maricopa County Medical Society** (☎ 602/252–2844) and the **Arizona Osteopathic Medical Association** (☎ 602/840–0460) offer referrals during business hours on weekdays.

DENTISTS

The **American Dental Association Valley** chapter (☎ 602/957–4864) has a 24-hour referral hot line.

LATE-NIGHT PHARMACIES

Walgreens has fourteen 24-hour locations throughout the valley. The easiest way to locate the one nearest you is to call 800/WALGREENS. **Osco Drug** (☎ 800/881–6726) has four 24-hour outlets including central Phoenix (3320 N. 7th Ave., ☎ 602/266–5501) west Phoenix (35th and Glendale Aves., ☎ 602/841–7861), Scottsdale (Scottsdale and Shea Rds., ☎ 602/998-3500), and Mesa (1836 W. Baseline Rd., ☎ 602/831–0212).

WEATHER

Pressline (☎ 602/271–5656, then press 1010) gives up-to-date valley conditions and three-day forecasts, as does the **U.S. National Weather Service** (☎ 602/265–5550).

Visitor Information

The **Phoenix and Valley of the Sun Convention and Visitors Bureau** (Arizona Center, 400 E. Van Buren St., Suite 600, ☎ 602/254–6500) has a satellite office in the Hyatt Regency Phoenix (2nd and Adams Sts., ☎ 602/254–6500). The **Phoenix Chamber of Commerce** (Bank One Plaza, 201 N. Central Ave., #2700, 85073, ☎ 602/254–5521) is in the heart of downtown.

6 Tucson and Southern Arizona

Tucson may have buried most of its Mexican roots, but you'll find remnants of the adobe days in its El Presidio neighborhood. And there is great Mexican food. Outside of town, the Mission San Xavier del Bac is a masterpiece, set in the midst of the Tohonó O'odham Reservation. Farther from the city, visit the legendary Tombstone and other mining towns, or pop over the border to Agua Prieta, Mexico. Lovers of nature should head for Ramsey Canyon, Organ Pipe National Monument, and Chiracahua National Monument.

By Edie Jarolim
and Trudy
Thompson Rice

A WONDERFUL ASSEMBLAGE of mountains, deserts, canyons, and dusty cowboy towns, southern Arizona remains largely undiscovered by travelers. The vast majority of the state's tourists head north for the Grand Canyon, often neglecting the southern half of the state. But it would be a pity to miss southern Arizona. It's uncrowded, the weather is usually mild, and there is plenty to see and do. Among the area's myriad attractions are historic Tombstone, Yuma, and Bisbee, where you can indulge in Old West fantasies galore; the huge, oddly shaped cacti of Saguaro National Park; the ominous, towering rock formations of Chiricahua National Monument; the lively shops and restaurants in Nogales, across the Mexican border; and, of course, Tucson. A gateway to southern Arizona, Tucson offers travelers history, culture, and sports: fascinating Spanish colonial adobe architecture; ballet, symphony, and the University of Arizona's photography museum (which has one of the largest 20th-century collections in the country); golf, tennis, and Hi-Corbett Field, where the Colorado Rockies compete with seven other major-league baseball teams during spring training.

Although it is Arizona's second-largest city, Tucson feels like a small town—one enriched by its deep Mexican and Old West roots. It is at once a bustling center of business and a kicked-back university and resort town. Metropolitan Tucson has more than 700,000 year-round residents, increased by "snowbirds" who come to the area in winter to enjoy the warm sun that shines on the city more than 320 days a year. Winter temperatures hover around 65°F during the day and 38°F at night. Summers are unquestionably hot—with July averaging 101°F during the day and 73°F at night—but not as hot as in Phoenix. In spite of a similar basin-and-range setting, Tucson is cooler in summer because of its higher altitude (2,400 feet, compared with Phoenix's 1,100 feet). And because Tucson averages only 11 inches of rain a year (more than half of which falls from July to September), low humidity makes even July's heat feel far more comfortable than one would expect.

In a part of the world where everything seems new and buildings more than 50 years old are viewed as historic places, Tucson is an exception. Historians have dated Tucson's earliest citizens to AD 100, when the Hohokam Indians made their home in the fertile farming valley. During the 1500s, Spanish explorers arrived to find Pima Indians enjoying the mild weather and growing crops.

The name Tucson came from the Indian word *stjukshon* (pronounced "*stook*-shahn"), meaning "spring at the foot of a black mountain." (The springs at the foot of Sentinel Peak, made of black volcanic rock, are now dry.) The name became Tucson (originally pronounced "*tuk*-son") in the mouths of the Spanish explorers who built the *presidio* (walled city) of San Augustin del Tuguison in 1776 to keep Native Americans from reclaiming the city. The walled city was affectionately called the Old Pueblo by early settlers, and the nickname has stuck till this day.

Father Eusebio Francisco Kino, a Jesuit missionary, first visited the village in 1687 and returned a few years later to build missions in the area. His influence is still strongly felt throughout the region, especially at the noteworthy Mission San Xavier del Bac south of Tucson on the Tohonó O'odham reservation.

Four flags have flown over Tucson—those of Spain, Mexico, the U.S. Confederacy, and the Union. Arizona didn't become a state until 1912, and its colorful days as a territory are still very much a part of the area's lore. In the 1850s the Butterfield stage line was extended to Tucson, bringing adventurers, a few settlers, and more than a handful of outlaws. Much of the city's growth was shaped by the University of Arizona, opened in 1891 on land "donated" by two gamblers and a saloon keeper (their benevolence was reputed to have been inspired by a bad hand of cards).

Tucson's growth really took off during World War II, thanks to Davis-Monthan Air Force Base. It was also around this time that air-conditioning made the desert hospitable to visitors and residents alike. Today the city's economy relies heavily on tourism, the university, and high-tech industries. The resident population is now almost one-quarter Hispanic, and some of the best Mexican food north of the border is served in restaurants here. The influence of Spanish and Mexican settlers is also strongly felt in the city's architecture and culture.

Tucson is a good jumping-off point for a visit to southern Arizona. Several day trips can be coordinated from the city, but to fully experience towns like Bisbee, Tombstone, or Douglas, plan on an overnight stay. As you might expect, the desert areas are popular in winter, and the cooler mountain areas are more heavily visited in summer months.

Check plane fares carefully when you're planning your trip. Though you may not want to spend time in Phoenix, sometimes it's cheaper to fly into that city and then take a scenic 2½-hour drive down the Pinal Pioneer Parkway (U.S. 79), or a speedier trip on I–10, to Tucson.

TUCSON

Tucson covers more than 500 square miles in a valley ringed by mountains. Touring the area requires having a car. The central part of town, where most shops, restaurants, and businesses are located, is roughly bounded by Wilmot Road on the east, Oracle Road on the west, River Road to the north, and 22nd Street to the south. The older downtown section, accessible just east of I–10 off the Broadway–Congress exit, is much smaller and easy to navigate on foot. (Streets there don't run true to any sort of grid, however, so it's best to get a good, detailed map.) If you're out walking in the hot weather, stop for frequent breaks to drink fluids: Tucson's climate is nothing if not dry, especially for those accustomed to living in humid areas. Alcohol aggravates dehydration, and be sure to wear sunscreen and a hat (even in winter months.

Exploring

Tour 1: El Presidio District

Numbers in the margin correspond to points of interest on the Tucson: Tours 1 and 2 map.

Originally the center of town, the downtown area is home to three historic districts: Barrio Historico, Armory Park, and El Presidio. The first two, somewhat spread out, are best explored by car. A map available from the Metropolitan Tucson Convention and Visitors Bureau (*see* Visitor Information *in* Tucson Essentials, *below*) marks a number of noteworthy sites. The El Presidio district, which has the greatest concentration of historical structures, can easily be explored on foot.

The area between Franklin and Pennington streets on the north and south and by Church and Main avenues on the east and west encompasses more than 130 years of the city's architectural history, and

dates from the original walled El Presidio del Tucson, a Spanish fortress built in 1776, when Arizona was still part of New Spain. The largest
❶ plaza in this historical area is now called **El Presidio Park,** bordered on the south side by several modern high-rise government buildings
★ **❷** and on the east side by the mosaic-dome **Pima County Courthouse.** This Spanish Colonial–style structure, perhaps Tucson's most beautiful historic building, was built in 1927 on the site of the original single-story adobe court of 1869; a portion of the old Presidio wall can be seen on the courthouse's second floor, and another section of the fort was recently discovered in front of the building. The park itself, an attractive open area with a large modern sculpture in the center, is shared by a combination of city workers and homeless people.

Head north and cross Alameda Street to the Tucson Museum of Art and Historic Block. You can walk around the area on your own, but it's worth asking at the museum for one of the free docent tours. The five historic buildings on this block are listed in the National Register of Historic Places and include La Casa Cordova, the Fish House, and the Stevens Home (*see below*). The other two residences, the **Romero House,** believed to incorporate another section of the Presidio wall, and the **Corbett House,** occupied for 56 years by the influential Tucson family for whom Hi-Corbett Field is named, are not open to the public. In the center of the museum complex is the **Plaza of the Pioneers,** honoring Tucson's early citizens.

❸ If you're ready to go inside, the **Tucson Museum of Art** houses a collection of pre-Columbian art, as well as a permanent display of 20th-century art depicting the West—some wonderful, some less than inspiring—and hosts some interesting traveling shows. The museum's gift shop features a fine variety of works (jewelry, silk scarves, weavings, ceramics) by local artisans. *140 N. Main Ave.,* ☎ *520/624–2333.* ☛ *$2 adults, $1 senior citizens and students, children under 12 free; Tues. free. Free docent tours available upon request.* ۞ *Mon.–Sat. 10–4, Sun. noon–4. Closed national holidays.*

❹ When you leave the museum, walk down Main Avenue to the corner of Alameda (less than a block away) to the **Edward Nye Fish House,** built in 1868 of adobe by the early Tucson merchant for whom it is named. Fish, a merchant, entrepreneur, and politician, and his wife, Maria Wakefield Fish, a prominent educator, shaped much of early Tucson history; they hosted such visitors as President and Mrs. Rutherford B. Hayes here. Their residence, notable for its 15-foot beamed ceilings and saguaro-cactus-rib supports, now houses the El Presidio art gallery, which sells contemporary and traditional Southwestern oils, watercolors, bronzes, and ceramics. *120 N. Main Ave.,* ☎ *520/884–7379.* ☛ *Free.* ۞ *Mon.–Sat. 10–4, Sun. noon–4. Closed Sun. June–Aug.*

❺ Also on Main Avenue, just north of the Fish House and architecturally similar, is the 1865 **Stevens Home.** Here wealthy politician and cattle rancher Hiram Stevens and his Mexican wife, Petra Santa Cruz, entertained many of Tucson's leaders—including Edward and Maria Fish—during the 1800s. A drought brought the Stevenses' cattle ranching to a halt in 1893, and Stevens killed himself in despair, after unsuccessfully attempting to kill his wife. The house was restored in 1980 and now hosts one of Tucson's most elegant restaurants, Janos (*see* Dining, *below*).

❻ For one of the best examples of simple but elegant adobe architecture, head across the Plaza of the Pioneers to **La Casa Cordova.** One of the oldest buildings in Tucson, with the original part built in about 1848, it is now home to the Mexican Heritage Museum. When you enter La Casa

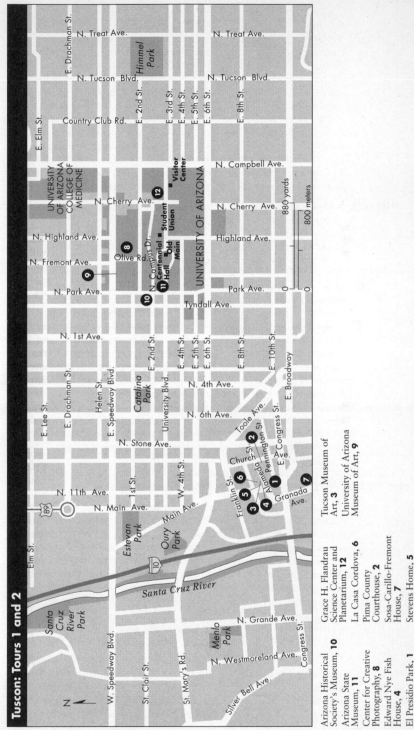

Tuscon: Tours 1 and 2

Arizona Historical
Society's Museum, 10

Arizona State
Museum, 11

Center for Creative
Photography, 8

Edward Nye Fish
House, 4

El Presidio Park, 1

Grace H. Flandrau
Science Center and
Planetarium, 12

La Casa Cordova, 6

Pima County
Courthouse, 2

Sosa-Carillo-Fremont
House, 7

Stevens Home, 5

Tucson Museum of
Art, 3

University of Arizona
Museum of Art, 9

Cordova through the double doors on Meyer Avenue, the room on your right has an exhibit of the history of the Presidio; three rooms off the patio display furnishings of the Indian and pioneer settlers of the period. If you are lucky enough to be here from November through March, don't miss the Naciemento, a traditional Dec. 25 display filling an entire room with miniatures arranged in elaborate scenes from the Old and New Testaments and from Mexican rural life. When you visit the museum, you'll understand why adobe—brick made of mud and straw, cured in the hot sun—was so widely used in early Tucson. It offers a natural insulation from the heat and cold, and it is durable in Tucson's dry climate. In some cases the woody cactus ribs built into the walls and ceilings for extra support poke through the hard-packed adobe. *175 N. Meyer Ave.,* ☎ *520/624–2333.* ☛ *Free.* ☉ *Sept.–Apr. Mon.–Sat. 10–4, Sun. noon–4. Closed Mon. June–Aug. and on national holidays.*

TIME OUT   **Old Town Artisans,** across Meyer Avenue from Casa Cordova, is a 13-room marketplace set in a 19th-century adobe building, with a focus on Southwestern and Mexican crafts. The pretty **Courthouse Grill** (186 N. Meyer Ave., ☎ 520/622-0351) on the patio, mist-cooled in summer, is a fine place to enjoy a salad or a sandwich.

❼ Not, strictly speaking, in the Presidio district, the nearby **Sosa-Carillo-Fremont House** is worth a short detour south. The only building spared when the surrounding barrio was torn down to build the Tucson Convention Center, this is one of Tucson's oldest adobe residences. Originally purchased by José Maria Sosa in 1860, it was owned by the Carillo family for 80 years. Arizona's territorial governor, John C. Fremont, may have spent a night or two here when the place was briefly rented out to his daughter in 1880. The restored house, now a branch of the Arizona Historical Society, is furnished in 1880s fashion and has rotating displays of territorial life. *Convention Center Complex, between the Music Hall and the Arena (parking at 151 S. Granada Ave.),* ☎ *520/622–0956.* ☛ *Free; walking tours of the Presidio and Tucson Historic District: $4 adults, children under 7 free.* ☉ *Wed.–Sat. 10–4; tours Oct.–Apr., Sat. at 10.*

Tour 2: University of Arizona Neighborhood

A university—especially in the Southwest—might not seem to be the most likely spot for a vacation visit, but this one is unusual. Not only is the institution itself of historical importance, but it also hosts museums for special interests ranging from astronomy to photography. If you're visiting during the week when classes are in session, parking in the university area is a hassle. You're best off leaving your car in a university lot. A central one, on 2nd Street between Highland and Mountain avenues, charges $5 from 7 to 1, $3 from 1 to 5, and $2 from 5 to 8. There's no fee for parking on weekends, and you shouldn't have a problem finding a legal spot during the summer, when most of the students leave campus.

The U of A, as the University of Arizona is known locally (versus ASU, its rival state university in Phoenix), covers 325 acres and is a major economic influence on the city. Approximately 38,000 students attend graduate and undergraduate classes here. The original land for the university was "donated" by a couple of gamblers and a saloon owner in 1891, and $25,000 of territorial money was used to build Old Main (the original building) and hire six faculty members. Money ran out before the Old Main's roof was placed, but a few enlightened local citizens pitched in with the funds to finish it. Most of the city's populace was less enthusiastic about the institution: They were disgruntled when the 13th Territorial Legislature granted the University of Arizona to Tucson and awarded rival Phoenix with what they considered to be the real prize—an insane asylum and a prison.

Note: For all of the university's institutions, it's best to call ahead and verify opening and closing hours; budget cuts have caused schedule changes in a number of cases. The *Tucson Official Visitors Guide,* available from the Tucson Convention and Visitors Bureau (*see* Visitor Information *in* Tucson Essentials, *below*) includes a detailed map of the campus.

★ ❽ Start your tour on the northwestern corner of campus, at the junction of Speedway Boulevard and Park Avenue, where you'll find a large parking garage. A pedestrian underpass leads to the **Center for Creative Photography,** located in a gray concrete building on the left. Set up to house the university's extensive Ansel Adams holdings, the center houses a superb collection of 20th-century photography, including works by Dorothea Lange, Paul Strand, Eudora Welty, W. Eugene Smith, and Edward Weston. Changing exhibits in the main gallery highlight various holdings of the collection, but if you'd like to spend an hour looking at the pictures of a particular photographer in the center's archives, call to arrange an appointment. *1030 N. Olive Rd.,* ☎ *520/621–7968.* ☞ *Free.* ☉ *Weekdays 11–5, Sun. noon–5. Closed Sat., national and state holidays.*

❾ Catercorner from the center on the right-hand side is the small **University of Arizona Museum of Art,** with a wide-ranging collection of European paintings from the Renaissance through the 17th century. Two of the museum's highlights are the 26 astounding panels of Fernando Gallego's 1488 Ciudad Rodrigo altarpiece and the second largest collection in the world of bronze, plaster, and ceramic sculpture by Jacques Lipschitz. *Fine Arts Complex, Bldg. 2,* ☎ *520/621–7567.* ☞ *Free.* ☉ *Sept.–mid-May, weekdays 9–5, Sun. noon–4; mid-May–Aug., weekdays 10–3:30, Sun. noon–4. Closed Sat., national and state holidays.*

❿ From the back of the museum, head directly south two blocks on Park Avenue and then go east on 2nd Street to reach the **Arizona Historical Society's Museum.** (If you're driving and this is your first stop, park your car in the lot at the corner of 2nd and Euclid streets and then inquire at the museum about the token system.) Well-displayed exhibits transport visitors through Arizona history, starting with the Hohokam Indians and Spanish explorers and highlighting important influences such as mining and cattle ranching. Children will especially enjoy the dark (and slightly spooky) replica of a mine shaft and the old cars and wagons in the transportation section. A gift shop includes items from the late 1800s (many reproductions, but also antiques) as well as Native American crafts and Mexican folk art. The library houses an extensive collection of historical Arizona photographs and sells reprints of most of them for a small fee. *949 E. 2nd St.,* ☎ *520/628–5774.* ☞ *Suggested donation: $3 adults, 50¢ children.* ☉ *Mon.–Sat. 10–4, Sun. noon–4. Closed national and state holidays.*

⓫ One block to the south on University Boulevard, just inside the main gate of the university, is the **Arizona State Museum,** the oldest in the state, dating from territorial days (1893). Exhibits in the original (south) building focus on the state's ancient history, including fossils and a fascinating sample of tree-ring dating. In the north building, Phase I of the extensive "Paths of Life: American Indians of the Southwest" exhibit, occupying some 10,000 square feet, opened in late 1993. The cultural traditions, origins, and contemporary lives of native tribes of Arizona and of Sonora, Mexico, are explored through a variety of displays and video programs. The museum's new gift shop is also in this building. *Park Ave.,* ☎ *520/621–6302.* ☛ *Free.* ☉ *Mon.–Sat. 10–5, Sun. noon–5. Closed national holidays.*

TIME OUT Just outside the campus gate, University Boulevard is lined with student-oriented eateries. You won't find sophisticated fare, but portions tend to be hearty and prices low. **Geronimoz** (800 E. University Blvd. at Euclid, ☎ 520/623–1711) stands out for its good burgers and salads. Beer aficionados should head over to **Gentle Ben's** (843 E. University, ☎ 520/624–4177), the only microbrewery in Tucson.

⑫ Back on campus, as you head east, University Boulevard turns into the grassy University Mall. Continue on to Cherry Avenue to reach the **Grace H. Flandrau Science Center and Planetarium.** (Note that this is a long walk. You may want to get back in your car and park closer if it's very hot out.) Tucson is a major center for astronomy. City ordinances allow viewing of the usually clear desert skies at night, even in the center city. Planetarium attractions include a 16-inch public telescope; the impressive Star Theatre, where a multimedia show brings astronomy to life; an interactive meteor exhibit; and, in the basement, a small Mineral Museum, which exhibits more than 2,000 rock and gem samples, some rather rare. Laser light shows are held at night. Bring a camera—special adapters allow you to take pictures through the telescopes. *Cherry Ave. and University Blvd.,* ☎ *520/621–4515.* ☛ *Exhibits $2, laser light show $5, exhibits plus theater $4.50 adults, $4 senior citizens and students, $3 children 3–13, no children under 3.* ☉ *Mon.–Tues. 10–5, Wed.–Thurs. 10–5 and 7–9, Fri. 10–5 and 7–midnight, Sat. 1–5 and 7–midnight, Sun. 1–5. Show times vary; call 520/621–7827 for recorded message. Telescope hrs: in summer, Tues.–Sat. 8–10 PM; in winter, Tues.–Sat. 7–10 PM.*

Tour 3: Tucson Mountain Park and Saguaro National Park

Numbers in the margin correspond to points of interest on the Tucson: Tours 3–5 map.

If you are interested in the flora and fauna of the Sonora Desert—as well as some of its appearances in the cinema—this is an ideal trip for you. Your best plan is to head out in the cooler early morning to Saguaro National Park, which has no shaded areas to duck into later in the day. Just south of Saguaro National Park, the 17,000-acre **Tucson Mountain Park** contains the **Arizona–Sonora Desert Museum** and **Old Tucson Studios** theme park. Spend the rest of the morning at the Desert Museum, where you can have lunch on the terrace of the Desert Museum's new restaurant. Unfortunately, a fire in the spring of 1995 at the nearby Old Tucson Studios, where more than 250 Westerns have been shot over the past 50 years, has destroyed much of the place. Call ahead to find out what has reopened (*see below*). If you don't drive, consider taking one of the many tours to the Arizona–Sonora Desert Museum (*see* Guided Tours *in* Tucson Essentials, *below*).

From Tucson, take Speedway Boulevard west to where it joins Anklam Road and becomes Gates Pass Road. Here you will see signs for Old Tucson Studios. At this juncture Gates Pass Road becomes Kinney Road. Continue on for about 12 miles (passing signs for the Arizona–Sonora

★ **⑬** Desert Museum) until you come to **Saguaro National Park.** It was upgraded from its status of national monument in October 1994, and signs bearing the old name still remain around town. The two portions of the park are separated by the city of Tucson. The eastern portion covers more than 67,000 acres and climbs through five climate zones; the smaller western portion, the one explored on this tour, has more than 24,000 acres, all approximately at the same elevation. Both sections of the park are populated by the huge saguaro (pronounced "suh-*war*-oh") cactus, which is native to the Sonora Desert and known for its towering height (often 50 feet) and arms that reach out in weird configurations. The cactus is ribbed vertically with accordion-like pleats that expand to store water gathered through its shallow roots during the infrequent desert rain showers. In the springtime (usually April or May), the giant succulent sports a tiny party hat of white blooms. At any time of year, the sight of these kings of the desert ruling over their quiet domain is awe-inspiring.

The slow-growing cacti (they can take up to 15 years to grow 1 foot) are protected by state and federal laws, so enjoy but don't disturb them. In recent years, they have suffered a decline because a decrease in the coyote population has led to an abundant rabbit population. Rabbits and other small animals nibble at the base of the young saguaro, gathering nutrients and water for survival and thereby hindering or halting the cactus's slow growth.

You'll see the most wildlife if you go through the park early in the morning, when the animals are at their liveliest. Desert critters such as snakes and scorpions aren't necessarily hostile unless you crowd them, so just watch your step and respect their habitat.

Before you venture into the desert, it's worth stopping in at the impressive new visitor center that opened on the west side of Saguaro National Park in 1994. A sophisticated slide show in the auditorium ends with a spectacular look at the landscape outside the window. An extremely lifelike display simulates the flora and fauna of the region, and an expanded sales area carries a large array of books and maps. Walkways from the side of the center lead out onto short nature trails, and you can get information about longer hiking trails that wind through the park. Ask how to get to Signal Hill, where you can explore petroglyphs (rock drawings) left by the Hohokam Indians centuries ago. *Westside:* ☎ *520/733–5158.* ☛ *Free.* ☉ *Visitor center: daily 8–5; park roads: 7–sunset. Eastside:* ☎ *520/733–5153.* ☛ *$4 per vehicle, $2 individuals entering by bicycle or foot. Same hrs as westside. Both centers closed Dec. 25.*

★ ⑭ About another half mile south of the visitor center, on Kinney Road, the **Arizona–Sonora Desert Museum** is not to be missed. The name "museum" is misleading for this site, which is more like a beautifully planned zoo. In this microcosm of a desert environment, hummingbirds, cactus wrens, rattlesnakes, scorpions, bighorn sheep, and prairie dogs all busy themselves in natural habitats ingeniously planned to allow the visitor to look on without disturbing them. Besides wildlife exhibits, there is also an Earth Sciences Center, which features a damp limestone cave and meteor and mineral displays that encourage visitors to feel the texture of the stones and inspect them under magnifying glasses. Exhibits and interactive programs change with the season. For example, during the spring visitors are invited to help identify local wildflowers.

Allow at least two hours for your visit to the museum, longer if you have nature lovers with you. You'll be outdoors most of the time, so take a jacket if you're visiting in winter and take frequent water breaks if you're visiting in summer. It can get really hot and dry here. The new

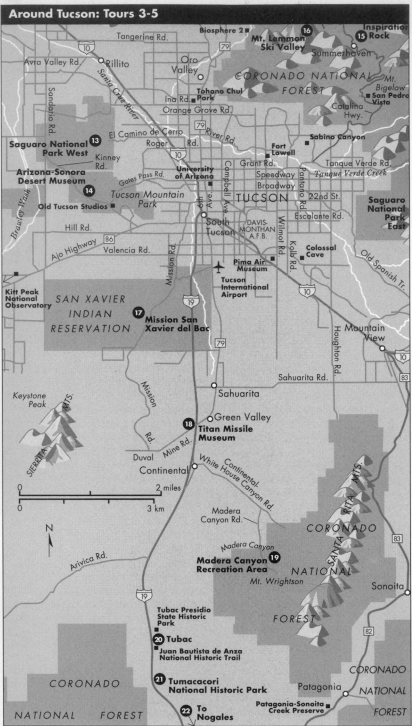

Ironwood Terrace restaurant, near the hummingbird exhibit, offers a variety of hot and cold sandwiches, along with burgers, soups, salads, and Mexican entrées. There's also a small coffee bar near the gift shop (which carries a tempting array of Native American jewelry as well as many terrific items made from minerals). Wheelchairs and strollers are available at the museum, but pets aren't allowed, so just don't take them along. Confining them to the car in Arizona heat can kill them. *2021 N. Kinney Rd.,* ☎ *520/883–2702.* ☛ *$8.95 adults, $1.75 children 6–12.* ☉ *Mar.–Sept., daily 7:30–6; Oct.–Feb., daily 8:30–5. Last ticket sales 1 hr before closing. MC, V.*

Once again, Old Tucson Studios was seriously damaged by fire in 1995. To find out which of the former activities and exhibits will be reopened in 1996—among them gunfights, magic shows, stunt shows, a petting farm, stagecoach rides, trail rides, and souvenir shops—call ahead for details. *201 S. Kinney Rd. (inside Tucson Mountain Park),* ☎ *520/883–6457.* ☛ *$12.95 adults, $8.95 children 4–11; after 5 PM $8.95 adults and children.* ☉ *Daily 9–9.*

Tour 4: Mt. Lemmon

This tour takes you to the southernmost ski slope of the continental United States, but you don't have to be a skier to visit. During warm months, you can enjoy hiking and picnicking in this lovely area. The mountain's 9,157-foot elevation brings welcome relief from summer heat, and in winter, the craggy old mountain often dons a cap of snow that draws all levels of enthusiasts.

Mt. Lemmon is one of the Santa Catalina Mountains, which stand guard at the northern rim of the valley that is Tucson (the main surrounding ranges are the Santa Ritas to the south, the Rincons to the east, and the Tucson Mountains to the west). Every 1,000 feet of elevation in these mountains is equivalent to traveling 300 miles north—thus the vegetation at the top of Mt. Lemmon is similar to that found in southern Canada. Standing in a forest of pines blanketed by snow, you might have trouble remembering that there's a desert with cacti and wildflowers less than 35 miles away.

If you're making the trip in the winter, check road conditions by calling 520/741–4991. On temperate days, consider packing a picnic lunch. Wear layers of clothing so you can cool or warm yourself as you change elevation. And be sure to fill up the tank before you leave town, because there are no gas stations on Mt. Lemmon Highway.

If all's clear, take Grant Road to the east side of town, where you can pick up Tanque Verde Road. Follow that until you reach Catalina Highway, which becomes Mt. Lemmon Highway as you head north. Drive this road for 30 twisting, climbing miles until you come to Mt. Lemmon Ski Valley—unless the heat inspires you to turn off a little side road to the cool, charming village of Summerhaven (you'll come to it right before you reach the ski area). It's not a good idea to take trailers and recreational vehicles on this mountain road, and it's best for all drivers to travel during daylight hours. Safety aside, it would be a pity to miss seeing the rock formations along the way. They look as though they were carefully balanced against one another by architects from another planet. There are a couple of pleasant lodges in Summerhaven if you don't want to descend the mountain on the same day that you drive up.

Hikers can take any number of side trips on this tour. There are some 150 miles of well-marked and well-maintained trails in the Mt. Lemmon area, for all levels of expertise. Of the several trails around San Pedro Vista, a good one for beginners is the **Green Mountain Trail,** which starts a half mile past the Rose Canyon turnoff from Mt. Lemmon Highway. The route takes you 4 miles (one-way) from San Pedro Vista— with lovely mountain views to the east—to General Hitchcock Campground. Hikers will enjoy the half-mile trek ascending more than 600 feet to the top of **Mt. Bigelow** from the Palisades Ranger Station. Coming down is the hard part. The ranger station (☎ 520/749–8700, open daily 9–5 in summer, Fri.–Sun. 9–5 in winter) can give you current information on hiking trails; it's also a good place to buy maps and books.

⑮ If you've brought your lunch, watch for **Inspiration Rock** just after milepost 22.5 on Mt. Lemmon Highway. There are picnic areas and plenty of room to stretch out under a tree for a siesta. The variety of birds here is astounding—watch for electric-blue Steller's jays and an assortment of hummingbirds.

⑯ Mt. Lemmon Highway ends at **Mt. Lemmon Ski Valley** (☎ 520/576–1321, or 520/576–1400 for a recorded snow report). Skiing here depends on natural conditions—there's no artificial snow—so call ahead. Some winters there is plenty of powder, and others it's pretty scarce. There are 16 runs, open daily, ranging from beginner to advanced. Lift tickets cost $25 for an all-day pass and $20 for a half day (starting at 1 PM); children 12 and under ski for $10. Ski equipment can be rented, and private instruction starts at $30 an hour. A $36 first-time skier's package includes equipment rental, a lesson, and a lift pass upon completion of the lesson. Even in off-season, visitors will enjoy a ride on the double chairlift that whisks them to the top of the slope—some 9,100 feet. The cost is $5 for adults and $2 for children 12 and under. Many ride the lift and then head out on one of several trails that crisscross the summit.

TIME OUT The **Iron Door** (☎ 520/576–1321) in Mt. Lemmon Ski Valley is open weekends 10–5:30, weekdays 10:30–5:30 (give or take half an hour, depending on the weather). In winter, the focus is on burgers, chili, corn bread, and soups; in warmer weather, lots of salads turn up on the menu. This place is popular on the weekends—parking can be tough.

Tour 5: Along I–19

There's something for everyone en route from Tucson to Nogales along I–19—history buffs, bird-watchers, hikers, Mexican-food lovers, and folks whose idea of heaven is to shop until they drop. The tour roughly follows the Camino Real (King's Road) that the conquistadors and missionaries took from Mexico up to what was once the northernmost portion of New Spain.

Drive southwest on I–19 from Tucson about 9 miles and get off on San Xavier Road. About three-quarters of a mile west, you'll come to the
★ **⑰** shining White Dove of the Desert, or **Mission San Xavier del Bac** (☎ 520/294–2624). The oldest Catholic church in the United States still serving the community for which it was built, San Xavier was founded in 1692 by Father Eusebio Francisco Kino, who established 22 missions in northern Mexico and southern Arizona. It was constructed out of native materials by Franciscan missionaries between 1777 and 1797. Today it is owned by the Tohonó O'odham Indian tribe (the name means "Desert People Who Have Come from the Earth").

The beauty of the mission, with elements of Spanish, Baroque, and *mudejar* (Spanish Islamic) architectural styles, is highlighted by the stark desert landscape against which it is set. Inside, there's a wealth of painted statues, carvings, and frescoes. The mission has been called the Sistine Chapel of the United States by Paul Schwartzbaum, who worked on restoring Michelangelo's masterwork in Rome and is helping to supervise the restoration of the mission's artwork. Begun in 1992, the project is not expected to be completed until 1997. A visitor center in the front part of San Xavier del Bac offers displays of the history and architecture of the church. It's adjoined by a gift shop, open 9–5 in winter, 8–6 in summer.

Across the parking lot from the mission, San Xavier Plaza has a number of shops that sell fine Native American crafts. Look especially for jewelry, pottery, and baskets featuring man-in-the-maze designs, and for friendship bowls, both particular to the Tohonó O'odham tribe. Works of the northern Arizona Hopi and Navajo are also represented.

TIME OUT   For wonderful Indian fry bread—large, round pieces of dough brought up fresh from the hot oil and topped with all sorts of delicious possibilities—stop in **The Wa:k Snack Shop** (☎ 520/573-9191) at the back of the plaza. You can also have breakfast or a Mexican lunch here.

Mass is celebrated daily at San Xavier. On Sunday and religious holidays, there's often a mariachi band—one of the many Mexican influences in evidence here. Call ahead for information about special celebrations.

 Get back on I–19 and drive south some 20 miles. At exit 69 you'll come to the **Titan Missile Museum,** site of the only one of 54 Titan II missiles left intact when the Salt II treaty with the Soviet Union was signed. Guided tours take visitors down into the command post where a ground crew of four lived. Among the fascinating—and sobering—sights is a 114-foot, 165-ton, two-stage liquid-fuel rocket. Now empty, it originally held a nuclear payload with 214 times the explosive power of the bomb that destroyed Hiroshima. *1580 W. Duval Mine Rd.,* ☎ *520/791–2929.* ☞ *$6 adults, $5 senior citizens and active military personnel, $4 children 10–17.* ☉ *Nov.–Apr., daily 9–5; May–Oct., Wed.–Sun. 9–5 (last tour at 4). Closed Thanksgiving and Dec. 25.*

Bird-watchers and hikers will want to get off I–19 at exit 63 and drive along White House Canyon Road, which turns into Madera Canyon Road. It veers south into Coronado National Forest and the Santa Rita Mountains—among them Mt. Wrightson, the highest peak in southern Arizona at 9,453 feet. With approximately 200 miles of scenic trails, the **Madera Canyon Recreation Area** (☎ 520/281–2296 in Nogales, 520/670–5464 in Tucson) is a favorite destination for hikers. Higher elevations and thick pine cover make it especially popular in summer with Tucsonans looking to escape the heat. Birders flock here year-round. About 400 avian species have been spotted in the area. As you enter the recreation area, you'll see a small visitor center, open only on weekends and operated by the volunteer Friends of Madera Canyon. Nearby, the Box Springs campground has 13 sites with toilets, potable water, and grills, available on a first-come, first-served basis (cost: $5 per vehicle per night).

★ ⑳ Forty-five miles south of Tucson at exit 34 you'll come to **Tubac,** site of the first European settlement in Arizona in 1726. A year after the Pima Indian uprising in 1851, a military garrison was established here to protect early Spanish settlers, missionaries, and peaceful Indian converts of the nearby Tumacacori Mission (*see below*) from further attack. It was from here that Juan Bautista de Anza led the expedition of 240 colonists across the desert that resulted in the founding of San Francisco in 1776. Arizona's first newspaper, *The Weekly Arizonian,* was printed here in 1859, and in 1860 Tubac was the largest town in Arizona. Today, the quiet little town is a popular art colony. Crafts sold in the more than 80 shops—mostly staffed by the artists who make the goods sold in them—range from carved wooden furniture and hand-thrown pottery to delicately painted tiles and silk-screen fabrics. The annual **Tubac Festival of the Arts** has been held in February for more than 30 years. For dates, contact the Tubac Chamber of Commerce (☎ 520/398–2704).

There's an archaeological display of portions of the original 1752 fort at the **Tubac Presidio State Historic Park and Museum** in the center of town. In addition to the visitor center, which has an exhibit area detailing the history of the early colony, the park includes Tubac's 1885 schoolhouse and a pleasant picnic area. *Presidio Dr., ☎ 520/398–2252.* ☛ *$2 adults, $1 children 12–17.* ⊙ *Daily 8–5. Closed Dec. 25.*

TIME OUT   Just north of Tubac on the road paralleling I–19, the **Tubac Country Market** (410 E. Frontage Rd., ☎ 520/398–9532 or 520/398–9870) has a patio where you can enjoy a tasty breakfast or lunch and a stunning vista. Reasonably priced and well-prepared dinner is available by reservation only. A large gift shop carries well-priced crafts from Arizona and Mexico. There's also a deli and a grocery.

You can tread the same road as the conquistadors to get to the next site: The first 4½ miles of the de Anza National Historic Trail from Tumacacori to Tubac were dedicated in 1992. You'll have to cross the Santa Cruz River (which is usually pretty low) three times in order to complete the hike, and the path is rather sandy, but it's a pleasant journey along the tree-shaded banks of the river.

㉑ Another option is to drive 3 miles south along the east frontage road of I–19 to reach **Tumacacori National Historic Park.** The site was visited by missionary Father Eusebio Francisco Kino in 1691, but the Jesuits didn't build a church here until 1751. Visitors can still see some ruins of this simple structure, but the main attraction is the mission of San José de Tumacacori, built by the Franciscans around 1799–1803. A combination of circumstances—Apache attacks, a bad winter, and Mexico's withdrawal of funds and priests—caused the friars to flee in 1848, and persistent rumors of wealth left behind by both the Franciscans and the Jesuits led treasure-seekers to unsuccessfully pillage the site. It was finally protected in 1908, when it became a national monument.

Information about the mission and the de Anza trail is available at the visitor center. Guided tours are also offered daily (more in winter than in summer). A small museum displays some of the mission's original artifacts, and the patio garden boasts a variety of native plants. In 1990, when Tumacacori became a national historic park, two mission ruins were added, both about 15 miles to the southwest. They are currently being excavated, however, and are not open to the public. In addition to a Christmas Eve service, costumed historical high masses are held at Tumacacori in spring and fall. An annual fiesta held here in the first week of December features arts and crafts and food booths. *Exit 29 off I–19, ☎ 520/398–2341.* ☛ *$2 adults 17 and older, free for children under 17 and Golden Age, Golden Eagle, and Golden Access cardholders.* ⊙ *Daily 8–5. Closed Thanksgiving and Dec. 25.*

Those who want a glimpse of present-day Hispanic culture can continue on to **Nogales,** a bustling border town. It can get fairly rowdy on weekends, when underage Tucsonans head south to drink, but it offers some good restaurants and fine-quality crafts and furnishings in addition to the usual border schlock. If you're just coming for the day, it's best to park on the Arizona side of the border (you'll see many guarded lots that cost about $4 or $5 for the day) and walk across. Practically all the good shopping is within easy strolling distance of the border.

The shopping area centers mainly around Avenida Obregón, which begins a few blocks west of the border entrance and runs north–south—just follow the crowds. You'll find a wide selection of handicrafts, furnishings, and jewelry here. Except at shops that indicate otherwise, bargaining is not only acceptable but expected. **El Zarape Curios** (Av. Obregón 161) specializes in sterling-silver jewelry and designer clothing. For upscale imports, particularly French perfumes, try **Mickey's** (Av. Obregón 128), **Via Veneto** (Aves. Obregón and Aguirre), and **Versailles** (Av. Obregón 111). **Continental Curios** (Av. Obregón 98) is a large department store with a wide selection of rebozos (shawls), appliquéd and embroidered clothing, hand-blown glassware, and leather huaraches. **El Changarro** (Calle Elías 93) specializes in high-quality furniture, antiques, pottery, and handwoven rugs. Most of the good restaurants near the border are also on Obregón.

TIME OUT   Large, friendly **Elvira** (Av. Obregón 1, ☎ 631/2–47–73) has long been a favorite for day-trippers to Mexico. It's been cleaned up and expanded in recent years, but a free shot of tequila still comes with each meal. Try any of the excellent fish dishes, the chicken mole, or the chile rellenos.

What to See and Do with Children

There are plenty of things to occupy children in Tucson and southern Arizona. Besides the activities listed here, a number are cited in Participant Sports, *below.* (Remember, however, that when you take children outdoors, their skin is especially prone to sunburn and windburn. Protect them with hats and sunscreen, and offer liquids frequently to prevent dehydration.) Many resorts also have activities designed to entertain children while their parents sightsee. Inquire when you make reservations.

Arizona–Sonora Desert Museum (*see* Tour 3, *above*).

Biosphere 2. This is a trip for school-age children. Smaller ones will enjoy being outdoors but won't really appreciate the tour. (*See* Off the Beaten Track, *below*.)

The dry limestone **Colossal Cave,** 20 miles east of Tucson and 6 miles north of I–10, is filled with stalagmites and stalactites. The cave has never been fully explored, and legend has it that gold is hidden in the dark recesses. *Old Spanish Trail Rd., ☎ 520/647–7275. ☛ $6.50 adults, $5 children 11–16, $3.50 children 6–10. ☉ Oct.–mid-Mar., Mon.–Sat. 9–5, Sun. and holidays 9–6; mid-Mar.–Sept., Mon.–Sat. 8–6, Sun. and holidays 8–7.*

Children love the old-fashioned melodramas at the **Gaslight Theatre,** where hissing the villain and cheering the hero are part of the audience's duty. There is free popcorn, and beer, wine, soft drinks, and pizza are sold. *7010 E. Broadway, ☎ 520/886–9428. ☛ $12.95 adults; $10.95 students, senior citizens, and active military; $6 children under 13.*

At **Golf 'n' Stuff Family Fun Centers,** children can play video games and miniature golf, ride bumper boats, and drive little race cars. *6503 E. Tanque Verde Rd.,* ☎ *520/296–2366.* ☛ *Free; each attraction priced separately.* ☉ *Sun.–Thurs. 10–10, Fri.–Sat. 10 AM–1 AM.*

International Wildlife Museum allows youngsters to touch and feel different animal skins, and teaches them many other things about more than 200 species of birds and mammals from all over the world via interactive computers. There's a theater that shows wildlife films, a gift shop, and a vending machine area (the restaurant is currently closed, but may be open by the time you read this). *4800 W. Gates Pass Rd.,* ☎ *520/624–4024.* ☛ *$5 adults, $3.75 senior citizens and students, $1.50 children 6–12.* ☉ *Daily 9–5. Closed major holidays.*

Kids interested in aerospace technology will enjoy the walk through U.S. aviation history at the **Pima Air Museum.** The huge collection of historic aircraft includes a full-scale replica of the Wright brothers' 1903 Wright Flyer and a mock-up of the X-15, the world's fastest aircraft. *6000 E. Valencia Rd.,* ☎ *520/574–9658.* ☛ *$6 adults, $5 military personnel and senior citizens, $4 children 10–17.* ☉ *Daily 9–5 (last admission at 4). Closed Thanksgiving and Dec. 25.*

The small but well-designed **Reid Park Zoo** won't tax the children's— or your—patience. Ask who's new when you arrive; the many baby animals born here each year are adorable. The zoo is being expanded by 2½ acres to include a South American enclosure, replete with rain forest and exotic birds. If you're visiting in the summertime, go early in the day when the animals are active. *Reid Park, Lake Shore Lane, off 22nd St. between Alvernon Way and Country Club Rd.,* ☎ *520/881– 4753.* ☛ *$3.50 adults, $2.50 senior citizens, 75¢ children 5–14.* ☉ *Daily 9–4. Closed Dec. 25.*

At **Tucson Children's Museum,** kids are encouraged to touch and explore the exhibits, which are oriented toward science, language, and history. Ages one through 12 will enjoy this 8,000-square-foot playground. *200 S. 6th Ave.,* ☎ *520/884–7511.* ☛ *$3 adults, $1.50 senior citizens and children 3–16.* ☉ *Sat. 10–5, Sun. noon–5; call for weekday hrs.*

Off the Beaten Track

Parks and Museums

You may have heard some of the publicity surrounding the once-controversial project taking place in the little town of Oracle, some 45 minutes north of central Tucson. The least flattering accounts described it as eight cultists locked up together in a terrarium for two years in preparation for colonizing Mars. But the original "crew" has left the enclosure, and, since 1994, **Biosphere 2** has gone completely legit, with distinguished scientists on staff to do research on the sealed ecosystem.

The miniature world created within Biosphere includes tropical rain forest, savanna, desert, thorn scrub, marsh, ocean, and agricultural areas, including almost 4,000 plant and animal species. Guided walking tours, which last about two hours, don't enter the sealed sphere, but a film and cut-away model explain the project, and visitors are able to look inside through observation areas. The Canyon Café, overlooking the Santa Catalina Mountains, offers health-oriented meals and snacks. Reasonably priced hotel suites with excellent views are available on Biosphere's premises. Pets and picnicking are not permitted on the site. *Hwy. 77, mile marker 96.5,* ☎ *520/896–6200 or 800/828–*

2462. ☛ *$12.95 adults, $10.95 senior citizens, $6 children 5–17.* ⊙ *Daily 9–5; guided tours 10–4. Closed Dec. 25.*

On the way back into town from Biosphere, you might want to stop off at **Tohono Chul Park** (less traveled than the similar Arizona–Sonora Desert Museum), which is making its own effort to preserve our environment—specifically the desert region. On its 37 acres, a demonstration garden, greenhouse, geology wall, and other exhibits educate visitors about the unique area, while shady nooks and nature trails allow for leisurely sitting or strolling. Two gift shops, a small art gallery, a tearoom (*see* Dining, *below*), and, next door, the Haunted Bookshop (*see* Shopping, *below*) are additional reasons to visit this lovely landscaped setting. *7366 N. Paseo del Norte,* ☎ *520/742–6455.* ☛ *$2 donation suggested.* ⊙ *Park: daily 7 AM–sunset; building: Mon.–Sat. 9:30–5, Sun. 11–5.*

★ All year round, but especially during summer, locals flock to **Sabino Canyon** in the northeast corner of town. Part of the Coronado National Forest but filled with saguaros and other desert flora and fauna, this is a good spot for hiking, picnicking, or enjoying the waterfalls, streams, natural swimming holes, and shade trees that provide a respite from the heat. No cars are allowed, but a narrated tram ride (about 45 minutes round-trip) takes you to the top of the canyon. You can get off and on at any of the nine stops. There's also a tram ride to adjacent Bear Canyon. Nighttime tram tours are offered when there's a full moon and the weather is warm enough. *Sabino Canyon Rd. in the Santa Catalina foothills,* ☎ *520/749–2861 (recorded tram information) or 520/749–8700 (visitor center).* ☛ *Tram fare: $5 adults, $2 children 3–12.; Bear Canyon tram fare: $3 adults, $1.25 children. Call for schedules, which change throughout yr.* ⊙ *Visitor center: weekdays 8–4:30, weekends 8:30–4:30.*

Fort Lowell Park and Museum, now a city park, was once the site of a Hohokam Indian village and, many centuries later, a fort. At a small museum run by the Arizona Historical Society, the reconstructed commanding officers' quarters gives visitors a glimpse of military life in territorial days. There are also rotating exhibits of photographs and frontier artifacts. *2900 N. Craycroft Rd.,* ☎ *520/885–3832.* ☛ *Free.* ⊙ *Wed.–Sat. 10–4.*

Funded by the National Science Foundation and managed by a group of more than 20 universities, **Kitt Peak National Observatory** is part of the Tohonó O'odham reservation. After much discussion back in the late-1950s, tribal leaders agreed to share their 4,400 square miles with the observatory's 19 telescopes. Among these is the McMath, the world's largest solar telescope, which is cooled by piped-in coolant. From a visitors' gallery, you can see into the telescope's light-path tunnel, which goes down hundreds of feet into the mountain. In addition to the vital research into aspects of the sun carried out here, Kitt Peak scientists have also observed distant galaxies. The scientists and staff are friendly and knowledgeable and keen to share their enthusiasm for astronomy. Nor will the superb setting, including a closeup of the imposing Baboquivari Peak, sacred to the Tohonó O'odham people, fail to impress.

The museum's visitor center has exhibits on astronomy and information about the telescopes at the facility. Tapes, mostly about the cosmos, run continuously in a minitheater. Free guided tours, which take about an hour, depart from the center daily at 11, 1, and 2:30. Complimentary brochures enable you to take self-guided tours. A gift shop sells excellent examples of Tohonó O'odham handiwork as well as astronomy-related items. To reach Kitt Peak from Tucson, take I–10 to I–19 south, exit at Ajo Hwy/AZ 86. After 44 miles on AZ 86, turn left at the AZ 386 junction and follow the winding mountain road up to the observatory. (In inclement weather, contact the highway department to confirm that the road is open.) There's a picnic area about 1½ miles below the observatory. Aside from vending machines in the observatory buildings, there's no place to get food or gas within 20 miles of Kitt Peak. *Kitt Peak National Observatory,* ☎ *520/318–8726 or 520/318–7200 for recorded message.* ☞ *Suggested donation: $2 per person.* ☺ *Visitor center: daily 9–3:45. Closed major holidays.*

Art galleries and boutiques coexist with real Western saloons in **Patagonia,** a tiny, tree-lined town some 82 miles southeast of Tucson, surrounded by rolling hills and choice cattle-grazing land. For the most scenic route here, take I–10 to AZ 83 south, and then pick up AZ 82 in Sonoita. The cheerful Ovens of Patagonia (corner 3rd Ave. and AZ 82, ☎ 520/394–2483) is a pleasant place to stop for a quiche or a cappuccino, and the Mesquite Grove Gallery (371 McKeown Ave., ☎ 520/394–2358) carries an appealing array of local crafts. Both are in the center of town. At the Patagonia–Sonoita Creek Preserve (☎ 520/394–2400), 750 acres of riparian habitat are protected along the Patagonia–Sonoita Creek. More than 260 bird species have been sighted here, along with deer, javelina, coatimundi, desert tortoise, snakes, and more. To get here, make a right on 4th Avenue, which comes to a dead end, and then make a left. This paved road soon becomes dirt and leads to the preserve in about ¾ mile. The preserve is open Wednesday through Sunday 7:30–3:30. Guided tours are offered Saturday at 9. Patagonia is also a good jumping-off point for a tour of southern Arizona's wineries (*see below*).

De Grazia's Gallery in the Sun is the museum, gallery, workshop, former home, and grave site of the Arizonan artist Ted De Grazia, who depicted southwest Indian and Mexican life. Built by the artist himself with the help of Native American friends, the sprawling, spacious single-story museum utilizes only natural material from the surrounding desert. None of De Grazia's original oil paintings, sculptures, or watercolors are for sale, but the museum's gift shop offers a wide selection of cards, prints, lithographs, ceramics, and books by and about the colorful artist. *6300 N. Swan Rd.,* ☎ *520/299–9191.* ☞ *Free.* ☺ *Daily 10–4.*

Wineries

Wyatt Earp might have been hooted out of town if he had swaggered up to a bar and ordered a glass of cabernet, but wine is in these days in cowboy country. Connoisseurs debate the merits of the various wineries that have sprung up in this area since 1974, but if you want to decide for yourself, you might start a tour with **R.W. Webb** (13605 E. Benson Hwy., ☎ 520/762–5777). Take I–10 east about 12 miles, and get off at Vail, exit 279. Most of the other growers are in the area where Routes 82 and 83 intersect: Get back on I–10 for two more exits, then drive south on Route 83 for 24 miles to Sonoita. Growers in the scenic ranching region nearby include the kosher **Santa Cruz Winery** (☎ 520/455–5373); **Sonoita Vineyards** (3 mi southeast of Elgin, ☎ 520/455–5893); and **Arizona Vineyards** (1830 Patagonia Hwy., 3 mi northeast of Nogales on Rte. 82, ☎ 520/287–7972). Most of them give tours and tastings Thursday through Sunday; call for hours. Tiny Elgin hosts two surprisingly sophisticated but reasonably priced restaurants. **Karen's Wine Country Cafe** (☎ 520/455–5282) could be straight out of Sonoma, California, with its Country French–style patio and innovative menu focusing on salads and pasta dishes—and of course a good selection of wines by the glass. **Er Pastaro** (☎ 520/455–5821), a homey, low-key place established by a former manager of Regine's in New York, offers a variety of sauces for its pastas, as well as a good choice of Italian wines. Hours at both restaurants are limited, so call ahead.

Casinos

After a long struggle with the state of Arizona, two Indian tribes now operate casinos on their Tucson-area reservations. The Pascua Yaqui tribe runs the **Casino of the Sun** (7406 S. Camino de Oeste, ☎ 520/883–1700 or 800/344–9435), which has lots of slot and video-gambling machines, as well as keno and high-stakes bingo. The Tohonó O'odham tribe's **Desert Diamond Bingo and Casino** (7350 S. Old Nogales Hwy., ☎ 520/295–9790) offers 500 one-arm bandits and live keno in addition to bingo. No alcohol is sold or permitted at either casino.

Shopping

There are a lot of special gifts and souvenirs to be found in the Tucson area. Native American crafts range from exquisite jewelry and basketry to the more pedestrian (but still authentic) tourist items. You'll see an abundance of both varieties in shops and even in some department stores. **San Xavier Plaza,** across from San Xavier mission, carries the work of a variety of native peoples, including the Tohonó O'odham upon whose reservation the church is located. Those looking for work by other regional artists might drive down to **Tubac,** a community 45 miles south of Tucson. Hard-core bargain hunters usually continue south to the Mexican border and **Nogales.** (*See* Tour 5 *in* Exploring, *above,* for details on all three areas.

In Tucson itself, much of the retail activity is focused around malls, but you'll find shops with more character in two areas. The **downtown** district hosts a number of art galleries, antiques shops, and crafts stores. Congress Street is a particularly good block to browse, and the **Old Town Artisans complex** (186 N. Meyer Ave., ☎ 520/623–6024), near the Tucson Museum of Art, has a large selection of Southwestern wares. The adjoining **4th Avenue** neighborhood, near the University of Arizona, is also fertile ground for unusual items. The **Fourth Avenue Merchants Association** (329 E. 7th St. at 4th Ave., ☎ 520/624–5004) represents the many artsy boutiques and restaurants that line 4th Avenue between 2nd and 9th streets.

Specialty Shops

ART GALLERIES

Check the **Cabat Studio** (627 N. 4th Ave., ☎ 520/622–6362) for exceptional life-studies and regional paintings by the late Ernie Cabat and shimmering ceramics by his wife, Rose. The more cutting-edge downtown galleries include **Etherton/Stern** (135 S. 6th Ave., ☎ 520/624–7370) and **Dinnerware** (135 E. Congress St., ☎ 520/792–4503). *Art Life* (Box 36777, Tucson 85740, ☎ 520/797–1271), published twice a year, lists local galleries and artists.

BOOKS

Tohono Chul Park (*see* Off the Beaten Track, *above*) is home to the **Haunted Bookshop** (☎ 520/297–4843), with its outstanding selection for bibliophiles of all ages. There's a coffeepot on the porch in the wintertime, plenty of nooks for a quiet read, and a tunnel for children to crawl through. In central Tucson, the **Book Mark** (5001 E. Speedway Blvd., ☎ 520/881–6350) also has very well-stocked shelves, covering a wide range of topics.

Near the University of Arizona, the **Audubon Nature Shop** (300 E. University Blvd., Suite 120, ☎ 520/629–0510) carries field guides, bird-feeders, and binoculars, along with a wide range of natural history books. Also in the neighborhood is **Books West Southwest** (2452 N. Campbell Ave., ☎ 520/326–3533), focusing on regional works. The store often hosts signings by local authors. Pick up your topographical maps and specialty guides to Arizona at **Tucson's Map and Flag Center** (3239 1st Ave., ☎ 520/887–4234). Seekers of books by and about women should stop in at **Antigone** (600 N. 4th Ave., ☎ 520/792–3715), which also sells creative feminist cards and T-shirts.

CACTI

You won't need to stick a cactus in your suitcase, if you want to take back a spiny souvenir (it's illegal anyway): **B&B Cactus Farm** (11550 E. Speedway Blvd., ☎ 520/721–4687), on the far eastern side of town, has a huge selection of desert plants and will ship all over the country.

GIFTS

Desert House Crafts (2837 N. Campbell Ave., ☎ 520/323–2132) has been part of the Tucson art scene for more than 40 years. Designs are inspired, and execution is flawless. **Sangin Trading Co.** (300 N. 6th Ave., ☎ 520/882–9334) is set in a historic warehouse filled with baskets, home furnishings, dried flower arrangements, and jewelry—some imported, some made by local artists. Very reasonably priced ethnic jewelry, clothing, and crafts can be purchased at the **United Nations Center** (2911 E. Grant Rd., ☎ 881–7060).

NATIVE AMERICAN ARTS AND CRAFTS

Bahti Indian Arts (St. Philip's Plaza, 4300 N. Campbell Ave., ☎ 520/577–0290) specializes in Native American art, including high-quality jewelry, pottery, baskets, and more. **Huntington Trading Co.** (111 E. Congress, ☎ 520/628–8578) carries masks and pottery made by the Yaqui and Tarahumara Indians. The **Kaibab Shops** (2841 N. Campbell Ave., ☎ 520/795–6905) have been selling a wide variety of Native American crafts in Tucson for more than 40 years.

WESTERN WEAR

Corral Western Wear (4525 E. Broadway Blvd., ☎ 520/322–6001), with a large array of shirts, hats, belts, jewelry, and boots, caters to both urban and authentic cowboys and cowgirls. **Stewart Boot Manufacturing** (30 W. 28th St., South Tucson., ☎ 520/622–2706) has been making handmade leather boots for more than 50 years. Factory imperfects are available.

Malls and Shopping Centers

Tucson Mall (4500 N. Oracle Rd. at Wetmore Rd., ☎ 520/293–7330) is probably the most heavily shopped mall in town, serving both the sophisticated and the family shopper with two floors of stores, including Foley's, Dillard's, Broadway Southwest, Mervyn's, Sears, JCPenney, and almost 200 specialty shops. For tasteful Southwestern T-shirts, belts, jewelry, and posters, try Señor Coyote, on the first floor of the mall near the food court.

El Con Mall (3601 E. Broadway at Alvernon Way, ☎ 520/795–9958) is Tucson's oldest mall and has more than 130 stores, including JCPenney, Foley's, Dillard's, and Montgomery Ward. One of its most popular stores is a huge House of Fabrics, headquarters for craftspeople and needleworkers of all persuasions.

Park Mall (5870 E. Broadway at Wilmot Rd., ☎ 520/747–7575) is a family shopping mecca, one of those utilitarian places where you can get all that practical stuff checked off your list in one trip. It has more than 120 stores, including Sears, Dillard's, and Broadway Southwest.

Foothills Mall (7401 N. La Cholla Blvd. at Ina Rd., ☎ 520/742–7191), the most upscale of the malls, isn't usually very crowded. In addition to such department stores as Dillard's and Foley's, it features a variety of tony boutiques. A cup of the coffee at the Java House might cure shopper's fatigue. A multiplex cinema and a good restaurant, Keaton's, are other retail-break options.

St. Philip's Plaza (4280 N. Campbell Ave. at River Rd., ☎ 502/529–2775) arranges its chic shops around a series of Spanish-style outdoor patios. After shopping such boutiques as Nicole Miller or Obsidian, El Presidio, and Turquoise Door galleries, you can enjoy a meal at Cafe Terra Cotta, Ovens, or Daniels, all among Tucson's top eateries.

Sports and the Outdoors

Participant Sports

Ballooning

What better way to take advantage of Arizona's mild winter months than to take a quiet hot-air-balloon ride in the early morning hours and get a bird's-eye view of the frisky desert wildlife down below? Two reputable companies in the region are **Balloon America** (Box 31255, Tucson 85751, ☎ 520/299–7744; Oct.–June only) and **Southern Arizona Balloon Excursions** (Box 5265, Tucson 85703, ☎ 520/624–3599; Sept.–May only). Both welcome individuals and groups and offer champagne celebrations and daily flights by pilots who are licensed by the Federal Aviation Administration (FAA). Prices range from about $115 to $250 per person, depending on the season and the length of the flight.

Bicycling

Tucson has designated bikeways, routes, lanes, and paths for bikers all over the city—through rugged terrain, up and down winding roads, or along frequently used byways in the Tucson area. The Tucson Transportation Department (☎ 520/791–4372) will mail you city bike maps, or you can pick them up at the office of the **Pima Association of Governments** (177 N. Church St., Suite 405, 520/792–1093). If you want even more isolated and scenic locations, try biking in southern Arizona. Tour maps are available at the **Metropolitan Convention and Visitors Bureau** (*see* Visitor Information *in* Tucson Essentials, *below*).

Most bike stores in Tucson carry the monthly newsletter put out by the Tucson chapter of **GABA** (Greater Arizona Bicycling Association, Box 34273, Tucson 85733), which lists rated group rides. Visitors are welcome. Reliable, centrally located bike renters include **The Bike Shack** (940 E. University Ave., ☎ 520/624–3663) and **Full Cycle** (3232 E. Speedway Blvd., ☎ 520/327–3232).

Bird-Watching

In the Huachuca Mountains, the Nature Conservancy's 300-acre **Ramsey Canyon Preserve** (90 mi southeast of Tucson, off AZ 92, ☎ 520/378–2785) is home to more than 200 species of birds, as well as dozens of species of butterflies, deer, snakes, frogs, and mountain lions. Even closer to Tucson, in the nearby Santa Rita Mountains, **Madera Canyon** (*see* Tour 5 *in* Exploring, *above*) is another bird-lovers' haven. **The Wild Bird Store** (3522 E. Grant Rd., ☎ 520/322–9466) is the best resource in town for bird-watching books, maps, and trail guides. Tours can also be arranged from the store.

Camping

There are at least 100 camping areas scattered throughout the southern region of Arizona. Though it can get very chilly at night in the desert, the weather's usually good enough year-round to make sleeping out under the vast, starry night sky an appealing option. Summertime is the time to camp in the state's cooler higher-altitude campgrounds.

The closest public campground to Tucson is probably at **Catalina State Park** (11570 N. Oracle Rd., ☎ 520/628–5798), about 9 miles north of town on AZ 77. Located in the desert foothills of the Santa Catalinas, the campground accommodates tents as well as RVs. It fills up quickly in good weather because it's close to town. Unfortunately, there is no reservation system.

Recreational vehicles can park in any number of facilities around town. The **Metropolitan Tucson Convention and Visitors Bureau** (130 S. Scott Ave., ☎ 520/624–1889 or 800/638–8350) can provide information about specific locations.

CAUTION: Be careful not to camp in low-lying areas, which are subject to extremely dangerous flash flooding in sudden summer rains (*see* Lodging *in* The Gold Guide's Smart Travel Tips for more information).

Golf

You can easily dedicate a vacation to golf in Tucson, which has some of the best desert courses in the country and more than 320 days of sunshine in which to play them. *The Tucson & Southern Arizona Golf Guide,* published by Tucson Guide Quarterly, Inc. (Box 42915, Tucson 85733, ☎ 520/322–0895), describes and rates all the local courses; send $2.50 for a copy. For a golf package based on your budget, interests, and experience, you might contact **Tee Time Arrangers** (6286 E. Grant Rd., ☎ 520/296–4800 or 800/742–9939). If you're planning to stay a week or more, **Tucson's Resort Golf Card** (6286 E. Grant Rd., Tucson 85712, ☎ 520/886–8800), offering year-round discounts at seven of the area's best courses, is a good deal. Write or call for information.

RESORTS

Many avid golfers check into one of the tony local resorts (described in more detail *in* Lodging, *below*) and do nothing but tee off for a week. Golf vacation specialists include **Tucson National Golf & Conference Resort**, co-host of the PGA's Northern Telecom Open, with 27 holes; **Westin La Paloma,** which has a 27-hole layout designed by Jack Nicklaus (rated among the top 75 resort courses by *Golf Digest*); **Sheraton El Conquistador,** its 45 holes in the Santa Catalina foothills affording 360° views of the city; and the 36-hole Tom Fazio–designed **Loews Ventana Canyon** course. Those who don't mind getting up early to beat the heat will find some excellent golf packages at these places in the summer. In high season (Jan. 15–Apr. 15) only guests can play the courses, but the rest of the year all but Westin's La Paloma course are open to the public.

MUNICIPAL COURSES

The flagship of the five low-priced municipal golf courses within the city of Tucson (Randolph North, Randolph South, El Rio, Fred Enke, and Silverbell) is **Randolph North,** which hosted the PGA and LPGA Tour for many years. For details about these city-operated courses, contact the Tucson Parks and Recreation Department (☎ 520/791–4336). Call a week in advance for weekday reservations at any of the courses.

PUBLIC COURSES

In Tucson the Arnold Palmer–managed **Starr Pass Golf Club** (3645 W. 22nd St., ☎ 520/622–6060) was developed as a Tournament Player's Course. A co-host of the Northern Telecom Open with Tucson National (*see* Resorts, *above*), it offers 18 highly rated holes. Two executive courses, **Cliff Valley** (5910 N. Oracle Rd., ☎ 520/887–6161) and **Dorado Golf Course** (6601 E. Speedway, ☎ 520/885–6751), are good for those who just want to play a few short rounds.

South of Tucson, near Nogales, **Rio Rico Resort & Country Club** (1550 Camino a la Posada, ☎ 520/281–8567) was designed by Robert Trent Jones, Jr. An excellent 18-hole course, it's one of Arizona's lesser-known gems. In Green Valley, **San Ignacio Golf Club** (4201 S. Camino del Sol, ☎ 520/648–3468), designed by Arthur Hills, is a challenging desert course in a beautiful setting. Nearby **Canoa Hills** (1401 W. Calle Urbano, ☎ 520/648–1880) is a good choice for average golfers.

Hiking

Tucson is a wonderful place for hiking. There are many desert trails to explore in the winter, and in summer the nearby mountain ranges offer cooler trekking options. The Exploring section (*see* Tours 3, 4, and 5 *and* Off the Beaten Track, *above*) offers some options for day trips that include good hiking opportunities: **Tucson Mountain Park, Mt. Lemmon, Madera Canyon,** and **Kitt Peak. Sabino Canyon** (*see* Off the Beaten Track, *above*) has a variety of trails closer to town. In addition, for hiking inside Tucson city limits, you might test your skills climbing trails up Sentinel Peak, generally called **"A" Mountain** (it sports a huge *A* first painted on it by fans of a victorious university football team in 1915). State and city parks in the area also offer a variety of hiking experiences. There are literally hundreds of trails in the immediate Tucson area. **Catalina State Park** (*see* Camping, *above*) is crisscrossed by hiking trails.

If you want to go a bit farther afield, head south past the Huachuca Mountain range, where you can wander in and out of old **ghost towns** such as Fort Duquesne, Pearce, and Washington Camp in the Patagonia Mountains. To the east of Tucson, beyond the Rincons and the Whetstone Mountains, the Dragoon Mountains are both beautiful and of historical interest. **Cochise's Stronghold** was the Apache chief's hideout with his people during 11 years of battle with U. S. troops. Farther east, **Chiricahua National Monument** (*see* Southeastern Arizona, *below*) offers a number of well-marked trails in a striking setting.

The local chapter of the **Sierra Club** (738 N. 5th Ave., Suite 214, Tucson 85705, ☎ 520/620–6401) welcomes out-of-town visitors on their weekend hikes around the area. There's a $2 suggested donation per person for nonmembers. For hiking on your own, a good source of information is **Summit Hut** (5045 E. Speedway Blvd., ☎ 520/325–1554), which has an excellent collection of hiking reference materials and a friendly staff who will help you plan and outfit your trip. Packs, tents, bags, and climbing shoes can be rented here.

CAUTION: Be sure to bring plenty of water with you when hiking and drink often. Dehydration can become a life-threatening condition. (*See* Hiking *in* The Gold Guide's Smart Travel Tips for more information.)

Horseback Riding

What's a trip to the Southwest without at least one ride on the back of a horse? In the northwest part of town, **Desert-High Country Stables** (6501 W. Ina Rd., ☎ 520/744–3789) offers trail rides, hayrides, and cookouts. **Pantano Stables** (4450 S. Houghton Rd., ☎ 520/751–

4235) holds special holiday and birthday rides—and even Western weddings—in addition to regular trail rides on the far east side of Tucson. **Pusch Ridge Stables** (13700 N. Oracle Rd., ☎ 520/825–1664) is adjacent to Catalina State Park, and its riders may see coyotes, javelina, and jack rabbits in the Santa Catalina foothills.

Rockhounding

Although the heyday of mining has passed, there are still plenty of gems and minerals to be found in these parts, if you know what you're looking for. Just be sure to check in advance that you're not removing anything from protected areas such as national parks or Indian reservations. Amateur traders and buyers might consider joining the thousands of professionals who come to town in February for the huge **Tucson Gem and Mineral Show** (Box 42543, Tucson 85733, ☎ 520/322–5773), the largest of its kind in the world. Many precious stones as well as affordable samples are displayed and sold here, and even if you don't buy a thing, it's fun to look at all the fascinating rocks and gems. The main show, sponsored by the Tucson Gem and Mineral Society, is held at the Tucson Convention Center, but many satellite shows run at the same time—some as informal as dealers operating out of hotel rooms. If you do plan to attend, make reservations far in advance. In 1996 every hotel and car-rental agency in town is likely to be booked up from February 8 through February 11—as well as the week before.

Tennis

A number of the hotels and resorts in town have tennis facilities. Many courts are at Loews Ventana Canyon, Sheraton El Conquistador, Westin La Paloma, Westward Look, and Canyon Ranch resorts (*see* Lodging, *below*). The **Randolph Tennis Center** (100 S. Randolph Way, ☎ 520/791–4896) offers 25 courts, 11 lighted, at very reasonable rates. Nonmembers can play at one of the 33 lighted courts at the **Tucson Racquet Club** (4001 N. Country Club Rd., ☎ 520/795–6960) for a $10 fee ($2.50 extra for night play). You might also check with the **Tucson Parks and Recreation Department** (☎ 520/791–4873) to see if there are courts at one of the city parks near where you're staying.

Spectator Sports

Cactus League Baseball

In 1993 Tucson's **Hi-Corbett Field** (3400 E. Camino Campestre) welcomed the Colorado Rockies to their inaugural season of Cactus League practice games (*see* Pleasures & Pastimes *in* Chapter 1, Destination: Arizona). Call 520/327–9467 for information about the team schedule and about tickets. Hi-Corbett Field is also home to the Tucson Toros (☎ 520/325–2621), a minor-league team. Picnickers and squirrels sit side by side in adjacent Randolph Park to enjoy the games of both teams. Inside the stadium, during training games, beer is sold behind first and third bases. Parking isn't easy to come by in the area, so park in any of the Randolph Park lots west of Hi-Corbett Field and take a short, pleasant walk through the park to get to the stadium.

Dining

Tucson's culinary reputation is growing, and there are restaurants in town to satisfy every appetite. Southwestern cuisine, in its element here, ranges from barbecue and cowboy steaks to light nouvelle recipes that use such innovative ingredients as cactus and blue corn.

Tucson's residents have long boasted about their city's Mexican food, some rather grandly proclaiming their town "Mexican Food Capital of the U.S." (a title regularly challenged by San Antonians and Phoenicians). Most of the Mexican food in Tucson is Sonoran style—that is, derived from the cooking native to the adjoining Mexican state of Sonora. It's the type that's familiar to most Americans, featuring cheese, mild peppers, corn tortillas, and beef or chicken. Although Sonoran Mexican food has a well-earned reputation for being high in calories and saturated fats, many restaurants in Tucson now feature otherwise authentically prepared dishes cooked without lard. (Note that the salsa served with baskets of tortilla chips may be spicier than what you are used to. Proceed with caution. Similarly, when you ask the staff whether a dish is "hot," remember that their definition may be quite different from yours.) If you enjoy the heat, this is the place.

Dress is more casual in Tucson than in many cities its size. Very few restaurants request that men wear jackets to dinner. The issue of whether to wear a tie takes on a new slant here—there's at least one cowboy steak house where anyone caught wearing such formal neckwear will have it snipped off and added to the restaurant's collection of city-slicker garb.

Late fall, winter, and early spring make up the high season for travel here. It's a good idea to call ahead for reservations during these busy months. Some restaurants close for a portion of the summer, taking advantage of the slow time to make repairs or give staff vacations. Again, it's wise to call ahead, this time to ensure that your intended destination is open and hasn't altered its hours. Don't assume, incidentally, that you'll have to dine indoors in summer—many Tucson restaurants cool their outdoor patios with a misting system.

While Tucson's variety of restaurants is akin to that of its big-city cousins, the city doesn't offer much in the way of late-night dining. Most restaurants in town are shuttered by 10 PM. Some spots that keep later hours are noted below. In addition, two locations of **Coffee, Etc.** (2830 N. Campbell Ave., ☎ 520/881–8070; 6091 N. Oracle Rd., ☎ 520/544–8588), which has great coffee and a varied menu, are open 24 hours.

CATEGORY	COST*
$$$$	over $35
$$$	$25–$35
$$	$15–$25
$	under $15

*per person, excluding drinks, service, and 7% sales tax (5% state plus 2% city)

American

$$$ **Rancher's Club.** The four wood grills on which most of the foods are prepared are the key to the success of this upscale Western-style restaurant—pink tablecloths contrast nicely with dark wood, mounted animal heads, and sidesaddles. As the friendly staff explains, different woods impart different flavors to foods, so diners must be ready to make a choice from two grills: mesquite wood is offered every day, and hickory, sassafras, and wild cherry alternate during the week. The lobster is especially good, and the steaks are excellent, too (a note on the menu advises "Our steaks are copious and we encourage you to share"). An array of sauces, butters, and condiments provides diners with interesting ways to flavor their food. ✕ 5151 E. Grant Rd., ☎ 520/321–7621. Reservations advised. AE, DC, MC, V. Closed Sun. No Sat. lunch.

$$–$$$ **The Kingfisher Grill.** Opened in late 1993, the Kingfisher has drawn
★ critical kudos and a loyal following for its fine regional American cuisine. The chic setting—low lighting, bright turquoise and neon con-

trasting with warm brick walls and comfy black banquettes—is matched by the innovative menu (which changes seasonally). You might find jerked pork tenderloin, in a tangy Caribbean marinade, or mesquite grilled cabrilla in lemon-herb butter. From 10 to midnight, a "lite" menu features soups, salads, burgers, and selections from the oyster bar. ✕ *2564 E. Grant Rd.,* ☎ *520/323–7739. Reservations advised for dinner. AE, D, DC, MC, V. Closed Sat. No Sun. lunch.*

Continental

$$$$ **Ventana Room.** This lovely dining room in the Loews Ventana Canyon
★ Resort is a triumph of understated elegance. Muted colors and low ceilings don't compete with the spectacular views, either of the lights of Tucson or the towering waterfall on the resort property. The contemporary Continental menu, which changes seasonally, has a California-inspired emphasis on lower-fat, lower-cholesterol preparation and beautiful presentation. Daily specials might include medallions of venison with dried cherry sauce or grilled Norwegian salmon with leeks and creamy horseradish. The wine list meets the high standards of the menu, and service is impeccable without being overbearing. ✕ *7000 N. Resort Dr.,* ☎ *520/299–2020. Reservations advised. Jacket and tie. AE, D, DC, MC, V. No lunch.*

$$$$ **Anthony's.** *The* special-occasion restaurant for many Tucsonans, Anthony's offers elegance and a superb view of the city. Pink linen, stemmed crystal, pink-rim china—and, on the glassed-in terrace, lighting that precludes you seeing your dining companion very well—add to the romantic atmosphere. Such dishes as the Arizona roll appetizer (a shrimp-and-pork spring roll with ceviche sushi) or the prickly pear pork tenderloin put a Southwestern spin on what is basically a Continental menu. Chateaubriand and lamb Wellington are classic examples. The wine list is the largest in Arizona, and service is uncharacteristically formal for Tucson. A classical pianist who plays from 7 PM nightly draws locals to the cocktail lounge. ✕ *6440 N. Campbell Ave.,* ☎ *520/299–1771. Reservations advised. AE, DC, MC, V. No Sun. lunch.*

$$$ **Arizona Inn Restaurant.** This confident, friendly establishment, a Tucson classic, welcomes old friends and new visitors alike. Sit out on the patio for a lovely view of the grounds of this historic adobe inn, or enjoy the view through huge windows in the dining room, a light, airy place with many 1930s Southwestern details. On chilly evenings there's a fire. Steamed fish of the day served with ginger and leeks is a specialty, and the mesquite-smoked quail is also popular. For dessert, try a slice of the terrific apple or pecan pie. Breakfast here is also a treat. ✕ *2200 E. Elm St.,* ☎ *520/325–1541. Reservations advised. Jacket and tie. AE, MC, V.*

$$$ **The Landmark Cafe.** Come to this pretty, intimate restaurant on the northwest side of town at dinnertime for the well-prepared Continental standards—flambé of roast duck, say, or chateaubriand for two—served tableside. Lunch is a more casual affair, with a variety of sandwiches and salads on offer along with well-priced specialty plates such as veal liver with bacon and onion or stuffed pork loin. Whenever you come, save room for dessert. The Landmark Cafe is a consistent winner of Tucson's annual Taste of Chocolate competition. ✕ *7117 N. Oracle Rd.,* ☎ *520/575–9277. Reservations advised at dinner. AE, D, DC, MC, V.*

French

$$$–$$$$ **Le Rendez-vous.** The clientele is a bit blue-haired and the service a tad hovering, but what can you expect from the most expensive French restaurant in town? Well, excellent food, among other things, and Le

Rendez-vous doesn't fail to deliver on that score either. The duck a l'orange is as crispy as it should be and the veal medallions with Calvados as tender. If you start with the garlicky escargot, you won't be disappointed, but be prepared if you decide to finish with the excellent *tarte tatin:* All eyes will be draw to your table when your dessert is immolated in brandy. The lunch menu is wide-ranging and rather moderately priced. The intimate dining rooms are light, with colorful art deco prints, and the sommelier is as entertaining as he is helpful. ✕ *3844 E. Fort Lowell Rd.,* ☎ *520/323–7373. Reservations advised for dinner. AE, D, DC, MC, V. Closed Mon. No weekend lunch.*

$$$ **Le Bistro.** Set in a nondescript building on a busy road near the university, Le Bistro is one of the prettiest restaurants in town: Towering palms preside over pink lace-covered tables, burgundy chairs, and Art Nouveau–style etched mirrors. The setting is matched by the creations of young chef-owner Laurent Reux. Born in Brittany, he offers many fish and shellfish dishes inspired by the seascape of his native region, such as supreme of salmon in a ginger crust with lime butter. Another popular specialty is Long Island duck in a raspberry vinaigrette. A revolving glass dessert display at the entrance will leave you pondering throughout the meal whether to opt for the triple-chocolate mousse cake, say, or the Key-lime tart. Lunch prices are very reasonable. ✕ *2574 N. Campbell Ave.,* ☎ *502/327–3086. Reservations advised on weekends. D, MC, V. No weekend lunch.*

$$$ **Penelope's.** Devotees of Patricia Sparks' place on Speedway Boulevard were bereft when a street-widening project left the chef-owner temporarily without a restaurant, but she's back now and better than ever in a more spacious northeast location. Four dining rooms decorated in Country French–style make a lovely setting for the prix-fixe menus (four or six courses, with or without wine, ranging from $26 to $42.50). The selections change often, but soups might include onion or cream of mushroom, entrées filet mignon *au poivre* (with crushed peppercorns) or sauteed boneless chicken breast with green-grape sauce. Desserts are uniformly excellent. ✕ *3071 N. Swan Rd.,* ☎ *520/325–5080. Reservations advised. MC, V. Closed Mon. No weekend lunch.*

Greek

$$ **Athens.** A Greek island of tranquility off bustling 4th Avenue, Athens creates a serene Mediterranean atmosphere with its lace curtains, wooden wainscoting, white stucco walls, and potted plants. Order a dish of creamy *taramousalata* (Greek caviar). Follow it with *kotopoulo stin pita* (grilled chicken breast with a yogurt-cucumber sauce on fresh-baked pita), a better deal than the skewered version of the same dish. If it's Greek comfort food you're after, go for the moussaka or the *pastitsio* (a pasta-, meat-, and bechamel-filled lasagna), both done just right here. A nice selection of retsina wine make a good complement. ✕ *500 N. 4th Ave., No. 6,* ☎ *520/624–6886. Reservations advised for dinner on weekends. AE, D, DC, MC, V. Closed Sun. No lunch Sat.*

$$ **Olive Tree.** In an appealing Santa Fe–style building, the Olive Tree serves up fine versions of such Greek standards as moussaka, shish kebab, and stuffed grape leaves, but also includes more unusual dishes on its menu. The Lamb Bandit is baked in foil with two types of cheese, potatoes, and vegetables. Daily fresh-fish specials are broiled in garlic, oregano, and olive oil, and served with a well-prepared orzo. This is not light cuisine. If you don't have room for supersweet baklava, a cup of strong Greek coffee makes for a satisfying finish. ✕ *7000 E. Tanque Verde Rd.,* ☎ *520/298–1845. Reservations advised. MC, V. No Sun. lunch.*

Guatemalan

$ **Maya Quetzal.** This friendly, family-owned restaurant on trendy 4th Avenue is inexpensive enough to allow those unfamiliar with Guatemalan food—and who isn't?—to sample lots of different dishes. Try the vegetarian *paches* (potato-meal tamales topped with a mild red pepper sauce) or the *pollo en jocón* (chicken with cilantro-flavor green sauce). Friday's chicken special comes in a rich, yogurt-based sauce. A large, brightly colored mural, Guatemalan crafts, and a pleasant patio all add to the congenial atmosphere. The food may be a bit bland for palates expecting Mexican fire, but you'll be eating for a good cause. A portion of all profits go to help Guatemalan refugees. ✕ *429 N. 4th Ave.,* ☎ *520/622–8207. No reservations. MC, V. Closed Sun.*

Indian

$–$$ **New Delhi Palace.** Vegetarians, carnivores, and seafood lovers will all find something to enjoy at this elegant Indian restaurant. The congenial staff is helpful in explaining the menu, which features a wide variety of tandoori dishes, curries, rice, and breads. The "heat" of each dish can be adjusted to individual preference by the chef. If you're undecided, a lunch buffet and complete dinners offer nice samplings of several dishes. The atmosphere is quiet, with Indian music played softly, and tasteful displays of Indian objets d'art. ✕ *6751 E. Broadway,* ☎ *520/296–8585. Reservations advised. AE, DC, MC, V.*

Italian

$$$ **Daniel's.** A fine northern Italian menu, an excellent wine and beer list, the largest selection of single-malt Scotches in town, and service that is attentive but not overbearing draw a sophisticated crowd to this chic art deco–style restaurant. The grilled shrimp and Gorgonzola appetizer, *spaghetti alla putanesca* with olives, capers, and tomatoes, and *bistecca alla florentina* (a tender rib-eye steak marinated in olive oil and herbs) are among the many recommended standards. Dining on the terrace during one of St. Phillips Plaza's outdoor concerts is a real treat. ✕ *St. Phillips Plaza, 4340 N. Campbell Ave.,* ☎ *520/742–3200. Reservations advised. AE, DC, MC, V. No lunch.*

$$–$$$ **Boccata.** In a tasteful mall in the foothills of the Santa Catalina Mountains, this pretty restaurant serves excellent northern Italian cuisine, with ★ some southern French dishes for good measure. The flowered tablecloths match the delicate aubergine and Tuscan-yellow walls, and the artwork ranges from contemporary to Victorian whimsy. A good wine list complements such entrées as penne *ciao bella* (with grilled chicken and a delicate white wine and Gorgonzola sauce) and a veal chop topped with a wild-mushroom sauce, and a steamed mussel appetizer is plentiful. Go Gallic for dessert: The profiteroles, with fresh-made vanilla ice cream and dripping warm chocolate sauce, are superb. ✕ *5605 E. River Rd.,* ☎ *520/577–9309. Reservations advised. AE, MC, V. No lunch.*

$$–$$$ **Vivace.** Daniel Scordato has had his hand in some of the best Italian restaurants in town, and his latest venture has become a quick hit. During high season, Vivace fills up even on weekday nights, mostly with a well-heeled, well-turned out crowd. It's all very industrial chic—grey columns, black iron chairs, open kitchen—but this is still Arizona, which means the black-and-white clad servers are not SoHo frosty to match. Appetizers are a little pricey compared to the rest of the menu, though the grilled eggplant and zucchini with goat cheese is hard to resist. Go for one of the good salads or a wonderful side dish of sauteed spinach with garlic if you're looking to economize. The veal special of the day is usually worth trying, and the linguine with grilled salmon makes a nice, light dinner—the better to leave room for spumoni, made on the

premises to perfection. ✗ *4811 E. Grant Rd., Suite 155,* ☎ *520/795–7221. Reservations strongly advised. AE, D, DC, MC, V. No Sun. lunch.*

$–$$ **Ciao Italia.** Don't be put off by the location on the busy Stone Avenue motel strip or by the generic looking green-and-white sign. It's far from sterile inside, and the friendly Sardinian-born couple who own the place will take care of you like family, especially if you come back a second time. And you'll want to, what with such well-priced, tasty pasta dishes as ziti with a zesty vodka, tomato, and chili cream sauce, or a spaghetti carbonara as caloric as you could hope for. Main courses such as classic shrimp scampi or fra diavolo come with a large salad, expertly cooked vegetables, and a side of ziti marinara. This is one of Tucson's hidden treasures. ✗ *1535 N. Stone Ave.,* ☎ *520/884-0000. Reservations advised for dinner on weekends. AE, MC, V. Closed Sun.*

$ **Pappy's.** Come here for huge portions of Italian standards served in a pleasant atmosphere—plush booths, white tablecloths, and a small, tree-shaded patio. You can order a variety of pastas with assorted chicken, seafood, meat, or vegetable toppings, or opt for the hearty lasagna or fettuccine Alfredo. Prices are generally very reasonable, and the cold pasta primavera with chicken is a serious bargain at $4.95. Just down the block from the Temple of Music and Art, Pappy's is ideal for a pre-theater dinner (just leave the garlic-redolent doggy bag in the car when you go to the show). ✗ *375 S. Stone Ave.,* ☎ *520/882-8908. Reservations advised on weekends. DC, MC, V. Call ahead for hrs, which vary throughout wk and season.*

Japanese

$$ **Yamato.** Colorful paper lanterns line the walls of this modest eatery, tucked away in a strip mall near the university. A sushi bar serves fish flown in daily from California, and a number of combination dinners such as shrimp tempura and teriyaki chicken are available. *Yaki soba* (beef and vegetables heaped on wheat noodles) makes a tasty, hearty meal. Many of Yamato's Japanese patrons gather on Saturday night from 10 PM to 1 AM for laser karaoke sing-alongs. ✗ *857 E. Grant Rd.,* ☎ *520/624–3377. Reservations accepted. AE, MC, V. Closed Sun. No lunch Sat.*

Malaysian

$ **Seri Melaka.** Malaysian food, like Thai, uses plenty of curry, coconut, and other tasty condiments in its sauces. This popular restaurant on the east side of town is an excellent place to try the cuisine, and to indulge in good versions of such dishes as *satay* (grilled meat on a skewer with peanut sauce) and *lemak* (shrimp or chicken with vegetables in a sweet curry sauce). An extensive selection of well-prepared Chinese dishes is also on the menu. There's a buffet at lunchtime seven days a week. ✗ *6133 E. Broadway,* ☎ *520/747–7811. Reservations accepted. AE, D, DC, MC, V.*

Mexican

$–$$ **Café Poca Cosa.** Arguably Tucson's best restaurant, it's certainly one
★ of the most interesting, serving consistently innovative Mexican fare in a marvelously colorful (hot pink, bright green, and tropical orange), lively setting. Eschewing the cheese-saturated Sonoran standbys, Mexico City–born chef-owner Susana Davila turns to many different regions of her native land for recipes and always comes up with something exciting. The menu, which changes daily, might include *pollo á mole* (chicken in a spicy chocolate-based sauce) or pork *pibil* (made with a tangy Yucatan barbecue seasoning). Consider a breakfast of green-chili tamales on the outdoor patio when the weather is fine. Locals, who discovered this place before the tourists, are happy for Susana's success

after she got a huge writeup in *Gourmet* magazine, but grumpy because it's so much harder to get a table now. You might have to call a few days in advance to get reservations for dinner. The tiny original restaurant across the street (20 S. Scott Ave.), also a lively treat, is open for breakfast and lunch during the week. ✕ *88 E. Broadway,* ☎ *520/622– 6400. Reservations strongly advised for dinner. MC, V. No dinner Sun.*

$–$$ El Charro Café. Started by Monica Flin in 1922, and run by her grand-niece and her grandniece's husband today, El Charro still serves excellent versions of the American-Mexican staples Flin claims to have originated—chimichangas (flour tortillas rolled around seasoned beef or chicken and deep-fried) and cheese crisps, most notably. Daily "fitness-fare" specials such as seafood enchiladas are delicious as well as healthful. You can dine outside on the front porch or inside in one of the bright, cheerful dining rooms. A lounge serves appetizers and drinks. Next door, a gift shop sells mementos of this Tucson classic. ✕ *311 N. Court Ave.,* ☎ *520/622–1922. Reservations advised. AE, MC, V.*

$–$$ El Minuto Café. This brightly decorated, bustling restaurant in Tucson's historic barrio is a good bet for those seeking a late meal downtown. It's open until 2 AM Friday and Saturday, 11 PM the rest of the week. In business for more than 50 years, El Minuto serves up crispy chimichangas, huge burritos, and green corn tamales (in season) made just right. The spicy menudo is a great hangover remedy (just don't ask what's in it if you don't already know). All the ingredients are fresh and the Mexican beer selection is large. ✕ *354 S. Main Ave.,* ☎ *520/882– 4145. Reservations required for 8 or more. AE, D, DC, MC, V.*

$–$$ South Tucson/4th Avenue. Every Tucsonan you meet will argue the merits of a favorite "real" Mexican restaurant, but invariably it's on or near 4th Avenue in South Tucson. Technically a separate city, South Tucson has a large Mexican-American population and thus many authentic and inexpensive places to find good south-of-the-border cuisine. Among the most popular: **Crossroads** (2602 S. 4th Ave., ☎ 520/624–0395); **Gran Guadalajara** (2527 S. 4th Ave., ☎ 520/620–1321); **Guillermo's Double L** (1830 S. 4th Ave., ☎ 520/792–1585); **La Hacienda** (4207 S. 6th Ave., ☎ 520/889–6613); **Micha's** (2908 S. 4th Ave., ☎ 520/623–5307); and **Mi Nidito** (1813 S. 4th Ave., ☎ 520/622–5081), all open for both lunch and dinner. You'd be hard-pressed to have a bad meal—or a bad time—at any of these friendly, informal places. Many have mariachi bands on the weekends. MC and V are accepted at most.

Southwestern

$$$–$$$$ Janos. Comfortably situated in the Hiram Stevens House, an adobe home built in 1855, this downtown restaurant—adjacent to the Tucson Museum of Art—offers innovative and superlative Southwest menus created by chef-owner Janos Wilder. A series of small, flower-filled dining rooms create an intimate, elegant atmosphere. Typical offerings include a mushroom-and-Brie stuffed chile appetizer, and an adobe of grilled salmon entree served with lobster *chipotle beurre blanc.* Combinations are usually very successful but the high prices make the occasional failure all the more disappointing. The summer and fall $12.95 dinner specials allow the less well-heeled to indulge in a meal here. Service can be somewhat scattered. ✕ *150 N. Main Ave.,* ☎ *520/884–9426. Reservations advised. AE, DC, MC, V. Closed Sun. Nov.–mid-May; Sun. and Mon. late May–Nov.*

$$$–$$$$ The Tack Room. This restaurant has won many awards for its food, and the setting—in a rustic but elegant old adobe on the grounds of a former resort—is romantic, but the service is a tad overfussy and the menu a bit safer than those of other first-rate restaurants in town. It's also irritating to pay extra for such standard accompaniments to expensive entrees as potatoes and vegetables. That said, it's still worth coming here for a splurge. Dark-wood beams and furnishings and a blue-and-maroon color scheme are complemented by the lighter dusty-rose linen. Walls are hung with Southwestern landscapes by local artists. Arizona four-pepper steak flavored with different chilies is a favorite, as is the rack of lamb for two, prepared with mesquite honey, cilantro, and Southwestern limes. ✗ *2800 N. Sabino Canyon Rd., ☎ 520/722–2800. Reservations advised. Jacket required. AE, D, DC, MC, V. Closed Mon. mid-May–mid-Dec., and 1st 2 wks of July. No lunch.*

$$–$$$ Café Terra Cotta. Everything about this restaurant says Southwest—from the decor, with its bright pastels and bleached woods, to the food, which features such contemporary Southwest specialties as prawns stuffed with herbed goat cheese, pork tenderloin with black beans, and pizza with artichokes and herbed mozzarella. The garlic-custard appetizer is superb. The place for native yupsters as well as their out-of-town guests, Café Terra Cotta offers an impressive by-the-glass California wine list and a tasty Sunday brunch. It's open daily for breakfast, too. Note: This reviewer has never had a bad meal here but has received some mixed reports from others. ✗ *St. Philip's Plaza, 4310 N. Campbell Ave., ☎ 520/577–8100. Reservations strongly advised for dinner, accepted for 5 or more at lunch. AE, D, DC, MC, V.*

$$–$$$ Presidio Grill. If it weren't for the saguaro cactus flanking the window, you might at first think you were in one of New York's chic downtown haunts, with stylish black booths and art deco light fixtures. But the food is Southwestern all the way. Blue-corn pancakes with prickly-pear syrup appear on the Sunday brunch menu. Lunch and dinner entrées include chicken Santa Fe, served with black beans, flour tortillas, grilled scallions, and two types of salsa; and an eggplant, artichoke heart, onion, and sun-dried tomato pizza. In the University of Arizona area and across the street from the city's main art cinema, this place is open unusually late (for Tucson) on weekends. A cabaret-style supper club is offered in the restaurant's banquet room every month or so (high season only), when four-course dinners are coordinated with such entertainment as flamenco, jazz, blues, or opera. ✗ *3352 E. Speedway Blvd., ☎ 520/327–4667. Reservations advised for dinner; tickets available for supper club. AE, MC, V.*

$$ Li'l Abner's. This Old West institution in the Butterfield Express stagecoach rest stop, which dates from the early 1800s, draws locals, who go straight for the mesquite-broiled two-pound porterhouse steaks. There's nothing here for vegetarians, except for the salad, beans, and salsa that come with all the entrées. On weekends, you can chow down to the sounds of a live country band. It's about a 20-minute drive from downtown. ✗ *8501 N. Silverbell Rd., ☎ 520/744–2800. Reservations advised. MC, V. No lunch.*

$$ Pinnacle Peak Steakhouse. No nouvelle-cuisine fans welcome here: Anybody caught eating fish tacos or cactus jelly would probably be hanged from the rafters—along with all the ties snipped from loco city slickers. This is a cowboy steak house that the tourists love. It's fun, it's Tucson, and the food ain't half bad, either, partner. Excellent mesquite-broiled steak comes with salad, baked potatoes, and pinto beans. If you can handle more after all that, try the hot apple cobbler with vanilla ice cream. The restaurant is part of Trail Dust Town, a re-creation of a turn-of-the-century town, complete with an "opera" house featuring cancan girls and a barbershop quartet, souvenir shops, and an old-time photographer's studio, where you can have your picture taken in Western garb. ✗ *6541 E. Tanque Verde Rd., ☎ 520/296–0911. No reservations. AE, D, DC, MC, V.*

$$ Tohono Chul Tea Room. The food is fine, though it's not the reason to make the drive to the northwest part of town. What's unique here is the setting. The tearoom is nestled in a wildlife sanctuary and surrounded by a fantastic cactus garden. Although the tearoom is typically Southwestern, with lots of Mexican tile and light wood and a cobblestone patio, the menu covers Southwestern, Mexican, and American dishes. House favorites include chicken enchiladas made with Monterey Jack cheese, corn, and green chilies, and a sliced-tomato-and-basil sandwich served on French sourdough bread. Sunday brunch is especially good—which can mean long waits in high season. ✕ *7366 N. Paseo del Norte,* ☎ *520/797–1711. Reservations accepted for 8 or more Mon.–Sat., no reservations accepted Sun. AE, MC, V. No dinner.*

$ Jack's Original Bar-B-Q. For those who like their Southwest cuisine in big, messy portions, this is the place to come. Jack's ribs are smoky, meaty, and without equal in these parts, and the sauce is rich and subtly flavored. The beans are also a real treat. Jack's impresses through good, honest food, not atmosphere—the floor is linoleum. Chairs and flowers are plastic. ✕ *5250 E. 22nd St.,* ☎ *520/750–1280. No reservations. MC, V.*

Vegetarian

$ Govinda. One of two places in town with a strictly nonmeat menu, this Hare Krishna–run restaurant offers reasonably priced all-you-can-eat lunch and dinner buffets that include vegan options. Selections of hot and cold dishes vary daily, but ingredients are consistently fresh and the food is tasty if not particularly spicy. There are three areas to eat: one with low tables and cushions (diners must remove their shoes to eat in here); an adjoining light wood dining room; and an outdoor patio, from which you can hear the squawks of the resident peacocks. No alcohol is served or permitted. ✕ *711 E. Blacklidge Dr.,* ☎ *520/ 792–0630. No reservations. MC, V. Closed Sun.–Tues.*

Lodging

In Tucson you can enjoy the luxury of a desert resort or the more basic accommodations offered by small motels. A number of guest ranches—some of them from the 1800s when they were real working cattle ranches—can be found on the outskirts of town.

There is also a variety of bed-and-breakfasts in the area, ranging from bedrooms in modest homes to private cottages nestled on wildlife preserves. The **Arizona Association of Bed and Breakfast Inns** (Box 7186, Phoenix 85711, ☎ 602/277–0775) can provide referrals to member inns in the area. Seven of the larger, more professionally run inns in town have formed **Premier Bed & Breakfast Inns of Tucson** (316 E. Speedway Blvd., 85705, ☎ 520/628–1800 or 800/628–5654, FAX 520/792–1880). Write or call for a brochure. **Old Pueblo HomeStays** (Box 13603, Tucson 85732, ☎ 520/790–0030 or 800/333–9776, FAX 520/790–2399) specializes in smaller, more casual B&Bs in southern Arizona and northern Mexico but also lists a number of the larger inns.

Prices vary widely between seasons. Room rates in summer—generally defined as April 15 through October 1—are sometimes as much as 60% lower than those in the winter, and visitors who don't mind warmer weather can get real deals at resorts that are quite pricey during the busy time. Note: Unless you book months in advance, you'll be hard-pressed to find a hotel room at any price in Tucson the week before and during the huge gem and mineral show (February 8–11 in 1996).

CATEGORY	COST*
$$$$	over $160
$$$	$110–$160
$$	$70–$110
$	under $70

All prices are for a standard double room, excluding room tax (9.5% in Tucson and 6.5% in Pima County). Prices given here are winter, or high-season, rates.

Hotels

$$$$ **Arizona Inn.** Although this landmark 1930s-era inn is close to the uni-
★ versity and downtown, you feel as though you're away from it all on
its 14 lushly landscaped acres. All rooms have patios and lovely period furnishings. Many have fireplaces. Service is excellent—friendly
but unobtrusive. The staff hosts small conferences beautifully, attending to the details without fuss. Locals as well as guests frequent the
hotel's restaurant (*see* Dining, *above*) and its cocktail lounge, which
often has a piano player. ☎ *2200 E. Elm St., 85719,* ☎ *520/325–1541
or 800/933–1093, FAX 520/881–5830. 80 rooms. 2 restaurants, lounge,
pool, 2 tennis courts, croquet, Ping-Pong, library. AE, MC, V.*

$$$ **Doubletree Hotel.** Convenient to the airport and to the center of town,
this comfortable, contemporary-style property is also across the road
from the municipal golf course at Randolph Park, which hosts the LPGA
tournament every year. Most of the participants stay here. Rooms are
large, and done in earth tones with Southwestern-style furnishings. The
pretty Cactus Rose Restaurant serves excellent nouvelle Southwestern
cuisine and the Javelina Cantina in the lobby is a fun place in which
to have a beer. ☎ *445 S. Alvernon Way,* ☎ *520/881–4200 or 800/222–
8733, FAX 520/323–5225. 295 rooms. Restaurant, bar, pool, beauty salon,
tennis courts. AE, D, DC, MC, V.*

$$$ **Embassy Suites Tucson–Broadway.** This centrally located hotel is 10
miles from Tucson International Airport, 5 miles from downtown, and
a bit less than 5 miles from the University of Arizona. Accommodations are two-room suites (with a kitchenette) opening onto an atrium
full of plants. Furnishings are tasteful if not exciting. Among the extras are a free cooked-to-order breakfast every morning and complimentary happy hour every evening. Transportation to the airport and
parking are also on the house. ☎ *5335 E. Broadway, 85711,* ☎ *520/
745–2700 or 800/362–2779, FAX 520/790–9232. 142 suites. Pool, coin
laundry. AE, D, DC, MC, V.*

$$$ **Tucson Hilton East.** This east-side property is convenient to Sabino
Canyon and Saguaro National Monument East as well as to Davis–Mon-
than Air Force Base. An airy glass-atrium lobby takes full advantage
of the view of the Santa Catalina Mountains. Rooms are nicely fur-
nished, with modern light-wood fittings, pastel carpeting, and vibrant
Southwestern bedspreads. The VIP level offers extra service and lux-
uries such as complimentary hors d'oeuvres, and deluxe Continental
breakfast. ☎ *7600 E. Broadway, 85710,* ☎ *520/721–5600 or 800/648–
7177, FAX 520/721–5696. 225 rooms. Restaurant, bar, pool. AE, D,
DC, MC, V.*

$$ **Holiday Inn Tucson Airport Hotel and Convention Center.** Favored by
businesspeople, this property is 10 minutes from the airport and ad-
jacent to I–10. The decor is a mix of Mexican and Spanish, with dark
print bedspreads and carpets throughout. In contrast, the light, cheerful lobby has a plant-filled atrium with a waterfall. Saltillo-tile floors
and white stucco walls give it an open, Southwestern feel. There are
free shuttles to the airport and to the large El Con mall. ☎ *4550 S.*

212

Tucson Dining and Lodging

Dining

Anthony's, **10**
Arizona Inn Restaurant, **25**
Athens, **28**
Boccata, **42**
Café Poca Cosa, **34**
Café Terra Cotta, **11**
Ciao Italia, **17**
Daniel's, **12**
El Charro Café, **30**
El Minuto Café, **32**
Govinda, **15**

Jack's Original Bar-B-Q, **53**
Janos, **33**
The Kingfisher Grill, **21**
The Landmark Cafe, **5**
Le Bistro, **20**
Le Rendez-Vous, **43**
Li'l Abner's, **1**
Maya Quetzal, **31**
New Delhi Palace, **55**
Olive Tree, **48**
Pappy's, **36**

Penelope's, **42**
Pinnacle Peak Steakhouse, **47**
Presidio Grill, **26**
Rancher's Club, **46**
Seri Melaka, **54**
South Tucson/ 4th Avenue, **37**
The Tack Room, **50**
Tohono Chul Tea Room, **2**
Ventana Room, **40**
Virace, **45**
Yamato, **19**

Lodging

Arizona Inn, **25**
Canyon Ranch, **51**
Casa Alegre, **24**
Casa Tierra, **22**
Catalina Park Inn, **27**
Doubletree Hotel, **39**
El Presidio Bed and Breakfast Inn, **31**
Embassy Suites Tucson-Broadway, **52**
Flamingo Travelodge, **18**

Holiday Inn Tucson
Airport Hotel and
Convention
Center, **38**

Hotel Congress, **35**

Lazy K Bar Guest
Ranch, **41**

Loews Ventana
Canyon Resort, **40**

Park Inn/ Santa
Rita, **34**

Peppertrees, **29**

Ramada Downtown
Tucson, **23**

Ramada Inn
Foothills, **49**

Rodeway Inn Tucson
North, **16**

Sheraton Tucson El
Conquistador, **8**

Tanque Verde
Ranch, **57**

Triangle L Ranch Bed
& Breakfast, **9**

Tucson Hilton
East, **56**

Tucson National
Golf & Conference
Resort, **4**

Westin La Paloma, **14**

Westward Look
Resort, **6**

White Stallion
Ranch, **3**

The Windmill Inn at
St. Phillip's Plaza, **13**

Palo Verde Blvd., 85714, ☎ *520/746–1161 or 800/465–4329,* FAX *520/ 741–1170. 299 rooms. 2 restaurants, bar, pool, sauna, tennis court, exercise room. AE, D, DC, MC, V.*

$$ Ramada Downtown Tucson. Convenient to the freeway, downtown, and to west side sights, this friendly hotel has an appealing pink Spanish-style lobby and a cheerful restaurant and lounge. Rooms are standard motel style but well maintained. Many look out on the inviting pool, surrounded by greenery. ⊞ *475 N. Granada Ave., 85701,* ☎ *520/622– 3000, 800/446–6589 (on-site reservations) or 800/228–2828 (central reservations),* FAX *520/623–8922. 300 rooms. Restaurant, bar, pool. AE, D, DC, MC, V.*

$$ Ramada Inn Foothills. Families as well as business travelers stay in this more upscale and slightly more expensive Ramada Inn on the north-eastern side of town, close to restaurants, Sabino Canyon, and mall shopping. An attractive light stucco building with rounded corners, this property has the expected generic rooms, but they're fairly new and more than serviceable. A Continental breakfast is complimentary, as are beer and wine in the afternoon. Free passes to a local health club are available, and golf and tennis facilities are nearby. ⊞ *6944 E. Tanque Verde Rd., 85715,* ☎ *520/886–9595 or 800/228–2828,* FAX *520/721–8466. 113 rooms. Restaurant, lounge, pool, sauna. AE, D, DC, MC, V.*

$$ Rodeway Inn Tucson North. Near I–10, and just west of the university area, this hotel caters to business as well as leisure travelers. The basic boxy motel architecture has been adapted to local style—a stucco exterior is accented with tasteful, low-key stripes of turquoise and pink. The pool is in a nicely landscaped courtyard studded with umbrella-shaded tables. Rooms are nothing fancy, but they are adequate. ⊞ *1365 W. Grant Rd., 85745,* ☎ *520/622–7791 or 800/424–4777,* FAX *520/ 629–0201. 146 rooms. Restaurant, lounge, pool, coin laundry. AE, D, DC, MC, V.*

$$ The Windmill Inn at St. Phillip's Plaza. Located in a chic shopping plaza
★ filled with glitzy boutiques and good restaurants (*see* Daniel's *and* Café Terra Cotta *in* Dining, *above*) this all-suites hotel, built in 1992, offers attractive, Southwest-contemporary accommodations. Each suite has a separate sitting area, microwave, wet bar, minifridge, two TVs, and three telephones. A few dollars extra will buy you a view of the pool rather than the parking lot. Complimentary coffee, muffins, and a newspaper are delivered to your door. All in all, it's a good deal for the price. ⊞ *4250 N. Campbell Ave., 85718,* ☎ *520/577–0007 or 800/547–4747,* FAX *520/577–0045. 122 rooms. Pool, bicycles, laundry, library. AE, D, DC, MC, V.*

$ Flamingo Travelodge. When the Flamingo was built in 1953, it was the closest thing to a resort in town: Bing Crosby and his brothers opened up an act at the lounge, and hotel guests included Rudy Valle, Gene Autry, John Wayne, and Elvis Presley. Reopened in 1994 after massive renovation, the property now offers comfortable standard rooms with Southwestern-style furnishings. Some suites have microwaves and coffeemakers. If it doesn't have the cachet of its earlier heyday, captured in photos lining the lobby, the hotel is convenient to both downtown and the university and sports the swell original neon sign. ⊞ *1300 N. Stone Ave., 85705,* ☎ *520/770–1910 or 800/300–3533,* FAX *520/770– 0750. 79 rooms. Pool, coin laundry. AE, D, DC, MC, V.*

$ Hotel Congress. Loved by many for its idiosyncratic charm, this downtown hotel was built in 1919 and restored to its original western version of Art Deco style. The renovated rooms, which vary in size, are individually furnished: All have black-and-white tiled baths and the original iron beds. Some have desks and tables. Some unrenovated rooms are available for rock-bottom rates, but they're pretty grim, with cracked walls and bathtubs that need recaulking. Near the Greyhound and Amtrak stations and the main Sun Tran terminal, and close to downtown art galleries and restaurants, this is an excellent choice for those who don't have a car. The downside of this convenient location is noise, compounded on weekend nights when music from the popular Club Congress filters up to the rooms. ⊞ *311 E. Congress St., 85701,* ☎ *520/622–8848 or 800/722–8848,* FAX *520/792–6366. 40 rooms. Restaurant, bar, hair salon, nightclub. AE, MC, V.*

$ **Park Inn/Santa Rita.** When this hotel became a Park Inn in 1991 (it had been a Days Inn during the late 1980s), it also reclaimed the name by which it had been known in Tucson for years—the Santa Rita. The property was spiffed up during the past decade—modern furnishings, hand-painted Mexican tile, and stuccoed walls brighten the lobby— but rooms are still fairly generic and the place sometimes shows its age in the plumbing. Still, the price is right, and the hotel is conveniently located near the downtown arts district and across the street from the visitor center. It's also home to the excellent Café Poca Cosa (*see* Dining, *above*). Continental breakfast, happy hour, and local phone calls are all on the house. ⊞ *88 E. Broadway, 85701,* ☎ *520/622–4000 or 800/437–7275,* FAX *520/620–0376. 163 rooms. Restaurant, pool, beauty salon, sauna. AE, D, DC, MC, V.*

Bed-and-Breakfasts

$$–$$$ **Catalina Park Inn.** Classical music plays softly in the living room of this beautifully restored 1927 neoclassical house, still a bastion of civilization though Tucson is no longer the rough-and-tumble desert town it was when this home was built. The original Art Nouveau tilework and butler's pantry are among the many architectural details you're likely to ogle. Lots of niches and porches afford views of tranquil Catalina Park or the pretty back garden. A newspaper and Continental breakfast delivered to your door allow you to be as antisocial as you like in the morning. Terry robes, irons, and hairdryers in all the rooms are among other luxurious touches at this conveniently located lodging. ⊞ *309 E. 1st St., 85705,* ☎ *520/792–4541 or 800/792–4885,* FAX *520/792–0838. 2 rooms with bath, 1 suite. TV and telephones in rooms. AE, MC, V.*

$$–$$$ **Peppertrees.** This restored Victorian just off the University of Arizona campus allows guests their privacy along with the usual B&B camaraderie. Two lovely Southwestern-style guest houses in the back of the tree-shaded main house have full kitchens, washers and dryers, and individual patios; 1½ baths are shared by two bedrooms in each unit. Rooms are also available in the more formal main house, and a separate studio apartment was recently added. Host Marjorie Martin, a gourmet cook, prepares elaborate morning repasts for her visitors. ⊞ *724 E. University Blvd., 85719,* ☎ *520/622–7167 or 800/348–5763,* FAX *520/622–5959. 3 rooms with bath, 2 2-bedroom guest houses, 1 studio apartment. MC, V.*

$$ **Casa Alegre.** You'll enjoy poking around the knickknacks and antiques—
★ everything from a hand-hewn Mexican mine shovel to an ornate 19th-century French clock—in friendly Phyllis Florek's "Happy House," as comfortable as it is fascinating. The 1916 Craftsman-style bungalow is near the university, 4th Avenue, and downtown, and it's a straight shot west from here to the desert museum and other west side attractions. A plunge into the pool and hot tub in the ramada-shaded backyard are an ideal end to a day of sightseeing. Breakfasts are copious and delicious. ⊞ *316 E. Speedway Blvd., 85705,* ☎ *520/628-1800 or*

800/628–5654, FAX *520/792–1880. 4 rooms with bath. Pool, hot tub, parking. D, MC, V.*

$$ Casa Tierra. For a real desert experience, head out to this bed-and-break-
★   fast on 5 acres of land near the Arizona–Sonora Desert Museum and
Saguaro National Monument West. For the last 1½ miles you'll be driving
along a dirt road. This adobe house built by Lyle Hymer-Thompson
in 1989 expressly to serve as a B&B has three guest rooms with pri-
vate bath and kitchenettes; all look out onto a lovely central courtyard
with a paloverde tree and other desert foliage. Each guest room has a
private entrance from individual back patios. The Southwestern-style
furnishings include Mexican *equipales* (chairs with pigskin seats), tiled
floors, and viga-beam ceilings. The delicious breakfasts prepared by
Karen Hymer-Thompson might include blue-corn pancakes, breakfast
burritos, or oatmeal apple waffles. There is always a lot of fresh fruit
and baked goods to accompany them. ⌖ *11155 W. Calle Pima, 85743,*
☎ *and fax 520/578–3058. 3 rooms with bath. Hot tub, minifridges.
No credit cards. 2-night minimum stay. Closed June–Aug.*

$–$$ The Triangle L Ranch Bed & Breakfast. Out near Biosphere 2 and
Catalina State Park, a 45-minute drive northeast of Tucson at an ele-
vation of 4,500 feet, Triangle L offers four private cottages scattered
about the property's 80 acres. Buffalo Bill was among the regular visitors to the ranch, which was built in the 1880s. The cottages are furnished with comfortable antiques. All offer porches and one has a
fireplace. Co-owner Tom Beeston repairs stringed instruments (there's
an amazing collection of historic ones on the premises) and will take
you out to see his studio. This place is a birdwatcher's paradise; song-
birds, hawks, ravens, and quail abound in the area. A hearty ranch breakfast of eggs, homemade breads, and fresh fruit is accompanied by
plenty of terrific coffee. ⌖ *2805 N. Triangle L Ranch Rd., Box 900,
Oracle 85623,* ☎ *520/896–2804 or 800/266–2804. 4 private cottages
with bath. D, MC, V.*

Guest Ranches

Note: Unless otherwise indicated, price categories for guest ranches include all meals and most activities.

$$$$ Lazy K Bar Guest Ranch. In the Tucson Mountains, 16 miles northwest
of town at an altitude of 2,300 feet, this family-oriented guest ranch
will please children as well as adults. Steak cookouts are held every
Saturday night, and the daily fare in the community dining room is
hearty and good. As you might expect, horseback riding is a focus, with
mounts available for greenhorns as well as those with experience. Riders are entertained with tales of the Old West as they explore the
Saguaro National Monument on horseback. Guest rooms are situated
in eight *casitas,* or cottages. Those in the older structures, made of Mexican Indian stucco, feature fireplaces and wood-beam ceilings, while
rooms in the newer, adobe-brick buildings are larger and more modern. Rates for children 17 and under are very reasonable. ⌖ *8401 N.
Scenic Dr., 85743,* ☎ *520/744–3050 or 800/321–7018,* FAX *520/744–
7628. 23 rooms. Pool, library. AE, D, MC, V. 3-day minimum stay.*

$$$$ Tanque Verde Ranch. The most upscale of Tucson's guest ranches and
★   one of the oldest in the country, Tanque Verde sits on more than 600
beautiful acres in the Rincon Mountains between Coronado National
Forest and Saguaro National Monument. There's plenty to do, from
guided nature walks and trail rides to tennis and swimming. Rooms
in the main ranch house or in private casitas are all furnished in tasteful Southwestern style; most have patios and some have fireplaces. Ser-

vice is relaxed but very attentive. Cookouts and indoor meals are delicious. Many of the guests have been coming here for years. It's not unusual for more than two generations of a family to visit together. ✉ *14301 E. Speedway Blvd., 85748,* ☎ *520/296–6275 or 800/234–DUDE,* 𝔽𝔸𝕏 *520/721–9426. 65 rooms. Indoor and outdoor pools, 5 tennis courts, spa, exercise room, basketball, horseback riding, horseshoes, volleyball, fishing. AE, D, MC, V.*

$$$$ **White Stallion Ranch.** If you feel as if this place is right out of the film
★ *High Chaparral,* you won't be imagining things. Many scenes from the movie were shot on the ranch, which sits on 3,000 acres of desert mountain land. The True family—Cynthia, Russell, and Michael—has run the White Stallion for almost 30 years, and it feels very homey. Children are welcome and large groups are easily accommodated. Horseback rides, a weekend rodeo, cookouts, and hikes along mountain trails are just a few of the activities offered. A herd of longhorn cattle and a wide variety of birds, desert cottontail rabbits, and peacocks make their home on the grounds. Children will enjoy the petting zoo, where llamas, potbellied pigs, and miniature horses are among the residents.There are no ☎s or TVs in the spare but comfortable rooms. ✉ *9251 W. Twin Peaks Rd., 85743,* ☎ *520/297–0252 or 800/782–5546,* 𝔽𝔸𝕏 *520/744–2786. 29 rooms. Bar, pool, hot tub, 2 tennis courts, basketball, horseback riding, Ping-Pong, shuffleboard, volleyball, billiards. No credit cards. Closed May–Sept.*

Resorts

$$$$ **Canyon Ranch.** Opened in 1979 on the site of the old Double U Guest
★ Ranch, Canyon Ranch draws an international crowd of glitterati to its superb spa facilities. Set on 70 acres in the desert foothills northeast of Tucson, two activity centers include a 62,000-square-foot spa complex and an 8,000-square-foot Health and Healing Center, where dietitians, exercise physiologists, behavioral-health professionals, and medical staff attend to body and soul. The unobtrusively healthful food has proved so popular that it's sold outside the spa. This is a wonderful place to be pampered, but beware: Unless you're seriously rich, the benefits of the stress reduction programs may be wiped out when you get the bill. ✉ *8600 E. Rockcliff Rd., 85715,* ☎ *520/749–9000 or 800/742–9000,* 𝔽𝔸𝕏 *520/749–1646. 67 standard rooms, 45 deluxe rooms, 41 luxury suites. Indoor pool, 3 outdoor pools, 8 tennis courts, exercise room, basketball, squash, racquetball. AE, D, MC, V.*

$$$$ **Loews Ventana Canyon Resort.** One of the newer desert resorts, Ventana Canyon is unquestionably luxurious, but also snootier than most Tucson properties (a new general manager may mean improved service). The setting is spectacular: Expect to see desert cottontails around the 93-acre grounds, along with hummingbirds, quail, and other birds. Don't be surprised if you find yourself sharing the golf course with a cottontail or two. Rooms are modern and chic, furnished in soft pastels and light woods, and each bath has a miniature TV. The center of this open, airy property is an 80-foot waterfall that cascades down the Catalina Mountains into a little lake. Four restaurants offer guests a choice of casual poolside snacks and elegant dining. The upscale Ventana Room (*see* Dining, *above*) serves first-rate Continental cuisine. ✉ *7000 N. Resort Dr., 85715,* ☎ *520/299–2020 or 800/234–5117,* 𝔽𝔸𝕏 *520/299–6832. 398 rooms. 4 restaurants, bar, tea shop, 2 pools, spa, beauty salon, 2 golf courses, 8 tennis courts, exercise room, hiking. AE, D, DC, MC, V.*

$$$$ **Sheraton Tucson El Conquistador.** You'll know you're in the Southwest
★ when you step into the cathedral-ceiling lobby of this golf and tennis

resort: It has a huge copper mural filled with cowboys and cacti, as well as a wide-window view of one of the pools set against a backdrop of the rugged Santa Catalina Mountains. This friendly, relaxing place draws families and out-of-town conventioneers as well as locals, who take advantage of summer rates for the Sheraton's excellent sports facilities. Rooms, either in private casitas or the main hotel building, have stylish light-wood furniture with tinwork and pastel-tone spreads and curtains, as well as balconies or patios (some suites have kiva-shaped fireplaces). The White Dove, the resort's dining room, has an innovative Italian menu, presided over by a chef who looks like Alec Baldwin. Biosphere 2 is a 10-minute drive up the road from here. ☎ *10000 N. Oracle Rd., 85737,* ☎ *520/544–5000 or 800/325–7832,* FAX *520/ 544–1222. 432 rooms. 4 restaurants, piano bar, 4 pools, sauna, 3 golf courses, 31 tennis courts, 2 fitness centers, basketball, horseback riding, racquetball, volleyball, bicycles. AE, D, DC, MC, V.*

$$$$ **Tucson National Golf & Conference Resort.** Perfect for couples with separate sybaritic interests, Tucson National features both an excellent golf course (it hosts the PGA's Northern Telecom Open annually) and a full-service spa where you can be coifed, waxed, wrapped, worked over, and scrubbed to your heart's content. Smaller than most of Tucson's major resorts, it's also closer to town and thus to sightseeing and shopping. Guest rooms are in the process of a complete overhaul. Oddly, of the three levels of accommodations available, the most expensive (executive casitas) are the least attractive. The Catalina Grill, the resort's new fine-dining room, has a good American regional menu and a great view of the lush greens, while the Legends Bar & Grill is a classic sports bar, replete with pool table and happily guzzling golfers. ☎ *2727 W. Club Drive, 85741,* ☎ *520/297–2271 or 800/528–4856,* FAX *520/742-2452. 167 rooms. 3 restaurants, pool, 3 bars, beauty salon, spa, 27-hole golf course, 2 tennis courts, exercise room, basketball, croquet, volleyball, bicycles. AE, D, DC, MC, V.*

$$$$ **Westin La Paloma.** Vying with the Sheraton and Loews Ventana for convention business, this sprawling pink resort offers lots of options for individual and family relaxation. The resort's golf, fitness, and beauty centers are top-notch; a huge pool has the only swim-up bar in Tucson and Arizona's longest water slide; and reasonably priced child care at a special play lounge helps both parents and kids enjoy their stay. Accommodations make tasteful use of Southwestern colors and copper tones, and views from private balconies are of the city lights, golf course, or grounds. The casual Desert Garden restaurant affords wonderful views of the Santa Catalina Mountains (its lounge also has a good tapas menu), while the more upscale La Villa specializes in freshly imported seafood. ☎ *3800 E. Sunrise Dr., 85718,* ☎ *520/742–6000 or 800/876–3683,* FAX *520/577–5878. 487 rooms. 5 restaurants, 2 bars, pool, beauty salon, 3 spas, golf course, 12 tennis courts, aerobics, croquet, exercise room, jogging, racquetball, volleyball, bicycles, shops, business services. AE, D, DC, MC, V.*

$$$ **Westward Look Resort.** Set on 80 acres in the Santa Catalina foothills
★ north of town, Westward Look has been a resort since 1943 (it was a guest ranch before that) but it is continuously being refurbished. Either a city or a mountain view is available from the well-appointed rooms spread across the landscaped grounds, traversed by golf carts driven by hotel staff to transport guests. The resort is dimly but beautifully lit at night, the better for guests to stargaze. In-room hot-beverage makers, irons and ironing boards, and refrigerators are among the many special touches. The resort's Gold Room restaurant is excellent , and the lobby lounge features live entertainment every night but Monday. Although it offers a full range of facilities, Westward Look is more in-

timate (and less expensive) than the other Tucson resorts, drawing many repeat visitors. ⚐ *245 E. Ina Rd., 85704,* ☎ *520/297–1151 or 800/722–2500,* ℻ *520/297–9023. 244 rooms with bath. 2 restaurants, bar, grill, lobby lounge, 3 pools, 3 spas, 8 tennis courts. AE, D, DC, MC, V.*

The Arts and Nightlife

The Arts

Tucson, known as the most cultured of Arizona's cities, is one of only 14 cities in the United States that is home to a symphony as well as to opera, theater, and ballet companies. Winter is the high season for most of Tucson's cultural activities because that's when most of the visitors come, but there's something going on all the time.

Summer is when **Downtown Saturday Night,** a year-round event, really comes alive. On the first and third Saturday nights of each month (about 7–10 PM), Tucson's downtown arts district opens up its galleries, studios, and cafés. There's dancing in the street—everything from calypso to square dancing—and musical performances ranging from jazz to gospel. Most of the activity takes place along Congress Street and Broadway (from 4th Avenue to Stone Street) and along 5th and 6th avenues, but the action radiates in all directions. For information about this event and about festivals, free workshops and classes, and performances in the downtown arts district, contact the **Tucson Arts District Partnership, Inc.** (☎ 520/624–9977), which also offers material on self-guided gallery and historic district walking tours.

The cost of attending any cultural event in Tucson will be a pleasant surprise to anyone who's accustomed to paying East or West Coast prices—symphony tickets can be purchased for as little as $5 for some concerts, and tickets to a touring Broadway musical can often be had for $22. Parking is frequently free. Most of the city's cultural activity takes place either downtown in the arts district, where the **Tucson Convention Center** (260 S. Church St., ☎ 520/791-4101 or 791–4266 [box office]) complex and the El Presidio neighborhood are, or at the University of Arizona, where the UA Presents series is held at **Centennial Hall** (off Park Ave. and University Blvd., ☎ 520/621–3341). The 1995 season includes everything from the New York City Opera's *La Traviata* to the national tour of *Angels in America.* Tickets to Tucson arts and entertainment events can often be purchased through **Dillard's Box Office** (☎ 800/638–4253).

The free *Tucson Weekly,* published every Wednesday and found in most supermarkets and convenience stores, and the Friday edition of *The Arizona Daily Star* both have complete listings of what's on in town.

Dance

Tucson shares its professional ballet company, **Ballet Arizona** (☎ 520/882–5022), with Phoenix. Performances, which range from classical to contemporary, are held at the Music Hall in the Tucson Convention Center (*see above*). The most established of the modern companies, **Orts Theatre of Dance** (930 N. Stone Ave., ☎ 520/624–3799), schedules a variety of outdoor and indoor performances.

Music

The **Tucson Symphony Orchestra** (443 S. Stone Ave., ☎ 520/882–8585 [box office] or 520/792–9155 [main office]), part of Tucson's cultural scene since 1929, holds concerts in the music hall in the Tucson Convention Center complex and at the Pima Community College Center for the Arts (12202 W. Anklam Rd.). A variety of concerts and recitals, many of them free, are offered by the **University of Arizona's School of Music** (☎ 520/621–2998 for a recorded listing of events in the upcoming week). A chamber-music series is hosted by the **Arizona Friends of Music** (☎ 520/298–5806) at the Leo Rich Theater in the Tucson Convention Center from October through April. The **Arizona Opera Company** (☎ 520/293–4336), centered in Tucson, puts on four major productions each year at the Tucson Convention Center's Music Hall.

From late February through late June, the Tucson Parks and Recreation Department hosts a series of **free concerts,** most of them held on the weekend at the De Meester Outdoor Performance Center in Reid Park. The Tucson Pops Orchestra and the Arizona Symphonic Winds alternate performances much of the time, but there are also special events, such as concerts by the Old Time Fiddlers and the Civic Orchestra. It's smart to arrive at least an hour before the music starts (usually at 7:30) so that you can position your blanket exactly where you want it. Call 520/791–4079 for the schedule.

The **Southern Arizona Light Opera Co.** (1202 N. Main Ave., ☎ 520/323–7888 [east-side ticket office] or 520/884–1212 [west-side ticket office]) is becoming increasingly popular. Most of the performances are at the Tucson Convention Center's Music Hall.

Tucson's jazz scene encompasses everything from afternoon jam sessions in the park to Sunday jazz brunches at resorts in the foothills. The **Tucson Jazz Society Hot Line** (☎ 520/743–3399) offers information about the many events around town.

Poetry

The **Tucson Poetry Festival** is held in early spring. A large range of poets, some internationally acclaimed—Allen Ginsberg and Amiri Baraka have been participants—come to town for three days of readings and related events. Call 520/321–2163 or 520/881–3206 for details.

The **University of Arizona Poetry Center** (1216 N. Cherry Ave., ☎ 520/321–7760) runs a free series open to the public. Phone during fall and spring semesters for information on scheduled readers.

Theater

Theater groups in town include Arizona's state theater, the **Arizona Theatre Company** (☎ 520/884–8210), which performs everything from classical to contemporary drama at the Temple of Music and Art (330 S. Scott Ave., ☎ 520/622–2823) from November through May. It's worth coming just to see the beautifully restored Spanish Colonial/Moorish–style theater, and dinners served at the adjoining SRO restaurant, coordinated to show times, are tasty preludes to a performance. The department of theater arts at the University of Arizona (☎ 520/621–1162) also puts on productions of all styles and periods through the **Contemporary Theatre Series** and through the **University Theatre.** The **a.k.a. theatre** (125 E. Congress St., ☎ 520/623–7852) specializes in avant-garde productions, and **Invisible Theatre** (1400 N. 1st Ave., ☎ 520/882–9721) presents contemporary plays and musicals.

Nightlife

Although Tucson doesn't have the huge selection of bars and clubs available in some major cities, there's something here to suit nearly every taste. Even if you can't two-step, it's worth stopping into one of the many local country-western clubs. A number of them offer free dance lessons, and the crowd is friendly to city slickers and cowpokes alike.

Most of the major resorts have night spots that offer late-night drinks and sometimes dancing.

Rock/Variety

Club Congress (311 E. Congress St., ☎ 520/622–8848) is the main venue in town for cutting-edge rock bands. **The Outback** (296 N. Stone Ave., ☎ 520/622–4700) hosts performers like Kansas, Electric Light Orchestra, or Mick Fleetwood, who wouldn't fill the convention center but draw a good crowd. At the **Cushing Street Bar and Restaurant** (343 S. Meyer Ave., ☎ 520/622–7984) the focus is on blues, though live jazz and rock acts are also booked. The **Chicago Bar** (5954 E. Speedway Blvd., ☎ 520/748–8169) features reggae on Wednesday and Thursday nights, rocking blues on Friday and Saturday nights, and a variety of live bands the rest of the week. Nearby **Berky's** (5769 E. Speedway Blvd., ☎ 520/296–1981) also has live music—R&B and rock 'n' roll—every night.

Jazz

Of the various clubs around town, **Cafe Sweetwater** (340 E. 6th St., ☎ 520/622–6464) is the most consistent in the quality of its jazz acts—and the food's pretty good, too.

Country and Western

An excellent house band gets the crowd two-stepping every night except Sunday at the **Maverick** (4702 E. 22nd St., ☎ 520/748–0456). On Sunday night the **Cactus Moon Cafe** (5470 E. Broadway Blvd., ☎ 520/748–0049) has a terrific all-you-can-eat buffet for $3 and free dance lessons. It's worth a drive to the **Wild Wild West** (4385 W. Ina Rd., ☎ 520/744–7744), the Southwest's largest country-and-western nightclub, with two dance floors, pool tables, and video games.

TUCSON ESSENTIALS

Arriving and Departing

By Plane

Tucson International Airport (☎ 520/573–8000) is 8½ miles south of downtown, west of I–10 off the Valencia exit. Carriers include **Aeromexico** and its subsidiary, **Aerolitoral** (☎ 800/237–6639), **American** and its subsidiary, **American Eagle** (☎ 800/433–7300), **America West** (☎ 800/235–9292), **Arizona Airways** (☎ 800/274–0662), **Continental** (☎ 800/525–0280), **Delta** (☎ 800/221–1212), **Northwest** (☎ 800/225–2525), **Reno Air** (☎ 800/736–6247), **Southwest** (☎ 800/444–5660), and **United** (☎ 800/241–6522).

BETWEEN THE AIRPORT AND DOWNTOWN

In addition to the modes of transportation listed below, many hotels provide courtesy airport shuttle service; inquire when making reservations.

By Car. It makes sense to rent at the airport. Parking is not a problem in most parts of town. All the major rental-car agencies—Avis, Budget, Hertz, and National Interrent—are represented at the airport, along with Alamo, Dollar, and Value. The driving time from the airport to the center of town varies, but it's usually less than half an hour; add 20 minutes during rush hours (7:30–9 AM and 4:30–6 PM).

By Taxi. Taxi rates vary widely; they are unregulated in Arizona. It's always wise to inquire about the cost of a trip before getting into a cab. You shouldn't pay much more than $18 from the airport to central Tucson. A few of the more reliable cab companies are **Airline Taxi**

(☎ 520/887–6933), **Yellow Cab** (☎ 520/624–6611), and **Fiesta Taxi** (☎ 520/622–7777), whose drivers speak both English and Spanish.

By Van or Bus. Arizona Stagecoach (☎ 520/889–1000), with an office at the airport, takes groups and individuals to all parts of Tucson for $8.50–$26, depending on the location.

If you're traveling light and aren't in a hurry, you can take a city **Sun Tran** (☎ 520/792–9222) bus to central Tucson for only 75¢. Bus 11, which leaves every half hour from a stop at the left of the lower level as you come out of the terminal, goes north on Alvernon Way, and you can transfer to most of the east–west bus lines from this main north–south road; ask the bus driver which one would take you closest to the location you need. You can also transfer to a variety of lines from Bus 25, which leaves less frequently from the same airport location and heads to the Roy Laos center at the south of town. You must have exact change, but transfers are free (you need to ask for them as you pay your fare).

By Car

From Phoenix, 111 miles northwest, I–10 east is the road that will take you to Tucson. Also a major north–south traffic artery through town, I–10 has well-marked exits all along the route. At Casa Grande, 70 miles north of Tucson, I–8 connects with I–10, bringing travelers into the area from the west. From Nogales, 63 miles south on the Mexican border, take I–19 into Tucson.

By Bus

Buses to Los Angeles, El Paso, Phoenix, Flagstaff, Douglas, and Nogales (Arizona) depart and arrive regularly from Tucson's **Greyhound Lines** terminal (2 S. 4th Ave. at E. Broadway, ☎ 800/231–2222). For travel to Phoenix, **Arizona Shuttle Service, Inc.** (☎ 520/795–6771) runs express service from three locations in Tucson every hour on the hour, 4 AM–9 PM every day; the trip takes approximately 2½ hours. One-way fares are $19 for adults, $10 for children under 12. Call 24 hours in advance for reservations.

By Train

Amtrak serves the city with westbound and eastbound trains three times a week; the station is downtown at 400 East Toole Street (☎ 800/872–7245).

Getting Around

A car is almost a requirement if you're really going to explore Tucson and southern Arizona. You can get around the small downtown area on foot and by bus or taxi, but Tucson is generally very spread out and public transportation is somewhat limited when it comes to sightseeing.

By Car

Much of the year, traffic in Tucson isn't especially heavy, but during the busiest winter months (December through March) streets in the central area of town can get congested. There's a seat-belt law in the state, as well as one that requires children under the age of four to ride in a secure child-restraint seat. Don't even think of drinking and driving; if you do, you'll spend your vacation in jail. Arizona's strict laws against driving under the influence are strongly enforced.

If you haven't rented a car at the airport (*see* Between the Airport and Downtown, *above*), you might try **U-Save Auto Rental** (☎ 520/790–8847 or 520/745–2119), **Enterprise** (☎ 520/747–9700 or 520/881–9400) or **Rent-A-Ride** (☎ 520/750–1900) in the city center. In addition,

Carefree Rent-A-Car (☎ 520/790–2655) offers reliable used cars at good rates. If you think you might be interested in driving to nearby Mexico, check in advance to make sure that the rental company will allow you to bring the car over the border.

CAUTION: When driving off major highways in low-lying areas, watch for rain clouds. Flash floods from sudden summer rains can be deadly (*see* Driving Precautions *in* The Gold Guide's Smart Travel Tips for more information).

By Bus and Trolley

Within the city limits, public transportation is available through **Sun Tran** (☎ 520/792–9222), Tucson's bus system. On weekdays, buses start running at around 5 AM; some lines operate until 10 PM, but most only go until 7 or 8 PM. Service is more limited on weekends. A one-way ride costs 75¢; transfers are free, but be sure to request them when you pay your fare, for which exact change is required. Those with valid Medicare cards can ride for 25¢. Call for information on Sun Tran bus routes.

The city-run **Van Tran** (☎ 520/620–1234) offers transportation in specially outfitted vans for riders with disabilities. Call for information and reservations.

Guided Tours

Orientation Tours

Great Western Tours (☎ 520/721–0980) and **Tucson Tour Company** (☎ 520/297–2911 or 520/544–2664) take individuals and groups to such popular sights as Old Tucson, Sabino Canyon, and the Arizona–Sonora Desert Museum and also offer in-depth tours of the city and its neighborhoods. **Old Pueblo Tours** (☎ 520/575–1175), with a slightly different itinerary—including "A" Mountain and San Xavier del Bac Mission—provides a fine historical overview of the area. Many tour operators are on limited schedules (or close altogether) during the summer, but **Off the Beaten Path Tours** (☎ 502/529–6090) has excellent customized excursions year round. **Sunshine Jeep Tours** (☎ 520/742–1943) and **Trail Dust Jeep Tours** (☎ 520/747–0323) both offer trips to the Sonoran Desert in open-air four-wheel-drive vehicles.

Special-Interest Tours

In the spring and fall, those interested in visiting the area's historic missions can contact **Southwest Mission Research Center** (☎ 520/628–1269), which has professional historians and bilingual guides on staff. Tours of a number of ghost towns in Southern Arizona depart from the **Stage Stop Inn** (☎ 520/394–2211) in Patagonia (*see* Off the Beaten Track *in* Exploring, *above*) whenever eight or more people are interested.

Walking Tours

Tucson's historic districts make for great walks. For one easy-to-follow self-guided tour, head for the **Convention & Visitors Bureau** (130 S. Scott Ave., ☎ 520/624–1817 or 800/638–8350). The friendly, knowledgeable docents of the **Arizona Historical Society** (☎ 520/622–0956) conduct walking tours of **El Presidio** neighborhood (departing from the Sosa-Carillo-Fremont House) every Saturday at 10 AM from October through April (price: $4 for adults). A self-guided tour of **Chicano Murals** in **El Barrio** neighborhood is part of a brochure available from the **Tucson-Pima Arts Council** (240 N Stone Ave., 520/624–0595). **Old Pueblo Walking Tours** (☎ 520/323–9290) gears its weekend strolls around historic neighborhoods to visitors' interests—for example, architecture or photography; the cost is $10.

Out-of-Town Tours

Several tour companies offer bus or van excursions to points throughout southern Arizona. **Gray Line Tours** (Box 1991, Tucson 85702, ☎ 520/622–8811) takes groups or individuals to such destinations as Bisbee, Tubac, and Nogales.

Opening and Closing Times

The majority of central-city businesses, including shops and some restaurants, close at the end of the office workday, sometimes as early as 5:30 or 6; most offices open at 8. Malls have more extended hours; most stores are open weekdays 10–9, weekends 10–6. Banking hours vary widely; most Tucson banks are open weekdays 9–4 (inside lobby services) and 9–5 (drive-in service); on Saturday some lobbies are open 8–2. Almost all banks have automated teller machines (ATMs), so customers with a banking network card can get cash when the banks are closed.

Radio Stations

The following are a few of the many popular stations in Tucson.

AM

KNST 790: News, talk; **KTKT 990:** Sports Entertainment Network; **KJYK 1490:** Top 40; **KUAT 1550:** National Public Radio, jazz.

FM

KUAT 89.1: National Public Radio, jazz; **KUAZ 90.5:** Classical; **KXCI 91.3:** Alternative rock, folk, blues; **KLPX 96.1:** Rock; **KIIM 99.5:** Country.

Important Addresses and Numbers

Emergencies

For the **police, ambulance, fire department,** dial 911, a free call from public pay phones.

DOCTORS AND DENTISTS

The Pima County Medical Society (☎ 520/795–7985) will refer visitors to Tucson physicians; the Arizona State Dental Association (☎ 520/881–7237) can recommend a dentist in the area.

HOSPITALS

El Dorado Hospital and Medical Center (1400 N. Wilmot Rd., ☎ 520/886–6361), **Northwest Hospital** (6200 N. La Cholla Blvd., ☎ 520/742–9000), **St. Joseph's Hospital** (350 N. Wilmot Rd., ☎ 520/296–3211), **Tucson General Hospital** (3838 N. Campbell Ave., ☎ 520/327–5431), **Tucson Medical Center** (5301 E. Grant Rd., ☎ 520/327–5461), **University Medical Center** (1501 N. Campbell Ave., ☎ 520/694–0111).

LATE-NIGHT PHARMACIES

Several **Walgreen's** drugstores in the city have 24-hour prescription service; for the location nearest you, call 800/WALGREENS (800/925–4733). A number of Osco Drug stores also offer 24-hour prescription service; if you phone 800/654–OSCO and give the zip code of the place where you're staying, you'll be referred to the closest open pharmacy.

Visitor Information

Located downtown, the **Metropolitan Tucson Convention and Visitors Bureau** (130 S. Scott Ave., 85701, ☎ 520/624–1817 or 800/638–8350), is open weekdays 8–5 and weekends 9–4.

SOUTHEASTERN ARIZONA

The southeastern corner of Arizona is a mix of ghost towns, rugged rock formations, dense, deep forests, and mountain mining towns. It's the site of Chiricahua National Monument, one of Arizona's best-kept secrets, and a paradise for birders, hikers, and antiquers—and anyone who has an interest in frontier history. Many consider this to be Arizona's most scenic region.

Much of this area is part of **Cochise County**, named in 1881 in honor of the chief of the Chiricahua Apache. Cochise waged war against troops and settlers for 11 years, but he was respected by Indian and non-Indian alike for his integrity and leadership skills. Today Cochise County is dotted by small towns, many of them much smaller—and all much tamer—than they were in their heyday. It's hard to imagine now, but Tombstone, headquarters for most of the area's gamblers and gunfighters, was once bigger than San Francisco. These days it derives most of its revenue from tourism, and the wildest visitor is usually a six-year-old traveling with Granny and Gramps on a winter vacation from North Dakota.

The area's terrain ranges from the rugged forests of its mountains to the desert grasslands of Sierra Vista. Cochise County is home to six and part of the seventh of the 12 mountain ranges—including the Huachucas, Mustangs, Whetstones, and Rincons—that compose the 1.7-million-acre Coronado National Forest.

Exploring

The loop suggested below includes hiking and an excursion from Douglas across the border to the pleasant town of Agua Prieta in Mexico. If you have only one day, consider a driving trip through Texas Canyon to Tombstone and Bisbee or traveling via Willcox to Chiricahua National Monument.

Numbers in the margin correspond to points of interest on the Southeastern Arizona map.

❶ From Tucson, head east on I–10 for approximately 63 miles, where signs tell you that you're entering **Texas Canyon.** Rock formations here are exceptional—huge boulders appear to be delicately balanced against one another.

Texas Canyon is also the home of the **Amerind Foundation** (a contraction of "American" and "Indian"), founded by amateur archaeologist William Fulton in 1937 to foster understanding about Native American cultures. Located off I–10 at Exit 318 (Dragoon Road), the research facility and museum is housed in a beautiful Spanish-style structure built between 1930 and 1959.

Visitors to the museum are given an overview of Native American cultures of the Southwest and Mexico through well-designed rotating displays of archaeological materials, crafts, and photographs. The museum store is well-stocked with books on history and Native American cultures, as well as items created by Native American craftspeople. The adjacent Fulton–Hayden Memorial Art Gallery offers an interesting assortment of art collected by William Fulton, mostly from the Southwest. The natural setting and the quality of the exhibits at the foundation make a visit here delightful as well as educational. *Dragoon Rd. one mile southeast of I–10, ☎ 520/586–3666. ☛ $3 adults, $2 senior citizens and children 12–18. ⊙ Sept.–May, daily 10–4; June–Aug., Wed.–Sun. 10–4.*

From the Amerind Foundation, return to I–10 and backtrack 12 miles to **Benson,** once the hub of the Southern Pacific Railroad and a stop on the Butterfield Stagecoach route, but now a fairly sleepy little town. With the start-up of the **San Pedro & Southwestern Railroad** in early 1995, Bensoners hope to draw a few more visitors. The 3½-hour round trip departs from Benson's new depot and follows the San Pedro River to Charleston, a ghost town between Tombstone and Sierra Vista. *796 E. Country Club Dr., ☎ 520/586–2266. ☛ $15 one-way, $25 round-trip adults; $12 and $21 senior citizens; $9 and $15 children 2–12. Call ahead for schedules. Trains run Fri.–Sun.*

As you pass through Benson on I–10, watch for Ocotillo Avenue, Exit 304. Take a left and drive about 2¼ miles, where a mailbox with a backward SW signals that you've come to the turnoff for **Singing Wind Bookshop** (Ocotillo Ave., ☎ 520/586–2425). Make a right at the mailbox and drive ¼ mile until you see a green gate. Let yourself in, close the gate, and go another ¼ mile to the store. If you don't see the proprietor, who also runs the ranch, ring the large gong out front and she's sure to come out and welcome you. This unique bookshop-on-a-ranch has an excellent selection of books on Arizona wildlife, history, and geology.

TIME OUT   For a good green-chili burrito or a patty melt, stop in at the **Horseshoe Cafe** (154 E. 4th St., ☎ 520/586–3303), which has occupied its current site on Benson's main street for more than 50 years. The neon horseshoe on the ceiling, the macramés of local cattle brands, and the large Wurlitzer jukebox all give this casual restaurant and lounge a unique Western character.

At Benson turn south on U.S. 80 and drive 24 miles through rolling ❷ hills to **Tombstone,** the legendary headquarters of Wild West rowdies. The area was called Goose Flats in the late 1800s and was prone to attack by nearby Apache tribesmen. The intrepid prospector, Ed Schieffelin, wasn't discouraged by those who cautioned that "all you'll find there is your tombstone." In 1877 he struck one of the West's richest veins of silver in the tough old hills and gave the town its name as an "I told you so." He called the silver mine Lucky Cuss, figuring that he fit the description himself.

The promise of riches attracted all types of folks, including the outlaw type. Soon gambling halls, saloons, and houses of prostitution sprang up all along Allen Street. In 1881 the Earp family and Doc Holliday battled to the death with the Clanton boys at the famous shoot-out at the OK Corral. Over the past 100 years or so, scriptwriters and storytellers have done much to rewrite the exact details of the confrontation, but it's a fact that the town was the scene of several gunfights in the 1880s. On Sunday, visitors are treated to replays of some of these on Allen Street.

Tombstone's rough-and-ready heyday was popularized by Hollywood in the 1930s and capitalized on by the local tourist industry in the decades that followed, but there's more to the town than the OK Corral, the souvenir shops on Allen Street, and the staged shoot-outs. "The town too tough to die" (it survived two major fires, an earthquake, the clos-

ing of the mines, and the moving of the county seat to Bisbee) was also a cultural center, and many of its original buildings remain intact. Check with the **Tombstone Office of Tourism** (*see* Southeastern Arizona Essentials, *below*) for a walking tour that includes several of the town's currently unmarked sights.

As you enter Tombstone, stop at **Boot Hill Graveyard,** where the victims of the OK Corral shoot-out are buried. It's on the northwestern corner of town, facing U.S. 80. The commercialism of the place may turn you off (you enter through a gift shop that sells novelty items in the shape of tombstones), but the site itself is interesting. Chinese names in one section bear testament to the laundry and restaurant workers who came from San Francisco during the height of Tombstone's mining fever. About a third of the more than 350 graves dug here from 1879 to 1974 are unmarked.

Once you've bought your tombstone-shaped yard sign, drive into town (less than 3 miles) on U.S. 80, which turns into Fremont Street. When you reach 3rd Street, head two blocks south to Toughnut Street, where the **Tombstone Courthouse State Historic Park** offers an excellent introduction to the town's—and the area's—past. The largest settlement between San Francisco and St. Louis in 1881, Tombstone was chosen as the seat of the newly established Cochise County. The courthouse built the next year was an expensive, stylish affair. Displays include a reconstruction of the original courtroom, numerous photographs of prominent—and notorious—town figures, and such area artifacts as the dozens of types of barbed wire used by local cattle ranchers. *Toughnut and 3rd Sts.,* ☎ *520/457–3311.* ✆ *$2 adults, $1 children 12–17.* ☉ *Daily 8–5. Closed Dec. 25.*

Go one block east on Toughnut and turn right onto 4th Street for the **Rose Tree Inn Museum.** Originally a boardinghouse for the Vizina Mining Company and later a popular hotel, this museum, with its 1880s period rooms and huge rose bush on the patio (listed in the Guinness Book of Records as the largest in the world), displays the gentler side of life in Tombstone. *Toughnut and 4th Sts.,* ☎ *520/457–3326.* ☛ *$2 adults, $1.75 senior citizens, children under 14 accompanied by adult free.* ☉ *Daily 9–5. Closed Thanksgiving and Dec. 25.*

You'll get a more dramatic version of the town's history, narrated by Vincent Price, in the **Historama** on Allen Street, a block to the north. At the adjoining **OK Corral,** a recorded voice-over details the town's most famous event, while life-size figures of the gunfight's participants stand poised to shoot. Photographer C.S. Fly, whose studio was next door to the corral, didn't record this bit of history, but Geronimo and his pursuers were among the historical figures he did capture with his camera. Many of his fascinating Old West images may be viewed at the **Fly Exhibition Gallery.** *Allen St. bet. 3rd and 4th Sts.,* ☎ *520/457–3456.* ☛ *Historama $2, OK Corral and Fly Exhibition Gallery $2; children under 6 free.* ☉ *Daily 8:30–5; Historama shows every hr on the hr 9–4.*

Allen Street, the town's main drag, is lined with restaurants and curio shops. Many of the street's buildings still bear bullet holes from their livelier days, and some of the remaining artifacts are interesting—including the **original printing presses** for the town's newspaper, the *Tombstone Epitaph* (9 S. 5th St., ☎ 520/457–2211), founded in 1880 and still publishing. (If the town's other newspaper, *The Nugget,* had survived instead, the Clanton boys might be mourned as martyrs today, but it was the Earp-supporting *Epitaph* and its version of history that endured.)

Another Tombstone institution is **The Bird Cage Theater,** a former music hall, where Caruso, Sarah Bernhardt, and Lillian Russell—among others—performed. The displays are dusty and chaotic, but if you poke around, you can find such treasures as the 1881 Black Maria hearse that brought all the victims of the OK Corral shoot-out—and everyone else who died in Tombstone—to the Boot Hill cemetery. *6th and Allen Sts.,* ☎ *520/457–3421).* ☛ *$3.50 adults, $3 seniors, $1.75 children 13–17, $1 children 8–12.* ☉ *Daily 8–6 or 6:30. Closed Dec. 25.*

TIME OUT   Sightseeing is thirsty work, and what better place to wet your whistle than one of Tombstone's saloons? The **Crystal Palace** (Allen and 5th Sts., ☎ 520/457–3611) sports a beautiful mirrored mahogany bar, wrought-iron chandeliers, and tinwork ceilings. Locals come here on weekends to dance to live country-and-western music. Those seeking solid refreshment in a historic setting might stop in for a burger at **Nellie Cashman's** (5th and Toughnut Sts., ☎ 520/457–2212), a restored 1879 building.

From Tombstone, take U.S. 80 south 24 miles to Bisbee. The drive here is a scenic one, climbing another 1,000 feet to a final elevation of more than a mile.

Bird and nature lovers will want to take a detour between Tombstone and Bisbee—or make a separate day trip—to **Ramsey Canyon Preserve,** managed by The Nature Conservancy, located off AZ 92 a few miles north of Nicksville. Between April and October, 14 species of hummingbird come to the area, and coati and white-tail deer are among other wildlife who make it their home. There are, of course, hiking trails through the preserve as well. Reservations are required on weekends and federal holidays, and the 13 parking spots fill up quickly on week-days in the busiest months of April, May, and August. Reserve well in advance for one of the Conservancy's fully-equipped cabins in the preserve. Register at the visitor center, where maps and books on the area's natural history, flora, and fauna are available. ⊠ *27 Ramsey Canyon Rd., Hereford 85615,* ☎ *520/378–2785.*

❸ Like Tombstone, **Bisbee** was a mining boomtown, but its wealth was in copper, not silver, and its success much longer-lived. It wasn't until 1975 that the last mine closed and the city went into decline. However, it was rediscovered in the early 1980s by burned-out city dwellers and revived as a kind of Woodstock West. The permanent population is a mix of re-tired miners and their families, aging hippie jewelry-makers, and enter-prising young restaurateurs and antiques dealers. The three rather disparate groups seem to get along fine—Bisbee is that kind of place.

When you drive through Mule Mountain Tunnel on U.S. 80, you'll be getting close. You'll see the pretty, compact town hugging the steep moun-tainside on your left. If you want to head straight into town, get off at Brewery Gulch interchange. You can park here and cross under the high-way, taking Main or Commerce or Brewery Gulch streets, all of which meet here.

Another option is to continue driving on U.S. 80 about ¼ mile to where it intersects with AZ 92. Pull off the highway on the right into a gravel parking lot, where a short, typewritten history of the **Laven-der Pit Mine** can be found attached to the hurricane fence surround-ing the area (Bisbee isn't big on formal exhibits). The hole left by the copper miners is huge, with piles of lavender-hue "tailings," or waste, creating mountains around it. Arizona's largest pit mine yielded some 94 million tons of copper ore out of more than 280 million tons of raw materials before the town's mining activity came to a halt. If you're interested in buying jewelry made from Bisbee Blue, the pretty turquoise stone still extracted from Lavender Pit, walk across the park-ing area toward the mountains to the right of the **Bisbee Blue shop.**

For a real lesson in mining history, however, you need to take the **Cop-per Queen mine tour.** The mine is less than a half mile to the east of the Lavender Pit, across U.S. 80 from downtown at the Brewery Gulch interchange. Tours are led by one of Bisbee's several retired copper min-ers, who are wont to embellish their official spiel with tales from their mining days. They're also very capable, safety-minded people (any miner who survives to lead tours in his older years would have to be), so don't be concerned about the precautionary dog tags (literally—they're do-nated by a local veterinarian) issued to each person on the tour.

The tours, which depart daily at 9, 10:30, noon, 2, and 3:30 (you can't enter the mine at any other time), last anywhere from 1 to 1½ hours, and visitors go into the shaft via a little open train, like those the min-ers rode when the mine was active. Before you climb aboard, you're outfitted in miner's garb—a yellow slicker and a hard hat that runs off a battery pack strapped to your waist. You may want to wear a sweater or light coat under your slicker because the temperature in the mine is a brisk 47°F on the average. You'll travel by train thousands of feet into the mine, up a grade of 30 feet (not down, as many visi-tors expect). Those who are a bit claustrophobic might consider tak-ing one of the surface tours that depart from the building at the same times as the mine tours (excluding 9 AM). They cover Old Bisbee and the perimeter of the Lavender Pit mine, as well as the old leaching plant. *478 N. Dart Rd.,* ☎ *520/432–2071.* ☛ *Mine tour $8 adults, $3.50*

children 7–11, $2 children 3–6; surface tour $7 for everyone over 3.
☉ *Daily. Closed Thanksgiving and Dec. 25.*

Right across the street from the mine, in Copper Queen Plaza, is the **Mining and Historical Museum,** housed in the old redbrick Phelps Dodge general office (Phelps Dodge was the operator of the town's copper mines). The museum is filled with old photographs and artifacts from the town's mining days, and explores other aspects of the first 40 years of Bisbee's history, from 1887 to 1920. It's fun to walk out of the museum and view the same buildings you've just seen depicted inside. *No. 5 Copper Queen Plaza,* ☎ *520/432–7071.* ☛ *$3 adults, $2.50 senior citizens, children under 18 free.* ☉ *Daily 10–4. Closed Dec. 25 and Jan. 1.*

Behind the museum is the venerable old **Copper Queen Hotel** (*see* Lodging, *below*), built a century ago. It has housed the famous as well as the infamous: "Black Jack" Pershing, John Wayne, Teddy Roosevelt, and mining executives from all over the world made this their home away from home.

The Copper Queen is adjacent to **Brewery Gulch,** today a short street running north and south (walk out the front door of the Copper Queen, make a left, and you'll be there in about 20 paces) that's largely abandoned and lined with boarded-up storefronts. In the old days, the brewery housed there allowed the dregs of the beer that was being brewed to flow down the street and into the gutter.

TIME OUT **Café Maxie** (☎ 520/432–7063), in No. 2 Copper Queen Plaza, once the Phelps Dodge General Mercantile Store and now the town's convention center, is a good place for homemade soups and sandwiches. Brightly colored parachutes are suspended from the ceiling, creating a festive, airy atmosphere. Take a trip upstairs to the rest rooms for a view of the lobby down below, with its rich copper (what else?) light fixtures and handrails.

There are no boarded-up storefronts on Bisbee's **Main Street,** which is very much alive and retailing. This hilly commercial thoroughfare is lined with appealing crafts shops, boutiques, and restaurants, many of them in well-preserved turn-of-the-century brick buildings.

❹ From Bisbee, continue southeast on U.S. 80 until you reach **Douglas,** on the U.S.–Mexico border. The town was founded in 1902 by James Douglas to serve as the copper-smelting center for the mines in Bisbee. Douglas's house, now owned by the Arizona Historical Society, is open to the public as the **Douglas/Williams House Museum** (1001 D Ave., ☎ 520/364–7370 or 520/364–2636). There's not much to see here and hours are limited, but there are some interesting old photographs and mementos.

The must-see historic landmark in town and still the center of much of Douglas's activity is the **Gadsden Hotel** (*see* Lodging, *below*), built in 1907. The lobby contains a solid white Italian-marble staircase, two authentic Tiffany vaulted skylights, and a 42-foot stained-glass mural. One thousand ounces of 14-karat gold leaf were used to decorate the capitals. When you leave the hotel and walk out onto G Street, Douglas's main thoroughfare, you'll be taking a stroll back through time. A film company shooting here had to do very little to make the restaurants and shop fronts fit its 1940s plot line.

Before Douglas became the smelter for Bisbee, the site was the annual roundup ground for local ranchers, Mexican and American—among them John Slaughter, who was the sheriff of Cochise County after Wyatt Earp. The 300-acre **John Slaughter Ranch/San Bernardino Land Grant** offers a glimpse of life near the border in the late 19th and early 20th centuries. This National Historic Landmark includes the Slaughter family ranch house, filled with period furnishings and old photographs, as well as a number of the ranch's original outbuildings. A car shed holds a 1915 Model T Ford identical to the one owned by John Slaughter. You can also visit ruins of a military outpost established here in 1911 during the Mexican civil unrest and maintained by the U.S. Army until 1923. Much of the ride out to the ranch is via a graded dirt road that traverses a strikingly Western landscape of rolling hills and desert scrub. *16 mi east of Douglas (from town, go east on 15th St., which turns into Geronimo Trail and leads to the ranch)*, ☎ *520/558–2474.* ☛ *$3 adults, children under 15 free.* ☉ *Wed.–Sun 10–3.*

Neither Douglas nor Agua Prieta nearby in Mexico fits the stereotype of a border town—both are clean, pleasant places. **Agua Prieta** offers well-priced Mexican goods, and shopping here involves neither haggling nor hassling. But it's easy to imagine you're far from the States when you sit in the leafy plaza at the center of town.

After touring Douglas, get back on U.S. 80 in the direction of Bisbee. It's less than a half mile to the turnoff for U.S. 191. Go north on this road for about 41 miles until you reach the intersection with AZ 181, where signs will direct you to Chiricahua National Monument, approximately 10 miles away. En route, just past the town of Elfrida on U.S. 191, you'll see a turnoff for the ghost towns of **Gleeson** and **Courtland.** There's little to see here now except a few adobe ruins, but it's an interesting side trip if you've got time—and good shocks. As you approach Gleeson, the paved road becomes rutted dirt.

➎ The vast fields of desert grass you've passed during most of the drive are suddenly transformed into a landscape of forest, mountains, and striking rock formations as you enter the 12,000-acre **Chiricahua National Monument.** Dubbed the "Land of the Standing-Up Rocks" by the Chiricahua Apache—who lived in the mountains for centuries and, led by Cochise and Geronimo, tried for 25 years to prevent white pioneers from settling here—this is an unusual site for a variety of reasons. The vast outcroppings of volcanic rock worn by erosion into strange pinnacles and spires are set in a forest where autumn and spring occur at the same time. Because of the particular balance of sunshine and rain in the area, in April and May visitors will see brown, yellow, and red leaves coexisting with new green foliage. Summer in Chiricahua National Monument is exceptionally wet: From July through September, there are thunderstorms nearly every afternoon. In addition, few other areas in the United States have such a variety of plant, bird, and animal life. Along with the plants and animals of the Southwest, the Chiracahua Mountains also host a number of Mexican species. Deer, coatimundis, peccaries, and lizards live among the aspen, ponderosa pine, Douglas fir, oak, and cypress trees—to name just a few. This is a natural mecca for bird-watchers, and hikers have more than 17 miles of scenic trails, ranging from ½-mile to 13 miles long. At the visitor center, you can purchase a brochure describing the trails for 10¢. Lists of the mammals, snakes, and birds in the region are also available, and in spring and summer rangers give interpretive talks at the visitor center or at the campground amphitheater. *Chiricahua National Monument, Dos Cabezas Route, Box 6500, Willcox 85643,* ☎ *520/824–3560.* ☛ *$4 per car.* ☉ *Visitor center: daily 8–5. Closed Dec. 25.*

In Chiricahua National Monument, AZ 181 turns into AZ 186. Continue north on this road for about 5 miles. You'll see signs directing

6 you to the well-maintained gravel road leading to Bowie and the **Fort Bowie National Historical Site,** in the Dos Cabezas (Two-Headed) Mountains. The fort and the nearby **Butterfield stage stop** played important parts in Arizona's history. The stage stop, in the heart of Chiricahua Apache land, was a crucial link in the journey from East to West in the mid-19th century. Chief Cochise and the stagecoach operators ignored one another until sometime in 1861, when hostilities broke out between U.S. Cavalry troops and the Apache. After an ambush by the chief's warriors at Apache Pass in 1862, U.S. troops decided a fort was desperately needed in the area, and Fort Bowie was built within weeks. There were skirmishes for the next 10 years, followed by a peaceful decade. Renewed fighting broke out in 1881. Geronimo, the new leader of the Indian warriors, finally surrendered in 1886. The fort was abandoned eight years later and fell into disrepair.

In order to get to the fort from the parking lot at the trailhead you must take a 1½-mile unpaved footpath. The site is virtually in ruins now, but there's a small ranger-staffed visitor center (☎ 520/847–2500) with a book-sale area, some historical displays, and rest rooms. The center is open daily 8–5 and admission to the site is free. Bring along lunch if you want to picnic at the spot where the last of Arizona's battles between Native Americans and U.S. troops was fought.

When you get back to the gravel road, take it another 6 miles north until you reach Bowie, where you'll pick up I-10. If you head west for

7 15 miles, you'll arrive at the turnoff for the town of **Willcox.** With fewer than 4,000 residents, Willcox is a major cattle-shipping center. Its downtown looks like an Old West movie set. An elevation of 4,167 feet renders the climate here moderate in summer and a bit chilly in winter. Apple-pie fans from all over Arizona know this little town as apple-growing headquarters. Enterprising Willcox cooks bake pies for customers as far away as Phoenix. If you visit in winter, you can see some of the more than 10,000 sandhill cranes that roost at the Willcox Playa, a 37,000-acre area resembling a dry lake bed some 12 miles south of Willcox. They migrate in late fall and head north to various nesting sites in February. Also near Willcox is the headquarters for the **Muleshoe Ranch Cooperative Management Area** (☎ 520/586–7072), nearly 49,000 acres of riparian desert land in the foothills of the Galiuro Mountains that are jointly owned and managed by the Nature Conservancy, the U.S. Forest Service, and the U.S. Bureau of Land Management. It's a 30-mile drive on a dirt road to the ranch. It'll take about an hour to get there, but the scenery, wildlife, and hiking are well worth the bumps. Backroad Jeep tours or horseback rides and pack trips can be arranged by the ranch, and a variety of overnight accommodations are also available (*see* Lodging, *below*).

Stay on the I–10 frontage road and follow the signs to Willcox's historic district. Here you'll find the **Rex Allen Arizona Cowboy Museum,** set up as a tribute to Willcox's most famous native son, cowboy singer Rex Allen. He starred in several rather average cowboy movies during the '40s and '50s for Republic Pictures, but he's probably most famous as the friendly voice that narrated Walt Disney nature films. In 1994 the Willcox Cowboy Hall of Fame, saluting local cattlemen and rodeo riders, was moved here. *155 N. Railroad Ave.,* ☎ *520/384–4583.* ☛ *Suggested donation: $2 single, $3 couple, $5 family.* ☉ *Daily 10–4. Closed major holidays.*

Less than a block down the street is the **Willcox Commercial Store.** Established in 1881, it's the oldest retail establishment in Arizona that's still operating in its original location. Locals like to boast that Geronimo used to shop here. Today it's a clothing store, with a large selection of Western wear.

As you leave town, stop at **Stout's Cider Mill** (it's on the frontage road to I–10—roll down your windows and follow the aroma of apples and nutmeg). Across the parking lot from Stout's, the Chamber of Commerce hosts the **Museum of the Southwest,** which focuses on the Native American and military history of the area. You can see a sword belonging to Civil War General Orlando Willcox, for whom the town was named, though his only contact with it was a single ride-through on the train. *1500 N. Circle I Rd.,* ☎ *520/384–2272 or 800/200–2272.* ☛ *Free.* ☉ *Mon.–Sat. 9–5, Sun. 1–5.*

To return to Tucson from Willcox, take I–10 west for 78 miles. It's an easy drive, unless you're doing it in the summertime toward the end of the day. It's best to wait until the sun has gone down and is out of your eyes.

Dining and Lodging

Bisbee

DINING

$$–$$$ **Stenzel's.** Although this small, attractive restaurant, set in a wooden cabin off the side of the road, is touted by locals for its seafood specialties, they're not really Stenzel's strongest suit. The barbecued ribs and grilled chicken breast are fine, however, and the fettuccine Alfredo is outstanding. There's a decent wine list. ✗ *207 Tombstone Canyon,* ☎ *520/432–7611. Reservations advised for dinner. MC, V. Closed Wed. No weekend lunch.*

$$ **Café Roka.** Opened in early 1993, Roka is the deserved darling of the
★ hip Bisbee crowd. The constantly changing northern Italian–style evening menu is small, but you can count on whatever you order— chicken with ricotta and basil cannelloni, sea scallops with spinach pasta—to be wonderful. Portions are generous, and the entrée price ($8.50–$15.50) includes soup, salad, and a pasta-based main course preceded by a sorbet. The dining room, with exposed brick walls and the original 1906 tinwork ceiling, looks onto a central bar, which offers a nice selection of wines and cognacs. ✗ *35 Main St.,* ☎ *520/432–5153. Reservations advised. No smoking. MC, V. Closed Sun.–Tues. No lunch.*

LODGING

$$ **Copper Queen Hotel.** Built by the Copper Queen Mining Company
★ (which later became the Phelps Dodge Corporation) at a time when Bisbee was the biggest copper-mining town in the world, this hotel in the heart of downtown Bisbee has been operating since 1902. The upstairs halls are lined with photos of its early days. Some of the accommodations are small or oddly laid out and the walls between them are thin, but all have a Victorian charm. Ask for a room that's been renovated. Guests over the years have included a host of wild and crazy prospectors as well as more respectable types. Today's visitors are also a varied lot, as likely to include a film producer scouting locations as a retired snowbird from Minnesota. ▦ *11 Howell Ave., Drawer CQ, 85603,* ☎ *520/432–2216 or 800/247–5829,* ℻ *520/432–4298. 43 rooms with bath. Dining room, bar, pool. AE, D, DC, MC, V.*

$–$$ The Bisbee Grand Hotel. Restored to Victorian excess in 1986, this 1906 structure on Main Street has 11 elaborately decorated accommodations. Some feature huge brass beds, others beds with lush red-velvet canopies. One suite even has a fountain with running water in its sitting room. The lodging section, with flocked wallpaper and gilding galore, is adjoined by a Western saloon and pool room. Rates include a full breakfast. ⌧ *61 Main St., Box 825, 85603,* ☎ *520/432–5900 or 800/ 421–1909. 4 rooms with bath, 4 rooms share 3 baths, 3 suites. Bar. AE, D, MC, V.*

$–$$ The Clawson House. Terrific views of the town from the sun porch, a light-filled kitchen, and generous but health-conscious breakfasts are among the reasons to seek out this B&B on Old Bisbee's Castle Rock. The owners' art and antiques collections grace a beautifully restored former residence, built in 1895 for the superintendent of the Copper Queen Mine. ⌧ *116 Clawson Ave., Box 454, 85603,* ☎ *520/432– 5237 or 800/467–5237. 1 room with bath, 2 rooms share bath. AE, D, MC, V.*

Douglas

LODGING

$–$$ The Gadsden Hotel. Although recently refurbished, the rooms at this hotel—declared a National Historic Monument in 1976—are rather strangely decorated: Some fine antique pieces are thrown in among mismatched rugs, bedspreads, and drapes. Shower curtains are discordantly modern. And you'll sometimes hear clinking radiators at night. But the accommodations, which include suites and apartments with kitchenettes, are clean, comfortable, and very reasonably priced, and the art deco public areas are beautifully maintained. The hotel bar, with its array of local brands and local characters, looks as if it's straight out of *The Life and Times of Judge Roy Bean,* which was filmed here. ⌧ *1046 G Ave., 85607,* ☎ *520/364–4481,* ℻ *520/364–4005. 160 rooms with bath. Restaurant, bar, coffee shop, beauty salon. AE, DC, MC, V.*

Pearce

DINING AND LODGING

$$$–$$$$ Grapevine Canyon Ranch. This guest ranch in the Dragoon Mountains,
★ approximately 80 miles southeast of Tucson, adjoins a working cattle ranch. Visitors get the chance to watch—and, in some cases, participate in—real day-to-day cowboy activities. Horses for all levels of experience are on hand, and there are lots of trails for hiking this quintessentially Western terrain. Grapevine is also a good base from which to explore towns such as Douglas, Tombstone, and Bisbee, and nearby Chiricahua National Monument. Accommodations, either in adjacent cabins or private casitas, vary—some are rather plain, while others have striking Southwestern-style furnishings—but all have spacious decks and porches. ⌧ *Box 302, 85625,* ☎ *520/826–3185 or 800/245–9202,* ℻ *520/826–3636. 12 rooms with bath. Pool, hot tub, horseback riding. AE, D, MC, V. 4-night minimum in peak season, 2-night minimum off-season.*

Tombstone

DINING

$$ Bella Union. A good spot for a leisurely dinner—service is none too swift here—the Bella Union offers well-priced American standards such as steaks and chops in a nice setting. The 1881 building, off the main commercial drag, has a tastefully restored front saloon with a piano and low-key dining-room decor. An old gazette-style menu highlights breakfast combinations, blue-plate lunch specials, and a wide range of dinner entrées. A country-western singer croons on weekend evenings. ✗ *401 E. Fremont St.,* ☎ *520/457–3656. Reservations accepted. AE, D, MC, V.*

$ **Longhorn Restaurant.** Like most of the places in town, this one has been rigged up to give city slickers an idea of what it was like to grab some grub about 100 years ago in these here parts. Done in dark woods, the Longhorn is decorated with posters and artifacts from Tombstone's wilder days. Burgers, sandwiches, steaks, and Mexican dishes are available here. Service is very efficient. ✗ *Allen and 5th Sts.,* ☎ *520/ 457–3405. No reservations. MC, V.*

LODGING

$–$$ **The Best Western Look-Out Lodge.** Set off U.S. 80 on the way into town, this motel has a lot of character. The rooms feature Western-print bed-spreads, Victorian-style lamps, and locally made wood-hewn clocks. All have views of the Dragoon Mountains and desert valley. A Conti-nental breakfast is included in the rate. The front desk and switchboard close at 10 PM, so you'll need to check in and receive any phone calls before then. ⊠ *U.S. 80 West, Box 787, 85638,* ☎ *520/457–2223 or 800/528–1234,* FAX *520/457–3870. 40 rooms with bath. AE, D, DC, MC, V. Pool.*

$ **Tombstone Boarding House.** Two meticulously restored 1880s adobes sit side by side in a quiet residential neighborhood. Guests of this friendly B&B sleep in one house and go next door to have a hearty country breakfast. It's ideal for those who like the intimacy of a B&B but feel a bit odd about staying in someone's house. Complimentary drinks are offered in the afternoon at a nearby restaurant. ⊠ *108 N. 4th St., Box 906, 85638,* ☎ *520/457–3716. 8 rooms with bath. No credit cards.*

Willcox
LODGING

$–$$ **Muleshoe Ranch.** A former late-19th-century health spa is now a uniquely appealing property run by the Arizona chapter of the Nature Conservancy. Accommodations vary—four furnished housekeeping casitas have kitchens or kitchenettes, baths, and linens, while one is more rustic—but all are in a beautiful natural setting on a dirt road. There's a camping area ($6 per night per vehicle, with water and cold showers provided) as well as a visitor center, a nature trail, natural hot springs (for use by casita guests only), and a common room. The Con-servancy runs natural-history workshops and, occasionally on Satur-day, guided hikes. Overnight horseback riding packages are available in fall and spring. A 50% deposit is required when you make your reser-vation. ⊠ *30 miles northwest of Willcox, R.R. 1, Box 1542, 85643,* ☎ *520/586–7072. 5 cabins, camping area. 2-night minimum Sept.–May and holiday weekends. No credit cards.*

Southeastern Arizona Essentials

Getting There
BY CAR
From Tucson, take I–10 east to reach the southeast. When you reach the town of Benson, take U.S. 80 south (turn off at Benson) to reach Tombstone, Bisbee, and Douglas.

CAUTION: When driving off major highways in low-lying areas, watch for rain clouds. Flash floods from sudden summer rains can be deadly (*see* Driving Precautions *in* The Gold Guide's Smart Travel Tips for more information).

Greyhound Lines (☎ 800/231–2222) has service from Tucson to Douglas and Bisbee. You'll need to book a tour if you want to take the bus to Tombstone.

Amtrak (☎ 800/872–7245) trains run three times a week from Tucson to Benson.

Visitor Information
Benson–San Pedro Valley Chamber of Commerce (363 W. 4th St., Box 2255, Benson 85520, ☎ 520/586–2842).
Bisbee Chamber of Commerce (7 Main St., Box BA, Bisbee 85603, ☎ 520/432–5421).
Douglas Chamber of Commerce (1125 Pan American, Douglas 85607, ☎ 520/364–2477).
Tombstone Office of Tourism (Box 917, Tombstone 85638, ☎ 520/457–3548 or 800/457–3423).
Willcox Chamber of Commerce & Agriculture (1500 N. Circle I Rd., Willcox 85643, ☎ 520/384–2272 or 800/200–2272).

SOUTHWESTERN ARIZONA

Many people just speed through southwestern Arizona on their way to California, but the area has much to offer travelers willing to slow down for a closer look. The turbulent history of the West is writ large in this now-sleepy part of the state. It's home to the Tohonó O'odham Indian reservation (largest in the country after the Navajo Nation's) and site of such towns as Ajo, created—and almost undone—by the copper-mining industry. Yuma, abutting the California border, was a major crossing point of the Colorado River as far back as the time of the conquistadors.

Natural history is also a lure in this starkly scenic region: Organ Pipe Cactus National Monument provides a number of trails for desert hikers, while birders and other nature-watchers will revel in the many unusual species to be observed at the little-visited Imperial National Wildlife Refuge on the lower Colorado.

Exploring

Numbers in the margin correspond to points of interest on the Southwestern Arizona map.

On warm weekends and especially during semester breaks, the 130-mile route from Tucson to Ajo is well traveled by cars headed southwest to Puerto Penasco (Rocky Point), Mexico, the closest outlet to the sea for Arizonans. Much of the time, however, one can go for long stretches west on AZ 86 without seeing another vehicle. A great part of the way the landscape is flat, abundant with low-lying scrub and cactus as well as mesquite, ironwood, paloverde, and other desert trees.

About 36 miles out of Tucson, you'll come to the turnoff for Kitt Peak (*see* Off the Beaten Track *in* Exploring Tucson, *above*). To the south, the 7,730-foot Baboquivari Peak is considered sacred by the Tohonó O'odham as the home of their deity, I'itoi ("elder brother"). Baboquivari sits on the eastern boundary of the Tohonó O'odham reservation, which covers some 4,400 square miles between Tucson and Ajo, stretching south to the Mexican border and north almost to the city of Casa Grande.

A little less than halfway between Tucson and Ajo, **Sells,** the tribal capital of the Tohonó O'odham, is a good place to stop for gas or a soft drink. Much of the time there's little to see or do here, but in March an annual rodeo and fair attract thousands of visitors. For details, call 520/383–2978.

At **Why** (I don't know), approximately 60 miles from Sells, AZ 86 forks off into the north and south sections of AZ 85. Originally the name of the community at this Y-shaped intersection was spelled, simply and descriptively, "Y," but in 1950 the town was told that it had to have a three-letter name in order to be assigned a postal code. Hence the querulous appellation that has kept travelers wondering ever since.

❶ Take AZ 85 north for 10 miles to reach **Ajo,** another town with a curious name. "Ajo" (*Ah*-ho) is Spanish for garlic, and some say the town got its name from the wild garlic that grows in the area. Others claim the word is a bastardization of the Indian word "au-auho," referring to red paint derived from a local pigment.

For many years Ajo, like Bisbee to the east, was a thriving Phelps Dodge company town. Copper mining had been attempted in the area in the late-19th century, but it wasn't until the 1911 arrival of John Greenway, general manager of the Calumet & Arizona Mining Company, that the region began to be developed profitably. Calumet and Phelps Dodge merged in 1935, and the huge New Cornelia pit mine produced millions of tons of copper until the mine finally closed in 1985. With the town's main source of revenue gone, Ajo looked for a time as though it might shut down, but many retirees are now being lured here by the warm climate and low-cost housing.

Set in a desert valley flanked by low mountain ranges to the north, south, and west, Ajo is indeed a very pretty place in which to live. At the center of town and of community activities is a sparkling white Spanish-style **plaza,** designed in 1917 by Isabella Greenway, wife of the Calumet mine manager and an important figure in her own right: In the 1930s she opened the Arizona Inn in Tucson, and she was friends with such dignitaries as Eleanor Roosevelt. The shops and restaurants that line the plaza's covered arcade today are rather modest. Unlike Bisbee, Ajo hasn't yet drawn an artistic crowd—or the upscale boutiques and eateries that tend to follow.

On Indian Village Road at the outskirts of town, the **New Cornelia Open Pit Mine Lookout Point** provides a panoramic view of the town's huge open pit mine, almost 2 miles wide. Some of the abandoned equipment remains in the pit, and various stages of mining operations are diagrammed at the visitors' ramada, which doubles as a real estate office. The number of buildings listed for sale—including the town hospital—comment poignantly on the gaping hole that was once the town's source of revenue.

Nearby, the **Ajo Historical Society Museum** has collected a mélange of articles related to Ajo's past from local townspeople. The displays are rather disorganized, but some of the historical photographs and artifacts are fascinating, and the museum is inside the Territorial-style St. Catherine's Indian Mission, built around 1916. *160 Mission St.,* ☎ *520/387–7105.* ☛ *Free.* ☼ *Generally 10–4 in high season; call ahead to confirm. Closed May 1–Oct. 1.*

Twenty minutes from Ajo, the 860,000-acre **Cabeza Prieta National Wildlife Refuge** was established in 1939 as a preserve for endangered bighorn sheep and other Sonoran Desert wildlife. A permit is required

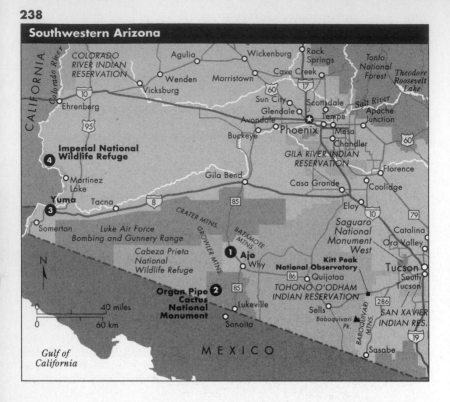

Southwestern Arizona

to enter, and only those with four-wheel-drive vehicles, needed to traverse the rugged terrain, can obtain one. For additional information
or for an entry permit, contact the refuge office (1611 N. 2nd Ave.,
Ajo 85321, ☎ 520/387–6483).

Anyone interested in exploring the flora and fauna of the Sonoran Desert
② should head for **Organ Pipe Cactus National Monument,** abutting
Cabeza Prieta but much more accessible to visitors. From Ajo, backtrack to Why and take AZ 85 south for 22 miles to reach the visitor
center. The monument is the largest gathering spot north of the border for organ pipe cacti. These multiarmed cousins of the saguaro are
fairly common in Mexico but rare in the States. Because they tend to
grow on south-facing slopes, you won't be able to see many of them
unless you take one of the two scenic loop drives, the 21-mile **Ajo Mountain Drive** or the 53-mile **Puerto Blanco Drive,** both on winding, graded
dirt roads. The latter trail, which takes half a day to traverse, brings
you to Quitobaquito, a desert oasis with a flowing spring. *Rte. 1, Box
100, Ajo 85321, ☎ 520/387–6849. ☛ $4 per vehicle. ☉ Visitor cen-
ter: daily 8–5. Closed Dec. 25.*

The drive from Ajo to Yuma is quick if not very picturesque: Take AZ
85 north for 40 miles to Gila Bend to pick up I-8 west. You'll come
to three freeway exits for Yuma just before the California border.

③ Many people tend to think of **Yuma** as a convenient en-route stop—
these days, between San Diego and Phoenix or Tucson—and this was
equally true in the past. It's difficult to imagine the lower Colorado River,
now dammed and bridged, as either a barrier or a means of transportation,
but up until the early part of the century, this section of the great waterway was a force to contend with. Records show that since at least

1540 the Spanish were using Yuma (then the site of a Quechan Indian village) as a ford across a relatively shallow juncture of the Colorado.

Some three centuries later, the advent of the shallow-draft steamboat made the settlement a point of entry for fortune seekers heading up through the Gulf of California for mining sites in eastern Arizona. Fort Yuma was established in 1850 to guard against Indian attacks, and by 1873 the town was a county seat, a U.S. port of entry, and an army quartermaster depot. The building of the Yuma Territorial Prison in 1876 helped stabilize the economy.

The steamboat shipping business, undermined by the completion of the Southern Pacific Railroad line in 1877, was finished off by the building of Laguna Dam in 1909, which controlled the overflow of the Colorado River and made agricultural development in the area possible. In World War II, Yuma Proving Ground was used to train bomber pilots, and General Patton readied some of his desert war forces for battle at a number of classified areas near the city. Many people who served here during the war returned to Yuma to retire, and the city's economy now relies largely on tourism. According to weather statistics, the sun shines more on Yuma than on any other U.S. city.

Most of the interesting sights in Yuma are at the north end of town. Stop in at the Convention and Visitors Bureau (*see* Visitor Information *in* Southwestern Arizona Essentials, *below*) and pick up a walking tour guide to the **historic downtown area.** Highlights include the Century House, which now hosts the **Arizona Historical Society Museum.** This adobe structure, built around 1870 and once owned by prominent businessman E.F. Sanguinetti, exhibits artifacts from Yuma's territorial days and details the military presence in the area. It's in a pretty complex with rose gardens, an aviary, small shops, and a restaurant. *240 S. Madison Ave.,* ☎ *520/782–1841.* ☞ *Free.* ⊙ *Tues.–Sat. 10–4. Closed Sun., Mon., state holidays.*

If you cross the railroad tracks at the northernmost part of town, you'll come to **Yuma Crossing National Historic Landmark,** which consists of the Quartermaster Depot, the Territorial Prison, and Fort Yuma to the north. The mess hall of the former fort, later used as a school for Indian children, now serves as the **Fort Yuma Quechan Indian Museum.** Historical photographs, archaeological items, and Quechan arts and crafts, including beautiful beadwork, are on display here. *On CA 24, 1 mi north of town,* ☎ *619/572–0661.* ☞ *$1 adults, children under 12 free.* ⊙ *Weekdays 8–5, Sat. 10–4. Closed holidays.*

On the other side of the river from Fort Yuma, the **Quartermaster Depot,** created toward the end of the Civil War period, was responsible for resupplying army posts to the north and east. Freight brought upriver by steamboat was unloaded here and distributed by wagon overland to Arizona forts. The depot's earliest building (1853) originally served as the home of riverboat captain G.A. Johnson. Dubbed "the Williamsburg of the West" by *Arizona Highways* magazine, the site has costumed interpreters who adopt the roles of people who might have made the crossing. Historical events are reenacted on weekends. There's a museum in the quartermaster's office, which is furnished in period pieces, as is his former residence. Five covered wagons dating from the 1850s stand outside. *Off 4th Ave. between 1st St. and the Colorado River Bridge,* ☎ *520/329–0404.* ☞ *$3 adults, $2.50 senior citizens, $2 children 6–15, $8 per family (2 adults and up to 5 children).* ⊙ *Daily 10–5. Closed Dec. 25.*

Head a few blocks east under the I–8 overpass to get to the most no-torious—and fascinating—tourist sight in town, **Yuma Territorial Prison.** Built largely by the convicts themselves, the prison operated from 1876 until 1909, when it outgrew its usefulness. The hilly site on the Col-orado River, chosen for security purposes, precluded further expansion.

Visitors gazing today at the tiny cells that held six inmates each, often in 115°F heat, are likely to be appalled, but the prison was once con-sidered a model of enlightenment: In an era when beatings were com-mon, the only punishments meted out were solitary confinement and assignment to a dark cell. The complex housed a hospital as well as the only library in Yuma, open to the public. The 25¢ fee charged towns-people for a prison tour financed the acquisition of new books. The inmates' food was sufficiently varied and plentiful to inspire locals to dub the place the "Country Club of the Colorado."

The 3,069 people who served time at this penal institution, the only one in Arizona territory during its tenure, included men and women from 21 different countries. They came from all social classes and were sent up for everything from armed robbery and murder to violation of the Mexican Neutrality Act and polygamy. R.L. McDonald, incar-cerated for forgery, had been the superintendent of the Phoenix pub-lic school system. Chosen as the prison bookkeeper, he absconded with $130 of the inmates' money when he left. Pearl Hart, convicted of stagecoach robbery, gained such notoriety for her crime that she at-tempted a career in vaudeville after her release.

Different groups continued to come, more or less voluntarily, after the prison closed. When the local high school burned down, classes were held for four years (1910–14) in the former hospital. In the 1920s rail-riders took a break from the freights to sleep in the unsupervised buildings, and during the Depression the abandoned cells provided shelter for many homeless people. A number of films, including *Red River Valley,* were shot here in the 1930s and '40s. The site of the for-mer mess hall opened as a museum in 1940, and the entire prison com-plex was designated a State Historic Park in 1961. *Near Exit 1 off I–8, Box 10792, Yuma 85366,* ☎ *520/783–4771.* ☛ *$3 adults, $2 children 12–17. Free interpretive programs at 11, 2, and 3:30.* ☉ *Daily 8–5. Closed Dec. 25.*

A drive to the far southern end of town will take you past citrus or-chards and ranches to the 40-acre **Saihati Camel Farm.** The landscape near Yuma inspired Saudi Arabia native Abdul-Wahed Saihati to raise and breed his favorite animals here, along with Arabian horses and more exotic desert-loving breeds such as oryx (antelope) and wildcats. It's fun to help feed the well-groomed, friendly dromedaries—not a biter or spitter among 'em—and to see some rare animal species, many of them purchased from the San Diego Zoo, at close range. *15672 S. Ave. 1 E (between County 15th and County 16th Sts.),* ☎ *520/627–2553.* ☉ *Guided tours ($3) Mon.–Sat. at 10 and 2, Sun. at 2. Reservations advised. Closed Thanksgiving and Dec. 25.*

Although shallow river steamers are no longer in operation, you can still take a boat ride up the Colorado with **Yuma River Tours** (1920 Ari-zona Ave., Yuma 85364, ☎ 520/783–4400). Twelve-person jet-boat excursions run by Smokey Knowlton, who has been exploring the area for more than 35 years, offer a unique look at the formerly ac-tive life of the river. Speed past Indian petroglyphs as well as abandoned steamboat landings and mining camps. The options are a three-hour trip ($25 per person, including lunch or dinner) or a full-day excursion ($49, including lunch), both departing from Fisher's Landing at Martinez Lake, 23 miles north of Yuma.

❹ These full-day tours are the best way to visit the 25,765-acre **Imperial National Wildlife Refuge,** created by backwaters formed when the Imperial Dam was built. Something of an anomaly, the refuge is home both to species indigenous to marshy rivers and to creatures that inhabit the Sonoran Desert, which lines its banks here—desert tortoises, coyotes, bobcats, and bighorn sheep. Most of all, though, this is bird-lovers' heaven. Thousands of waterfowl and shorebirds live here year-round, and migrating flocks of swallows pass through in the spring and fall. During those seasons, expect to see everything from pelicans and cormorants to Canadian geese, snowy egrets, and a variety of rarer species. Canoes can be rented at Martinez Lake Marina, 3½ miles southeast of the refuge headquarters. It's best to visit from mid-October through May, when temperatures are lowest and the ever-present mosquitoes least active. *40 mi north of Yuma off U.S. 95,* ☎ *520/783–3371.* ☞ *Free.* ☉ *Visitor center: mid-Apr.–mid-Oct. weekdays 8–4:30; mid-Oct.–mid-Apr. weekdays 8–4:30, weekends 10–4.*

Dining and Lodging

Ajo

LODGING

$$ The Mine Manager's House Inn. Another remnant of the town's Phelps Dodge heyday, this 5,000-square-foot, 1919 mansion overlooks the entire town from its site atop the highest hill in Ajo. The high-ceiling guest rooms have period furnishings and artwork. Full breakfasts are served on linens and fine china in the former mine superintendent's light-filled formal dining room. ☎ *1 Greenway Dr., 85321,* ☎ *520/387–6505,* FAX *520/387–6508 5 rooms with bath. Coin laundry. MC, V.*

$ Guest House Inn. Built in 1925 to accommodate visiting Phelps Dodge VIPs, this lodging is one of six Southwest "Bird 'n' Breakfast Fly-Inns": Guests can head out early to nearby Organ Pipe National Monument or just sit on the patio and watch the quail, cactus wrens, and other warblers that visit the Sonoran Desert. Rooms are furnished in a range of Southwestern styles, from light Santa Fe to rich Spanish colonial. ☎ *3 Guest House Rd., 85321,* ☎ *520/387–6133. 4 rooms with bath. AE, DC, MC, V.*

Yuma

DINING

$ Chretin's Mexican Food. A Yuma institution, Chretin's opened as a dance hall in the 1930s before it became one of the first Mexican restaurants in town in 1946. Customers enter through the back, passing the kitchen and cashier's stand, into three large dining areas. The food is all made on the premises, right down to the chips and tortillas. Try anything that features *machaca* (shredded spiced beef or chicken). If you're really hungry, go for the enchilada-style burritos, smothered with cheese and sauce. ✕ *485 S. 15th Ave.,* ☎ *520/782–1291. Reservations accepted except Jan.–Mar. D, MC, V.*

$ Lutes Casino. Almost always packed with locals at lunchtime, this large, funky restaurant and bar, at the historic North End of town, claims to be the oldest pool hall and domino parlor in Arizona. Decorated with photos of the bad old days, this is the place for a brew and a burger. Try potato tacos or "Especial" hot dog/cheeseburger combo, which tastes a lot better than it sounds. ✕ *221 S. Main St.,* ☎ *520/782–2192. No reservations. No credit cards.*

LODGING

$$ ★ **Best Western Coronado Motor Hotel.** This Spanish tile-roof lodging, convenient to both the freeway and downtown historical sights, was built in 1938 and is run by the son of the original owner. Bob Hope used to stay here during World War II, when he entertained the gunnery troops training in Yuma. Photos of Yuma's territorial days line the walls of the hotel's restaurant, where guests enjoy a free Continental breakfast. The rooms have such extras as VCRs (with two free films each night), refrigerators, microwaves, hair dryers, and modem phone jacks. Some have Jacuzzis. Family suites with full kitchens are available. ☒ *233 4th Ave., 85364,* ☎ *520/783–4453 or 800/528–1234,* ℻ *520/782–7487. 49 rooms, including 20 family suites. Restaurant, lobby lounge, pool, coin laundry. AE, D, DC, MC, V.*

$ **Holiday Inn Express.** Rooms in this motel, located near a large shopping center, are generic but comfortable. Many complimentary extras are included in the rate: breakfast, cocktail hour, airport shuttle, and newspaper (Monday to Friday). All rooms have coffeemakers and refrigerators, and a number offer microwaves. ☒ *3181 4th Ave., 85364,* ☎ *520/344–1420 or 800/HOLIDAY,* ℻ *520/341–0158. 120 rooms. Pool, coin laundry. AE, D, DC, MC, V.*

Southwestern Arizona Essentials

Getting There

BY CAR

Ajo lies on AZ 85 (north–south), Yuma at the junction of I–8 and AZ 95. For a scenic route to Ajo from Tucson (126 miles), take AZ 86 west to Why and turn north on AZ 85. Yuma is 170 miles from San Diego on I–8, and it is 300 miles from Las Vegas on NV and AZ 95.

CAUTION: When driving off major highways in low-lying areas, watch for rain clouds. Flash floods from sudden summer rains can be deadly (*see* Driving Precautions *in* The Gold Guide's Smart Travel Tips for more information).

BY BUS

You can get to Yuma from a variety of directions via **Greyhound Lines** (☎ 800/231–2222). The **Ajo Stage Line** (☎ 800/242–9483) has bus service from Tucson and Phoenix to Ajo three times a week.

BY TRAIN

Amtrak (☎ 800/872–7245) runs trains to Yuma from Tucson and Los Angeles three times a week.

BY PLANE

Both **Sky West**(☎ 800/453–9417), a Delta subsidiary, and **America West** (☎ 800/235–9292) have frequent direct flights to Yuma from Phoenix. Sky West also flies nonstop from Los Angeles.

Guided Tours

Ajo Stage Line (410 N. Malacate St., No. 4, Ajo 85321, ☎ 800/942–1981) runs naturalist-guided van tours to Rocky Point, the Pinacate volcanic field, the Kino missions, and other sites in northern Mexico and western Arizona.

Visitor Information

Ajo Chamber of Commerce (Hwy. 85, just south of the plaza, 321 Taladro, Ajo 85321, ☎ 520/387–7742). ☉ Monday–Saturday 9–3 in high season, more limited hours during the summer.

Yuma Convention and Visitors Bureau (377 S. Main St., Box 10831, Yuma 85366, ☎ 520/783–0071). ☉ Weekdays 9–5.

7 Portraits of Arizona

The First Arizonans

The What and the Why of Desert Country

Arizona Crafts

More Portraits

THE FIRST ARIZONANS

HUMAN HISTORY in the Southwest is one of human ingenuity brought to bear on a most unforgiving environment. Considering the aridity of the region, the flourishing of its different civilizations—and the tremendous cultural productivity of each—is not simply a fascinating anthropological fact, it is also one of the best examples of humankind working with the challenges of nature to produce a meaningful existence. Over time, tribal interaction became a vital, even necessary, part of that existence. It is easy to think of such interaction in terms of the trade of goods, and troves of goods would come into the Southwest from as far away as southern Mexico—macaw feathers, for example. But truly dramatic social change resulted from the influence of Mesoamerican ritual practice and agricultural techniques on native Southwesterners. That influence sparked the wondrous achievements visible in pottery and cliff dwellings, informed peoples' spiritual beliefs, and planted its legacy in the Pueblo cultures of today. As understanding of native cultures deepens, then, the patterns of Southwestern life are revealed as a rich interweaving of human experience. Arizona is the single best place to learn about that experience, both past and present.

Following Ice Age migrations from Asia to North America over the land bridge that has become the Bering Strait, nomadic peoples began populating the Southwest. Three Paleo–Indian groups (*paleo* meaning "old") are the earliest recognizable inhabitants. One group hunted large game, first wooly mammoth until they became extinct, then bison. They carved their spear points and knives roughly and used *atlatls*, spear-and-stick throwing weapons, to bring down their prey. Evidence of their presence from Clovis, New Mexico, dates back 11,500 years. One thousand years later, they moved east to follow the bison. Fossil remains from Fulsom, New Mexico, suggest another group with different hunting techniques. Other sites around the Colorado–New Mexico border indicate an even wider variety of activities and tools used for them.

Traces of more permanent settlements appear from 9,000 years ago in what archaeologists call the Archaic Period. New groups moved south into deserts and canyonlands that Paleo-hunters couldn't use, taking smaller game and gathering extensively. They were still quite mobile and took full advantage of seasonal plants, fruit, and nuts to supply their nourishment. And they prospered—there is quite an abundance of sites from the Archaic Period. Just how the groups at different sites interacted may not be clear, but similarities among artifacts suggest patterns of intertribal communication that would continue for thousands of years.

The next stage of development in the Southwest, about 4,000 years ago, marks a major transition in cultures around the world as people gradually adopted agriculture and a more sedentary way of life. Mesoamerican influences spread into the region from agricultural pioneers cultivating corn, squash, and beans. But Archaic peoples were slow to change. For over a couple of thousand years they mostly continued to gather the bulk of their diet from wild plants and animals. The social foundations for the next major changes, however, were in place.

One group in particular is seen to have spurred that next phase. Opinions differ as to exactly how this culture took shape, but the Hohokam developed a highly productive agricultural system in an area straddling the Arizona–Mexico border. Some archaeologists believe that they migrated from northwestern Mexico with knowledge of planting, growing, and irrigation. Others picture an evolution of Archaic peoples who gradually absorbed Mesoamerican practices. Either way, they had great success and in turn came to influence their northern and eastern neighbors for over a thousand years. Their artisans produced ritual objects, jewelry, and stone and ceramic wares with great skill. They continually traded with Mesoamerican tribes, and Pacific coast trade brought in raw materials for their own and other regional artisans.

The flowering of Hohokam culture began around 2,300 years ago. The period of their growth, expansion, and eventual decline, when the pattern of cultural influence turned back toward them from the north, lasted about 1,500 years—twice as long as the Roman Empire. During that time, they cultivated corn, beans, squash, agave, and cotton using remarkable irrigation methods. Some of their networks of canals stretched 3 miles from the Salt and Gila rivers to planted fields. Regular contact with Mesoamerican cultures periodically brought new strains of corn to the Southwest as well as religious beliefs, ritual practices, and the ball game and ball courts well-known from the Maya. The Hohokam essentially fertilized the cultures of the region, providing raw material for the Pueblo culture that has survived into the modern era.

The Mogollon were another group, occupying an area stretching from eastern central Arizona into New Mexico from 2,000 to 500 years ago. They absorbed the Hohokam and northern Ancestral Pueblo (so-called Anasazi) cultural patterns, but they never fully embraced an agricultural lifestyle. They became skillful potters, especially those living near the Mimbres River. Contact with the Anasazi resulted in the production of some of the Southwest's most outstanding pottery. The principle Mogollon site, in the Mimbres River area, is the Gila Cliff Dwellings National Monument in New Mexico.

ROMANTICIZED, mythicized, and perhaps misunderstood, the so-called Anasazi left wondrous architectural remains, most notably at Mesa Verde in Colorado, Chaco Canyon in New Mexico, and Canyon de Chelly, Betatakin, and Keet Seel in Arizona. Composed of separate groups living around the Four Corners area, they have generated the most intense interest. We take up with them 2,000 years ago where we left off with the Archaic peoples. While for centuries they lived semi-nomadically, hunting, gathering, and marginally cultivating corn, squash, and beans, they eventually settled into villages and adopted

substantially more of the Hohokam culture than did their Mogollon neighbors.

These various Ancestral Pueblos were not pueblo dwellers yet, however. At first they were slow to establish year-round communities. Perhaps they weren't convinced that the Hohokam model would work in their rugged, dry canyonlands. With fewer and smaller rivers, they wouldn't have been able to irrigate on the Hohokam scale. Then about 1,500 years ago the Pueblo cultural pattern called Anasazi suddenly began to take shape, owing, perhaps, to the introduction of a new, more productive strain of corn.

Ancestral Pueblo peoples made a significant contribution to Southwestern culture with their architecture. Their remarkable stone masonry evolved out of the pithouse style used by Archaic peoples. A precursor of the kiva, the pithouse was constructed around a shallow, circular dugout with mud walls packed around vertical pole supports. The new stone-and-mortar houses, on the other hand, were very often rectangular in plan. In small communities they were built on a scale to house groups of a few families. These groups would have individual clan *kivas* (the Hopi word for underground ceremonial chambers) or single great kivas.

The soaring cliff dwellings of Canyon de Chelly, Betatakin, Keet Seel, and Mesa Verde represented another type of settlement, more protected from the elements and, perhaps, raiders. Villagers cultivated the land around them. The wholly different, massive, free-standing structures of Chaco Canyon may have housed a few thousand people at that civilization's height. All of these communities had kivas, central ritual spaces in the lives of deeply spiritual people.

Ancestral Pueblo culture reached its height about 1,000 years ago. Hitherto they had continued to refine their use of water, not actually irrigating, but using the region's sporadic rainfall to greatest advantage. They would line stones across slopes and cut arroyos to distribute rainfall and limit erosion. Occasionally they dug canals in order to channel rainwater into planted fields. Unquestionably, they were expert "dry farmers," coaxing abundance out of a harsh environment.

At the time of this climax, some people began moving from smaller, widespread communities into larger, denser settlements. The volume of trade in nearly all directions was tremendous, and Pueblo artisans were making superb pottery. Decorative techniques varied from region to region: black-on-white, black-on-red, black-on-orange, red-on-orange, and expressive combinations of these. They also etched petroglyphs into, and painted pictograms onto, rock faces. Rock art is found at almost all Anasazi and Sinagua sites. The quantity of artifacts that they left behind—utility and ceremonial items alike—is unparalleled among Native North American groups.

Around 850 years ago, a cultural decline began. Drought and climatic change put pressure on the Pueblos' settled, agricultural lifeways. Longer winters shortened growing seasons in which less rain fell. Villagers continued to move into denser settlements. By the late 1200s, Canyon de Chelly was unoccupied. Chaco Canyon had been vacant for 100 years. Settlements at Wupatki continued a little longer, into the 1300s. The Hopi mesas, on the other hand, first built in the 1100s, were growing. They absorbed some of their migrating neighbors, and their traditions testify to their assimilation of ancient Pueblo culture.

There are also a great number of transitional settlements, many yet to be excavated, that accommodated groups leaving the immediate Four Corners area. Some of them are quite substantial. Archaeologically speaking, then, the scenario that used to be construed as the disappearance of a vast culture can now take a more human shape. The Anasazi didn't vanish, they chose to move. Over a couple of centuries they gradually migrated to new locations, slightly altering their lifestyles. (Some of them may have been doing that sporadically for hundreds of years anyway.) In the process they passed on their knowledge to the people they joined, the Hopi, the New Mexican Zuñi, the Acoma, or other Pueblos. And while archaeologists look for external forces that might have caused this movement—drought, climatic change, deforestation, disease, warfare— the Zuñi see the migration as a process of searching for "the center place," a place of spiritual rightness. That center place is where present-day Pueblos are living.*

MANY OTHER PEOPLES also lived within current Arizona borders in the pre-European Southwest. One of them, the Sinagua (meaning "without water" in Spanish), belonged to a diverse group called the Hakataya, spread out across central Arizona. Wupatki, Walnut Canyon, Tuzigoot, and the inappropriately named Montezuma Castle are all Sinagua sites. These people absorbed Hohokam, Mogollon, and Anasazi cultural patterns: agriculture, village life, and the Mesoamerican ball game; stone masonry and cliff-dwelling architecture; and pottery.** Situated in the middle of these three groups, they became a composite but separate culture.

The next Native Arizona peoples to thrive in the former Anasazi territory were the Navajo and the Hopi. An Apachean group linguistically related to the Athabascans of western Canada, the Navajo gradually moved into the Southwest 500 years ago. Migrating southward along the Rocky Mountains, they finally settled in unoccupied places around Pueblo villages. Hunting and gathering were just about all that the land would support. Over time they learned farming techniques from the Pueblos and traded with them, and as a result took on a character distinct from other Apachean groups, such as the 19th-century Chiracahua and Mescalero Apache. Living in small, dispersed groups, Navajos also raided Pueblo farms and villages—a practice in retrospect notoriously Apachean.

Then came the Spanish. After overrunning Mesoamerica, they invaded the Southwest early in the 16th century. Unlike Anglo-European conquerors, they did allow elements of Native cultures to survive, provided that they accept a transfusion of Catholicism and alien governance. Of course, their intrusion into Southwestern life was far from cordial. Their first contact was with New Mexican Pueblos, whose understandable lack of interest in accepting Spanish rule met with the sword. Pueblo retaliation brought further hostility from the invaders, who murdered hundreds of Natives and destroyed villages. But because the Pueblo lands did not have the wealth that the Spanish had dreamed of, they didn't wholly occupy the region until about 400 years ago.

The Apacheans were slightly less bothered by the Spanish, in part because their scattered settlements were more difficult to locate than pueblos. Some of the eastern Apaches entered into slave trade with the conquerors, selling them captives taken during raids. Then after the Pueblo Revolt of 1680, which drove the Spanish away only to have them return 12 years later, the Navajo periodically housed Pueblos seeking refuge from reprisals. In return, the Pueblos taught them rituals, customs, agricultural techniques, and arts—in some of which, like weaving, they eventually surpassed their teachers. In the 1700s, drought led many Hopis to seek refuge among the Navajo in the formerly vacated Canyon de Chelly—a poignant example of the long-standing cooperative relationship of the two groups.

The Navajo also picked up European skills, some of them from the Pueblos. Directly from the Spanish they learned about silversmithy, raising cattle, and riding horses—and they became superior horsemen. Horses extended their gathering range and gave them greater mobility for trading and raiding. It's important to stress, however, that the Navajo were not nomadic. Many of them had different seasonal residences, log-and-earth hogans, as they continue to do today. But these are maintained as permanent dwellings.

After independent Mexico ceded New Mexico to the United States in 1848, the Southwest's new "owners" decided to put an end to Indian raids. Over the next 16 years U.S. troops and the Navajo clashed repeatedly. The United States set up army posts within Navajo territory. They attempted to impose treaties, but since U.S. agents often arranged them with headmen who had no overall authority, the treaties didn't cover all Navajo groups.

This misunderstanding of Navajo organization had tragic results for them. When raids continued, the U.S. territorial governor believed he had been betrayed and decided that drastic measures were necessary to safeguard the "frontier." He called in Colonel Kit Carson to destroy Navajo crops and livestock. Over the next few months, "The People," as the Navajo call themselves, began to give themselves up.*** In early 1864, the first couple of thousand Navajo made the grueling "Long Walk" to captivity in Fort Sumner, 300 miles to the southeast.

U.S. policies forced them into four years of concentration camp life. When The People returned to their land in 1868, fewer in number and greatly demoralized, they had to reconstruct their lives from scratch, rebuilding customs and lifestyles that had been impossible, if not forbidden, in the camps. When a reservation was granted to them, there were fewer than 8,000 Navajo. Since then, Navajo ingenuity and an impressive ability to seize opportunities have gained them a measure of success in modern America. Their democratically governed community—they call it Navajo Nation—numbers over 250,000.

THE HOPI didn't suffer that kind of brutality. The Spanish had set up a mission at Hopi by 1629. But the Hopi drove them out in an all-Pueblo revolt in 1680. Spanish missionaries returned to attempt another conversion, and again the Hopi got rid of them. They accomplished this by destroying the Christianized village of Awatovi, thus maintaining the purity of Hopi ritual. Because of their otherwise noncombative stance, the Hopi were never viewed by the U.S. government as hostile. Until this century, their lives have consequently been less disrupted by Eur-American interference than have those of other so many other Native Americans.

It is clear from their beliefs and rituals that the Hopi are descended from the so-called Anasazi. In their proper observance of tradition and ritual they are unique even among traditional Native Americans. In fact it was to Hopi spiritual leaders that many Native American traditionals turned in the 1950s in what eventually became the "Indian Unity Movement." Hopi beliefs focus on the relationship between the people, the land, and the Creator, whose "Life Plan" locks them all in balance. In this strict moral order, prayer and ritual—including the kachina "rain power being" dances—are necessary to keep the natural cycle in motion and to insure the flow of life-sustaining forces. The earth is sacred, and they are its keepers.

The Hopi may well be the best dry farmers on the planet, successfully harvesting crops on a precarious 8 to 15 inches of rain per year. Doubtless they manage this because they have perfected ancient Ancestral Pueblo techniques. The mesas on which the Hopi chose to live contain precious aquifers, particularly essential to life in such an arid territory. These sources of water no doubt sustained them and their migrant guests as Pueblos peoples left places like Wupatki and Walnut Canyon and Canyon de Chelly 700 years ago.

Earlier this century, U.S. government efforts to make Indians across the country self-determined created a major rift at Hopi. The plan required the formation of a Tribal Council. Yet the eventual leaders of the council—those who were essentially most willing to work with whites—had no relationship to traditional Hopi leadership. Instead, council members were, and are, among the Christianized, progressive members of the Hopi. For over a decade in the '30s and '40s, the council was suppressed at Hopi, only to be resurrected in the early '50s. Since then, the council has acted in the interest of modernizing Hopi at the expense of traditional ways. Among other things, it has secretly sold sacred land to strip miners who in turn have destroyed parts of Black Mesa and depleted the aquifer. Those who have held fast to the Hopi way reside in the villages of Oraibi and Hotevilla and Shungapovi. They are, unfortunately but understandably, intolerant of whites. They follow the Hopi Way even as modern life and the "Tribal Council" pose ever greater threats to it.

The present-day Tohono O'Odham (called Papago by the Spanish) and the Pima, in central southern Arizona, are descendants of the Hohokam. The Spanish first encountered them in the 17th century cultivating former Hohokam territory, using some of the ancient irrigation canals. Both tribes are Pimans, and both continue some Hohokam practices: living in rancherías along canals and performing costume dances and other rituals that link them to Uto-Aztecan language groups nearby in Mexico. The Pima live on the Salt River Reservation south of Phoenix, and the Tohono O'Odham reservation stretches north from the Mexican border.

Like the Southwest's history, various perspectives on Native American cultures are complex and fascinating—and have become confused in the clash of Euro-American and Native American ways. Take, for example, the enchanting and mysterious word *Anasazi* that enters into almost any discussion of Native Arizonans. This Navajo word, meaning both "ancient ones" and "enemy ancestors," automatically implies one perspective. Another of equal cultural value is that of the Hopi, whose name for the ancient culture, *Hisatsinom,* means "people of long ago." Yet another perspective is that of the New Mexican Zuñi, who prefer the word *Enote:que,* "our ancient ones, our ancestors." *

To scientifically trained Euro-American archaeologists, *Anasazi* conveniently groups together a variety of ancient Pueblo peoples who had similar lifestyles but often divergent adaptations to Southwestern conditions. In past decades researchers encouraged the myth of a lost Anasazi civilization and posed virtually unanswerable questions about who the people were and how and why they "vanished" from the scene. Had they taken the beliefs and statements of the Hopi and of New Mexican Pueblos seriously—acting as both archaeologists and anthropologists—certain answers would have been clear. The *Hisatsinom–Enote:que–Anasazi* would have fit seamlessly into the continuity of Native American life.

The perspective we can never know is that of the Ancestral Pueblos themselves—we don't even know the language they spoke. Yet we can try to get a sense of their worldview by listening to contemporary Pueblos. If we project their uniquely American customs into the past, aspects of their ancestral culture come to life. And while Western tradition has its own ancient echoes, in a world rushing to keep up with continually accelerating values, traditional Pueblo ways speak of a balanced life, rooted in its relationship with the earth.

Sources
Ancient Ruins of the Southwest: An Archaeological Guide. David Grant Noble. Flagstaff: Northland Publishing Co., 1981.

Indian Country. Peter Mathiessen. New York: The Viking Press, 1984.

*** *The Navaho.* Clyde Kluckhon and Dorothea Leighton. Cambridge, Mass.: Harvard University Press, 1974.

North American Indians: A Comprehensive Account. Alice Beck Kehoe. Englewood Cliffs: Prentice-Hall, Inc., 1981.

** *Those Who Came Before: Southwestern Archaeology in the National Park System.* Robert H. Lister and Florence C. Lister. Flagstaff: Southwestern Parks and Monuments, 1983.

* *What Happened to the Anasazi? Why did they leave? Where did they go? A panel discussion at the Anasazi Heritage Center.* Jerold G. Widdison, ed. Albuquerque: Southwest Natural and Cultural Heritage Association, 1990.

— *Stephen Wolf*

Stephen Wolf is the editor of this and other travel books.

THE WHAT AND THE WHY OF DESERT COUNTRY

ON THE BRIGHTEST and warmest days my desert is most itself because sunshine and warmth are the very essence of its character. The air is lambent. A caressing warmth envelops everything in its ardent embrace. Even when outlanders complain that the sun is too dazzling and too hot, we desert lovers are prone to reply, "At worst that is only too much of a good thing."

Unfortunately, this is the time when the tourist is least likely to see it. Even the winter visitor who comes for a month or more is likely to choose January or February because he is thinking about what he is escaping at home rather than of what he is coming to here. True, the still-warm sun and typically bright skies make a dramatic contrast with what he has left behind. In the gardens of his hotel or guest ranch, flowers still bloom and some of the more obstreperous birds make cheerful sounds, even though they do not exactly sing at this season. The more enthusiastic visitors talk about "perpetual summer" and sometimes ask if we do not find the lack of seasons monotonous. But this is nonsense. Winter is winter, even in the desert.

At Tucson's elevation of 2,300 feet it often gets quite cold at night, even when shade temperatures during the day rise to 75°F or higher. Most vegetation is pausing, though few animals hibernate. This is a sort of neutral time when the desert environment is least characteristic of itself. It is almost like late September or early October, just after the first frost, in southern New England. For those who are thinking of nothing except getting away, rather than learning to know a new world, this is all very well. But you can't become acquainted with the desert itself at that time of year.

By April the desert is just beginning to come into its own. The air and the skies are summery without being hot; roadsides and many of the desert flats are thickly carpeted with a profusion of wildflowers such as only California can rival.

The desert is smiling before it begins to laugh, and October or November are much the same. But June is the month for those who want to know the true desert. That is the time to decide once and for all if it is, as for many it turns out to be, "your country."

It so happens that I am writing this not long after the 21st of June, and I took special note of that astronomically significant date. This year, summer began at precisely 10 hours and no minutes, mountain standard time. That means that the sun rose higher and stayed longer in the sky than on any other day of the year. In the North there is often a considerable lag in the seasons as the earth warms up, but here, where it is never very cold, the longest day and the hottest are likely to coincide pretty closely. So it was this year. On June 21 the sun rose almost to the zenith so that at noon it cast almost no shadow. And it was showing what it is capable of.

Even in this dry air, 109°F in the shade is pretty warm. Under the open sky the sun's rays strike with an almost physical force, pouring down from a blue dome unmarked by the faintest suspicion of even a fleck of cloud. The year has been unusually dry (even for the desert). During the four months just past, no rain—not even a light shower—has fallen. The surface of the ground is as dry as powder. And yet, when I look out of the window, the dominant color of the landscape is an incredible green.

On the low foothills surrounding the steep rocky slopes of the mountains, which are in fact 10 to 12 miles away but in the clear air seem much closer, this greenness ends in a curving line following the contour of the mountains' base, inevitably suggesting the waves of a green sea lapping the irregular shoreline of some island rising abruptly from the ocean. Between me and that shoreline the desert is sprinkled with hundreds, probably thousands, of evenly placed shrubs, interrupted now and then by a small tree—usually mesquite or what locals call a cat's-claw acacia.

More than a month ago all the little perennial flowers and weeds, which spring up after winter rains and rush from seed to flower and to seed again in six weeks, gave up the ghost at the end of their short lives. Their hope of posterity lies now invisible, either upon the surface of the bare ground or just below it. Yet even when summer thunderstorms come in late July or August, these seeds will not make the mistake of germinating. They are triggered to explode into life only when they are both moist and cool—which they will be February or March when their season comes again. Neither the shrubs nor the trees seem to know that no rain has fallen during these long months. The leathery, somewhat resinous leaves of the dominant shrub—the attractive plant unattractively dubbed "creosote bush"—are not at all parched or wilted. Nor are the deciduous leaves of the mesquite.

Earlier in the year the creosote was covered with bright yellow pealike flowers, the mesquite with pale yellow catkins. Now the former is heavy with gray seed and on the mesquite are forming long pods that Indians once ate and that cattle now find an unusually rich food.

It looks almost as though the shrubs and trees could live without water. But of course they cannot. Every desert plant has its secret, though not always the same one. In the case of mesquite and creosote it is that their roots go deep and that, below six feet, there is no wet or dry season in the desert. What little moisture is there is pretty constant throughout the year, in dry years as well as wet. Like the temperature in some caves, it never varies. The mesquite and creosote are not compelled to care whether it has rained for four months or not. And unlike many other plants they flourish whether there has been less or more rain than usual.

Plants with substantial root systems that do not reach very deep are more exuberant some years than others. Thus the Encelia, the brittlebush, which in normal years literally covers many slopes with thousands of yellow, daisylike flowers, demands a normal year. Though I have never seen it fail, I am told that in very dry years it comes into leaf but does not flower, while in really catastrophic droughts it does not come up at all, as the roots lie dormant and hope for better times. Even the creosote bush, which never fails, profits from surface water, and when it gets the benefit of a few thunderstorms in late July or August, it will flower and fruit a second time, sprinkling the desert expanse once again with yellow. . . .

On such a day as this, even the lizards, so I have noticed, hug the thin shade of the bushes. If I venture out, the zebratails scurry indignantly away, the boldly banded appendages that give them their name curved high over their backs. But I don't venture out very often during the middle of the day. It is more pleasant to sit inside where a cooler keeps the house at a pleasant 80 degrees. And if you think that an advocate of the simple life should not succumb to a cooler, it is you rather than I who is inconsistent. Even Thoreau had a fire in his cottage at Walden, and it is no more effete to cool oneself in a hot climate than it is to get warm before a stove in a cold one. The gadget involved is newer, but that is all.

In this country "inclemency" means heat. One is "sunbound" instead of snowbound and I have often noticed that the psychological effect is similar. It is cozy to be shut in, to have a good excuse for looking out of the window or into oneself. A really blazing day slows down the restless activity of a community very much as a blizzard does in regions that have them. Where there is either, a sort of meteorological sabbath is usually observed even by those who keep no other.

OBVIOUSLY the animals and plants that share this country with me take it for granted. To them it is just "the way things are." By now I am beginning to take it for granted myself. But being a man I must ask what they cannot: What *is* a desert, and why is it what it is? At 32° latitude one expects the climate to be warm. But the desert is much more than merely warm. It is a consistent world with a special landscape, a special geography, and, to go with them, special flora and fauna adapted to that geography and that climate.

Nearly every striking feature of this world, be it the shape of the mountains or the habits of its plant and animal inhabitants, goes back ultimately to the grand fact of dryness—the dryness of the ground, of the air, of the whole sum total. And the most inclusive cause of dryness is the simple lack of rain.

Some comparisons with wetter regions may bring that into sharper focus. Take, for example, southern New England. By world standards it gets a lot—namely some 40 inches—of rain per year. Certain southern states get even more: about 50 inches for east Tennessee, nearly 60 for New Orleans. Some areas on the West Coast get fantastic amounts, like the 75 inches at Crescent City, California, and the unbelievable 153 inches, nearly four times what New York City gets, recorded one year in Del Norde County, California.

Nevertheless, New England's 40 is a lot of water, either comparatively or absolutely. The region around Paris, for instance, gets little more than half that amount. Forty inches is, in absolute terms, more than most people imagine. One inch of rain falling on an acre of ground means more than 27,000 gallons of water. No wonder irrigation in dry regions is a formidable task even for modern technology.

In terms of vegetation, 40 inches is ample for the kind of agriculture and natural growth that we tend to think of as "normal." It means luxuriant grass, rapid development of second-growth woodland, a veritable jungle of weeds and bushes in midsummer. In inland America, rainfall tends to be less than in coastal regions. Moving west from the Mississippi, it declines sharply and begins to drop below 20 inches a year at about the one-hundredth meridian or, very roughly, at a line drawn from Sioux Falls, South Dakota, through Oklahoma City. This means too little water for most broad-leaved trees and explains why the southern Great Plains were as treeless when the white man first saw them as they are today.

OUR TRUE DESERTS lie further west still: the Great Basin Desert in Utah and Nevada, the Chihuahuan in New Mexico, the Sonoran in Arizona, and the Mohave in California. The four differ among themselves but they are all arid, and they all fulfill what is probably the most satisfactory definition of "desert": namely, a region where the ground cover is not continuous—where the earth remains bare of vegetation between the plants that manage to grow. Over these American deserts rainfall varies considerably, and with it the character and extent of vegetation. In southern Arizona, for instance, there are about 4 inches of rain at Yuma, nearly 11 around Tucson. Four inches means sand dunes that look like pictures of the Sahara that the word "desert" calls to most people's minds. Eleven means that where soil is suitable, well-separated individuals of such desert plants as cacti and paloverde trees will flourish.

But if scant rainfall makes for deserts, what makes for scant rainfall? To that there are two important answers. One is simply that most non-mountainous regions tend to be dry if they lie in that belt of permanently high atmospheric pressure extending some 30 or 35 degrees on each side of the equator where calms are frequent and winds erratic. Old sailors used to call this region "the horse latitudes," though nobody knows exactly why. (You can take your choice of three equally unconvincing explanations. One is that horses tended to die on ships lying long in the hot calms. Another: the boisterous changeableness of winds when they do come suggests unruly horses. A third is that they were originally named after an English explorer, Ross, whose name Germans mistook for their old word for "horse.") In any event, Tucson falls within the "horse latitudes." Most of the important deserts of the world, including the Sahara and the Gobi, lie within this belt.

Mountains lying across the path of moist winds also make for scant rainfall. In our case, the Coast Ranges of California lie between us and the Pacific. From my front porch, which looks directly across the desert to some of the southernmost Rockies, I can see, on a small scale, what happens. So many times a moisture-laden mass of air reaches as far as these mountains. Dark clouds form, sometimes the whole range is blotted out. Torrential rain is falling—but not a drop on me. Either the sky is blue overhead or the high clouds that have blown my way dissolve before my eyes as they reach warm air rising from the sun-drenched flats. I live in what geographers call a "rain shadow" cast by the mountains. At their summit rainfall is nearly twice as much as it is down here, and as a result they are clothed with pines from 6,000 or 7,000 feet right up to the 9,000-foot peak. When I do get rain in midwinter and midsummer, it is usually because winds have brought moisture up from the Gulf of Mexico by an unobstructed southern route, or because in summer a purely local thundershower has formed out of hot air rising from the sun-beaten desert floor. Most of the time the sun is hot, even in winter, and the air is usually fantastically dry, the relative humidity being often less than 10.

NATURALLY the plants and animals living in such a region must be specially adapted to survive under such conditions, but the casual visitor usually notices the strangeness of the landscape before he is aware of flora or fauna. Peculiar features of the landscape are also the result of dryness, even in ways that are not immediately obvious.

The nude mountains reveal their contours, or veil them as lightly as late Greek sculptors veiled their nudes, because only near the mountaintops can anything grow tall enough to obscure the outlines. A little less obvious is the fact that the beautiful "monuments" of northern Arizona and southern Utah owe their unusual forms to the sculpting of windblown sand—or that sheer cliffs often rise from a sloping cone of rocks and boulders because there is not enough draining water to break them down and distribute them over the surrounding plain, as they would be distributed in regions with heavier rainfall. But the most striking example of all is the greatest single scenic wonder of the region, the Grand Canyon itself. This narrow gash, cut a mile deep through so many strata that the river now flows over some of the oldest rock exposed anywhere on earth, could have been formed only in a very dry climate.

As recently as 200 years ago the best-informed observer would have taken it for granted that the river was running between those sheer walls at the bottom of the gorge simply because it had found them out. Today few visitors are not aware that the truth is the other way around, that the river cut its own course through the rock. But most laymen do not ask the next questions: Why is the Grand Canyon unique, or why are such canyons, even on a smaller scale, rare? The answer to those questions is that a set of very special conditions was necessary.

First there must have been a thick series of rock strata slowly rising during a period when a considerable river flowed over it. Second, that considerable river must have carried an unusual amount of hard sand or stone fragments in suspension so that it could cut downward at least as rapidly as the rock over which it flows rose. Third, that considerable river must have coursed through very arid country. Otherwise rain, washing over the edges of the cut, would widen it at the top as the cut went deeper. That is why broad valleys are characteristic of regions with normal rainfall and canyons require arid country.

And Grand Canyon is the grandest of all canyons because at that particular place all the necessary conditions were fulfilled more exactly than at any other place. The Colorado River carries water from a relatively wet country through a dry one, it bears with it a fantastic amount of abrasive material, the rock over which it flows has been slowly rising during several millions of years, and too little rain falls to rapidly (in geological time) widen the gash that it cuts. Thus in desert country everything from the color of a mouse or the shape of a leaf to the largest features of mountains is more likely than not to have the same explanation: dryness.

So far as living things go, all this adds up to what even an ecologist may call, forgetting himself for a moment, an "unfavorable environment." But like all such pronouncements this one doesn't mean much unless we ask "unfavorable for what and for whom?" For many plants, for many animals, and for some people it is very favorable indeed. Many of the first two would languish and die if transferred to some region where conditions were "more favorable." It is here, and here only, that they flourish. Likewise, many people feel healthier and happier in the bright dry air than they do anywhere else.

And since I happen to be one of them, I not unnaturally have a special interest in the plants and animals that share my liking for just these conditions. For many years now I have been amusing myself by inquiring of them directly what habits and what adjustments they have found most satisfactory. Many of them are delightfully ingenious and eminently sensible. . . .

I HAVE LIVED in this house and been lord of these few acres for nearly five years, and the creatures who share the desert with me have already summed me up as a softy and have grown contemptuously familiar. It is not only that the cactus wrens sit on the backs of my porch chairs. The round-tailed ground squirrels—plain, sand-colored, chipmunk-like animals—are digging rather too many burrows rather too close about the house. The jack rabbits—normally the most timid as well as the fleetest of creatures—take nibbles at the few plants I have set out and refuse to leave off until I arrive shouting and waving my arms a few feet from where they are. Sooner or later something may have to be done to discourage this impudent familiarity, but for the present I am getting some good looks at creatures who usually don't wait to be looked at. Yesterday, for instance, I saw what at first I thought was a bird eating seeds from the upper branches of a creosote bush. It turned out to be a ground squirrel belying his name by climbing several feet above ground among the slender swaying branches of the creosote to eat the small fuzzy seeds. This is doubtless no addition to Knowledge with a capital K. But it is an addition to my knowledge, and that is the next best thing. I like to investigate such matters for myself when I can. "What on earth do they live on?" is a common ques-

tion from those newcomers not too egotistical to notice that creatures other than those of their own kind do live here somehow. Obviously "creosote seeds" is one answer so far as the ground squirrel is concerned.

People of many races have been known to speak with scorn of those who live where nature makes things easy. In their inclement weather, the stoniness of their soil, or their rigorous winters, they find secret virtues to make even a thing like London fog praiseworthy. Making a virtue out of necessity is not itself a virtue. But there may be something of value in that process. We grow strong against the pressure of a difficulty and test our ingenuity by solving problems. Individuality and character are developed by challenge. We tend to admire trees, as well as people, who bear the stamp of success from struggles with adversity. People who have not had too easy a time of it develop character. And there is no doubt about the fact that desert life has character. Plants and animals are so clearly what they are because of the problems they have solved. They are part of some whole. They belong. Animals and plants, as well as people, become especially interesting when they fit their environment, when to some extent they reveal what their response to it has been. And nowhere more than in the desert do they reveal it.

— *Joseph Wood Krutch*

Joseph Wood Krutch (1898–1970), one of America's noted natural-history writers, contributed to The Nation *for many years as a drama and literary critic and lived his last 18 years outside Tucson.* The Voice of the Desert, *from which this essay was excerpted,* Grand Canyon, *and* Henry David Thoreau *are among Krutch's 21 books.*

ARIZONA CRAFTS

WHETHER YOU HAVE $10 or $1,000 to spend, shopping for crafts can make your trip to Arizona memorable, and not only for what you'll take home with you. The pursuit of local wares may take you down desert roads to remote studios, introduce you to snazzy urban galleries and historic trading posts, or involve you in lively festivals. Regional crafts also provide an intimate introduction to an area's history, culture, and peoples, as well as its contemporary interests and trends.

In the Southwest, several cultures have strong craft traditions, some predating European contact by more than 1,000 years. Native American, cowboy, and contemporary crafts—many made from native materials or by capturing local colors, themes, and spirit—are all well developed in this region.

Native American Crafts

Arizona visitors will see Native American crafts everywhere—in specialty shops, airports, motel gift shops, drugstores, and even gas stations. The problem is finding authentic work. Some so-called Native American crafts are made in Taiwan or Mexico. Others labeled "genuine Indian made" are mass-produced with shoddy material and inferior workmanship.

If you haven't read any books on the subject, study Native American collections at the Heard Museum (Phoenix) or the Museum of Northern Arizona (Flagstaff). These museums have their own gift shops which sell good-quality items at reasonable prices. Long-established trading posts, galleries, and Native American dealers are another option. Most first-rate shops will have a range of prices and knowledgeable salespeople who can answer your questions. If everything in a shop is inexpensive, it's probably attributable to the poor quality of the goods rather than to low overhead. It's a good idea to shop elsewhere.

One way to ensure authenticity and at the same time add an adventurous detour to your trip is to buy directly from craftspeople on the reservations. Look for signs that say "pottery," "rugs," or "baskets" hanging outside homes. Although visiting craftspeople is not a guarantee of quality, it does provide an opportunity to ask questions and learn about the work you are purchasing. And it's fun to watch artisans at work, to see their raw materials being turned into finished pieces.

Reservation gift shops are another option for authentic wares, although quality and prices vary tremendously. Crafts are also sold at Native American festivals, fairs, and powwows (ceremonial gatherings), which also have tribal dances and storytelling groups and serve food. One recommended event is Flagstaff's annual six-week Festival of Native American Arts held each summer at the Coconino Center for the Arts (2300 N. Valley Rd., U.S. 180, Flagstaff, ☎ 602/779–6921). This juried festival offers high-quality, traditional and contemporary tribal arts, including work rarely found elsewhere, such as colorful Pueblo moccasins and miniature pottery. Visitors can also watch jewelry-making, cloth- or basket-weaving demonstrations or participate in various workshops, including one that teaches children how to make Native American masks.

Arizona's 14 tribes each make distinctive art. The works of the Hopi, Navajo, and Tohonó O'odham (Papago) are best known, but the Chemehuevi, Maricopa, Mojave, Paiute, and Pima tribes create equally fine pieces.

Hopi pottery, baskets, and weaving reflect ancient traditions and techniques, while the tribe's silver work is of more recent vintage. Each of the reservation's three mesas has a craft specialty. First Mesa is home to potters who fashion hand-coiled vessels with pale cream or deep red glazes decorated with stylized birds and figures. Second Mesa's specialty is baskets of thickly coiled yucca joined with colorfully dyed lengths of yucca leaves; wicker baskets decorated with brightly colored designs can be found on Third Mesa. When buying pottery and baskets, look for symmetrical shapes, smooth rims, and neatly painted or evenly woven designs.

Hopi artisans also create kachina dolls, colorfully costumed, masked figures embellished with feathers, textiles, and leather. Modeled after the ceremonial kachina dancers, the dolls are used to teach children their religious heritage. Hopi men weave colorful sashes and narrow decorative bands used on clothing on belt looms. The vertical threads (warp) on these unusual looms stretch from one rod, tied to a tree, to another rod held taut by a belt wrapped around the weaver's waist. While making a sash, the weaver leans forward to loosen the warp and insert the woof, then backward to tighten it. Although Hopi woven fabrics are created primarily for their own use, some pieces are occasionally available through the reservation's crafts cooperative.

Hopi silver work, begun as a craft in the late 1890s, reflects a union of contemporary silver-working techniques and ancient motifs. Hopi silversmiths create some of the Southwest's finest jewelry. Two-layer designs use a number of motifs, ranging from simple sun shapes to those depicting elaborate tribal legends. Patterns are carefully cut through a top layer, which is then soldered to a bottom layer. Tiny parallel lines are chiseled into the design, and pieces are then oxidized to make motifs stand out from the polished silver surrounding it. Some of the best pieces have smoothly cut patterns with neatly stamped, parallel interior lines.

Navajo jewelry traces its origin to the mid-19th century. Tribal craftsmen learned smithery from Mexican artisans, later adding their own styles and designs. Early pieces were made from hammered silver coins and decorated with stamp work. Although turquoise beads date from prehistoric times, Navajos did not combine the stone with silver until the late 1800s. Today, in addition to turquoise, artisans incorporate coral, lapis, and other semiprecious stones into their designs.

Contemporary Navajo jewelry ranges from simple rings and cast silver bracelets to massive necklaces and concha belts (named for the stamped silver disks strung together on narrow leather strips). Because there are so many variables in the quality of stones and workmanship, purchase Navajo jewelry only from reputable dealers. Many Indian traders and jewelry shops throughout the Southwest have one case displaying items of Native American–made jewelry that have been pawned and not retrieved by their owners. Although you can occasionally find older pieces of exquisite quality in these cases, be wary about assertions as to an item's age or caliber.

The Navajo are also known for the variety and quality of their woven wool rugs. Sheepherders for centuries, they learned weaving skills from Pueblo peoples during the 18th century. At first they produced blankets and clothing in natural brown-and-white stripes. During the late 19th century, colors, particularly red, and a wide range of complex designs were added. At this time, most weavers also switched from making pieces for personal use to creating rugs for traders. Today Navajo rug patterns range from traditional eye dazzlers with bold zigzag patterns and pictorials featuring animals and other figures to *yei* rugs that duplicate sandpainting designs and two-faced rugs with different patterns on each surface.

If you purchase a Navajo rug, make sure that it is made entirely of wool (no linen or cotton threads), that the wool is of even thickness throughout the piece, that the design is neatly woven, and that colors are uniform throughout. A good source of Navajo rugs and other Native American crafts is the Hubbell Trading Post, a National Historic Site in Ganado, on the Navajo reservation 22 miles west of Window Rock. Established in 1878, the post looks exactly as it did in the 19th century when Navajos brought John Lorenzo Hubbell their rugs and jewelry to trade for groceries and other goods. These artisans still bring their crafts for sale or trade, but now they arrive in pickups instead of on horseback.

While Hopi and Navajo crafts are the best-known Arizona Native American arts, other tribes also produce good-quality items that provide an introduction to their cultural history. Among these, traditional Tohonó O'odham baskets are coiled, waterproof vessels with intricate designs using techniques and materials that have remained virtually unchanged for more than 11 centuries. Most baskets, made from two Southwestern desert plants, are broad and slightly sloping, with geometric patterns. Black designs, the most highly prized, are fashioned from black devil's claw, an increasingly rare plant that yields strong strips of jet-black fiber. Red motifs are woven with the root of banana yucca, a more common plant found in Arizona's higher elevations. One traditional Tohonó O'odham design is the legendary Man in the Maze, a stylized male figure standing at the top of the basket, about to enter a complex white-and-black labyrinth.

Baskets are also made by the Pima and Paiute. The Pima use coils of cattail stems bound with willow and favor complex zigzag designs. Traditional Paiute baskets have plain, functional shapes, reflecting the fact that they were once used to carry water, harvest or store seeds, and cradle babies. Mojave, Maricopa, and Chemehuevi tribal arts are more difficult to find, but they are worth the effort. Mojave beadwork can be exquisite, especially large, collar-shape necklaces created in traditional network designs resembling intricate lace. Maricopa artisans specialize in cream-color pottery, decorated with black designs that incorporate both geometric shapes and curvilinear symbols. Finely woven Chemehuevi baskets, another rare but exquisite craft, are made from coiled fiber, sometimes decorated with colorful feathers.

Cowboy Crafts

Even if you don't own horses or cattle, consider buying cowboy crafts: They can add vicarious fun to your wardrobe or decor. Watch them being created by talented artisans.

Arizona ranchers may use computers to keep track of their businesses, but no one has devised the technology to replace cowboys. Although his (and sometimes her) job may include time in a pickup, the daily routine is still dominated by horses, cattle, and traditional equipment rarely influenced by 20th-century innovations. Everyday cowboy trappings—saddles, spurs, bridles, and hats—form a craft tradition that spans centuries. Some items originated with Native Americans, while others were adopted from Mexican or California-Spanish styles.

Arizona cowboy crafts can be found in many shops, and even in department stores, but it's more fun to buy them directly from craftspeople or in tack shops that sell everything a horse and its rider need. Look in telephone books under tack shops, horse furnishings, or specific crafts such as saddlery or hats. For a thorough immersion, attend Flagstaff's annual 5½-week Trappings of the American West Festival, sponsored by the Coconino Center for the Arts; it runs from early May until the second week of June. The festival includes cowboy craft demonstrations and workshops where you can learn rawhide braiding and boot making.

Although cowboy crafts are often decorative, they are first of all functional tools of the trade. Hats protect the wearer from weather, branches, and rocks and double as containers for carrying water and feed. Boots, designed to be pulled off easily and fit comfortably in stirrups, protect feet from mud and brush. Chaps shield the legs from prickly cactus and other hazards. The brush in Arizona is particularly heavy, so cowboys here prefer Arizona bell-bottom chaps made from very heavy leather that is flared at the bottom so they bend with the leg. What is the best of each?— hats made from beaver-fur felt, custom-made boots, and used chaps with that trail-worn look.

Saddles, which are custom-made to fit horse and rider, are often covered with carved or stamped designs of elaborate floral and leaf motifs. Some cowboys claim that deep carving keeps them from slipping in the saddle. For urban cowpokes, many saddlers create stamped or carved leather purses, belts, wallets, and even wastebaskets.

The oldest cowboy craft is leather and horsehair braiding. Conceived by Native Americans, braiding was later adopted by Mexican and American cowboys. Complex patterns decorate braided horse gear, from bridles and reins to other items whose exotic names belie their practicality: bosals and hobbles, romals and quirts. Look also for braided hatbands, belts, and bracelets.

Other cowboy accoutrements include bits and spurs with ornate inlaid designs that are seen only by the cowboy and his horse. Texas cowboys generally favor massive inlaid silver stars and geometric patterns, while California and Arizona cowboys prefer gear embellished with flowers and flourishes. Many smiths also fashion decorative silver work for saddles, as well as buckles, money clips, and jewelry. Knives, another cowboy necessity, can be found in great variety. Look for those with handles made from exotic materials and engraved or inlaid with precious metal and stones.

Contemporary Crafts

Arizona's contemporary artisans work in every medium, but particularly in clay, textiles, and wood. Although the focus of their work varies from abstract to functional, many of the crafts reflect Arizona colors: the glowing hues of a desert sunset, the subtle pastels of cactus flowers, the myriad reds of Sedona's cliffs. There's also a healthy dose of humor in many items: prickly ceramic cactus vases, howling wood dogs, flirty roadrunner sculptures, chairs with coyote armrests. The use of native materials is also common— for example, you may come across cactus-spine baskets or mesquite armoires.

Phoenix, Scottsdale, and Tucson offer a bonanza of contemporary crafts galleries. On a smaller scale, Tubac, an artists' community 35 miles south of Tucson, has numerous crafts studios open to the public. Tubac artisans create everything from avant-garde jewelry and textiles to copper fountains shaped like cacti. To find galleries throughout Arizona, consult *Art Life,* two comprehensive guides (one covering northern Arizona, the other southern Arizona) that describe galleries, provide detailed maps, and include indexes arranged by style, subject, and medium. The guides are available free in many Arizona galleries and by calling Yoakum Publishing (☎ 602/797–1271).

— *Suzanne Carmichael*

Author of The Traveler's Guide to American Crafts, *Suzanne Carmichael also writes articles on travel and crafts for such publications as* The New York Times, USA Weekend, *and* Northwest magazine.

MORE PORTRAITS

Essays and Fiction

Going Back to Bisbee, by Richard Shelton, *Frog Mountain Blues,* by Charles Bowden, and *The Mountains Next Day,* by Janice Emily Bowers, are all fine personal accounts of life in southern Arizona. The hipster fiction classic *The Monkey Wrench Gang,* by Edward Abbey, details an ecoanarchist plot to blow up Glen Canyon Dam. *Stolen Gods,* a thriller by Jake Page, is set largely on Arizona's Hopi reservation and in Tucson. Three novels by Tucson-based writers skillfully evoke the interplay between Native American culture and contemporary Southwest life: *Pigs in Heaven,* by Barbara Kingsolver, *Almanac of the Dead,* by Leslie Marmon Silko, and *Yes Is Better Than No,* by Byrd Baylor. Wild West adventure, with all of the mythological glory that Hollywood has tried to capture, abounds in Zane Grey's novels—buy a new copy or look for any of the charming illustrated hardcover editions in used or out-of-print bookstores. Tony Hillerman's mysteries will put you in an equally Southwestern mood.

General History

Arizona Cowboys, by Dane Coolidge, is an illustrated account of the cowboys, Indians, settlers, and explorers of the early 1900s. Buried-treasure hunters will be inspired by *Lost Mines of the Great Southwest,* by John D. Mitchell, which is just enough of a nibble to start you sketching maps and planning strategy. First printed back in 1891, *Some Strange Corners of Our Country,* by Charles F. Lummis, takes readers on a century-old journey to the Grand Canyon, Montezuma Castle, the Petrified Forest, and other Arizonan "strange corners." For a dip into the backroads of the past, try the *Arizona Good Roads Association Illustrated Road Maps and Tour Book,* a 1913 volume, replete with hotel ads, reprinted by Arizona Highways magazine. The *Roadside History of Arizona,* by Marshall Trimble, will bring you up to date on many of the same thoroughfares. *Ghost Towns of Arizona,* by James E. and Barbara H. Sherman, gives historical details on the abandoned mining towns that dot the state and provides maps to find them.

Native American History

Two books provide excellent surveys of the ancient and more recent Native American past and cover in more depth sites mentioned in this guidebook. *Those Who Came Before: Southwestern Archaeology in the National Park System,* by Robert Lister and Florence Lister, provides a well-researched and completely accessible summary of centuries of life in the region informed by both contemporary Indian and archaeological perspectives, and it contains wonderful photographs and descriptions of numerous sites. David G. Noble's *Ancient Ruins of the Southwest* covers similar territory more briefly and portably and includes directions for driving to sites. *Hohokam Indians of the Tucson Basin,* by Linda Gregonis, offers an in-depth look at this prehistoric tribe. In *Hopi,* by Susanne Page and Jake Page, the daily, ceremonial, and spiritual life of the tribe are explored in detail. Study up on the history of Hopi silversmithing techniques in *Hopi Silver,* by Margaret Wright. The beautifully illustrated *Hopi Indian Kachina Dolls,* by Oscar T. Branson, details the different ceremonial roles of the colorful Native American figurines. Navajo homes, ceremonies, crafts, and tribal traditions are kept alive in *The Enduring Navajo,* by Laura Gilpin. Navajo legends and trends from early days to the present are collected in *The Book of the Navajo,* by Raymond F. Locke.

A superb new collection of Native American stories, songs, and poems, *Coming to Light,* edited by Brian Swann, includes material from all over the country, not only the Southwest. Introductions to individual pieces provide invaluable and fascinating cultural information.

Natural History

A Guide to Exploring Oak Creek and the Sedona Area, by Stewart Aitchison, provides natural-history driving tours of this very scenic district. In *100 Desert Wildflowers in Natural Color,* by Natt N.

Dodge, you'll find a color photo and brief description of each of the flowers included. Also written by Natt N. Dodge, *Poisonous Dwellers of the Desert* gives precise information on both venomous and nonvenomous creatures of the Southwest. *Cacti of the Southwest,* by W. Hubert Earle, depicts some of the best-known species of the region with color photos and descriptive material. For comprehensive information on Grand Canyon geology, history, flora and fauna, plus hiking suggestions, pick up *A Field Guide to the Grand Canyon,* by Steve Whitney. *Common Edible and Useful Plants of the West,* by Muriel Sweet, gives the layperson descriptions of medicinal and other plants and shrubs, most of which were first discovered by Native Americans. *Roadside Geology of Arizona,* by Halka Chronic, is a good resource for finding the causes of the striking natural formations you'll see throughout the state.

Crafts

The Traveler's Guide to American Crafts: West of the Mississippi, by Suzanne Carmichael, gives browsers and buyers alike a useful overview of Arizona's traditional and contemporary handiwork.

General Interest

Arizona Highways, a monthly magazine, features exquisite color photography of this versatile state. Useful general travel information, fine pictures, and well-written historical essays all make *Arizona,* by Larry Cheek, a good pretrip resource.

INDEX

NOTES

NOTES

NOTES

NOTES

NOTES

NOTES

NOTES

NOTES

NOTES

NOTES

Escape to ancient cities and

journey to  *exotic islands with*

CNN Travel Guide, a wealth of valuable advice. Host

Valerie Voss will take you to

all of your favorite destinations,

including those off the beaten

path. Tune-in to your passport to the world.

CNN TRAVEL GUIDE
SATURDAY 12:30 PMet   SUNDAY 4:30 PMet

Your guide to a picture-perfect vacation

Kodak and Fodor's join together to create the guide that travelers everywhere have been asking for—one that covers the terms and techniques, the equipment and etiquette for taking first-rate travel photographs.

The most authoritative and up-to-date book of its kind, **The Kodak Guide to Shooting Great Travel Pictures** includes over 200 color photographs and spreads on 100 points of photography important to travelers, such as landscape basics, under sea shots, wildlife, city street, close-ups, photographing in museums and more.

$16.50   ($22.95 Canada)

At bookstores everywhere, or call 1-800-533-6478.

Fodor's. The name that means smart travel.™

Fodor's Travel Publications

Available at bookstores everywhere, or call 1–800–533–6478, 24 hours a day.

Gold Guides
U.S.

Alaska	Florida	New Orleans	Santa Fe, Taos, Albuquerque
Arizona	Hawaii	New York City	
Boston	Las Vegas, Reno, Tahoe	Pacific North Coast	Seattle & Vancouver
California		Philadelphia & the Pennsylvania Dutch Country	The South
Cape Cod, Martha's Vineyard, Nantucket	Los Angeles		U.S. & British Virgin Islands
The Carolinas & the Georgia Coast	Maine, Vermont, New Hampshire	The Rockies	USA
	Maui	San Diego	Virginia & Maryland
Chicago	Miami & the Keys	San Francisco	Waikiki
Colorado	New England		Washington, D.C.

Foreign

Australia & New Zealand	Egypt	Madrid & Barcelona	Provence & the Riviera
Austria	Europe	Mexico	Scandinavia
The Bahamas	Florence, Tuscany & Umbria	Montréal & Québec City	Scotland
Bermuda	France	Moscow, St. Petersburg, Kiev	Singapore
Budapest	Germany	The Netherlands, Belgium & Luxembourg	South Africa
Canada	Great Britain		South America
Cancún, Cozumel, Yucatán Peninsula	Greece	New Zealand	Southeast Asia
Caribbean	Hong Kong	Norway	Spain
China	India	Nova Scotia, New Brunswick, Prince Edward Island	Sweden
Costa Rica, Belize, Guatemala	Ireland		Switzerland
Cuba	Israel	Paris	Thailand
The Czech Republic & Slovakia	Italy	Portugal	Tokyo
Eastern Europe	Japan		Toronto
	Kenya & Tanzania		Turkey
	Korea		Vienna & the Danube
	London		

Fodor's Special-Interest Guides

Branson	Fodor's London Companion	Shadow Traffic's New York Shortcuts and Traffic Tips	Where Should We Take the Kids? California
Caribbean Ports of Call	Gay USA		
The Complete Guide to America's National Parks	France by Train	Sunday in New York	Where Should We Take the Kids? Family Adventures
	Halliday's New England Food Explorer	Sunday in San Francisco	
Condé Nast Traveler Caribbean Resort and Cruise Ship Finder	Healthy Escapes	Walt Disney World, Universal Studios and Orlando	Where Should We Take the Kids? Northeast
Cruises and Ports of Call	Italy by Train	Walt Disney World for Adults	
	Kodak Guide to Shooting Great Travel Pictures		

Special Series

Affordables

Caribbean
Europe
Florida
France
Germany
Great Britain
Italy
London
Paris

Fodor's Bed & Breakfasts and Country Inns

America's Best B&Bs
California's Best B&Bs
Canada's Great Country Inns
Cottages, B&Bs and Country Inns of England and Wales
The Mid-Atlantic's Best B&Bs
New England's Best B&Bs
The Pacific Northwest's Best B&Bs
The South's Best B&Bs
The Southwest's Best B&Bs
The Upper Great Lakes' Best B&Bs

The Berkeley Guides

California
Central America
Eastern Europe
Europe
France
Germany & Austria
Great Britain & Ireland
Italy
London
Mexico
Pacific Northwest & Alaska
Paris
San Francisco

Compass American Guides

Arizona
Chicago
Colorado
Hawaii
Idaho
Hollywood
Las Vegas
Maine
Manhattan
Montana
New Mexico
New Orleans
Oregon
San Francisco
Santa Fe
South Carolina
South Dakota
Southwest
Texas
Utah
Virginia
Washington
Wine Country
Wisconsin
Wyoming

Fodor's Citypacks

Atlanta
Hong Kong
London
New York City
Paris
Rome
San Francisco
Washington, D.C.

Fodor's Español

California
Caribe Occidental
Caribe Oriental
Gran Bretaña
Londres
Mexico

Nueva York
Paris

Fodor's Exploring Guides

Australia
Boston & New England
Britain
California
Caribbean
China
Egypt
Florence & Tuscany
Florida
France
Germany
Ireland
Israel
Italy
Japan
London
Mexico
Moscow & St. Petersburg
New York City
Paris
Prague
Provence
Rome
San Francisco
Scotland
Singapore & Malaysia
Spain
Thailand
Turkey
Venice

Fodor's Flashmaps

Boston
New York
San Francisco
Washington, D.C.

Fodor's Pocket Guides

Acapulco
Atlanta
Barbados

Jamaica
London
New York City
Paris
Prague
Puerto Rico
Rome
San Francisco
Washington, D.C.

Rivages Guides

Bed and Breakfasts of Character and Charm in France
Hotels and Country Inns of Character and Charm in France
Hotels and Country Inns of Character and Charm in Italy

Short Escapes

Country Getaways in Britain
Country Getaways in France
Country Getaways in New England
Country Getaways Near New York City

Fodor's Sports

Golf Digest's Best Places to Play
Skiing USA
USA Today The Complete Four Sport Stadium Guide

Fodor's Vacation Planners

Great American Learning Vacations
Great American Sports & Adventure Vacations
Great American Vacations
National Parks and Seashores of the East
National Parks of the West

Before Catching Your Flight, Catch Up With Your World.

Fueled by the global resources of CNN and available in major airports across America, CNN Airport Network provides a live source  of current domestic and international news,  sports, business, weather and lifestyle programming. Plus two daily Fodor's features for the facts you need: "Travel Fact," a useful and creative mix of travel trivia; and "What's Happening," a comprehensive round-up of upcoming events in major cities around the world.

With CNN Airport Network, you'll never be out of the loop.

HERE'S YOUR OWN PERSONAL VIEW OF THE WORLD.

Here's the easiest way to get up-to-the-minute, objective, personalized information about what's going on in the city you'll be visiting—before you leave on your trip! Unique information you could get only if you knew someone personally in each of 160 destinations around the world. Everything from special places to dine to local events only a local would know about.

It's all yours—in your Travel Update from Worldview, the leading provider of time-sensitive destination information.

Review the following order form and fill it out by indicating your destination(s)

and travel dates and by checking off up to eight interest categories. Then mail or fax your order form to us, or call your order in. (We're here to help you 24 hours a day.)

Within 48 hours of receiving your order, we'll mail your convenient, pocket-sized custom guide to you, packed with information to make your travel more fun and interesting. And if you're in a hurry, we can even fax it.

Have a great trip with your Fodor's Worldview Travel Update!

Fodor's WORLDVIEW TRAVEL UPDATE

Insider perspective

Time-sensitive

Customized to your interests and dates of travel

DESTINATIONS

Worldview covers more than 160 destinations worldwide. Choose the destination(s) that match your itinerary from the list below:

Europe
Amsterdam
Athens
Barcelona
Berlin
Brussels
Budapest
Copenhagen
Dublin
Edinburgh
Florence
Frankfurt
French Riviera
Geneva
Glasgow
Lausanne
Lisbon
London
Madrid
Milan
Moscow
Munich
Oslo
Paris
Prague
Provence
Rome
Salzburg
Seville
St. Petersburg
Stockholm
Venice
Vienna
Zurich

United States (Mainland)
Albuquerque
Atlanta
Atlantic City
Baltimore
Boston
Branson, MO
Charleston, SC
Chicago
Cincinnati
Cleveland
Dallas/Ft. Worth
Denver
Detroit
Houston
Indianapolis
Kansas City
Las Vegas
Los Angeles
Memphis
Miami
Milwaukee
Minneapolis/St. Paul
Nashville
New Orleans
New York City
Orlando
Palm Springs
Philadelphia
Phoenix
Pittsburgh
Portland
Reno/Lake Tahoe
St. Louis
Salt Lake City
San Antonio
San Diego
San Francisco
Santa Fe
Seattle
Tampa
Washington, DC

Alaska
Alaskan Destinations

Hawaii
Honolulu
Island of Hawaii
Kauai
Maui

Canada
Quebec City
Montreal
Ottawa
Toronto
Vancouver

Bahamas
Abaco
Eleuthera/
  Harbour Island
Exuma
Freeport
Nassau &
  Paradise Island

Bermuda
Bermuda Countryside
Hamilton

British Leeward Islands
Anguilla
Antigua & Barbuda
St. Kitts & Nevis

British Virgin Islands
Tortola & Virgin
Gorda

British Windward Islands
Barbados
Dominica
Grenada
St. Lucia
St. Vincent
Trinidad & Tobago

Cayman Islands
The Caymans

Dominican Republic
Santo Domingo

Dutch Leeward Islands
Aruba
Bonaire
Curacao

Dutch Windward Island
St. Maarten/St. Martin

French West Indies
Guadeloupe
Martinique
St. Barthelemy

Jamaica
Kingston
Montego Bay
Negril
Ocho Rios

Puerto Rico
Ponce
San Juan

Turks & Caicos
Grand Turk/
  Providenciales

U.S. Virgin Islands
St. Croix
St. John
St. Thomas

Mexico
Acapulco
Cancun & Isla Mujeres
Cozumel
Guadalajara
Ixtapa & Zihuatanejo
Los Cabos
Mazatlan
Mexico City
Monterrey
Oaxaca
Puerto Vallarta

South/Central America
Buenos Aires
Caracas
Rio de Janeiro
San Jose, Costa Rica
Sao Paulo

Middle East
Istanbul
Jerusalem

Australia & New Zealand
Auckland
Melbourne
South Island
Sydney

China
Beijing
Guangzhou
Shanghai

Japan
Kyoto
Nagoya
Osaka
Tokyo
Yokohama

Pacific Rim/Other
Bali
Bangkok
Hong Kong & Macau
Manila
Seoul
Singapore
Taipei

INTERESTS

For your personalized Travel Update, choose the eight (8) categories you're most interested in from the following list:

1.	**Business Services**	Fax & Overnight Mail, Computer Rentals, Protocol, Secretarial, Messenger, Translation Services
	Dining	
2.	**All-Day Dining**	Breakfast & Brunch, Cafes & Tea Rooms, Late-Night Dining
3.	**Local Cuisine**	Every Price Range — from Budget Restaurants to the Special Splurge
4.	**European Cuisine**	Continental, French, Italian
5.	**Asian Cuisine**	Chinese, Far Eastern, Japanese, Other
6.	**Americas Cuisine**	American, Mexican & Latin
7.	**Nightlife**	Bars, Dance Clubs, Casinos, Comedy Clubs, Ethnic, Pubs & Beer Halls
8.	**Entertainment**	Theater – Comedy, Drama, Musicals, Dance, Ticket Agencies
9.	**Music**	Classical, Opera, Traditional & Ethnic, Jazz & Blues, Pop, Rock
10.	**Children's Activites**	Events, Attractions
11.	**Tours**	Local Tours, Day Trips, Overnight Excursions
12.	**Exhibitions, Festivals & Shows**	Antiques & Flower, History & Cultural, Art Exhibitions, Fairs & Craft Shows, Music & Art Festivals
13.	**Shopping**	Districts & Malls, Markets, Regional Specialties
14.	**Fitness**	Bicycling, Health Clubs, Hiking, Jogging
15.	**Recreational Sports**	Boating/Sailing, Fishing, Golf, Skiing, Snorkeling/Scuba, Tennis/Racket
16.	**Spectator Sports**	Auto Racing, Baseball, Basketball, Golf, Football, Horse Racing, Ice Hockey, Soccer
17.	**Event Highlights**	The best of what's happening during the dates of your trip.
18.	**Sightseeing**	Sights, Buildings, Monuments
19.	**Museums**	Art, Cultural
20.	**Transportation**	Taxis, Car Rentals, Airports, Public Transportation
21.	**General Info**	Overview, Holidays, Currency, Tourist Info

Please note that content will vary by season, destination, and length of stay.

Name

Address

City   State   Country   ZIP

Tel #   (   )   -   Fax #   (   )   -

Title of this Fodor's guide:

Store and location where guide was purchased:

INDICATE YOUR DESTINATIONS/DATES: You can order up to three (3) destinations from the previous page. Fill in your arrival and departure dates for each destination. <u>**Your Travel Update itinerary (all destinations selected) cannot exceed 30 days from beginning to end.**</u>

		Month	Day	Month	Day
(Sample) **LONDON**	From:	6	/ 21	To: 6	/ 30
1	From:		/	To:	/
2	From:		/	To:	/
3	From:		/	To:	/

CHOOSE YOUR INTERESTS: Select up to eight (8) categories from the list of interest categories shown on the previous page and circle the numbers below:

1 2 3 4 5 6 7 8 9 10 11 12 13 14 15 16 17 18 19 20 21

CHOOSE WHEN YOU WANT YOUR TRAVEL UPDATE DELIVERED (Check one):
❑ Please send my Travel Update immediately.
❑ Please hold my order until a few weeks before my trip to include the most up-to-date information.
Completed orders will be sent within 48 hours. Allow 7–10 days for U.S. mail delivery.

ADD UP YOUR ORDER HERE. SPECIAL OFFER FOR FODOR'S PURCHASERS ONLY!

	Suggested Retail Price	Your Price	This Order
First destination ordered	$ 9.95	$ 7.95	$ 7.95
Second destination (if applicable)	$ 6.95	$ 4.95	+
Third destination (if applicable)	$ 6.95	$ 4.95	+

DELIVERY CHARGE (Check one and enter amount below)

	Within U.S. & Canada	Outside U.S. & Canada
First Class Mail	❑ $2.50	❑ $5.00
FAX	❑ $5.00	❑ $10.00
Priority Delivery	❑ $15.00	❑ $27.00

ENTER DELIVERY CHARGE FROM ABOVE: +

TOTAL: $

METHOD OF PAYMENT IN U.S. FUNDS ONLY (Check one):
❑ AmEx ❑ MC ❑ Visa ❑ Discover ❑ Personal Check (U. S. & Canada only)
❑ Money Order/International Money Order

Make check or money order payable to: Fodor's Worldview Travel Update

Credit Card __/__/__/__/__/__/__/__/__/__/__/__/__/__/__/__/ **Expiration Date:** __/__

Authorized Signature

SEND THIS COMPLETED FORM WITH PAYMENT TO:
Fodor's Worldview Travel Update, 114 Sansome Street, Suite 700, San Francisco, CA 94104

OR CALL OR FAX US 24-HOURS A DAY
Telephone **1-800-799-9609** • Fax **1-800-799-9619** (From within the U.S. & Canada)
(Outside the U.S. & Canada: Telephone 415-616-9988 • Fax 415-616-9989)

(Please have this guide in front of you when you call so we can verify purchase.)
Code: FTG   Offer valid until 12/31/97